Golf Digest

Golf's Greatest Players, Courses and Voices

GolfDigest

50 years of the best, from the editors of GOLF DIGEST magazine

BEAUX ARTS EDITIONS

GolfDigest®

Published in association with The New York Times Company Magazine Group Inc.
Golf Digest® is a registered trademark of The New York Times Company Magazine Group Inc.
All text, illustration and photograph copyrights are owned by Golf Digest/The New York Times
Company Magazine Group Inc. unless otherwise specified. All rights reserved. The copyrights to
all other texts, illustrations and photographs are retained by the individual.

Pebble Beach, Spyglass Hill, Pebble Beach Golf Links, Spyglass Hill Golf Course, their
respective images, golf course and individual golf hole designs are trademarks, service marks
and trade dress of Pebble Beach Company used by permission.

Excerpt on pages 62–63 reprinted with the permission of Simon & Schuster, from *Little Red
Book* by Harvey Penick with Bud Shrake. Copyright © 1992 by Harvey Penick and Bud Shrake
and Helen Penick.

Design: Lori S. Malkin
Executive Editor, Golf Digest Special Projects: Robert Carney
Project Editor: James O. Muschett
Photo Research: Mary Rung and Julia Isabelle

ISBN 0-88363-372-8
Printed in Hong Kong

Photo credits:
PAGE 3: Pebble Beach Golf Links No.7 (Photo: Evan Schiller)
PAGE 5: Gene Sarazen (Photo: Golf World)

We wish to thank all of the Golf Digest contributors, editors, photographers and artists
whose stories and essays appear in the book. We offer special thanks to the people who had
the daunting task of pulling this material together, beginning with Mary Rung, Golf Digest's
Manager of Editorial Resources, and Julia Isabelle, Licensing Coordinator. They did an amazing
job. We are also grateful to the editors of the sections: Jerry Tarde, Roger Schiffman, Mike
O'Malley, John Barton, Peter McCleery, Scott Smith, Guy Yocom, Ron Whitten
and Mike Stachura; to our historian Cliff Schrock, and to copy editors and researchers Betsy
Van Sickle, Mike Johnson, Debby Zindell, Julie Ware and Brett Blackhall.

"*Dear Sir,*
I have read my book and
I like it very much."

—Gene Sarazen to
his collaborator
H. B. Martin

CONTENTS

Foreword: by Nick Seitz 8
Introduction: by Jerry Tarde 9

Section One: *A Sense of Place* 10

Reflections on Augusta, Peter Andrews, April 1987
Golf's Irish Blessings, Peter Dobereiner, March 1987
Monterey: How I was seduced by a peninsula, Cal Brown, January 1971
Southern Comfort: Pinehurst is a state of mind, Charles McGrath, June 1999
Pine Valley: A beauty and a beast, Tom Callahan, November 1989
The Holy Land: St. Andrews, Peter Andrews, July 1990
Seminole: Golf of the first order, Herbert Warren Wind, April 1980
In Celebration of Tradition, the Editors, May 1995

Section Two: *Playing the Game Right* 50

How to Play
What You Can Learn From the Greatest Players I Ever Saw, Sam Snead, February 1984
My Most Memorable Shots in the Majors, Jack Nicklaus, May 1985
The Secrets of Golf, Harvey Penick, with introduction by Tom Kite, May 1992
Shortcuts to Save Strokes, Golf Digest Pro Panel Staff, March 1992
How to Get the Killer Instinct, Dr. Bob Rotella, October 1985

The Swing
How to Develop a Swing that Repeats, Ben Hogan, April 1956
The Touch System for Better Golf, Bob Toski, July 1971
Swings of the Century: A Gatefold of Six of the All-Time Best Swing Sequences
How and When to Chip with Your 3-Wood, Tiger Woods, September 1997
Shape Your Swing the Modern Way, Byron Nelson, April 1976
I Can Get You Out of Sand with One Hand, Claude Harmon, September 1972
I Can Cure Your Slice, Lee Trevino, January 1992

Power
Bobby Jones on Power, Bobby Jones, February 1996
57 Keys to Distance, February 1996
Distance Through Resistance, David Leadbetter, May 1993

Section Three: *Characters and Character* 96

In Their Own Words
Conversations with golf's greatest personalities

Voices
There's no time to smell the roses today, Henry Longhurst, November 1975
Augusta's a nice place but it's not heaven, Frank Beard, April 1977
Missing old friends and good times, Dave Marr, November 1980
Will Greg Norman reach superstardom?, Peter Dobereiner, September 1984
Looking for golf courses my grandma would love, Peter Thomson, February 1987
The last days of Bobby Jones, Charles Price, April 1991
Why I hate family golf, Dan Jenkins, December 1994
We know who they are, Tom Callahan, August 1996

The man who stood up to Arnie and Jack, Jerry Tarde, April 1997
Golf and discipline, David Owen, October 1998
A sudden end to a love story, Dave Kindred, November 1998
Legend on the loose, Nick Seitz, January 1999

Characters
Ben Hogan Today, Nick Seitz, September 1970
How Hard It Is to Be Ken Venturi, Tom Callahan, April 1986
Nancy Lopez: Almost Too Good to Be True, Dwayne Netland, April 1978
How Bob Drum and I Invented Arnold Palmer, Dan Jenkins, August 1975
J.C. Snead: Bad Guy or Good Ol' Boy?, Mickey Herskowitz, September 1984

Section Four: *Major Voices, Major Events* 152
Is It Heaven or Is It Hell?, Dave Kindred, April 1995
Let Us Now Praise Amen Corner, Herbert Warren Wind, April 1984
Open-Minded Geniuses, Frank Hannigan, June 1995
Maurice Flitcroft: The Open's Don Quixote, Peter Dobereiner, July 1985
The Grand Slam That Almost Was, Dave Anderson, July 1987
How I Won One PGA and Lived Royally Ever After, Dave Marr, August 1973
Major Dan: Our Man Jenkins on the Scene, 1985–1999

Section Five: *From the Gallery* 186
Great letters, famous and otherwise, from our eloquent gallery
We Found Him! America's Worst Avid Golfer, Peter Andrews, September 1985
Field of Dreams: The Armchair Architect, Ron Whitten, December 1991

Section Six: *Crusades* 204
Let's Get Back to Real Golf, J. L. Briggs, May 1990
Caddies: Golf's Oldest Profession, Michael Bamberger, February 1993
Knocking on the Clubhouse Door, Marcia Chambers, June 1990

Section Seven: *The Rest of The Best* 216
Giving Voice to the Game: Chronology of 50 Years of GOLF DIGEST
The Cover of a Magazine is Like an Honest Face: Including a Gatefold of 50 of the Best Covers
50 Who Shaped the Game
Nongolf Celebrities
12 Greatest Shots of All Time
The All-Time America's Greatest Courses
Firsts & First Mentions
The Advertisers
Editorial Staff 1950-1999
Contributors

Index 238

Final Shot: *Nurtured Under Golf's Melodic Line* 240
Peter Dobereiner, December 1986

by Nick Seitz
Editor-at-Large

Top to bottom: *The founding fathers of* Golf Digest: *William H. Davis, Howard R. Gill, Jr. and John Barnett.*

Golf Digest and I landed in golf in the spring of 1950, quite independently of each other but both from modest Midwestern launching pads. Golf Digest began as a 16-page, pocket-size, black-and-white local publication produced out of golf-buff Bill Davis' bedroom in suburban Chicago.

It wasn't a guest bedroom—he slept amid the disarray of manuscripts and layouts. With Davis wearing more hats than the Northwestern University marching band, two issues were published that first year, the first selling for 15 cents and the second for a dime.

Meanwhile, your longtime correspondent was starting to play golf with a few other grade-school kids on the nine-hole Washburn University course in our Topeka, Kan., neighborhood—my warmest memory the heavy metal drag rakes for the sand greens, made scalding to the touch by the prairie sun. Several of us shared a skimpy canvas bag of hand-me-down clubs and swung them without benefit of instruction, lowering our baseball swings and producing mostly ground balls.

If you call that playing golf and call what Davis was doing publishing, we both were hooked, lined and sinkered for life.

Looking back on that year in the exact middle of the 20th century (is anybody ready to refer to it as "the last century"?), it appears notable for seminal news developments, though in hindsight I seem to have been only vaguely aware of them at the time. McCarthyism made its ugly debut in Washington, North Korea invaded South Korea, U.S. troops responded and the first American television war was under way. The first credit card was introduced, as was the first telephone answering machine. Elizabeth Taylor got married for the first time. Charles Schulz created the comic strip Peanuts. John Wayne was No. 1 at the box office, "Goodnight Irene" topped the hit parade and Ed Sullivan was reeeeeally big on weekend TV.

In golf, a grimly determined Ben Hogan won the 1950 U.S. Open in a playoff at Merion the year after narrowly missing death in a grisly car-bus accident. His victory has been dramatically preserved for posterity by the famous Hy Peskin photograph of his 1-iron shot to the 72nd green.

Hogan told me later that the Merion win was his most meaningful because he proved to himself he could be the best again despite his injuries, even though his nerves and short game were not as controllable and never would be. Davis and Golf Digest considered him the dominant player of the day, though Sam Snead was the leading money winner that year—with the lordly total of $35,000.

The game and the magazine were about to take off and propel each other to undreamed-of heights over the next half century. Consider the vacation-resort dimension the magazine has always covered and encouraged. In 1950 Myrtle Beach was a summer-only coastal strip with two courses. Today it's pretty much a year-round destination with 102 courses!

Golf Digest may have been smaller and less polished in its formative days, but Davis built its guiding spirit and essential appeal into the foundation. "From the beginning, we believed golf was a fun game that becomes more enjoyable the better you play it," he would say on the occasion of our 25th anniversary. "Our aim was to provide readers with a balance of easy-to-understand instruction and service articles along with entertaining and informative human-interest features."

There's been no major deviation from that simple mission statement. Refinement, yes, especially of presentation. Bigger budgets, certainly, to continue to hire the finest writers, teachers and players and devote more pages to the game's rich diversity—golf being subdivisible into more dimensions than a ball wears dimples, and, as every practitioner of our beloved black art knows well, stirring every emotion known to man as well as a few not yet categorized.

All-important continuity has been accomplished through only a handful of chief editors during the 50 years, their regimes overlapping smoothly. Davis and his longtime partner Howard Gill have passed on to that great driving range in the sky, while the third partner, Jack Barnett, years ago retired to become an on-line day trader before most of us knew what one was. Their legacy is alive and flourishing as this delectable smorgasbord of a book demonstrates.

Grassroots programs they established—like the one recognizing most improved golfers—go on, manifesting Golf Digest's long-held belief that golf is a fun game made more fun if you can play better. I remember Davis' words in 1975 and I remember Ben Hogan seconding the sentiment in an interview we did in the late 1980s.

"Most of the enjoyment in life is in improving," Hogan said with great conviction. "The weekend golfer gets more enjoyment out of the game than the tour player, because the tour player gets to a point where he can't improve anymore. But this fella who's a 90 shooter, he has a long way to go. The 90-shooter is going to find something every day to boost him up."

It will always be the best game in the world to play badly. And the best to read about. I think you'll agree after spending time with this joyful collection.

I don't know what ever happened to Davis' bedroom in Illinois, but that little Washburn University course with the sand greens was wiped out by the tornado of 1966 and subsequent rebuilding of the school. Golf Digest and I are on the East Coast now, but whenever I go back to Topeka, I make sure to drive by.

INTRODUCTION

by Jerry Tarde,

Editor

As we stand looking into the abyss of another 50 years of GOLF DIGEST, another 500 years of golf, another millennium of civilization, the question we ask ourselves inevitably is, will the grass be greener on the other side?

It is the ultimate golfer's dilemma. Some of us may be happy to find the grass just as green as it is on this side. Some may be hoping for bent over Bermuda. Some may be satisfied just to find there's grass at all.

The question brings to mind a story that comes by way of two GOLF DIGEST columnists. One of them was the Englishman, Henry Longhurst. Henry described himself as born to travel first class but without the price of a ticket. He was a Cambridge man, elected to Parliament in the 1940s, the former German amateur golf champion, and a very fine writer, but in the way television twists everything, he became best known for his eloquent reporting on golf for the BBC. He was the only golf commentator to work for two American networks at the same time, both ABC and CBS, which was just as inconceivable then as now. And he was one of the great gin drinkers, but I digress.

By the late 1970s, when Henry was in his 70s, he was dying of cancer and forced to stop working. He lived at the time in a pair of landmark windmills known as Jack and Jill, on the top of Sussex Downs. One of his closest friends and regular visitors was an even more legendary figure in English history, the World War II flying ace, Wing Commander Sir Douglas Bader.

Bader lost both his legs in an accident in 1931 when he slow-rolled his Bristol Bulldog fighter at an air show. Somehow he won another commission from the RAF in 1939, flying Spitfires specially converted with manual controls. At Dunkirk and the Battle of Britain, he destroyed 30 enemy aircraft but collided with a Luftwasse Messerschmidt over France, lost one of his artificial legs in parachuting and was captured by the enemy. He was so revered a figure in the war that Germany allowed Britain to airdrop in another set of tin legs, whereupon he used them to escape. Recaptured shortly thereafter, he attempted so many more escapes that his captors confiscated his legs each night. After the war, Bader turned his attention to golf and became an excellent player, reducing his handicap to 4. Needless to say, he was a man of indomitable spirit who moved a nation, the perfect companion for a dying friend.

In their weekly talks over glasses of gin, they solved the problems of golf and politics and life. When the bottle was empty, Bader went home. As Henry's days were drawing to a close, one afternoon he said to Bader, "Old friend, there is something I've always wondered about."

"What's that, Henry?" he replied.

"I've always wondered: Will the grass be greener on the other side?"

Neither being particularly religious men, they talked for a while to no conclusion and parted company. That very week, Henry died, and in his mourning Bader forgot all about the conversation.

Months later, Bader was in London to speak at the Lord's Taverner Dinner. When he emerged from his cab at the place of the banquet, there standing on the street was, by all appearances, a beggar woman. She approached and Bader put his hand to his pocket when she said, "I don't want your money. Are you Sir Douglas Bader?" He said he was.

She said, "I am a clairvoyant. I have a message from a friend of yours in the spirit world named Henry. I don't have his last name and I don't know what the message means. He said, 'Tell Bader, the grass is greener on the other side.' "

With that, she walked away, leaving Bader so shaken he did not stay for the dinner, but went home in the same cab that brought him.

The story was never told in Bader's lifetime. He revealed it to a friend who replaced Longhurst as the British columnist for GOLF DIGEST, Peter Dobereiner.

The details of what happened are presented here exactly as Bader related them to Dobereiner, who always wondered about the veracity of the story. He thought it might have been Henry's idea of an elaborate hoax. It remains one of the great mysteries of golf.

Will the grass be greener on the other side? We can only wait and see.

Golf courses, like fingerprints or snowflakes, are all unique; each has its own character, mood, sense of place. Pictured is Sycamore Hills Golf Club in Fort Wayne, Ind. (Photo: Chris John/PDI)

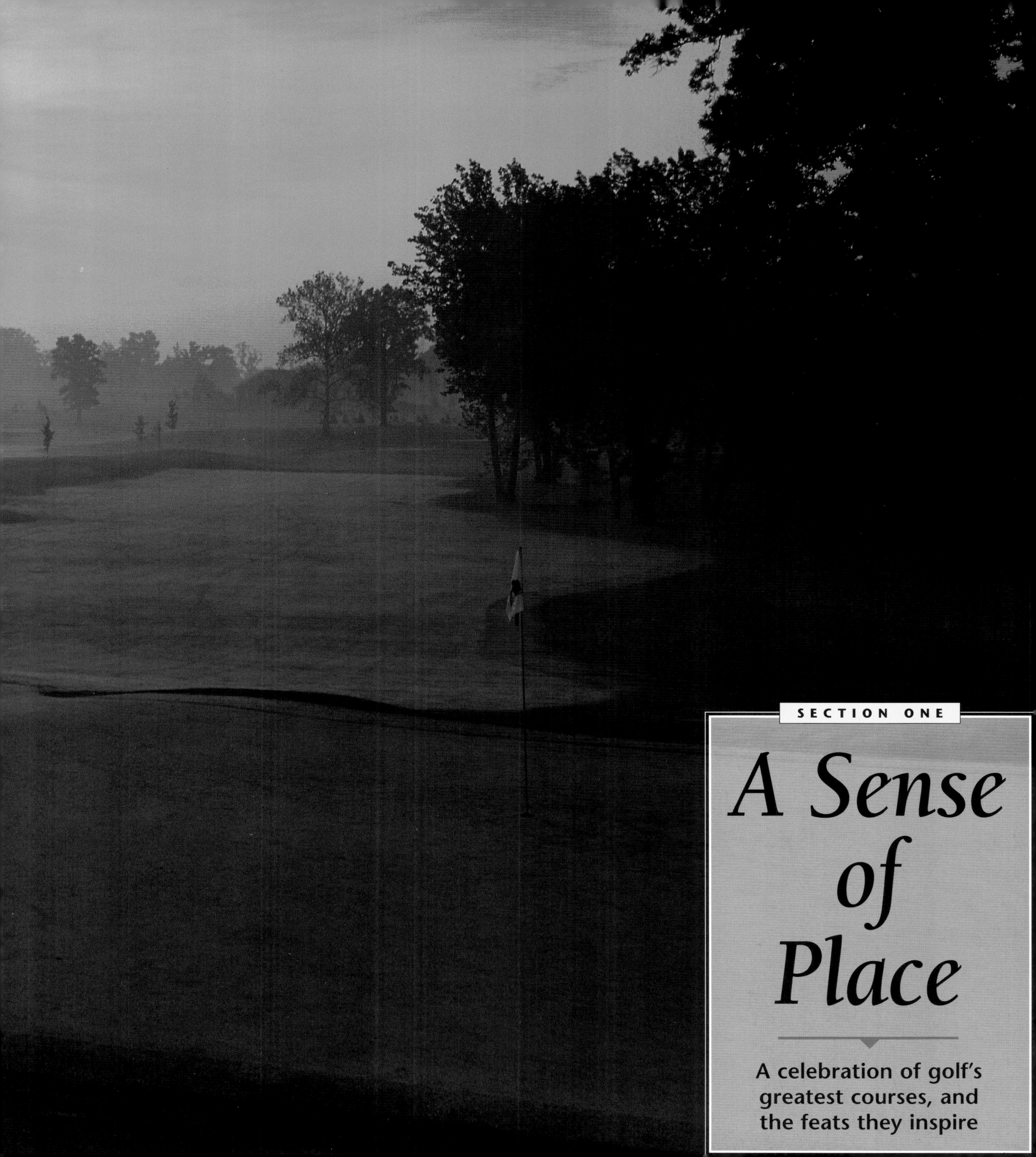

SECTION ONE

A Sense of Place

A celebration of golf's greatest courses, and the feats they inspire

by Ron Whitten, Architecture Editor

Ben Hogan knew the secret all along. It's out there in the dirt, he used to say. You've just got to dig it out.

Of course, he was talking about the perfect golf swing, but his wisdom applies equally as well to golf course architecture.

That's the secret of great golf course design. It's in the land.

That may seem logical, but it was never obvious. GOLF DIGEST spent much of its first 50 years searching the many facets of golf course design. In the postwar boom of the 1950s, our coverage was mainly previews of major tournaments, but by the end of the decade, we were documenting the explosion of new public courses in a column called "Places to Play."

In the technicolor 1960s, our cameras defined what a "spectacular golf hole" should look like, Places to Play became an annual directory, and Herbert Warren Wind penned the seminal treatise on course architecture, so massive in scope that it was spread over two issues.

In the Me Decade that followed, we began tracking the careers of many tour professionals who turned to golf design as an avocation, but the real stars were golf courses. Our biennial ranking of America's 100 Greatest (which had its roots in a 1966 feature) became the standard of the industry, ultimately spawning a number of imitators.

Our course ranking system was revamped in the mid-1980s, and we began boldly ranking America's greatest courses by number, one through 100. The evaluation system we instituted to determine those rankings became the measuring stick by which great golf courses are now determined around the globe, and a progeny, the annual Best New Courses survey, blossomed as the most desired honor of every new layout. We also turned 22,000 readers into Armchair Architects with a design contest judged by real golf architects and a trip to Bermuda as the top prize.

We reprised the contest in the early 1990s, promising immortality instead of Bermuda this time, but of the three winning entries, only the par-3 hole was able to be con-

The August 1972 issue featured a spectacular, new course on the cover—Pete Dye's Casa de Campo in the Dominican Republic.

structed, at Greystone Golf Club north of Detroit. The winning par-4 and par-5 holes, destined for other projects in other states, were strangled by environmental and zoning red tape. Places to Play became a reader event, too, soliciting judgments from actual customers of nearly every public course across America, ratings that filled several guide books.

In that 50-year span, America went from just a dozen full-time course architects to well over 300, from green fees of $1 all-day to $280 plus caddie, from hand-watering tees and greens to quadruple-row automatic irrigation.

Through it all, a handful of courses stood out. The same ones, year after year, decade after decade. At home, Pine Valley, Augusta National and Pebble Beach. Overseas, St. Andrews and Ballybunion.

But we were never really sure why.

From time to time, other courses would join them on the lofty perch of public acclaim. Some stayed, most didn't.

Cypress Point rose above a jab by Jimmy Demaret as "the best 17-hole golf course in the world," but Merion, even with a recent new set of back tees, can't shake its image as a quaint museum piece. Pinehurst No. 2, given up for dead in the 1980s, was vindicated by the 1999 U.S. Open, but its British Open counterpart that year, Carnoustie, in Scotland, was dubbed "Carnasty" in the aftermath of its Open carnage.

An observation in the late 1980s by Bill Davis, co-founder of this magazine and genius behind its course rankings, provided the first real clue to the secret of great architecture. Ever notice, he asked, how great courses seem to be clustered together? The cluster on California's Monterey Peninsula, in New York's Westchester County, on each coast of Scotland?

It's the land, he said. Great land begets great courses.

True enough, but that didn't explain why certain courses, the greatest of the great, endured. None of those courses have the same land. Not even close. Pine Valley is nothing like Pebble Beach.

So the secret wasn't the property used for the course. Great land doesn't automatically produce great golf courses. Some terrible land has been turned into fascinating layouts by imaginative architects.

Nor is the secret in how much earth is pushed around in creating tees, fairways and greens.Or how little dirt, for that matter.

No, the real secret to a great golf course is an architect remaining faithful to the locale. A great golf course gives all golfers who step upon it a sense of where they are. It reflects the best of what that particular piece of land has to offer. The great courses do that. Pretenders do not.

Sand Hills in Nebraska was one of the hottest new arrivals in the 1990s. Its appeal is that it looks like it's been there forever. (Photo: Stephen Szurlej)

Pine Valley captures the very essence of the sandy "pine barrens" just east of the Delaware River from Philadelphia. It does so through its long expanses of exposed sand, stretching from tee boxes to fairways on most holes, from fairways to greens on some. This is unraked sand, we should add, leaving the possibility that the footprints of Palmer and Nicklaus could literally precede us in the course of a round. Although most of New Jersey's pine barrens are now covered in concrete and asphalt, the past survives within the fencelines of Pine Valley. That timelessness is part of the joy of a round of golf there.

The site of Augusta National was once a deep South arboretum, though in truth its present-day dogwoods and azaleas provide far more dazzle than anything grown in its previous life as a modest nursery. Augusta is dominated by its towering cathedral pines, blanketed beneath by pine straw, as red as brick-clay earth, and its sweeping topography of steep slopes and banked turns. Stroll along Augusta National, and you know you're in Georgia.

Pebble Beach isn't merely a seaside course, it's an 18-hole encounter with the Pacific Ocean. The opening holes tease with occasional glimpses of Carmel Bay. Four through six take us along the surf, but high above it. The seventh green brings us to water's edge, where you can taste the sea spray, then we climb atop sheer cliffs once again. Pebble concludes memorably along the rocky coastline, among smashing waves, seagulls and sea lions.

What has made each of those courses great is that they have become a part of the land on which they exist. They're in the land.

The test holds true when applied to any great course. The auld grey town of St. Andrews, Scotland, is visible from any spot on the Old Course, except, perhaps, by players mired in one of its ferociously deep bunkers, like Hell or Strath. The merger of course and adjacent town is nearly seamless. There are no fences, it being a public common, and picnickers are free to stroll across the fairways to and from the beach, even during play.

The Irish Alps are no mere backdrop to the golf holes of Ballybunion, they are a part of them. Fairways rise along slopes and tumble into valleys, forever twisting and turning despite a snug fit between land

and course that has endured for more than 75 years.

Some architects have discovered this secret. The best ones neither overpower a site nor underplay it. They're able to strike the right tone and balance, providing not just challenging shots and testing putts, but also an appreciation for the landscapes on which they build.

It's in the land. The beauty of Prairie Dunes in Hutchinson, Kan., is not that it resembles some grand old Scottish links, but that it contains the best that Kansas has to offer. It offers rippling fairways strung out over sand dunes, bordering plum thickets, spiny yucca plants emerging from many bunkers, and even a

cove of sturdy cottonwoods—the state tree—at one bend of the course. Likewise, its more recent counterpart, Sand Hills Golf Club in central Nebraska, displays the awesome grandeur of the Great Plains. The bunkers at Sand Hills look as though carved by nature, and they were, for wind constantly resculpts their edges.

The great courses provide a sense of place. That's why they remain the greatest generation after generation. That has to be their secret. It's the only thing they have in common, other than little plastic cups, four and one half inches in diameter, sunk into each of their greens.

Below: *The Donald Ross-designed East Course at Oak Hill in Rochester, N.Y., has held three U.S. Opens, a PGA Championship, and the 1995 Ryder Cup. (Photo: Chris John/PDI)*

Bottom: *The Blue Course at Congressional, not far from the nation's capital, has long been a member of America's 100 Greatest Golf Courses. (Photo: Chris John/PDI)*

The par-3 seventh hole at the majestic Shinnecock Hills, Southampton, N.Y., is a classic example of a "Redan" hole, with a diagonal green that slopes from front right to back left, and a cavernous bunker protecting the left side. (Photo: Stephen Szurlej)

"Nature," someone once said, "is something man has been placed on this earth to rise above." Nowhere has this concept been more fully developed than at the Augusta National Golf Club.

Top: *Augusta National entrance. (Photo: Jim Moriarty)*
Bottom: *Augusta National's famously formidable No. 13.*
(Photo: Stephen Szurlej)

Reflections on Augusta

The first impressions of a first-time spectator at golf's greatest tournament
by Peter Andrews

You can't have a truly first impression of the Masters any more than you can have a first impression of the Grand Canyon or the Eiffel Tower. Its images have been filed in your memory bank for as long as there have been postcards and television. I know Amen Corner better than I know the boundary line on my own property, something my neighbor has remarked on more than once, and I am as familiar with Magnolia Lane as I am with Lexington Avenue. I don't have to journey to the Louvre to look at the Mona Lisa. I know the painting. I just want to see if they've got the light right.

They don't, by the way. But then again, the French Ministry of Culture doesn't have the kind of clout the people who run the Masters do. The Lord may have said, "Let there be light," but Clifford Roberts personally riffled through the swatches and picked out the exact shade of green he wanted.

"Nature," someone once said, "is something man has been placed on this earth to rise above." Nowhere has this concept been more fully developed than at the Augusta National Golf Club. It is not simply that no real rough grows on the course. It is that no imperfection will be tolerated. You get the feeling that once, probably during the Great Depression when there was a lot of aimless roaming around in the country, a few sprigs of crabgrass and perhaps a dandelion poked up somewhere on the back nine and the green-keeper came over and speaking very quietly, told them, "We don't want your kind around here," and they packed up and moved to a municipal course in Idaho. Do I exaggerate? One spring, I'm told, the azaleas started to bloom too early to suit the membership and in a gesture worthy of Olympus they had the offending plants packed in ice so the blossoms would be perfect for the tournament. It takes a certain presence to make Mother Nature wait in line for the Masters to begin along with the rest of us.

AN INAUSPICIOUS APPROACH

The approach to the course is not particularly imposing. The adjoining town of Augusta, which by Augusta National fiat is never photographed during the Masters, is a robust community of some 50,000. It is almost an editorial mandate to denigrate Augusta and describe it as a tacky, little Southern town swollen with fast-food restaurants unfit to host so grand an affair as the Masters. I do not recall reading a report on the place that did not make that point. Well, I am a New Yorker and I know tacky when I see it.

PEERLESS SERVICE

The Masters stands for service. There is no better $8 haircut available in the English-speaking world than the one provided by Leslie (Johnny) Johnson, who maintains his shop within the clubhouse. The next day I went back for that most civilized amenity, the barber's shave. You would have to go to Tramp's in London to find its equal. But then you probably wouldn't get a barber who has played Amen Corner in level par.

I didn't fully realize the extent of the Masters' dedication to service until the second day of the tournament when I had a raging toothache. I went to the press desk and was given an immediate appointment in Augusta with Dr. Emanuel Weisman, an avid golf enthusiast. I found out there was a team of dentists on round-the-clock standby for just such emergencies. Dr. Weisman had me back out on the course free of pain within an hour.

LOCAL FAUNA

Men away from home do odd things. In the interest of securing some local color we went one night to the Discotheque Lounge, a night spot in Augusta that promised a "Las Vegas Type Show." The show consisted of Wanda, Chirl, Dee Dee and Angie who took off their

"It is simply that no real rough grows on the course." Or so it seems, once the painstaking preparations are finished. (Photo: Jim Moriarty)

clothes while we sipped a $2.50 scotch and water. One in our company ordered a Chablis, but was told sharply, "This is not a white-wine place." Midway through the first act, a former U.S. Open champion walked in, stopped by our table to say hello and found a seat in the back. After a round we started to go and the doorman dressed in an Uncle Sam costume pleaded with us to stay for the grand finale in which one of the ladies would perform with two boa constrictors. But I am a city boy and I had seen enough fauna for the evening and we left. I may go back this year. I haven't seen a really good snake dance act since Tempest Storm.

ROMAN ECHOES
On the third day, I decided to trail well behind the field because I wanted to be alone on the course. The Palatine Hill in Rome must have sounded like this when the emperors staged their great victory parades. I could hear cheers rolling across the countryside. It did not seem to matter who was winning as long as the game was being played well.

Real estate, no matter how beautifully cultivated, is just property until you know what men have done there to give it value. Clayton Hoskins, a distinguished attorney and man of golf, said Augusta National sounds "like a place where you might bury a war hero." Hoskins knows whereof he speaks. He is almost certainly the only Navy pilot who flew in World War II with a mashie niblick in the cockpit of his airplane.

Augusta does resemble a great battlefield memorial. Just as you can go to Gettysburg and look up toward Cemetery Ridge and "see" General Armistead's black felt hat perched on a saber above the smoke of Pickett's charge as it breached the Union line in the last great moment of the Confederacy, you can tramp the course and "see" the moments of glory and folly that are part of the history of the Masters. Each hole has its own war story. Those stories change the nature of holes with charming names such as Pink Dogwood and Golden Bell into places of dark menace. That's the second hole where Doug Tewell misjudged a four-foot birdie putt 25 feet past the cup, and the 12th where Tom Weiskopf once tried to hit too exquisite a shot over the pond and put five into the water for a 13.

If Augusta were in Spain, the old women of the village would rend their garments and sing sad songs about such things. But self-pity has been banished along with crabgrass at the shrine of Bobby Jones and you smile and play the man and don't let anyone see how badly you're hurt. Not a bad lesson in any endeavor.

TRAILING THE PARADE
Behind every circus parade there are the people who follow and clean up. The mowers came rumbling out trimming and cutting and squads of young people with "Litter" written on their yellow caps slipped out of the woods and began picking up scraps of paper. I picked up a few myself and put them in my pockets. I don't know that I would pick up used drinking cups at Yankee Stadium.

17

Left: *The innocent-looking 170-yard 16th hole, called "Redbud," has dashed many hopes of glory. (Photo: Stephen Szurlej)*

EVENING PRIMROSE

Not everything about Augusta National is necessarily august. A distinguished-looking gentleman, not a member, pointed to a flowering azalea bush on the front nine and confided to me that this was where a member disported himself one evening with a woman to whom he was not legally bound.

"It was," he told me, "the most interesting thing that has ever happened around here after 6 o'clock in the evening since Jimmy Demaret."

LASTING FAME

I will not dwell on the final day. Its heroics have been captured in millions of words and thousands of yards of film already. The Iliad doesn't need a sidebar. But

there was one ancient lesson that was relearned. There is nothing harder to kill than an old idol. As Nicklaus was screaming his way to a final round of 65, I passed an elderly gentleman who remarked somberly to a friend, "I don't care what you say, he's not Arnold Palmer and I guarantee he never will be."

APPLAUSE, APPLAUSE

Augusta is a hard place to leave. As our airplane was heading home the pilot took a slow right turn over the grounds to give us one last look. We put our drinks down and suddenly all the passengers began clapping their hands as if to recapture the excitement of the previous day—an airplane full of grown people flying at 6,000 feet applauding a golf course.

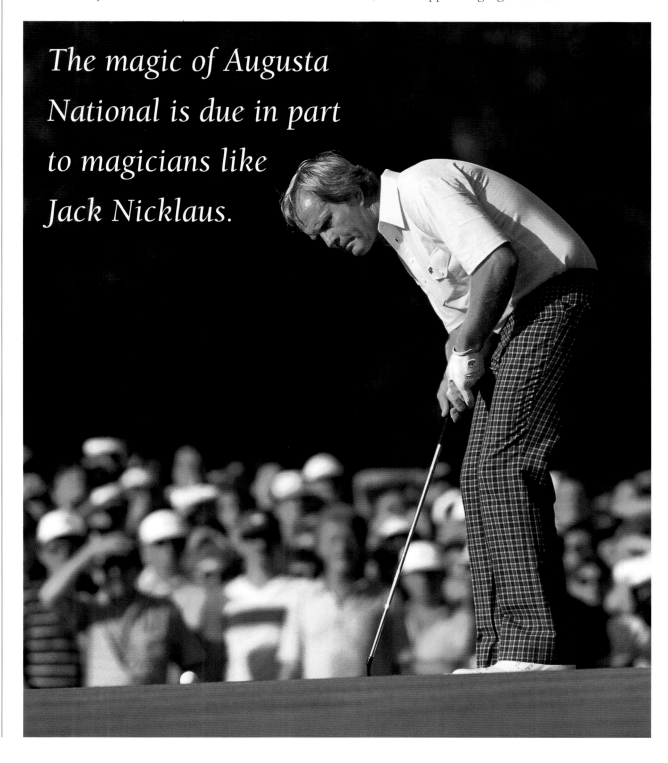

The magic of Augusta National is due in part to magicians like Jack Nicklaus.

Right: *The cheers ricocheted around the magnolias as Jack Nicklaus marched toward his sixth Masters title in 1986. (Photo: Jim Moriarty)*

Over Nelson's Bridge

The real Rae's Creek turns in front of the 13th tee. The water edging the left side of the hole and hugging the famed green is just a tributary.

Fade it to the green

It's tempting to go for the green from here, but the ground slopes right to left. That's a hook lie; the shape of the green requires a fade.

America's Greatest
Par 5

The winner: Augusta National's 13th is 485 yards of risk and reward

This 1933 collaboration of Bobby Jones and Alister Mackenzie is familiar to all Masters fans. Mackenzie patterned the tee shot as a mirror image of the drive at his par-4 17th at Cypress Point. The go-for-broke second was based on his 1914 contest-winning design of an ideal golf hole. (Photo: Stephen Szurlej)

A legend's ledge
Jack Nicklaus' green redesign in 1983 resulted in back pin placements perched above a steep swale. The hardest pin to attack is front right.

Up the creek
Once a moat, this was turned back to a babbling brook in 1996 so that players could again try recovery shots from the rocky creek bed.

If Portrush is rigorous, Ten Commandment Golf (Thou shalt not miss the fairways; Thou shalt not covet thy neighbor's wind-cheating 1-iron) then Newcastle is pure Song of Solomon.

Golf's Irish Blessings

May the green rise up to meet you, the wind be always at your back, and may you be in the clubhouse an hour before the storm breaks

by Peter Dobereiner

On a visit to Ireland a friend of mine remarked to the taxi driver that they seemed to be proceeding in the wrong direction along a one-way street. "Sure," said the driver cheerfully, "but it's bloody miles the other way round." That incident encapsulates two elements of the Irish character that help to make Ireland the finest destination in the world for the itinerant golfer.

First there is the genuine desire that the visitor should think well of Ireland, even if it means a betrayal of the universal taxi driver's code that no matter where the tourist wants to go he must be taken to the cleaners.

The second element is rather more subtle. On the face of it you might think that deliberately driving the wrong way down a one-way street showed a total contempt for the law. No, no. It is a highly sophisticated process. The Irish regard laws, rules and regulations as guidelines, to be judged against prior considerations of common sense. Say the law requires bars to close at 11 p.m. Well, if the bar is empty at the due closing time then the barman will dutifully lock up the premises. But if the bar is full at 11 and nobody is being disturbed in the neighborhood by the wavering tenor in the spit-and-sawdust, vibrantly observing the sun going down on Galway Bay, and most particularly if the tenor happens to be the village policeman, then the bar will stay open until 2 a.m., or breakfast time, or next Thursday.

That is not anarchy; that is the highest form of civilization. It also plays hell with schedules and itineraries and programs and, as I know to my cost, newspaper deadlines, which is why the visiting golfer should keep his plans flexible.

The absolutely best way to play golf in Ireland is to plan nothing. Gather together a convivial party, buy air tickets with open returns and just go. Pick up rental cars at the airport and make for the nearest golf course. Mention casually in the club that you have nowhere fixed up to stay and you will immediately become plugged into The System. This is an informal network based on the fact that Ireland is a small country populated by enormous families so, although everybody does not know everybody else, everybody has a cousin who has a contact who can reach the ear of someone who knows a man with enough influence to get to the man with real pull.

Once you are in The System nothing is impossible in Ireland. I once met a man who knew a man who knew a man and as a result a scheduled flight from Dublin to Lourdes was diverted to drop me off at Shannon to play golf at Ballybunion.

In your case, a man will know a man whose sister-in-law has the finest guest house in the district and cooks steaks like you wouldn't believe. She in turn will have an aunt who runs an even finer establishment in County Mayo and so, if you wish, you will be passed on indefinitely until you lose track of time and probably get yourself fired when you eventually get back to the office two weeks late.

On three separate occasions I have set out to visit Donegal, a place of legendary beauty. It remains legendary so far as I am concerned. In the six weeks I have devoted to that quest I must have played 50 courses and had as many adventures, but I have never made it to Donegal.

Americans have the reputation of liking everything cut and dried and organized down to the last detail, a slur on the American character from my observations in Ireland, but let it pass. Let us get down to some details.

The best golf is to be found around the edges of the island, on or near the coast. The ports of entry for international flights are Shannon or Dublin and in both cases I would

Ballybunion, "a journey through a wonderland of enormous dunes," is a must-play for any visitor to Ireland. (Photo: ALLSPORT)

tell golfers: "I wouldn't start from here." Take an internal flight on to Cork and pick up your car there. Then you are well sited for a clockwise tour of Ireland, working your way up the west coast and then down the east coast to Dublin.

In that case Waterville is the next logical stop. A rather humdrum start to the round is followed by 11 holes of the finest links golf you could imagine, with gorgeous views of the rocky Kerry coastline. On this seaboard the wind often whips in off the Atlantic at 60 miles per hour, making for exhilarating golf and if your yardage chart is whipped from your hand by the gale you need not fret; it is useless in this form of golf anyway.

Apart from freshly made potato cakes, a good reason for patronizing guest houses and the ubiquitous bed-and-breakfast homes is that you save enough to indulge yourself occasionally on a splurge at a luxury hotel. Waterville Lake Hotel is one such, if only for the finest view from any dining room in the world and fabulous fresh seafood. They also have a remarkably extensive wine cellar.

By now you may be ready for Ballybunion, with two of the greatest links in the world. Tom Watson drools over Old Ballybunion, a journey through a wonderland of enormous dunes. My own feeling is that Robert Trent Jones has produced his masterpiece in the New Course, where the dunes are even higher and the golf on a more heroic scale. Give it two more years to mature and it will be one of golf's wonders of the world, a judgment that is confirmed rather than shaken by many opposing opinions that it is so difficult as to be unplayable. Some people

say the same thing about the 16th at Cypress Point.

Lahinch must be the next destination, a lovely old-fashioned links with some absolute collector's items of blind shots and plenty of scope for cunning use of contours to coax your ball up to the flag, or bump-and-run golf as the distressing American phrase has it. The barometer in the clubhouse is broken and has pasted on it the legend: "See goats." If the club's herd of goats is huddled against the lee of the clubhouse it is going to rain hard. If they are nowhere to be seen, grazing on distant fairways, it means it is raining only lightly.

In keeping with our policy of staying near the coast where the sea air is lightly scented by the peat smoke from the grates of the whitewashed cottages, I would urge a dash north next to Rosses Point in County Sligo. It is a good drive so it might be worthwhile to fortify the inner man first with an overnight stop at Dromoland, a medieval castle beautifully adapted to lotus-eating luxury with the full four-poster bed treatment and browsing and sluicing of epicurean standard. Across the drawbridge Dromoland has its own golf course, but forget it. You could get more interesting golf at a driving range. This is a purely 19th-hole job.

Like a number of clubs in Ireland, Rosses Point is not the proper name. It is the Sligo Golf Club, but I have never heard an Irishman refer to it as such. Be that as it may, it offers yet another change of pace. It does not have the grandeur of Ballybunion's mighty dunes, suggesting rather a sandy promontory that might have been once used as a tank training ground and experimental station for land mines. It has a wild,

unkempt look about it that perfectly matches the prevailing weather. This is a genuine championship course with a long tradition of mighty men and mighty deeds, a tough test of a man's golf and character.

For some obscure reason based on ignorance or prejudice, the editors of GOLF DIGEST wish me to perpetuate the partition of Ireland and discuss Northern Irish golf separately, probably on a different page with an intervening ad for FootJoy to keep the combatants apart. In my suggested itinerary we would next move to Portrush, but orders are orders and we will continue our story at the end, in the east coast city of Dublin.

So far our golf has been friendly and informal, come as you please, when you like, and welcome, but in Dublin we are in dress-code territory, with jackets and ties required if you want to use the dining room, and advance arrangements to be made with the secretary for starting times. Portmarnock is one of the great championship courses of Europe, built on a headland of softly rolling links with water on three sides. Unusual for any golf course, it has 18 strong holes. Correction. Make that 17 strong holes and one absolute jewel, a par 3 along the beach to

compare with the 15th at Cypress Point and not dissimilar in character.

Royal Dublin is on an island reached by a causeway built by Capt. Bligh of the famous mutiny on the HMS Bounty. It is not as long as Portmarnock nor would it move Arnold Palmer similarly to describe it as "the finest natural golf in the world." What it has over its illustrious neighbor is charm. It is a captivating course, short and sporty links golf, and never more charming than in the spring when the hares go mad. The hares are a great feature of Royal Dublin, just as the goats are at Lahinch, and they have an uncanny knack of leaping from the rough just as you are on the backswing. Dead is he of soul who can observe their madcap antics without collapsing with mirth, especially if his opponent has been startled into whiffing his ball.

Dublin is richly endowed with golf courses of great variety, links, parkland, cliff-top, mountain and heath, but I would advise driving out of town for one last links course, near Drogheda. It is the County Louth Club, so naturally everyone calls it Baltray, a beautiful and testing links and one of the undiscovered gems of Irish golf.

GO NORTH, MY MAN

Overseas visitors are naturally wary about going into Northern Ireland because all they know of the country is the TV news image of the troubles, or the nonsense as some of us think of it. Is it safe? I cannot give any assurance but I can tell you that I feel safer in Belfast than I do in Newark, N.J., or Detroit, or Chicago, or New York, or St. Louis, where the hall porter of my hotel gave me a map showing two streets where it was safe to stroll after dark. I can tell you that no overseas golfer has ever received so much as a scratch in Northern Ireland. I can tell you that Belfast Airport has the best antiterrorist record in Europe, safety having been the major priority for 17 years. I can tell you that security is rigid but so unobtrusive that you do not notice it unless you search for it. I can tell you that I do not give these things a thought when I visit Northern Ireland. Like the Golf Union of Ireland, which amicably administers the game throughout the whole Emerald Isle, I happily endorse the principle that golf does not recognize lines drawn on maps unless they are marked with white posts and that the golf community is a harmonious international brotherhood under the protection of the god that looks after drunks and lunatics.

So let us fill in at least two notable gaps in the itinerary with a visit to Royal Portrush, the only Irish course to have held the British Open. That was in 1951 and England's Max Faulkner was the winner. He had only 108 putts and afterward spread his arms and boasted: "I shall never miss one of these again." Henry Longhurst wrote that when he heard these words he moved away in case the gods associated him with such heresy. Portrush is reckoned to be the supreme test of driving, probably because so many of the holes dogleg sharply through the dunes and the penalties for running through the fairway are severe.

Royal County Down, known as Newcastle, is at the opposite end of the golfing scale, and of the province. If Portrush is rigorous, Ten Commandment golf (Thou shalt not miss the fairways; Thou shalt not covet thy neighbor's wind-cheating 1-iron) then Newcastle is pure Song of Solomon. Behold thou art fair, my Love.

They tell me that Newcastle is actually a good test of golf. I wouldn't know. For me, Newcastle is golf's most powerful opiate and symbols written on a card under the influence of this beguiling drug do not bear scrutiny when I come down from my high.

Mackenzie mastery
In 1925, Alister Mackenzie moved the green back from the cliff and added the surrounding bunkers. The once-generous green is now tiny.

No easy lay up
These flanking bunkers were added in the early 1950s. Before that, there were cross bunkers in the fairway, complicating bailout shots.

America's Greatest
Par 4

*The winner: Pebble Beach's
No. 8 is a 431-yard
cliff-hanger*

With the profile of a roller coaster, up and over a hump, followed by a scary banked turn to the green, Pebble's "chasm" hole was a startling par 4 when Jack Neville and Douglas Grant finished it in 1917. Jack Nicklaus says the eighth has "the greatest second shot in the game." (Photo: Jim Moriarty)

Gobbling gulch
A few pebbles still show through the beach of golf balls at the foot of this gulch. The cove also has swallowed a dog and a golf cart.

Test of courage
The fairway here is 100 feet high. Johnny Miller once had a perilous lie right on the precipice. He wisely kept his weight on his right side.

On Monterey's rhinocerotic land mass, Pebble Beach, Spyglass Hill and Cypress Point compete for the golfer's soul.

Pebble Beach (No. 5 shown, top), Spyglass Hill (No. 6 shown, middle) and Cypress Point (No. 13 shown, bottom) form the holy trinity of golf on the Monterey peninsula. (Photos: Jim Moriarty [top]; Stephen Szurlej)

Monterey

How I was seduced by a peninsula

by Cal Brown

In the Bible it says that God made the world in six days and on the seventh, rested. But I think that on the seventh day he created the Monterey Peninsula. There cannot be another place on earth quite like it, nor another place that has three golf courses of such quality in so small a space.

It is as though every thundering emotion, every subtle line had been withheld from the rest of creation and then dumped in this one place to test our understanding of the superlative. One's response to this angular chunk of land, shaped like the snout of a rhinoceros and jutting into the Pacific about 90 miles south of San Francisco, is instant and elemental. Even on a gray, overcast day or during a winter storm, it is compelling and seductive.

Hills and craggy bluffs tumble into the sea, which ebbs and crashes against copper-brown rocks, casting huge white plumes and mist into the air above dozing seals and an occasional solitary beachcomber. Gray-boled and winter-green cypress trees cling to the soil in clumps or in stark individuality, bent and twisted by the wind and spray. Here and there the headland splashes down into uneven, white-faced dunes. Surmounting everything is a sense of quiet, a curious intimation of settled spirit on the raging coast.

Here are three of the world's greatest golf courses, and how could they be otherwise? Their names alone stir the juices—Pebble Beach, legendary, rugged and for all of its fame still a bridesmaid to U.S. Open competition; Cypress Point, shy and mysterious, a splendidly proportioned and artful mistress; and Spyglass Hill, diabolical, controversial and maddening in its newness.

Within 5,200 acres of private land known as the Del Monte Forest, the late Samuel F. B. Morse founded and developed some of the most expensive real estate and one of the most magnificent resorts in the world. The Del Monte property is encircled by a 17-mile drive over which visitors may travel, at $3 per car. No overnight camping is permitted, and no plant or animal may be "disturbed, injured or removed." Deer roam freely through the forest and across the golf courses.

Pebble Beach—rugged

Although the Bing Crosby National Pro-Am is held on all three of Monterey's great courses, people are most familiar with Pebble Beach, where play is seen on television, even though obscured, at times, by the rain and fog that regularly visit the peninsula.

Like many of our greatest courses, Pebble Beach was designed by amateurs. Jack Neville and Douglas Grant, both California amateur champions, laid out the 6,777-yard course in 1919. It has held three national amateur championships, the first in 1929. That was the year Johnny Goodman, then an unknown, came out from Omaha to beat Bobby Jones in the first round. The winner was unheralded Harrison Johnston of Minnesota, who bested a field that included Francis Ouimet, Chick Evans, Lawson Little, Chandler Egan and Cyril Tolley. In 1947 the cast included Dick Chapman, Bud Ward, Smiley Quick, Bob Rosburg and Frank Stranahan, but the winner was Skee Riegel, who walked like a fighter and played like a machine, smoking two packs of cigarettes per round, to beat Johnny Dawson in the finals. In 1961, Jack Nicklaus took the second of his amateur crowns here, beating Dudley Wysong 8 and 6 in the final.

Pebble Beach opens like a lamb, with four easy, very ordinary holes. The fifth is a short, quick thrust up through a sliver of light between the trees and then, suddenly, you are upon the ocean riding two terrifying shots along the crest of a massive bluff to the sixth green. To the right, nothing but emptiness and, far below, thrashing surf and rocks.

The sixth hole, a 515-yard par 5 that Byron Nelson thinks is the toughest hole on the course, begins a stretch of five of the most spectacular holes in golf, three of them on a narrow, craggy spit that overhangs the ocean. The seventh is a tiny, 120-yard downhill pitch that looks almost like a miniature golf hole. But when the wind blows, it can require a solid 4-iron into the gale. The eighth is a marvel, one of the great two-shotters in the world. After a blind tee shot to a plateau, you are faced with hitting 180 yards over a sheer cliff, across a chasm that resembles a shark's maw and to a green that is pitched into a depression and completely surrounded by bunkers.

The ninth stretches 450 yards along the ocean, its right margin eaten away by the surf. When the wind is up, the biggest hitters cannot get home even with two wood shots. During the 1963 Crosby, Dale Douglass took 19 blows here after landing on the steep bank, an even worse place to be than the rocky beach below.

There are many who believe the inland stretch from 11 through 16 is inferior and not at all in keeping with the hair-raising ocean holes. This is only partially true. Certainly 11 and 12 are routine holes, but 13, a straight-away par 4 of 400 yards, is perhaps the most underrated hole on the course. The second shot must fly true to avoid bunkers and trees guarding the green.

The 14th is a marvelously deft par 5 that curls away from the sea to the right and has been the scene of a few miserable encounters. Here Arnold Palmer, who has never won the Crosby, came a cropper in 1964. In going for the green on his second shot, Palmer hit a tree on the right and went out-of-bounds twice. He made 9 on the hole and dropped from contention. The next day, a storm knocked the tree down.

The 17th, a par 3 surrounded by sand and ocean, looks more beatable in real life than it appears on television—until you play it. The 18th, a journey that ends happily only after three very strong shots and two good putts, is among the most ballyhooed finishing holes in golf, and quite rightly.

Spyglass Hill—maddening

Spyglass Hill is a Robert Trent Jones layout that opened in 1966 and ever since has been the target of stronger words than Spiro Agnew at a gathering of New York Republicans. Most of the abuse comes from touring pros, who are not accustomed to shooting in the 80s.

Spyglass, in its youthful striving for greatness, is too new to be finally judged. Several things about it are evident, though. It is ruthlessly tough and on windy days almost impossible. In 1970 it was rated at 76.1 from the back tees (6,972 yards), but it has never been played in competition over its full length.

The course record is 70, two under par, made by Forest Fezler, a California amateur who played the ball "as it lies." The best professional score in competition was also 70, made by Bob Murphy in the 1968 Crosby. But he played from the middle tees (6,609 yards, which carries a rating of 74.1), and was improving his lies.

"People can't believe it's so tough," chortles Spyglass Hill's home professional, Frank Thacker. "The first five holes are more a case of fright than anything else." The first hole sweeps 604 yards through the pines down to the ocean, and the next four holes are played on the dunes from one island of grass to the next. The second, though a lay-up hole, is nevertheless an appealing two-shotter that wants a thoughtful golfer and is, for the medium hitter, a fearsome journey past waist-high spikes of pampas grass. The third and fifth are sand-locked par 3s sandwiched around the par-4 fourth, a partially blind hole.

These psychological thrillers are among the easier

Perhaps the most photographed hole in golf: the short but deadly 120-yard seventh at Pebble Beach. Depending on the wind, it can be anything from a half wedge to a full-blooded long iron. (Photo: Jim Moriarty)

No. 15 at Cypress Point plays over a small rocky inlet and back toward land, with crashing surf to the player's right when looking from tee to green. (Photo: Evan Schiller)

The first five holes at Spyglass Hill lull you with sweeping Pacific views. The course then heads into the trees, and shows no mercy. (Photo: Stephen Szurlej)

to design the course. Mackenzie, a Scot and former doctor in the British Army, later did the Augusta National course in Georgia with Bobby Jones.

Cypress is strictly a golf club, and its members are golfers. There are no pools, tennis courts or other distractions. Non-members are not permitted in the clubhouse, even during the Crosby tournament. For years the pros had to change their shoes outside. Now a separate room has been added for this purpose.

The first hole is a lazy dogleg to the right and, at 407 yards, long enough to loosen the muscles. Until recently the tee shot had to negotiate an old, dead pine tree that blew down in a storm and had been called "Joe DiMaggio"—it caught everything.

After a few holes, you are caught up in the pure joy of the place. You feel that every shot is just what you always knew golf should be. Soon you are heading toward the distant ocean over the rugged dunes from holes eight through 13. At 15, a mere 139 yards, you play across a narrow gorge where the water boils angrily as it cuts its way into the cliff. The ball must reach the putting surface, for there are trees, sand and clutching ice plant all around. The ice plant, thick, fleshy stuff, is like trying to escape from a vat of marshmallow.

Then comes the 16th, which has been called the ultimate test of golfing courage. From the back tees it is 233 yards of carry across the Pacific to a large green on the tip of the point. The average golfer must lay up short to the fairway on the left and then pitch to the green. Only on windless days do the pros try for it. The late Porky Oliver made 16 after going in the water four times, and Henry Ransom picked up after 16 attempts to move his shot from the beach up the sheer cliff to the green. Another pro, Hans Merrill, has the all-time record of 19. He made it all on the same ball, going from ice plant to ice plant for nearly half an hour.

The 17th is another heroic hole, a par 4 that runs along the cliff for 375 yards to a green that lurks behind a fat, sprawling cypress tree. The tee, set next to the 16th green on the point, looks into the cliff and you can take as much of the barrier as you like. Once in the fairway you must play either left or right of the tree and stop the ball very quickly. You can easily hit over it—and just as easily into it. Jimmy Demaret once played this hole in the wind by hitting two drivers; he aimed the second out over the ocean and let it blow back.

After the excitement of the ocean holes, the 18th is a soft dissolve swinging gently up through scattered trees to a flagstick silhouetted against the sky next to the clubhouse, of simple Spanish California style that looks so natural on the site it seems to have grown there among the cypress trees.

Opinion about a golf course can be a fragile thing. But taken all as a piece, the Monterey Peninsula and its golf courses are something to behold. There is enough variety to sate the most demanding golfing spirit. It is a special place where the tendons and mind can stretch on equal terms. In fact, if heaven isn't like Pebble Beach, I won't be going.

holes. Once the course turns inland it gets narrower and longer, and your breath and shoulder turn get shorter. Spyglass Hill's greens are huge, and you can three-putt all day long. Putts of 150 feet are possible. A lot of the criticism of the course centers around the greens, which have since been remodeled. The first time the course was used in the Crosby, on the 14th hole, a gem of a par 5 with an angled green perched on the left above a pond, one of the contestants putted off the green and into the water. On the same green, Jack Nicklaus once four-putted from 14 feet.

Is Spyglass tougher than Pebble Beach? Probably. Not long ago two doctors teed off at Spyglass Hill with three dozen golf balls between them and had to send the caddie in for a new supply after six holes. But though Spyglass is rated a stroke tougher, it lacks the wild, undisciplined spirit of Pebble Beach. Spyglass is a more refined article, with a harder, more sculptured look than either of the other two courses here.

Cypress Point—artful

"If I were condemned to play only one course for the rest of my life, I would unhesitatingly pick Cypress Point."

So says Joe Dey, former executive director of the USGA and now commissioner of the Tournament Players' Division of the PGA. Dey, no mean judge of golf courses, is not alone in this choice. Golfers fortunate enough to play this little masterpiece more often than not come away feeling that Cypress Point is more fun to play than any other on the peninsula.

The course was conceived in 1926 by Marion Hollins, the women's national amateur champion of 1921, and Roger Lapham, who was president of the California Golf Association and a member of the USGA executive committee. They bought property from Del Monte and commissioned Alister Mackenzie

Southern Comfort

It's more than a place: Pinehurst is a state of mind

by Charles McGrath

Of the many legendary American golf courses, Pinehurst No. 2 is the one that most resembles a muny: It's open to anybody, of whatever station or ability, who can foot the bill. But in a way No. 2 is also the most elusive of the classic layouts. Because in recent years it has played host to so few important tournaments, the course hasn't yet become television familiar, its lofty, pine-towered aisles memorized by the cameras, its puzzling greens computer-graphed and analyzed. All this is about to change, of course, but for now, in the imaginations of many of us, Pinehurst No. 2 still exists much as it did in the head of its creator, Donald Ross—as a kind of waking dream. Pinehurst, the locals like to say, is a state of mind.

Ross, whose kindly, steel-spectacled likeness is everywhere in Pinehurst, was actually the second, or maybe the third, visionary associated with the place. The first was James Walker Tufts, an apothecary from Medford, Mass., who in the years after the Civil War made a killing in the soda-fountain business. His fountains weren't just a spigot and a handle, they were marble and chrome monuments to the miracles of carbonation. Like so many New Englanders of his generation, Tufts was also a health nut, and he had a notion of founding a sanitary winter colony for God-fearing citizens who wished to escape the frigid, pestilential North. (The original applicants were required to submit letters from both their doctors and their ministers.)

In 1895 Tufts purchased 6,000 acres of virtual wasteland in the Sandhills of North Carolina—land that had been burned and clear-cut in the manufacture of tar and turpentine—and hired as his landscaper the illustrious Frederick Law Olmsted, designer of Central Park.

Olmsted found Tufts' site unpromising; it was little more than a desert. But he drew up a village master plan—a series of curving roads radiating from and returning, like lines of magnetic force, to a central village green—and he also dispatched one of his associates to oversee the planting of some 250,000 trees and shrubs. A gabled hotel, the Holly Inn, quickly went up, and so did dozens of "cottages"—shuttered and clapboarded single-family residences. Pinehurst was open for business. It looked—and still does—like a little slice of New England transplanted to the pinewoods.

The original sports at Pinehurst were tennis, shooting (Annie Oakley ran the gun club), lawn bowling, and—Tufts' favorite—a game called roque, which was a sort of one-armed version of croquet. Golf arrived, by accident, in 1897, after farmers complained that their cows were being disturbed by some of Mr. Tufts' guests whacking tiny white balls around the pasture. A little nine-holer and a clubhouse were promptly built, but the defining moment in Pinehurst history came in 1900, when Tufts hired Ross, newly emigrated from Scotland, to supervise his golf operations.

Ross' association with the resort lasted until his death, in 1948, and though he went on to build hundreds of courses, including several in the Sandhills area, none meant as much to him as his beloved No. 2, which was both his masterpiece and a constant work-in-progress. Ross' other great Pinehurst legacies were the first driving range ever—Maniac Hill, as Pinehurst's practice ground was called—and the Pine Crest Inn, on Dogwood Street in the village, which he owned and operated from 1921 until his death and which hasn't changed much at all in the years since.

Where the rest of Pinehurst, especially that part run by the resort, is proper and upscale, the Pine Crest is funky and pleasingly down at the heels. The lobby smells of stale cigarette smoke, and the cabbage-rose wallpaper in the main stairwell is due for a face-lift. But there is always something going at the Pine Crest—nightly chipping contests, for example, where guests hit off the carpet at a round target propped up in front of the fireplace, or the weekend appearances of Clarence and Tim, a piano player and Elvis impersonator, who by the end of the evening usually have everybody, college kids and geezers, up and dancing to "Blue Suede Shoes." If the Pine Crest isn't the heart of

"The man who doesn't feel stirred when he golfs at Pinehurst beneath those clear blue skies and with the pine fragrance in his nostrils is one who should be ruled out of golf for life."—TOMMY ARMOUR

Top: *The 1994 U.S. Senior Open showed that Pinehurst No. 2 was once again ready for the big time. (Photo: Bill Fields)* **Bottom:** *The first ever clubhouse at Pinehurst, circa 1898. (Photo: Tufts Archives)*

Pinehurst, exactly, it's easily the id. (The men's-room graffiti is simultaneously scatological and golf related, as in this entry: "Doug can't golf for s---.")

The collective memory of Pinehurst, on the other hand, is crammed into the back room of the Given Memorial Library. The Tufts Archive, as it's known, is in the process of being reorganized, and at the moment it resembles an overcluttered attic stuffed with bills, bric-a-brac, old dance cards and family albums. The collection includes John Hemmer's striking portraits not only of guests but of the working folk—the caddies and mule drivers and greenkeepers.

In some respects, the present-day village of Pinehurst is a little like Bedford Falls—it's almost too good to be true: You half expect to see Jimmy Stewart and Clarence (the *other* Clarence) shuffling down the street. Ross transformed the place, turning

what had been a kind of Chautauqua into a golf mecca—but enough of the small-town vision of Tufts and Olmsted persists that it still has an identity of its own, and is much less self-consciously a shrine than, say, St. Andrews. (A golf memorabilia store in town, Burchfield's Golf Gallery, sells not chotchkes and T-shirts but prints and photographs.)

In recent years, dozens of gated golf course communities have sprawled over the surrounding area, some tasteful, some tacky, and an adventurous golfer who didn't mind pitching over a few condos could probably play right through to Southern Pines, six miles away. In late afternoon, the traffic circle outside of town frequently approaches gridlock. But the village itself, now inhabited mostly by retirees, looks and feels much as it did at the turn of the century. (The action, such as it is—and the inevitable strip mall—is down the road in

Background: The 15th hole on Pinehurst No. 2. (Photo: Stephen Szurlej)

a brief history: THE MAKING OF A MECCA

1835: James Walker Tufts born in Charlestown, Mass.

1872: Donald Ross born in Dornoch, Scotland.

1891: Tufts merges his soda-fountain company with others to form the American Soda Fountain Co.

1895: Tufts buys 6,000 "worthless" acres from Henry Page of Aberdeen, N.C., for a dollar an acre. It's called Tuftstown, then renamed Pinehurst. First hotel, Holly Inn, opens.

1897: A visitor brings a set of clubs to Pinehurst; by fall, residents are hitting balls around area cow pastures.

1898: Tufts and Dr. LeRoy Culver lay out a nine-hole course.

1899: Ross arrives in U.S. Becomes professional at Oakley Country Club, Mass. Nine more holes built at Pinehurst.

1900: Harry Vardon plays exhibition match at Pinehurst; spreads favorable word about the club. Ross meets Tufts in Medford, Mass.; agrees to become Pinehurst professional.

1901: Ross starts redesign of No. 1 Course. Carolina Hotel opens on New Year's Day. First nine holes of No. 2 open, designed by Ross. First North & South Amateur played.

1902: Tufts dies, age 67. First North & South Open played.

1907: Eighteen holes of No. 2 completed (length: 5,860 yards). First nine of No. 3 opens, too, designed by Ross.

1910: No. 3 Course becomes 18-holer.

1912: Lucy Richards creates the famed bronze statuette, "The Putter Boy."

1916: Annie Oakley comes to Pinehurst, opens gun club.

1917: Bobby Jones, age 15, plays Pinehurst for first time.

1919: No. 4 Course opens, designed by Ross.

1935: No. 2 greens changed from clay-sand mix to grass.

1936: Denny Shute wins PGA Championship on No. 2.

1940: Ben Hogan wins first pro title, North & South Open.

1947: Babe Zaharias wins Women's North & South.

1948: Ross dies, age 75.

1949: Arnold Palmer loses, 12 and 11, to Frank Stranahan in semifinals of North & South Amateur.

1951: U.S. wins Ryder Cup Matches on No. 2.

1959: Jack Nicklaus wins North & South Amateur.

1961: No. 5 Course opens, designed by Ellis Maples.

1970: Pinehurst sold for $9.2 million to Diamondhead Corp., which "modernizes" No. 2 and destroys Ross look.

1973: Gibby Gilbert and Tom Watson both shoot course-record 62s on No. 2 in World Open.

1974: World Golf Hall of Fame opens.

1975: Nicklaus wins World Open. Curtis Strange wins North & South Amateur. He wins again the following year.

1977: Hale Irwin ties No. 2 Course record with 62 in Colgate Hall of Fame Classic.

1979: No. 6 Course opens, designed by George Fazio and his nephew, Tom.

1982: Resort Assets Corp. takes control of Pinehurst after Diamondhead fails to pay on multimillion dollar loan.

1984: Pinehurst purchased by Robert Dedman's Club Corporation of America for $15 million.

1986: No. 7 Course opens, designed by Rees Jones.

1989: Vicki Goetze wins U.S. Women's Amateur on No. 2.

1991-92: PGA Tour Championship played on No. 2.

1993: World Golf Hall of Fame closes doors.

1994: Simon Hobday wins U.S. Senior Open on No. 2.

1996: No. 8 Course opens, designed by Tom Fazio. Pinehurst named a National Historic Landmark.

1999: Payne Stewart wins the 99th U.S. Open on No. 2.

—*CLIFF SCHROCK*

Aberdeen.) Olmsted's street plan still works a kind of optical illusion, creating curving, expansive vistas, and strolling along the sandy roadsides, breathing in the sharp, piney fragrance, you can with no trouble at all imagine yourself in another, better world.

Every peaceable kingdom has its Dark Age. Pinehurst's began in 1970, when the Tufts family sold its interest to the Diamondhead Corporation, a real-estate outfit in Mississippi. The Diamondhead people aggressively marketed house lots and built condos along formerly pristine fairways. They ripped up Donald Ross' wire grass on No. 2 and replaced the famous sandy hardpan with rough and love grass; and at the end of the fifth fairway they built the ill-fated World Golf Hall of Fame—it stood for years as an empty, Ozymandias-like monument to failed dreams and poor planning, then was demolished earlier this year.

Diamondhead went bankrupt in 1981, and three years later Pinehurst was sold to the Dallas-based Club Corporation of America, which has restored the luster. (The final step, a renovation of the historic Holly Inn, was just completed.) ClubCorp added two more courses, including the Tom Fazio-designed No. 8, which (except for its mausoleum-like clubhouse) is worth a trip all by itself, and spiffed up all the facilities.

The main hotel, with its copper roof and rocking-chaired verandas, has been returned to its former glory as the one-time "Queen of the South," and re-christened with its original 1901 name of The Carolina. The ambience, for the most part, is relaxed rather than stuffy, but it's still the kind of place where the bellmen wear knickers and argyles, where they serve tea every afternoon in the lobby, and change the sand in the hallway ashtrays nightly, raking it like a bunker and then stamping it with the Pinehurst logo.

The Carolina Dining Room, the best of the resort's eateries, does the full monty—mirrors, drapes, chandeliers, live music even at breakfast—but the food is good, even adventurous.

You go to Pinehurst to play golf, not to eat, though, and the mid- and high-handicapper should be warned: Donald Ross intended No. 2 to be an examination of championship golf. It tests every club in your bag, demands nerve-racking precision (around the crowned greens especially), and will expose weaknesses in your game that you didn't even know were there. This isn't to say that it isn't fun. On the Saturday before the Super Bowl this year, when workmen had already begun snaking phone cables through the woods in preparation for the Open, I played a round at No. 2 that ranks among the two or three most memorable golf days of my life. At the end, however, I was so physically and emotionally spent that I was catatonic.

Then I repaired to Mulligan's sports bar, in the lobby of the Manor Inn, and by chance found myself sitting on a stool right between a group of three guys, businessmen from San Diego who had teed off immediately before me, and a pair of waste-management specialists from Canada who were in the foursome right after mine. "Howdja do, eh?" one of the Canadian guys said. "Pretty tough, if you're asking me."

We all nodded and then shyly exchanged scores and horror stories. You, too? Five putts on No. 9! In instant camaraderie, we drank a toast to each other—OK, a lot of toasts—like mustard-gassed veterans of Ypres or the Somme, happy to be among friends.

"*If a man can't break 90 on a good course, it's murder to send him across the sandy wastes down there.*"

—JOHN KIEMAN, WRITER

Top: *The expansive cross bunkering at Pine Valley's par-5 seventh hole is known as Hell's Half Acre. (Photo: Stephen Szurlej)*
Bottom: *The "D.A." bunker at the 10th is "named for Satan's least attractive body part." (Photo: Cal Brown)*

Pine Valley: A Beauty and a Beast

America's No. 1 course easily retains its title

by Tom Callahan

Located in the handsomest, homeliest state in the union—New Jersey—near the most cynical, sentimental city in the world—Philadelphia—Pine Valley is by reputation, acclamation, the most heavenly hell hole on earth. It is also the hardest golf course in creation.

A grump named Crump, sort of a turn-of-the-century Trump, is said to have spotted the potential development from a railroad car on the old Reading line that continues to snake about the piney woods below Camden en route to Atlantic City. Pine Valley's ordinarily forthright members exaggerate when they recollect how—gazing absently out the train window—George Crump envisioned the penal colony of his dreams. But he did foresee a lot of misery.

In more than the obvious ways, God's hand was involved too. Crump's favorite golfing partner and first consultant was Father Simon Carr, the Philadelphia amateur champion of 1908. As anyone can attest who has ever put in a Sunday afternoon at golf, there is no more sulphurous character in life or literature than a Roman Catholic priest who has just double-bogeyed. Maybe Father Carr had something to do with Pine Valley turning out to be such a dead-honest course. Or his influence might be detected in the remarkable number of unholy references that have come to dot the landscape. They range from "Hell's Half Acre," a terrible expanse of brimstone badlands strip-mined across the par-5 seventh hole, to a greenside sandpit at the par-3 10th vulgarly named for Satan's least attractive body part. So the legend goes at No. 5, a 232-yard par 3, "only God can make a 3." (The rules of modesty forbid but the laws of blasphemy require breaking in at this point to state, for the record, that any man pure of thought and possessed of extraordinary nerves need only drive normally and two-putt casually for his 3 at No. 5. This will be the last personal message.)

At that, Gene Littler was unlucky enough there to take a 7 before God and the "Shell's Wonderful World of Golf" TV cameras. He spent most of those shots extricating himself from the woods.

In the national debate on how much wilderness is absolutely necessary, Pine Valley consistently comes down on the side of just five yards more than you figured. The resident caddies, masters of satire and semaphore, are forever signaling back to the tee the distant results. They have one symbol for high rough and another for low rough. Sometimes they merely drag a forefinger expressively across their throats.

Except for a few mustachioed gents in ascots, there are no rakes on the course. The sand traps are heel-clomped scrub buckets sprouting derelict whiskers of bracken and broom. The natural effect is strangely pleasing, though, and a blind sand wedge (delicately struck) from the depths of a man-sized bunker at the ninth could end up right next to the cup for a marvelous par that wins the side. (But never mind that.)

Jack Nicklaus spent his honeymoon at The Valley, which verifies what a soapy romantic he is. But the only celebrated professional closely associated with the place is George Fazio, golf's renowned architect and face-lifter, who was once a teaching pro there. Few may recall him as a player, but Fazio was accomplished enough in 1950 to join Ben Hogan and Lloyd Mangrum in the U.S. Open playoff at Merion that lit Hogan's legend. At Pine Valley, Fazio was rumored to have hid his best scores from the community.

To a visiting hacker, the members are effusive hosts. In the dining room later, over a crock of snapper soup, it thrills them to hear the worst. The clammier you look, the smaller your voice has become, the more comically your legs cramp up as you try to climb the stairs, the warmer their embrace. If you happen to have struck one of them viciously on the ankle from more than 200 crooked yards away, he limps for you afterward with incandescent delight.

In a charming publication, a kind of class annual for sale in the golf shop, page after page of disasters are chronicled under the chapter heading "Pleasure-Pain." They commonly begin "A guest of Pete Stephens . . ." or "A guest of Ray Farley . . ." Some are anonymous entirely:

"An amateur golfer who had only recently before reached the semifinals of the United States Amateur championship was even par for seven holes and had a fine drive on the eighth. His second shot was shrugged off by the green. Then he went back and forth from sand to sand, finally holing out in 16 strokes. He gets better marks than a former British Amateur champion and famous writer who followed that script exactly until he picked up at the eighth after nine strokes. He didn't finish the round."

As long as they were bound to say "former British

Amateur champion and famous writer," they might as well have gone ahead and named Bernard Darwin, who responded in a different forum: "It is all very well to punish a bad stroke, but the right of eternal punishment should be reserved for a higher tribunal than a Greens Committee."

Babe Ruth had an easier way with the language. After nearly blowing a career of local good will by shooting a remarkable 85 (left-handed, of course) straight out of the box, the Bambino made it up to everyone the following day with a gracious 12 at the 15th and a line to his caddie that has reverberated through the pine trees ever since. "Hell, I don't need to know where the green is," he sighed. "Where is the golf course?"

Where it usually is. At the top of the list.

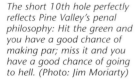

The short 10th hole perfectly reflects Pine Valley's penal philosophy: Hit the green and you have a good chance of making par; miss it and you have a good chance of going to hell. (Photo: Jim Moriarty)

The 17th at St. Andrews, the "Road Hole,"
is probably the toughest par 4 in golf.
Play for a 5 and stay out of trouble.
(Photo: Stephen Szurlej)

The Holy Land

For as long as golf is played, the town of St. Andrews will be its Mecca

by Peter Andrews

St. Andrews has always been something of a mythical town, so let's start with a bit of mythology. Back around the sixth century, in what we smugly refer to as the Dark Ages, a God-struck monk named Rule, then living in Greece, had a vision calling on him to take relics of the martyred St. Andrew to the land of Albion. Rule and a group of pilgrims sailed north and, after a violent storm, were washed ashore near the East Neuk of Fife with only their faith and a box of saintly bones to protect them. A Pict chieftain, hearing of their arrival, hustled over to loot and pillage, something Picts always did to newcomers, but was stopped by the sight of a white cross slashing across a blue sky. Even the surliest brigand knows when he is overmatched and the Pict became Christianized on the spot. The town of St. Andrews was born and a white cross on a blue field later became the national flag of Scotland.

Anthropologists will tell you that St. Andrews was first settled by hunters who drifted there on log boats from Scandinavia sometime around 8000 B.C. If you like that story better than the one about the monk and the great cross illuminating the sky, you're welcome to it.

That's the way it is at St. Andrews, a town that by anyone's reckoning reaches back to our oldest yesterday. Legend and history converge into a seamless web and a visitor is free to choose his own way.

When I first sat down to do this story I wanted to write about St. Andrews without ever mentioning the golf. That's the kind of idea writers like to come up with because we think it makes us look clever. It was impossible. Golf is not simply a recreation here. It's part of the heartbeat of the community. There was a time in the late 18th century when St. Andrews almost became a ghost town and its only industry was making golf balls. Craftsmen, using iron rods, stuffed wet feathers into small leather cases held hard against their chests. It was dreary labor and most of the men died of consumption doing it. But the town lived.

Golf and St. Andrews can't be separated. Visit the graveyard at St. Rule's Tower and there is the monument to the memory of Young Tom Morris. Gaze past to look at St. Andrews Bay and there is the municipal putting green. Admire the University College Tower on North Street and you are reminded that it's your line when hitting off the 15th tee on the Old Course. There is no escaping golf here.

So let us have a word or two about the golf before we look about the town. Like all the truly great and lasting offerings the British Isles have placed on the altar of civilization (Shakespeare and whisky come most swiftly to mind), golf at St. Andrews is at once ancient and modern. When first played here in the 14th century, St. Andrews golf sorted well with the fierce Scottish brand of Presbyterianism. Its names, Hell Bunker and the Elysian Fields, tell the story as men skulked about in the wind and rain picking their way between eternal damnation and perpetual bliss. The righteous prevailed; the wicked perished.

Today, we look on the Old Course differently. Its randomly placed hazards have no order, as we now understand the term. A good shot puts you in a bunker you had no reason to believe was there and a bad one leaves you with easy access home. Like the sea, the Old Course is indifferent to whether the people who approach it have come for good or evil. It has become a 20th-century enterprise that would warm the chilly heart of a French existentialist philosopher. If Jean-Paul Sartre had possessed the physical dexterity of a bubble-gum machine, he could have played St. Andrews well.

The town also puts on a modern face without forfeiting its heritage. At one end there are the ruins of St. Andrews Castle that took four centuries to build, and at the other there is a supermarket as well provisioned as any I know of in America. St. Andrews University serves as a reasonable microcosm of the community. Established in the 15th century, it is the oldest university in Scotland and ranks behind only Oxford and Cambridge as the oldest in the British Isles. Today, in addition to its divinity school, St. Andrews is famed as a center for the study of neo-conservative economics. Adam Smith, who was born not far

> *"Golf is not simply a recreation here. It's part of the heartbeat of the community."*

St. Andrews is awash in history, from the grave of Old Tom Morris (top) to antique stores that sell clubs. (Photos: Jim Moriarty)

away in Kirkcaldy, would be pleased. After a long and turbulent history, St. Andrews still works.

There is no easier town in the world to walk around in than St. Andrews. You can traverse its streets five times a day and not get tired. The basic layout has remained largely unchanged for 500 years. A friend of mine loaned me a copy of a town street map drawn up in 1530. As a guide to the main part of the town from Kinness Burn to St. Andrews Bay, it is still more than adequate.

What do you want to see in this old town: churches, good theater, architecture, bargain shopping, historical sites? Or are you content to have a pint in a pleasant saloon with the local populace talking treason against the Queen? St. Andrews has them all in profusion.

St. Andrews does not yield up all of its attractions at first blush to the casual visitor. Like its golf course, the town takes a bit of knowing. The house where Mary, Queen of Scots, once stayed is now part of St. Leonard's School and only open to the public when school is in session and then only on Thursdays from 2 to 3 in the afternoon. Walking its quiet, almost surgically neat streets today, it is difficult to realize that St. Andrews has as violent a history as any community in the realm. Henry VIII marked it for extinction to the last woman and child. But the clues are there if you want to look for them. The ruins of St. Andrews Cathedral are testaments of the power of fire and religious fervor. The initials of Patrick Hamilton (it took six hours to burn him) are etched in the cobblestones outside the entrance of St. Salvator's College. If you sometimes feel that Western civilization has not progressed as far as it should have in the last 500 years, take a look at St. Andrews Castle and pop down to the Bottle Dungeon, a Scottish detention facility that makes the Tower of London seem like a villa in Spain.

Do I dwell excessively on the grotesque? My defense is I am three quarters Scot myself and we naturally love mayhem. When the Romans threw up a wall across the length of the island just to keep us away, they knew what they were about. While others want to spend a quiet moment at the bucolic setting of the Law Mill by the Ladebraes, I want to nip over to Town Hall and look at the fine old headsman's ax in a glass case and be reminded of the days before the do-gooders spoiled everything and you could get a man in to do a really first-class job for about $2.

If St. Andrews were not so famous for its golf, it would be known as a university town. Relations between the school and the community have not always been smooth. There was a riot once when a divinity instructor at St. Mary's was practicing archery and missed the butt by a fair piece, hitting a passing maltster who was walking in the yard. Today everything seems serene and you get your best water views by strolling through university property along the Scores.

The thing to do at St. Andrews is just keep walking aimlessly and let the town happen to you. You can never get importantly lost. St. Rule's Tower stands at one

end and just about everything else lies along three streets below it. My system was to roam about and take a look at the Pends, a charming vaulted 14th-century gate house, and then hit a pub. Look in on the St. Andrews Preservation Trust Museum housed in a 17th-century fisherman's house on North Street and then hit another pub. Kept up like this for an afternoon, you get the sense of being on a part historic tour and part house party. If you are feeling energetic, you can stop by Auchterlonie's on Golf Place where they have been making clubs since the early 19th century and for £8 you can have an indoor lesson at the nets with John Nicoll.

There are pubs for every taste in St. Andrews. Most of them, such as the Castle Tavern and the Donvegal, manage to be comfortable and charming without trying to be quaint. Sometimes, however, the

The first hole at St. Andrews has one of the widest fairways in golf, but the green is guarded by the devilish Swilcan Burn. (Photo: Stephen Szurlej)

40

traditional Scottish spirit is broken by American accents. I dropped by Kate Kennedy's to find Oprah Winfrey's show playing on the television. The audience couldn't seem to make any more out of it than I did.

It used to be that looking for a good restaurant in Scotland was like looking for a good tailor in Zagreb. If you found one, it wasn't worth the trouble. Not so anymore. Rusack's, the hotel overlooking the Old Course, serves fine food, and a few miles away in Cupar is the Peat Inn, which is a great restaurant by any standard. David Wilson, the owner and chef, who plays a bit of golf when he gets the chance, is a master of nouvelle cuisine who actually has something to say. He takes local fish, game and vegetables and elevates them to the status of art.

That the Scots are dry and quick of speech is legendary. Their talk is the conversational equivalent of the poisoned ear dagger. You can be dead on the ground before you know you've even been hit. My grandmother was known to alienate entire wings of our family wishing them a happy Christmas. I was struck by this when I went into one of St. Andrews' many fine bookstores. I counted seven but there are more, I am sure. I bought a couple of Balzac novels to read on the plane home. When I took them to the woman at the counter she wrapped them for me and observed crisply, "I see. An American comes to Scotland to buy French novels. It seems an Irish thing to do."

For those of you who are connoisseurs of such matters, as I am, note the deftness of stroke and

Intense battles have been waged on the Himalayas putting green for more than a century, as this 1890 photograph shows. (Photo: St. Andrews University Archives)

economy of line. In a single aside, a white-haired lady from a small town in Scotland managed to dismiss the United States of America, the Republic of Ireland and the literature of France. Well bowled, Madam, well bowled.

Bowls, by the way, is a game to which I became addicted. When I was in St. Andrews, television gave more time to a bowls tournament than we do to the Super Bowl and all without a single "up-close-and-personal" view of anybody. It was most pleasant. Bowls is a game so languid a player may roll his ball down the carpet, lean over to tie his shoelaces, and still have plenty of time to witness the result of his effort. I watched the final one late afternoon at the St. Andrews Club with another enthusiast and discovered that bowls is the only sporting event that you can watch at a fever pitch of excitement and doze at the same time.

One thing I always do when visiting the British Isles is go to church. It just seems the proper thing to do. And so, on Sunday morning, as surely as if my grandfather were taking me by the hand, I found myself at the Hope Park Church and was reminded once again that churches are not simply places of architectural interest, but places to go to. For one

thing, they sing at Hope Park. I mean they really sing. I couldn't shake the feeling that by way of encouragement, vestrymen were prepared to pass among the congregation with rawhide whips, but the old songs came back easily enough:

For all the saints who from their labors rest
And when the strife is fierce and the warfare long
Steals on the ear the distant triumphant song
And hearts are brave again and arms are strong.

If I spent more time listening to that and less to sports psychologists I would be both a better person and a better golfer.

Genes tell. On my last day I was walking on Market Street dressed in my tweed jacket from the St. Andrews Woolen Mill and a proper cap when an American lady from Cleveland and her two children who were "doing the churches" asked me for directions to St. James. I think I told her correctly; I am not very good at giving or receiving directions to anywhere. I can get lost in a squash court. But it doesn't matter. Wherever she goes in St. Andrews, she's sure to find something terrific.

Seminole

Seminole proves that a course can be fun for the average player and still challenge the pros

by Herbert Warren Wind

eminole, which is situated on the Atlantic about 15 miles north of Palm Beach, is the work of a master architect, Donald Ross, a Scot from Dornoch. Ross had been in this country for about 30 years when he built Seminole. Subtropical in appearance, what with its dark green Bermuda grass fairways and greens, its brilliantly white bunkers and its palms and rubber trees, it is a far cry from the courses one generally associates with Ross—the original four at Pinehurst, his longtime headquarters, and the hundreds, literally, that he laid out on rolling countryside in the northern part of the country, mainly between Minnesota and Massachusetts.

Appearances can be deceiving. Seminole, along with Pinehurst No. 2, is the quintessential Ross course. It may look mild and manageable—the fairways are wide, the rough is civilized, the undulations restrained, the greens large and candid—and because of its reasonable length from the standard tees the average player can sometimes salvage a par after a poorish drive. Nonetheless, when all is said and done, the course demands golf of the first order. Unless a player positions his tee shots carefully, he will not be able to regularly hit and hold the splendid variety of stiffly bunkered greens, and strokes will inevitably start to slip away fast.

While the course measures only 6,778 yards from the back tees, when the long-driving tournament stars drop in, they find it all they can handle. Low scores are such a rarity that old Seminole hands are still a little aghast that Claude Harmon, the club professional for many years, once got around in 60. On a calm day Seminole is an enjoyable challenge for golfers of all degrees of skill, but it would not be the celebrated test it is were it not for the southeast wind off the Atlantic that sweeps across the holes. More about this later. First, a little background music.

The Seminole Golf Club is about the same vintage as Cypress Point: It opened its course for play in October of 1929. The two clubs share other similarities. The bulk of their members, aside from being well-off and social, have a considerable knowledge of golf and a deep affection for it. They have taste, too. Both clubs, for example, eschewed expansive adaptations of the Alhambra or Mount Vernon in favor of small, comfortable, charming clubhouses. Seminole's is Florida Spanish, built of terra-cotta-colored concrete. Designed by Marion Wyeth, it typifies the variations Wyeth made on the style that Addison Mizener established during Palm Beach's palmy days. Incidentally, Seminole has 325 members. Its entrance fee is $10,000 and the annual dues are $1,100. Cypress Point has 235 members, its entrance fee is $15,000 and the dues are $95 a month. Because of Florida's hot and humid summers, Seminole is closed from mid-May to November, which probably explains why it is less expensive than Cypress Point, which is playable the year round.

Allan Ryan, who came to Seminole in the early 1930s, has been its president since 1971. He knows the history of the course like few people. "When Ross arrived, the area was just a jungle," Ryan recalls. "The property had every kind of Florida wildness. A crew of 180 men worked on it for nine months. They went into the swamps with hip boots and hacked down the heavy brush. They used teams of mules to move the earth into place and they shaped the greens by hauling the earth in pans. The course is a triumph of drainage and irrigation. Ross, you know, constructed three small lakes, and they come into play, directly or indirectly, on nine of the holes. I am still thoroughly amazed by the job Ross did."

There are no weak holes at Seminole and many very good ones, but nearly everybody who knows the course agrees that the best and most representative hole is the sixth, a par 4 only 390 yards long that invariably shows up whenever someone lists the top 18 holes in the United States. An impressively original hole, it has a two-level fairway, the left side rising well above the right.

> *"If you can play Seminole, you can play any course in the world."* —BEN HOGAN

Top: *Seminole's modest Florida-Spanish clubhouse is charming both outside and within. (Photo: Dick Beattie)* **Middle:** *Seminole's No. 16.* **Bottom:** *The ocean winds can be a factor at the par-3 17th hole. (Photos: Stephen Szurlej)*

From the tee all the trouble on the sixth is on the left: four good-sized bunkers menace that edge of the fairway. It is a mistake, nevertheless, to simply play down the right side, for this increases the difficulty of the approach shot. Ross, you see, devised a green that slants out of the fairway from left to right at about a 1 o'clock angle. In order to get home from the right with your second, you must carry a chilling succession of bunkers. The bunker farthest from the green cuts deeply into the fairway, and the others patrol the entrance to the green on the right and then move along the righthand side of the green. To keep you honest, there are two bunkers to the left of the green.

The correct way to play the sixth, if you have the ability and the nerve, is to hit your drive as close as you can to the bunkers on the left. Then all you have to do is to play a crisp approach over the first or the second bunker in the long white line. From the back tees, the pro at Seminole, Jerry Pittman—he succeeded Henry Picard, who succeeded Harmon—usually hits a 3-iron or 4-iron for his second when the wind is against him and as little as an 8-iron or a 9 when it is with him.

Occasionally the wind at Seminole comes out of the north, but the prevailing wind, as noted earlier, is from the southeast. It changes direction and force quite often, but however it blows it has a decisive influence on how the holes play. On the 17th, a par 3 that is 175 yards long from the back, Pittman uses a 2-iron to a 5-iron. On the 18th, a 417-yard dogleg left on which the tee, like the one on 17, is set on a sand ridge above the beach and the ocean, he plays anything from a 3-wood to a 4-iron on his approach.

"The southeast wind sweeps across from left to right on both these holes," Pittman says. "It can be a strong wind, but you don't feel it on the 17th tee because you're sheltered by the growth of sea grape. When you move down the fairway, you feel its full force. By that time, of course, you've already seen what it's done to your shot." In a north wind the 18th can be a tartar. Pittman remembers playing in such a wind with Jack Nicklaus and George Burns, two of the most powerful hitters in the game. Neither of them was able to get home with two woods. In any wind, and from

There are no weak holes at Seminole, and many strong ones, such as the tough second. (Photo: Stephen Szurlej)

any of the tees, the last two holes at Seminole provide a properly rigorous finish.

One of Seminole's best-known members and staunchest admirers is Ben Hogan. No one is more effective in describing its appeal and its worth. "It's one of the few courses I know that I don't get tired of," Ben said last autumn. "The wind is different nearly every day, and that changes all the shots. I used to play Seminole for 30 straight days when I was preparing for the Masters, and I was just as eager to play it on the 30th morning as I was on the first.

"Seminole is a placement course," he continued. "Most of the holes bend one way or the other slightly, and you must place your tee shot on the right side or left side of the fairway to have the best angle to the green on your approach shot. I was always a spot player—that is, I played to a spot on the fairway and then to a spot on the green. That's the fascination of golf for me—placing the ball in the proper position and then coming as close as I can to playing precisely the kind of shot that's called for. You just don't hit a club— say, the 4-iron—the same way all the time. There are

10 different ways to hit a 4-iron. At Seminole you get the chance to play all the shots there are. I like that and the fact that you can visualize clearly what you have to do.

"If I were a young man going on the pro tour," Hogan added, "I'd try to make arrangements to get on Seminole. If you can play Seminole, you can play any course in the world."

One more thing. As Hogan and its other enthusiasts seldom fail to mention, the ingenious routing of the holes contributes immeasurably both to Seminole's enchantment and its difficulty. Seldom do two holes in a row move in the same direction. Quite the contrary. The sequence, full of twists and turns, varies so abruptly from hole to hole that it brings to mind the complex pass patterns that Lynn Swann of the Pittsburgh Steelers runs, and the unpredictable gyrations that John Havlicek of the Celtics used to resort to in order to lose his man and get free. Particularly on courses like Seminole and Cypress Point, where the wind is such a factor, a fine routing pattern can change a good course into a remarkable one.

Death or glory
From tee to front collar, it's a 190-yard carry over the blue Pacific. Intervening cliffs and bunkers make run-up shots unlikely.

Shadow of a cypress
The club's logo cypress tree is dead but not forgotten. Its leaning stump remains a hazard for those bailing out to the left.

America's Greatest
Par 3

The winner: Cypress Point's No. 16 is 219 yards of beauty, challenge and terror

The most feared, most photographed and least aced par 3 in the land, this 1928 Alister Mackenzie design is a fish hook come alive, with the tee on the point and the green not much bigger than a hook's eye. On this fish-or-cut-bait hole, many a golfer has been reeled out to sea. (Photo: Jim Moriarty)

Conspiracy theory
Skeptics have long insisted there's an abandoned tee atop this hill, proving Mackenzie intended the hole to be a par 4. Don't believe it.

Straight as an arrow
Bing Crosby, always the showman, aced the 16th from the white tees in 1947. It was the second hole-in-one ever recorded on the hole.

The 11th tee reminds us of Bobby Jones. (Photos: Dom Furore)

In Celebration of Tradition

May 1995

Age, wealth and social standing have nothing to do with it. Merion is a case study in what really matters.

by the Editors of GOLF DIGEST

Golf is the most traditional of games. It respects the past. It reveres its legends. It is handed down from one generation to the next by word of mouth, by the example of its players and—most important—by the lay of the land.

Golf courses at their best harken back to the origins of the game. Our playing fields celebrate tradition. The great ones endure the test of time, even give something back to the game.

What is this thing we call tradition?

First, you should know what it is not. Tradition is not "old money." The game came from the villages of Scotland where Everyman could play and no one was excluded.

It is not merely old age. Age alone is no more a prescription for tradition than it is for wisdom.

It is not big clubhouses and bigger locker rooms. It is not valet parkers dressed in kilts or a bagpiper drowning out conversation during the cocktail hour. It is not a "St. Andrews burger" for lunch or a dining room wallpapered in Scottish tartan.

It is not the ego of a rich man or the idiocy of a committee, although both have a long tradition in the sport.

So what is it?

Tradition is a game played afoot, with a caddie, or a bag slung over a shoulder or pulled by a trolley.

It is the feel of a persimmon head striking a balata ball.

Merion's history dates to 1896.

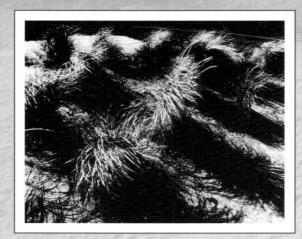

Clumps of grass add double jeopardy to Merion's bunkers.

Background: Merion No. 10 (Photo: Stephen Szurlej)

Like caddies everywhere, Merion's offer free swing tips.

It is wicker baskets that offer no clue as to the direction of the wind.

It is a game played on the ground as well as in the air.

It is turf that is never uniform, either in color or texture.

It is fairways kept firm and dry, putting surfaces maintained at a sensible pace.

It is unpredictable bounces of the ball, off slopes gentle and severe, sometimes into disheartening trouble, sometimes into undeserved success.

It is match play, where the course is not the opponent, only its canvas.

It is camaraderie in the clench of a stormy nassau.

It is holes that look as though they evolved from the terrain rather than were forced upon it.

It is a series of heart-skipping risks with commensurate rewards.

It is strategies that maintain our interest.

It is water hazards provided solely by nature.

It is the easy approach resulting from a well-positioned drive on a Donald Ross dogleg.

It is the wide berth we give to each A.W. Tillinghast bunker.

It is the glee in deciphering the complexities of an Alister Mackenzie green.

It is the puzzlement summoned by one of C.B. Macdonald's blind holes.

It is a simple clubhouse with massive showerheads and a modest menu.

It is the great theater of national championships—especially at well-preserved courses that offer a common ground upon which players of different eras can be compared.

It is the rush of adrenaline when we reach a spot where Ben Hogan once stood.

It is a shade tree under which Walter Hagen once paused (and relieved himself).

It is our sense of wonder when we're reminded of the accomplishments of Bobby Jones.

It is companionship, especially with those who first taught us the game. And with those to whom we pass it along.

It is a game that should be accomplished in three hours, not six.

It is the absence of cartpaths.

It is affordable for every man and woman.

It is not necessarily the game we play today. It is the game we'd like to play from now on.

Part of the clubhouse was a farmhouse in 1824.

The greatest showerheads in all of golf.

Wicker baskets are the club's trademark.

A simple locker room.

Rest for the weary after a three-putt.

John Elliott

Davis Love Jr.

Tim Mahoney

Mike LaBauve

Jack Lumpkin

Gale Peterson

Playing the Game Right

Bob Toski

Scott Davenport

Peter Kostis

DeDe Owens

The world's best teachers and players help us master this maddening game

MAKING YOUR GAME

by Guy Yocom,
Senior Editor

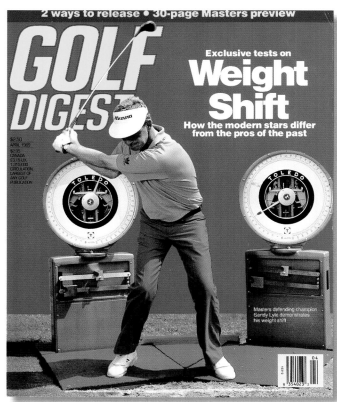

"It is the constant and underlying hope for improvement that makes golf so exquisitely worth the playing." This observation by Bernard Darwin, one of golf's greatest writers, rang with profundity back in the 1920s, when America as a nation took up the game in earnest and discovered there was something elusive about trying to nail a simple brassie shot squarely on the meat with some degree of consistency. But there is nothing profound about the statement today. The maddening challenge of playing the game well has been vocalized so loudly by the golfing public that every nongolfer takes up the game fully aware of the perils that lie ahead. The quest to strike the ball better has driven millions of golfers to practice ranges, lesson tees and equipment racks—and to the pages of GOLF DIGEST.

Instruction has always been the heart and soul of GOLF DIGEST. Feature stories may entertain and inform, service pieces can explain how to figure your handicap, travel articles will advise where to vacation, and equipment stories suggest which clubs to buy. But learning how to straighten your slice, play the long bunker shot, or handle the slippery downhill putt— that is the sweet stuff. The desire to achieve a better score or formulate a more handsome swing is endemic to the golfer's personality. GOLF DIGEST has always known that, and has gone to extraordinary lengths toward making improving possible.

We have appealed to every great player of the last 50 years to provide their secrets, and they have responded. Since GOLF DIGEST debuted in 1950, every male winner of every major championship has by-lined at least one instruction article in GOLF DIGEST, save for Ed Furgol, the 1954 U.S. Open Champ. (No one remembers why.) Some, like Jack Nicklaus, a hundred times at least. Most of the women champions have contributed too. Virtually every prominent instructor has authored lessons; Harvey Penick shared the content of what would become the *Little Red Book* a quarter of a century before the book itself became famous. Several U.S. Amateur champions have contributed, and our amateur authors have even included a few 22-handicappers.

There is no part of the game that hasn't been addressed, though some areas have been covered more thoroughly than others. From the beginning, there has been a reverberating cry for help on three subjects: curing the slice, hitting the ball farther, and gaining more consistency. On the slicing front alone, our teachers have utilized brooms (Hank Johnson, 1983 and 1992), stakes driven into the ground (Davis Love Jr., 1986), and other arcane devices such as beach balls, baseball bats, hammers, and automobile steering wheels. Through drills, imagery, swing thoughts and even a national campaign, we have sought to rid the public of this odious ball-flight pattern.

The challenge to fix any swing problem is formidable. Teaching someone how to install tile on a bathroom floor is simple, because every floor is flat. Not so with golf, for every golfer is built differently, possesses a different temperament, and has different levels of strength and coordination. The instruction also is a one-way dialogue; the author isn't there to observe the reader when he or she attempts to put the advice into practice. We've also learned, sadly and recently, that not all humans are capable of imitating things they see in pictures—they need to be trained physically, like elephants.

But it can be done. When John Daly won the 1991 PGA Championship, he eagerly explained he had learned to play by reading instruction articles in GOLF DIGEST. Buoyed by success stories like his, we have tried every device imaginable to convey swing advice in an intelligible manner. The thousands of instruction articles have run the gamut of communication styles. We have used high-speed photographs, art-illustrations, and text-only pieces with no graphic touches at all. The stories range in scale from one-paragraph tips to 30-page blockbusters. We've offered pull-out pocket tips booklets and poster-size gatefolds the reader can hang on the walls of the den.

Much of the innovation has been through new photographic processes. There is no camera angle that has not been tried or technique that hasn't been used. For example, GOLF DIGEST has reversed photos so right-handers appear to be swinging left-handed, so the reader can emulate exactly what he sees. We have shot upward through plexiglass stations (Tom Watson, 1979) and even photographed in the dark (Payne Stewart, 1991). In 1985, Tom Kite hit balls while wearing sensory wires and little else save for a pair of paper shorts. We've

Illustration by Jack Davis

Instruction has always been the heart and soul of GOLF DIGEST

employed cameras so small they are barely legal, and a high-speed camera so sophisticated that only one person in the world was capable of fixing it when it broke down. Our photographers have placed the viewfinder of their cameras against the eyes of the instructor as he demonstrates, so the reader can observe his positions from the perspective of the instructor.

What else? We've tried weight scales, magnetic resonance imaging and pressure gauges placed on the grip end of the club. We've used eye doctors, sport psychologists, physical trainers, biomechanics experts and nutrition specialists.

Innovation surely will continue, but there also is the tried and true. Perhaps the most popular ongoing instruction feature has been swing sequences. In terms of quality, they've come a long way since 1961 when a senior editor named John May photographed Ben Hogan with an 8-millimeter camera and we published the grainy images. Today, using a high-speed camera that spins film through the camera at a rate of 65 frames per second, we obtain tack-sharp images of the best players in the world, catching them all at the precise moment of impact. In addition to photographing the best men and women players extant, we've had fun with celebrities, politicians and athletes, ranging from Tip O'Neill to

Michael Jordan. The number we've published to date exceeds 150.

A sequence of a player like John Daly is for the most part entertaining. From a learning standpoint, however, the reader admittedly is left with the considerable task of trying to imitate that which he sees. What GOLF DIGEST has always done best is provide practical, hands-on, how-to help with specific problems. The simple, straightforward instruction pieces, the type you will see a lot of in this section, are what really shave strokes off your score. And in putting them together, we have utilized one of the great learning resources ever seen: The Golf Digest Schools. The first prominent commercial golf "camp," the Schools began in 1971 and had a dramatic and immediate impact on our instruction content. The Schools have employed some of the best instructors in history, including Bob Toski, Jim Flick, Peter Kostis, Davis Love Jr., DeDe Owens and Jack Lumpkin. These teachers, and the many who followed them, have proved expert at taking the information they gave their pupils and passing it along to our readers. From this "learning laboratory" came an inexhaustible well of story ideas generated by some of the most innovative minds in the business.

Not all of the great teachers taught full time, however. There also is the Golf Digest Pro Panel, that included such great players as Byron Nelson, Sam Snead, Dr. Cary Middlecoff and Paul Runyan. They have always been a unique lot, for they have drawn on their vast playing experience to provide insight into peripheral topics such as equipment, playing in wind and rain, strategy and course management, or the nature of competition.

Through it all, the star really has been the reader. That's why GOLF DIGEST started a series of recognition programs in the 1960s, some of which continue to this day. We've saluted the most improved golfers, club champions, age shooters, golfers who made holes-in-one and double eagles. We also have cast an eye to the future, awarding individuals and programs that have made contributions to junior golf.

In days past, GOLF DIGEST used to conduct a yearly gathering of Pro Panel members, who for two full days would discuss and debate freely the eternal issue of improving, and how we could do a better job helping readers lower their handicaps. At one point, Bob Toski, up to the gills in frustration over the pains we were taking, exclaimed, "You can't teach golf through the pages of the magazine!"

A day later, Toski suggested he may have been wrong. After you read his *Touch System for Better Golf* and other stories for this chapter, you'll probably agree.

February 1984

In alphabetical order, here are the best I've ever seen: Seve Ballesteros, Walter Hagen, Ben Hogan, Bob Jones, Jack Nicklaus, Byron Nelson, Arnold Palmer, Gene Sarazen, Lee Trevino and Tom Watson.

Illustrations by Jim Sharpe

What You Can Learn From the Greatest Players I Ever Saw

The game's senior statesman picks his personal top 10 and tells what their talents can do for you

by Sam Snead

Seve Ballesteros

Some folks might be surprised to see Seve Ballesteros' name on this list. After all, he's just 26. Hell, I've got golf shoes older than that.

But with two Masters wins and a British Open title behind him I think he's just scratched the surface of what he can do, especially now that he's decided to play on our tour more or less full time. I've always believed that if you want to be the best you've got to compete against the best.

Seve's great strength is that he has a lot of power and that's what you need to win today. There are no short hitters on tour anymore—just

long and unbelievably long. Just look at the record. Seve won at Augusta last year on the par 5s. My God, he reached No. 8 with an iron! He darn near won the Open at Oakmont without so much as saying "Hello" to his driver.

What sets Seve apart is that, for all his power, he's an extremely good putter. The two don't always go hand in hand. He's got good touch and imagination in his short game. That's also unusual, but I think he developed that as a kid when he'd play with just one club.

Seve's got one helluva swing, but one thing that really stands out in my mind is how well he uses his

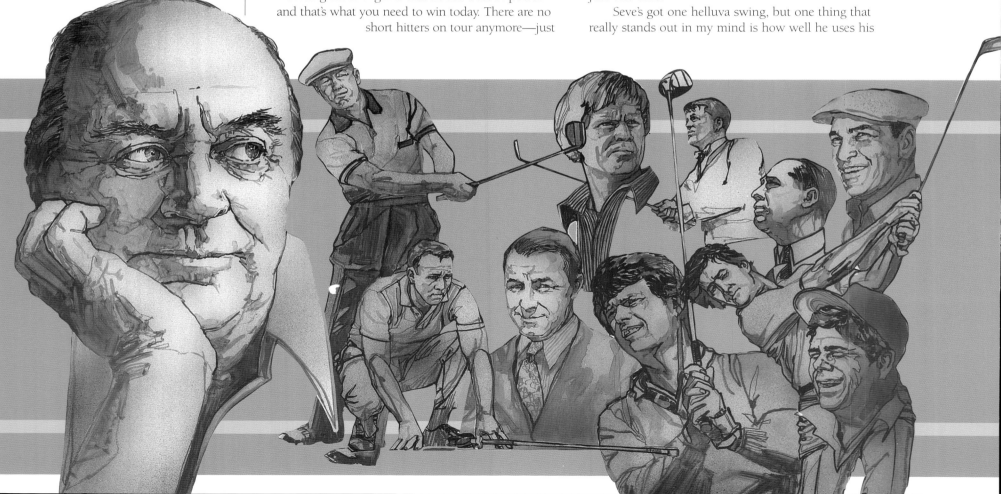

> **When Walter Hagen was on a golf course he was like a general on a battlefield—in total control.**

legs. The legs are a great source of power when used properly, but what most people don't realize is that the legs control the pace of the swing. I don't believe there's ever been a good golfer—or any athlete for that matter—who didn't have good footwork.

Once you've developed a feel for proper footwork and legwork go to the practice tee and hit some balls with a short iron. Forget about distance. Just try to concentrate on letting your legs pace your swing.

Walter Hagen

I don't believe that Walter Hagen had a single weakness in his game.

He drove the ball beautifully, could hit any kind of shot he needed to hit, and putted with the best of them.

What impressed me the most about Hagen wasn't what you'd call his mechanics, even though almost everyone could learn something from the way he made a pass at the ball. Hagen impressed me because he was always in control of the situation.

When Hagen was on a golf course he was like a general on a battlefield. He was in total control and there was nothing that could happen out there that could shake him.

Hagen could turn a 77 into a 67 as well as anyone who ever played. By that, I mean that he didn't panic when he had one of those rounds where nothing was going right.

For one thing, as I said, he was a great shotmaker so he was able to make up strokes during a round. For another, he was smart enough to realize that you're going to get some bad breaks and hit some off-color shots in every round and you have to learn to accept it. I see a lot of weekend players who get a bad break early in the round and by the time the smoke stops coming out of their ears they're out of the match. That never happened to Hagen. He played a round one shot at a time.

One last thing about Hagen. He knew the rule book inside and out. Most people think the rules are there to hurt them, but if you know the rules you can make them work in your favor. That's true of all really good players. You'll never see a Jack Nicklaus get hurt by not knowing a rule.

And I'll guarantee you that Walter Hagen never was.

Ben Hogan

A while back somebody asked me how I would rank Ben Hogan with the other great players I've known in my day, and I'd have to say that if Ben wasn't the best he was right up there near the top.

Ben didn't have the prettiest swing in the world. In fact, he'd set up to the ball and "woosh, woosh" it was over with. I'd watch where his shots went, but I'd never watch his swing. I was afraid what it might do to mine.

Ben and I played some pretty memorable head-to-head matches, though. I can remember every shot and every pin placement from our playoffs in the

1950 Los Angeles Open and the 1954 Masters. I won them both, and believe me, there was a special satisfaction in beating Ben. It wasn't so much that we were archrivals, like the press liked to write. It was more because when I beat Ben I knew I'd beaten about the best there was.

I liked playing with Ben. He'd wish you good luck on the first tee and then go about his business—and let you go about yours. He withdrew into his own world for however long the round took.

What always impressed me most about Ben was his ability to concentrate totally during a round. Concentration means different things to different people, but to me it means keeping yourself on an even keel no matter what happens. Don't get too high when things are going good; don't get too low when things go wrong.

The only other player I can think of who comes close to Ben's ability to concentrate is Jack Nicklaus. But if you watch Jack closely you can read his emotions. If he hits a bad shot or makes a bogey the red will rise up his neck and he'll walk a little slower. Believe me, I spent a lot of time trying to read Ben without much luck.

Ben used to be a professional card dealer in his early days to help make ends meet. If you do that for a living you learn pretty quickly to control your emotions and not show your feelings.

Ben learned his lessons very well . . . and, obviously, they paid off.

Bob Jones

Bob Jones was past his prime by the time I played with him, but there's no question in my mind that he was one of the best. His record speaks for itself.

Jones had a swing that he kind of wound up, like you'd wind up the spring on a watch. He got a lot of power out of that swing, though. I'd guess that he was about as long as anyone he played against and he was a deadly player with those fairway woods.

Bob was a great driver of the ball and about as good a putter as there was. Doc Middlecoff used to say that if you were a great driver and a

great putter then you were a "bodacious" player. I don't believe anyone else ever called Bob Jones "bodacious," but I guess Doc is pretty much on the money.

It's a funny thing. Most people don't realize that as great a player as Jones was, he wasn't a very good long-iron player. He drew the ball, and when the pins were tucked behind a right-hand bunker he had a tough time getting at them. He bogeyed a lot of par 3s, especially if they were longish holes.

Jones had a fine rhythm in his swing, but what stands out in my mind, especially when I look at pictures of his swing, was how well he coordinated his arms with his lower body. It was as though they worked as one unit. When one or the other lags behind is when you have trouble. That's where Jones' rhythm came into play. People who swing too fast have a tough time coordinating their arms and legs. Usually they throw their arms in high gear, race to what they think is the top of their backswing and then go like hell at the ball before their legs have a chance of working like they should. Think about it: Your legs can't move as fast as your arms can. You've got to give them time. Bob Jones did and it worked pretty well for him.

Jack Nicklaus

I don't think it ever occurred to Jack Nicklaus that he might not succeed.

Deep down inside of a lot of people is a fear of winning. It almost seems like they'll find a way to lose. People like Jack find a way to win.

I first met Jack when he was just a kid, maybe 15 or 16. We played an exhibition and if he was nervous or even the least bit intimidated you couldn't prove it by me. I knew then and there that this was a kid to watch.

With a player as great as Jack you can pick just about any part of his game and it will be good enough to copy. Jack is long off the tee and I guess there isn't much doubt that he was as good a putter as you'll ever come across. I'd have to say that, year in and year out, he was the best putter we had out on tour. People say that Jack's weakness was with his wedges, especially in the sand. That might be, but he was smart enough to avoid the traps and you can bet a bundle that, when push came to shove, Jack seldom hit a bad wedge shot under the gun. Like I said, champions are people who will find a way to win.

One thing I noticed about Jack is that, because he hit the ball so far off the tee, he was in the rough more often than you might expect for a player of his caliber. That's what people don't realize about hitting the ball a long way. A ball hit 3 degrees off line and 270 yards will be a lot farther from the fairway than a 200-yard drive that's 3 degrees off-line.

One reason Jack could recover from the rough so well is that he's always had a fairly upright swing. Too often I see amateurs with flat swings try to hit shots out of the rough and they don't have a prayer.

A flat swing gives the clubhead more time to get tangled up in the grass before it gets to the ball. A fairly upright swing like Jack's delivers the clubhead to the ball at a fairly steep angle, and that cuts down on

> **I don't think it ever occurred to Jack Nicklaus that he might not succeed.**

Left hand is key to great putting

by Arnold Palmer, November 1958

Right now I have settled on a style of putting and a putter that feel great to me. I am confident I will strike the ball in the direction and at the speed I intend. When I miss a putt, I feel it is because I have misread the green. My system hasn't failed—my thinking has. My whole putting system revolves around two things:

1. I want the back of my left hand to face the target throughout the stroke.

2. I do not want my left wrist to "cup," or break, on the follow-through.

If my left hand remains in the same position relative to the target throughout the stroke, I am certain my backswing will be consistently the same.

If my left wrist does not cup after impact, I am certain I will not pull the ball to the left of the target— the most common error in putting.

This all means my putting motion is more of an arm-and-shoulder swing than a wrist action.

If you are familiar with my current style, you will notice that the angle of my left wrist does not change between the address and the follow-through positions.

Palmer showing winning form in 1963. (Photo: Lester Nehamkin)

the chances of hitting the ball far or getting the club-head twisted around by the grass.

When I have a pro-am partner who has a tough time in the rough I tell him to think of Jack's swing—nice and upright—and then pop that clubhead right down on that ball.

You'd be amazed how thinking of Jack helps them.

Byron Nelson

Ben Hogan, Byron Nelson and I were born the same year and so there have always been a lot of comparisons made of our careers.

I always thought that Ben and Byron were pretty much equals as players, week in and week out. I think Byron was a better driver and long-iron player, but I believe Ben was better around the greens.

Looking back, I suppose it's not really so surprising that Byron left the tour when he did. He had proved that he was a great champion and I just don't think that all the travel and the pressure agreed with him as much as it did some of the other fellows.

Don't get me wrong. Byron loves golf and has given a lot back to the game. And I'm not saying he wasn't a helluva player and competitor or that his approach was wrong or right. It was his way and more power to him.

As I said, Byron was a great driver of the ball and an exceptional long-iron player, which was possible because he could generate a lot of clubhead speed. If you looked at his swing you'd notice that he did this without taking the club past parallel at the top. In fact Byron seldom got the club to parallel. He felt this gave him better control—and club control is the name of the game.

Too often I see players—even some pretty good touring pros—actually breaking their wrists at the top because they feel like they need that little bit extra.

If players would just think about setting that club at the top—not even at parallel—and maintaining their wrist cock as they start the downswing they'd be a lot better off.

It worked for Byron. He had plenty of accuracy and he never went hungry in the distance department either.

Arnold Palmer

Arnold Palmer is the best example of what I call a "hitter" of the ball as opposed to a "swinger."

Now in the long run I believe that a swinger will win out over a hitter, because hitters have a smaller margin for error. But when a hitter gets hot, watch out, it's Katy Bar the Door time—especially when it's a hitter that could putt like Arnold in his heyday.

Arnold didn't just think he'd make every putt he faced, he honestly *expected* to make them all. Hell, I played rounds with him where he'd run in five or six 30-footers and think nothing of it.

All that comes down to confidence and that's what good putters have a lot of. They have confidence in their ability to read a putt, set up properly to the ball and the target, and let their stroke do the work.

Most often, when I see people with putting problems, they lack that confidence. They read the putt, set up to the ball, and all of a sudden things begin to look a little funny. They move their feet, twist their shoulders, fine tune the putterblade and pretty soon are so confused they don't have a chance of making that putt.

When I think of Arnold in his prime what stands out is that he'd get set over the ball and he'd be locked in. He didn't move around or make adjustments. He had confidence in what he was doing and wasn't going to be moved. Period.

That brings me to one other point. People used to joke about Arnold's putting stance. They said he looked like a damned old praying mantis bent over the ball. But it was a comfortable position for Arnold. It worked for him. Putting is the most individual part of the game, but I've always told people that one thing all good putters have in common is that they get themselves in a position that's comfortable—and they putt with confidence.

Gene Sarazen

I guess Gene Sarazen was about as good a player as ever played, but I *know* he was as good a competitor as ever came along.

Gene isn't very big and a fellow his size might have a pretty tough time of it out on the tour now. But size or no size, Gene had that quality that it takes to win.

*I have a rule for pitch-
ing and chipping out of
tall grass that might
make some of your
shots from the rough
easier: "Deeper the
grass, tighter the grip."*

*If the rough is really
tall and thick, I
squeeze the club as
tightly as I can. Why?
So I can keep it moving
at a constant speed
through the thick
grass. And I want that
speed to be the same
on the downswing as it
is on the backswing. I
just start back gently,
and at the top I let it
go, allowing my arms
(with no wrist move-
ment) to lead the club-
head through the ball.*

*If you grip the club
too loosely, you're liable
to catch the clubhead
in the grass, slowing it
down and closing the
face. When you're try-
ing to get the ball close
that can be deadly.*

—Lee Trevino,
August 1985

There are a lot of people that, deep down, are afraid to win. I've always thought that, because they don't want anyone to dislike them. Gene didn't care very much about that. He didn't want to just win; he wanted to bury his opponent.

I think that's how you have to be. Once you start feeling sorry for your opponent then you're just asking for trouble. I don't believe Gene—or any of these other fellows—ever would let up.

Of course, Gene is going to be remembered as the inventor of the sand wedge, but by itself the club wouldn't have meant much unless you came up with a swing that complemented the design. Gene did that.

In the old days you'd play bunker shots with a niblick—a 9-iron—and cut under the ball, spinning it out of the sand.

You can't do that very well with a sand wedge because of the wide flange and the bounce it produces.

To make the sand wedge work properly you need to set up with your weight a little bit to the left, but the real difference is in the arc of the swing—it has to be more of an up-and-down motion.

If you can learn to play the right kind of shots with Gene's sand wedge, you can save yourself a lot of shots around the green.

If you learn to develop Gene's never-let-up attitude, you'll win yourself a lot more matches.

Lee Trevino

Let me say this right from the start: I honestly believe that Lee Trevino is one of the most underrated golfers in history—if not *the* most. I mean, here's a guy who won two U.S. Opens, two British Opens and a PGA Championship in a career that didn't really start until 1968 and has been plagued by injuries.

I'll go one step further. I think he's as good a pure shotmaker as there is on this list. You name the shot and he can hit it. He's got great feel and a natural instinct for imagining the right shot and producing it.

Like anyone else, Lee has his favorite shots—his bread-and-butter shots that he can go to when the pressure is on.

When he first came out on tour Lee hit a lot of low shots, which makes sense since he learned to play as a kid in Texas where if you get your ball up in that wind you're a goner. Don't get me wrong, he could hit the ball high with the best of them but it wasn't his natural shot.

All this worked two ways for Lee—for and against him.

It worked against him at a course like Augusta National. People say he can't win there because you need to work the ball right to left, but they're wrong on two counts. First, he can move the ball that way without hardly trying. Second, he still could win there because he's learned to hit his approaches with some height. That's the shot you need to win at Augusta.

If you ask him he'll tell you that he loves to play the British Open courses because the wind is a big

WATCH THE SAND, NOT THE BALL

Weekend golfers probably fear sand shots more than any others. That's because they understand them less, and practice them less. But you have a greater margin for error in the sand.

All you have to do is slice your sand wedge into the sand one inch to three inches behind the ball. If you open the face of the wedge and finish your swing, the ball will always come out of the bunker. Think of the sand as your ally.

Focus on the spot you want the clubhead to enter the sand, not on the ball. Practice by drawing a line in the sand behind the ball and starting your long, thin divot at that point. Watch that spot where you want to enter the sand.

The ideal divot for a normal sand shot is long and shallow— longer and shallower than most players ever envision. The divot should extend at least eight inches past the ball. In other words, the divot is about a foot long.

—Tom Watson, July 1997

greatest tips

Play the shot you can pull off
by Tom Watson, February 1979

No piece of advice, mechanical or mental, has ever benefited me more than the words I received from the late Leland (Duke) Gibson shortly before I joined the PGA Tour. At the time, Duke was head professional at the Blue Hills Country Club in Kansas City, my hometown.

"Know what your limitations are," he told me. "Understand what you can and what you can't do. Never try to execute a shot that you are not capable of."

What Duke was saying was that I must know when to take a risk and when to play it safe. For example, if I have a little pop wedge shot over a bunker or water hazard to a pin cut close to the hazard, do I gamble with a tricky finesse shot to get it close or do I merely get the ball safely onto the green? Some days you have a good touch with that shot, some days you don't. The decision on how to play it rests with my own knowledge of my capabilities and my limitations on any given day.

Every time I'm faced with one of those decisions, I remember Duke's words.

factor and the courses are perfectly suited to knock-down, bump-and-run approaches. Lee Trevino will be a threat to win the British Open for as long as he lives.

I think if weekend players could learn to hit low shots, and play bump-and-run approaches into greens they'd be much better off. It's a safer shot. The key is keeping your hands ahead of the clubhead through impact. Just concentrate on keeping the clubhead low to the ground. With a little practice you'll learn how far the ball will run with each club.

You may never need it to win the British Open, but it will sure come in handy a lot more often than you might think.

Tom Watson

It's a funny thing, but I suppose that no matter how many tournaments Tom Watson goes on to win, people will always remember him for the wedge shot he holed on 17 at Pebble Beach in the last round of the 1982 U.S. Open.

That's not bad, of course. There are a lot worse things to be remembered for. In a way, it makes sense that he should be remembered for that shot since it sort of symbolizes what I consider his greatest strength—he's an absolutely fearless scrambler.

Now some people might be

offended by that, but I mean it as a compliment. Tom is a fine ball striker. There's no doubt about that. But without his ability to get it up and down I don't believe he'd have won half the tournaments he's won—and I bet he'd be the first to agree.

I think the key to Tom's success is that he's a very aggressive player—off the tee and on the green. Tom's going at the hole every time. There's no lay up in that boy.

Now there's an old saying. "The good Lord hates a coward but he's not real fond of a fool, either." There's a big differ-ence between being aggressive and being crazy.

My point is that you'll seldom see Tom leave an approach putt or a chip shot short of the hole. The reason? He's got so much confi-dence in his ability to make those two- or three-footers coming back. Hell, he thrives on putts that have driven an awful lot of people off the tour.

If you go to a tournament, watch Tom on the practice green. He spends a lot of time working on those short putts—and I mean working. You can't say that about many high handicappers.

Tom's smart. He figured out a long time ago that those long approach putts are a lot easier if you have confidence in your ability to make the short ones coming back.

May 1985

My Most Memorable Shots in the Majors

From the Golden Bear's long-running series on his best and worst decisions in the majors

by Jack Nicklaus with Ken Bowden

The greater the pressure, the less you should try to *finesse* the shot. Go with the highest percentage club.

Even if it's Hogan, don't be intimidated

THE SITUATION: Walking after my 3-wood tee shot on the 385-yard 13th hole in the final round of the 1960 U.S. Open at Cherry Hills, a scoreboard indicates that I'm leading the championship by one stroke ahead of Arnold Palmer, Julius Boros and Jack Fleck. I've put the ball exactly where I want it, on level ground short of the creek intersecting the fairway, and loft an easy 9-iron 12 feet below the pin. My playing partner, for the first time ever, is Ben Hogan, going for a record fifth Open and now two shots adrift of me.

MY THOUGHT PROCESS: At only 20 years old, I'm still in awe of Hogan, although he's been very pleasant to me. Nevertheless, as I look over the birdie putt, it occurs to me that even he might have difficulty in making up three strokes in five holes. Pumped by that notion, I stroke the ball a little too hard and it slides 18 inches past the cup. Now there's a little indentation left by a poorly repaired ball mark between me and the hole.

THE SHOT: Excited, anxious, under as much pressure as I've ever known, I can't focus my mind clearly on whether the rules allow me to repair the ball mark (they do). Also, I'm too shy or embarrassed to admit this in front of Hogan or to hold up play by asking an official. So I go ahead and stroke the putt. The mark deflects the ball just enough to spin it out. I bogey, then three-putt the next green. Arnie, with his phenomenal historic charge, wins the Open with me second.

THE LESSON: There are three lessons here, which have stuck with me ever since. First: Repair ball marks as you'd like others to repair them for you. Second: Know the rules. Third: If in doubt, ask.

When to play a drive like an approach

THE SITUATION: With nine holes to go, I'm leading the 1963 Masters by two and feeling on top of the world. Less than an hour later, walking off the 12th green, I'm one back of Sam Snead and Gary Player, tied with Tony Lema and Julius Boros and thoroughly disgusted with myself. After three sloppy shots, only an

eight-foot putt has saved me from making a double bogey on the shortest hole on the course. As I get to the 13th tee, I learn that Snead has birdied the 15th and is now two shots ahead.

MY THOUGHT PROCESS: Augusta National's 13th, at 475 yards, is what I think of as a marvelous "par 4½." At that distance, it offers at least a birdie, and in any final Masters round when I'm contending I feel I must make one here to stay in the race. On the other hand, there's disaster all around on every shot from even a

Illustrations by Jim McQueen

**The 1960
U.S. Open
Championship**
Cherry Hills Country Club
Denver, Colo.
13th hole, par 4, 385 yards

**The 1963
Masters Tournament**
Augusta National Golf Club
Augusta, Ga.
13th hole, par 5, 475 yards

**The 1980
U.S. Open
Championship**
Baltusrol Golf Club
Springfield, N.J.
17th hole, par 5, 630 yards

slight miscue. For me, the key to a birdie or better is the tee shot. It must finish far enough around the dogleg to leave no more than a long iron from a reasonably level lie and approach angle, otherwise the creek becomes too great a hazard to go for the green in two. For maximum control, I'd usually hit a 3-wood from the tee. Now I tell myself this is no time for faintheartedness. It has to be the driver.

THE SHOT: I'm having trouble shaking off the shock of the 12th hole, and the danger at times like this is to abbreviate the next swing by rushing it. I tell myself: "Stay loose at address, set the club fully at the top and start down only as fast as you swung back." I align for the necessary draw: shoulders, hips, knees and feet slightly right, clubface fractionally closed. To minimize tension build-up, I begin the swing the moment I feel properly set up—no last-second delay or second-guessing. The shot turns out exactly as I've planned and visualized it. I hit the 2-iron to the green, two-putt for birdie and am right back in the thick of things. I go on to win by a stroke over Tony Lema.

THE LESSON: Never treat tee shots more lightly than the strokes that seem to more heavily influence your score—and especially when you're "hot." How you put the ball in play is as big a factor as how well you hole out. The "just-haul-off-and-fire" tee-shot approach very rarely produces winners.

Go with your shot

THE SITUATION: Final round of the 1980 U.S. Open at Baltusrol, the 630-yard par-5 17th. After a good drive and 2-iron, I'm 88 yards from the pin, which is set front and left. Miss the green left and it's big trouble. I'm two strokes ahead of Isao Aoki, who now hits his third shot five feet from the pin. I've played with Isao all four rounds and, the way he's putted, I just *know* he'll make this one. The final hole is another par 5, and I figure he'll birdie that, too.

MY THOUGHT PROCESS: I'm sure I need at least a birdie and a par on the last two holes to avoid a playoff,

and I'm feeling exceptional pressure. I've revamped my entire game, worked my tail off all season, but haven't won in almost two years. As well as I've played this week, it's been hard not to wonder whether the wheels will stay on—and pitching has never been my strongest suit. When you're uptight like this, there's a strong urge to relieve the tension by rushing. I force myself to think this shot through very deliberately. Finally I decide to play to the right of the pin, both to protect against the trouble to the left and to leave myself an uphill putt. But which club? I can hit the ball 88 yards with either a three-quarter pitching wedge or a full sand wedge.

THE SHOT: The faster the adrenaline flows, the tougher "part"-shots become. Pumped up, you tend to take too long a backswing, then either hit the ball way strong or involuntarily slow down through impact and leave it short or drag it off line, or both. Thus you're far better off with a club you can swing fully and freely, and that's why I choose the sand wedge in this case. I hit the ball pin-high 23 feet to the right of the cup, and when I make the putt suddenly all the tension evaporates. I'm able to play the final hole conservatively, luck out with another good putt for a final birdie, win my fourth U.S. Open, break my own 72-hole scoring record and enjoy one of the happiest evenings of my life.

THE LESSON: The greater the pressure, the less you should try to "finesse" the shot. Take your time in analyzing the situation, then go with the highest-percentage club—the one you can swing most normally.

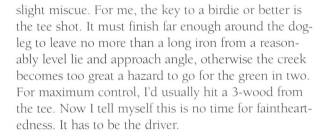

May 1992

The Secrets of Golf

For the first time, this legendary teacher reveals what's inside his Little Red Book

by Harvey Penick, with an introduction by Tom Kite

Whether or not you realize it, you are about to read an excerpt from one of the most important golf instruction books ever written. If you have never had the opportunity to take a lesson from Harvey Penick, that statement may surprise you some. But even better is the fact that these lessons will be enjoyable and you will learn something that should improve your game.

This is the effect Mr. Penick has had on his students. No one can help but enjoy being around Harvey. He is as comfortable as an old pair of jeans, as unpretentious as a young child, and yet is one of the smartest men I have ever had the pleasure to meet. No, not book smart, but people smart.

Even at this stage in his career, Harvey says he learns something new about golf every day. Contrast that to one of today's method teachers who says there is only one way to swing the club. Harvey allows the swing to fit the student. What other reason could there be for the tremendous numbers of great players who have worked with him? Davis Love Jr. and III, Mickey Wright, Betsy Rawls, Sandra Palmer, Kathy Whitworth, Judy Kimball, Terry Dill, and Don and Rik Massengale made the trip to Austin more than once.

Don't be misled into thinking that Harvey taught us all the same way. I have never seen him give a group lesson. To the contrary, he would shoo away any sideline watchers for fear they would overhear something that didn't apply to their games. In more than 30 years of playing golf with Ben Crenshaw, I have never been allowed to watch Ben take a lesson from Harvey, nor has he been allowed to watch me.

For more than 60 years, Harvey has compiled notes and observations about golf in a slender volume with a red cover. Intended as a teaching tool for his son Tinsley, who followed him as head professional at the Austin (Tex.) Country Club, he never let anyone else read his writing. Now, for the first time in print, we share with you excerpts from Mr. Penick's Little Red Book. —T.K.

THE THREE MOST IMPORTANT CLUBS

Herbert Warren Wind, the stylish and learned golf writer, came to see me at the club and asked what I think are the three most important clubs in the bag, in order.

I said, "The putter, the driver and the wedge."

Herb said he'd asked Ben Hogan the same question. Ben had replied, "The driver, the putter and the wedge."

My reasoning is that you hit the driver 14 times in an ordinary round. But on the same day, you may have 23 to 25 putts that are outside the "gimme" range, but within a makable distance.

A five-foot putt counts one stroke, the same as a 270-yard drive, but the putt may be much more significant to your score.

Psychologically, the driver is very important. If you hit your tee ball well, it fills you with confidence. On the other hand, if you smash a couple of drives into the trees, your confidence can be shaken.

But nothing is more important psychologically than knocking putts into the hole. Sinking putts makes your confidence soar, and it devastates your opponent.

A good putter is a match for anyone. A bad putter is a match for no one.

The woods are full of long drivers.

THE MOMENT OF TRUTH

Two proud parents came to me at the club and announced that their son had scored his first birdie. I agreed that was a wonderful event and asked them how long was the putt Junior made for the birdie.

The parents said the putt was only two feet long, so they gave Junior a "gimme" to assure his first birdie.

"I've got news for you," I said. "Junior still hasn't made a birdie."

Opposite: More than 60 years of teaching notes were the frame-work of Harvey Penick's Little Red Book. *(Photo: Dom Furore)*

Above, left: *Psychologically, the driver is very important. If you hit your tee ball well, it fills you with confidence. (Artist: Bernie Fuchs)*

Above, right: *Mr. Penick's rule is that a youngster should be required to hole every putt. (Artist: Bernie Fuchs)*

Not only did Junior not sink the birdie putt, it was now planted in his mind that he could pick up his ball two feet from the hole and announce the putt as made, not having to face the moment of truth.

When Junior reaches a higher level of play, where there are no "gimmes," he may develop an anxiety about short putts that will bother him the rest of his life.

My rule is that a youngster, no matter how small, should be required to hole every putt.

If Junior grows up knowing that he has to make all the short ones, it will automatically become part of his game. When he plays on higher levels and faces a two-footer to win an important match, he'll be ready.

THE MYTHICAL PERFECT SWING

Here is how to make the Mythical Perfect Swing that all golfers are always pursuing:

Stand a few paces behind the ball and look down the line toward the target.

Walk to the ball from behind, get a good grip, pass the club in back of the ball square to the target, then adjust your stance to fit.

Have a waggle and set the club in back of the ball again. Then make a forward press similar to what you would do swinging a bucket of water.

In the first move back as the club gets parallel to the ground, the toe of the club points directly up, and your left heel starts off the ground.

Let the club come on up, keeping your elbows in front of your body, to the top of your backswing, where the clubhead will be pointing almost to the ground.

Return your left heel to the ground and let your right elbow move back to your side as it comes down.

Weight has started shifting to your left side. Your forearms cross over as they swing. Your head stays behind the ball, perhaps even moving slightly more behind it.

Finish with your forearms in front of you. A good finish shows what has gone before it.

Let your head come up to look at the good shot.

On your follow-through, the right foot helps to hold your balance.

If you have lost your balance during this Mythical Perfect Swing, it is probably because your grip is too weak or tight or both.

Practice this at home in slow motion without a ball.

Be sure you don't watch the clubhead go back. Swing the clubhead at a spot every time.

Force yourself to approach the ball from behind, before every swing, even on the carpet.

Make 10 to 20 Mythical Perfect Swings each night, teaching your muscles what your brain wants.

greatest tips

Hit from the "high" foot on hilly lies

by Hardy Loudermilk, May 1964

Uphill and downhill lies needn't be a problem if a golfer simply remembers to play the ball off the "high" foot.

Because of the terrain, when you're playing from an uphill lie your clubhead reaches the ground a bit later in the swing—so you should position the ball toward your left foot. On a downhill lie the clubhead reaches the ground earlier in the swing—so play the ball back toward your right foot.

It also helps to keep most

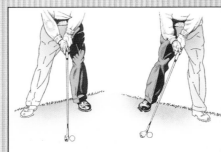

Illustration by Ed Acuna.

of your weight on the "high side" at the start of the swing. This offsets the normal gravitational pull toward the lower foot, which causes the tendency to hook from an uphill lie and slice from a downhill lie.

Remember that you get a higher and shorter flight from an uphill lie, so use a less-lofted club than usual—a 4- or 5-iron where you would normally hit a 6-iron. Hitting from a down-hill slope produces a lower flight, so be sure to use a more-lofted club.

March 1992

Shortcuts to Save Strokes

How to lower your scores without rebuilding your swing

by members of the Golf Digest Pro Panel Staff

Saving strokes is what golf is all about. Think about it. A birdie saves you at least a shot. So does getting up and down from a greenside bunker. Playing safe when you're tempted to go for the risky carry over the pond more often than not saves you at least one shot.

And that, in turn, is what this story will give you: the ability to save shots without totally rebuilding your game. None of our "strokesavers" call for a Faldo-like revamping of your technique, or Hoganesque dedication, or even any need to sacrifice job, family and friends in an effort to improve. Nor is it merely a group of quick tips that rarely last past the third tee.

No, the items that follow were chosen by Jack Lumpkin, Mike LaBauve, Paul Runyan, John Elliott and lefthander Dick Aultman, all noted members of the Golf Digest Schools Staff, because they apply directly to what really matters—shooting lower scores. Some deal with technique and so will require some practice. Others pertain to the mental side of the game. Properly executed, all will last for the rest of your golfing life.

Photo: Jim Moriarty

Decide where not to finish ▶
by Dick Aultman

The wise golfer instinctively plans shots with a negative approach. He decides where he does not want the ball to finish. Only then does he switch to the positive, planning where he does want it to finish.

Your red alert might kick in whenever you come to a green with the flagstick positioned close to the right side. You know that missing the green on that particular side would cost you a shot because the chances of you chipping close are remote. So play away from that side, adjusting your aim and/or swing accordingly.

It's fine to accentuate the positive. Just make sure that you eliminate the negative, too.

Photos: Jim Moriarty

◀ Improve your pivot
by Jack Lumpkin

If you have trouble making solid contact with the ball, the problem may be in your pivot.

Assume a correct address posture, bending forward from the hips with your back straight and knees slightly flexed. Retaining this posture, drop your club to the ground. Then grasp your left shoulder with your right hand and your right shoulder with your left hand. (1)

While retaining the angle of your spine, pull your left shoulder down and around with your right hand and push your right shoulder up and around with your left hand. Turn your shoulders until your right hand is under your chin. (2) Feel your weight shifting onto your right foot as you wind around your right leg.

Using your lower body—without applying pressure to your shoulders—unwind counterclockwise to the left until your hips and shoulders face the "target," your weight on your left foot.

Do this 12 to 15 times, then as if gripping a club and next with a club in your hands. Finally, hit balls. You'll soon be making better strikes.

Lower your chips—and scores
by Paul Runyan

Many golfers chip with very lofted clubs. That's risky. The more lofted the club is, the longer your swing must be to make the ball fly a given distance. And longer swings lessen your chance of making solid contact.

Lesser-lofted clubs allow shorter swings. So choose the least-lofted club that will land the ball safely on the green without its overrunning the hole. Experiment with various clubs to learn what trajectories they produce.

When in doubt between two clubs, however, choose the more lofted and play the ball back in your stance. The steeper downswing that produces makes catching the club in the grass behind the ball less likely.

Follow this plan when chipping from bad lies, too. The worse the lie, the more loft you should use and the farther back you should play the ball.

Play with post-impact picture
by John Elliott

Most golfers do not play well because they are thinking practice thoughts. When I practice, at least 90 percent of my thoughts are pre-impact, things like grip, posture, ball positioning, backswing and downswing.

I practice those so that I don't have to think about them when I'm under pressure out on the course. I'll play better if my focus is forward of impact and singular. I want only one thought per swing. I want it to be either post-impact technique or a visualization of the target or the ball's flight.

Practice with practice thoughts, then play with play thoughts.

Conquer these tough shots ▶
by Mike LaBauve

Although swinging out to in is not something I normally recommend, it can help on shots from:

1. Divots (inset).   2. Deep grass.
3. Fairway bunkers.   4. Downhill lies.

The biggest challenge on all of these shots is making certain that the clubhead is moving downward when it hits the ball, thus avoiding the grass or sand behind it.

To create the out-to-in path, assume your address position but align your shoulders to the left (*shown*), so your clubhead will be moving more leftward than normal at impact. Make your backswing more with your arms and less with your body, but be sure to turn your body through during your forward swing.

October 1985

How to Get the Killer Instinct

The difference between seeming tough and being tough

by Dr. Bob Rotella

> "You have to be a perfectionist. You have to hate playing badly more than you love playing well, and you have to hate losing more than you love winning."
>
> —AMY ALCOTT, ON WHAT IT TAKES TO BE A CHAMPION

Lee Trevino has told you which players, in his opinion, have the killer instinct. The question is, how do you get it?

With all due respect to Lee, my advice would be don't wait for Lee Trevino—or anyone else—to tell you whether you've got it or not. Lee didn't wait. When he came on tour he knew that the pros who were winning then were perfectly content to have him believe that they had something he didn't. The guys you play against, unless they are very, very good friends, will let you think that, too.

Am I saying that there may be a bit of gamesmanship in Lee's story? Is there gamesmanship in the whole concept of "killer instinct"? Sure. More importantly, good players aren't worried about what anybody else thinks of them. They don't want to appear to be mentally tough. They want to be tough. And they do that by playing their own game, shot by shot, at their own pace and tempo.

Poor players, I'm afraid, get distracted by the trappings of toughness. They throw a club, once in a while a la Craig Stadler, or go for all the pins like Lanny Wadkins. But that's like trying to be a great soldier by watching Rambo when you ought to be reading Eisenhower.

The great players, Nicklaus being a prime example, know that the battle is not between you and the next guy. The true battle is between you and yourself, you and the course.

Three qualities help you to win: confidence, concentration and composure.

How do you develop these qualities? By planning your round the night before a match and sticking to that plan; by building a precise preshot routine to take the sloppiness out of your alignment and setup and staying with it on every shot; by putting aside thoughts of score (yours or your opponents) and applying yourself to each shot equally; and by letting your emotions flow naturally on the course, accepting the game's joys and disappointments.

There are also attitudes that get in your way:

1. "The good ones are different from me." What I like about Lee's list of killers is that it includes Lee. Would you leave yourself off of yours? I also like his story about walking with Nicklaus in the '71 Open at Merion. Trevino decided early on that he would walk at his own pace, swing his way and interact with the gallery the way he liked. I've had pros confess that when playing with famous players they found themselves abandoning their game plans and preshot routines and adopting the other player's instead. A competitive golf round is one time when you have the right to be self-centered and even selfish.

2. "At least I didn't leave it short." A high school basketball coach brought me one of his best players because the boy, although a deft shooter from the floor, was missing all of his foul shots. He was banging them hard off the rim and backboard. I asked the young man what his main thought was prior to shooting a foul shot. "Not throwing an airball," he said. "Why?" I asked. "Because I did that once in a tournament and after that the crowd always yelled, 'Airball! Airball!' when I got to the line."

Golfers who say, "At least I didn't leave it short!" after bashing a critical putt six feet past are doing the same thing. Don't be so bold that you make sure you lose.

3. "I can't putt." How often have you heard that line? Or, should I say, how often have you said it? When pros tell me they are putting poorly, I want the evidence. If it turns out they missed a couple of 10-footers and asked another pro if their stroke looked suspect and he said yes, I don't buy it. People make all kinds of pronouncements about putting that only serve to unnerve them. If you have doubts about your putting stroke, go to a flat spot on the green and practice until you're making three- and four-footers consistently. And, remember, sometimes you can do everything right physically, mentally and emotionally and the other guy gets a hot putter and you lose. That doesn't mean he's a killer and you're not.

4. "I was holding the group up." If you have to admit that you've changed your tempo, swing pace or preshot routine because you're afraid that you would offend your playing partners, remember Lee walking with Jack or Jack playing at his own pace against "our hero" Arnold Palmer back in the 1960s. That doesn't mean play slowly. It means play your own game. At the club level social inhibitions are strong. You want to be friendly. You don't want to be too slow or too temperamental. But part of the killer instinct is being yourself out there. Find a style and pace you can be comfortable with no matter who your playing partners are.

In short, give yourself the satisfaction of playing your game, shot by shot, for one entire round. Learn to do that and someday when you are "in the hunt," you'll be surprised at the "killer" in you.

Opposite: Nicklaus and Trevino often found themselves paired—and atop the leader boards—on Sundays in the early '70s. (Photo: Al Satterwhite)

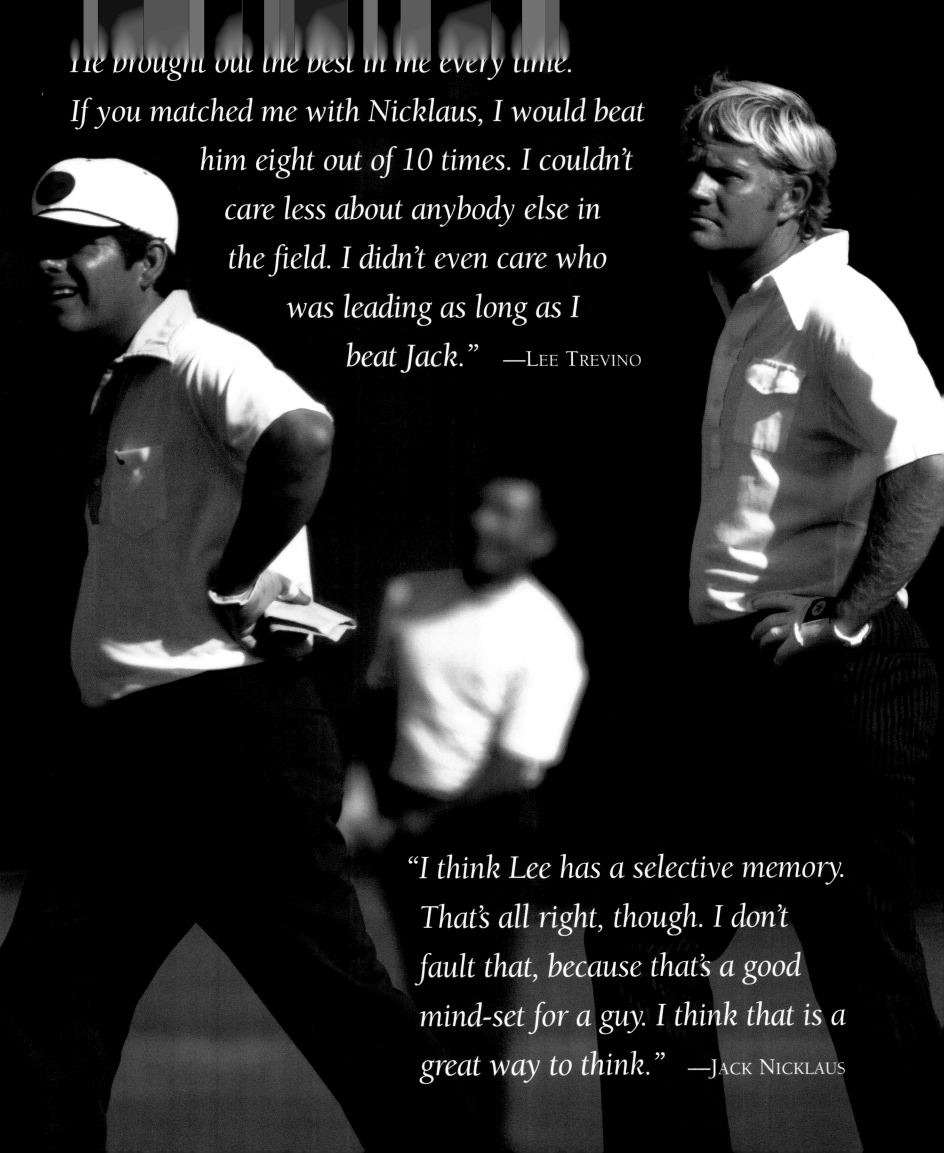

"He brought out the best in me every time. If you matched me with Nicklaus, I would beat him eight out of 10 times. I couldn't care less about anybody else in the field. I didn't even care who was leading as long as I beat Jack." —LEE TREVINO

"I think Lee has a selective memory. That's all right, though. I don't fault that, because that's a good mind-set for a guy. I think that is a great way to think." —JACK NICKLAUS

April 1956

How to Develop a Swing that Repeats

With practice, anyone can shoot in the 70s.
The key is finding a swing that repeats

by Ben Hogan

HOW TO BUILD A CONSISTENT PACE

After swinging without a ball, hit balls while maintaining that same swing length. Increase your swing speed until you exceed the pace at which you strike the ball well. Then throttle back to a controllable speed and identify the feel of that pace. Stay with it.

—DeDe Owen,
February 1985

Developing a good golf swing is a helluva tough chore—at least it was for me. First you must gather all the material together, sift through it and then throw away what's not good for *you*. It's something like making a mulligan stew.

However, there are several fundamentals that are applicable to *everyone*. These fundamentals are particularly important in developing a swing that REPEATS. And after all, that is what every golfer should strive for—a swing that will work the same ALL the time. I think anyone (who does not have a physical disability) can be a 70-shooter. But he has to want to do it—and he must work at it.

Here are the fundamentals I think are applicable to everyone:

1. Grip: The union of the two hands must be right and constant or all else is lost.

2. Posture: This is how you stand and look: Right foot straight, left toe pointing out, knees slightly flexed, back straight.

3. Arms: The position of the arms is very important. From the clubhead to the left shoulder there should be but one hinge—at the hands. With the left arm firm and the right arm loose you can be assured of always coming back to the ball in the same place. The right elbow points to the body.

4. Swing: The left arm continues to be straight all through the backswing. This permits the clubhead to travel the greatest distance. The right elbow points to the ground at the top of the backswing.

5. Follow-Through: As you swing through the ball the right arm straightens and—most important—the body FOLLOWS the swing.

I've noticed one thing that all good golfers do and all bad golfers do not do. The good ones have their left wrist leading at impact. It seems a small thing, but I've found it to be universally true. At impact the left wrist of a good golfer is slightly convex, while that of a poor golfer is generally concave. Which are you?

Ben Hogan preparing for the 1930 Texas Open in San Antonio. (Photo: The Institute of Texan Cultures)

July 1971

The Touch System for Better Golf

How your swing should feel:
First look at a revolutionary approach

by Bob Toski

The first thing I'm going to do to make you a better golfer is ask that before you read any further you find yourself a pen or pencil and a piece of paper. Seriously! Go ahead. I'll wait.

Now, if you've done that, I'd like you to write your name three or four times *as fast and as legibly as you can*. I will do the same.

Let's compare signatures. I've reproduced mine here in the actual size that I wrote it. Are your handwriting strokes as light and as consistent as mine? Are your letters as tall and as deep and as wide? Or are your lines heavier, or your letters smaller? Does your handwriting seem as "free" as mine, or does it appear more "controlled"?

Why swing so hard?
A 150-pound golfer weighs about 170 times as much as the club he's swinging and about 1,480 times as much as the ball he's striking. Most players fail to fully use this tremendous weight and size advantage, because they don't realize, subconsciously, just how light the ball really is. They lose distance because they swing with more effort than they need, and thus ruin their timing. They swing AT the ball, rather than THROUGH it. (Artist: Stan Drake)

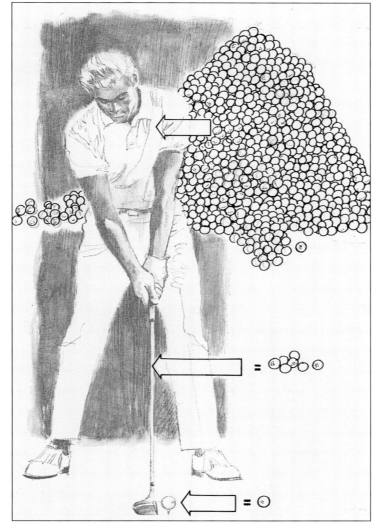

And who do you think wrote the fastest, you or me? I'd better warn you that I've raced against dozens of "signature signers," and only a handful have written faster than I did. And none of them wrote as legibly.

What does all of this mean? Why did I ask you to write your name? I did so because I believe—I *know*—that there is a definite link between the way a person writes his name and the way he, or she, plays golf. I can watch a person sign his name, and then, almost invariably describe correctly how he swings a golf club. The person who writes fast and smooth with big loops like I do usually makes a full, free, rhythmical swing, with his hands moving quite high on the backswing. The person who writes with a heavy-handed, jerky stroke and makes small letters usually has a relatively short, fast, jerky backswing.

Hold your pen or pencil as tight as you can and try to write your name. I'll bet that your writing suddenly becomes slower, and less legible, than normal. Why? Because you over-control the pen. The same thing happens when you over-control a golf club. Hold the club too tight and you'll lose clubhead speed and rhythm. You won't hit the ball as far, or as straight.

Why can I drive a golf ball 250 or 260 yards and keep it in play almost every time? Certainly not because of my size or strength; I weigh barely 135 pounds when my wallet is full. That's why Sam Snead calls me "Mouse." I hit the ball far and straight simply because I have developed a high degree of *feel* for the rhythm and motion and timing of a proper swing. It's the same sensitivity for rhythm and motion that lets me write so fast and so legibly.

I know that with your cooperation I can teach you a similar feel for the proper golf swing. Once you develop this feel, you will make golf shots you never dreamed you could achieve.

I believe there are a *few* "mechanics" of golf—note the stress on *few*—that anyone who hopes to play well must first master. If you haven't already done so, you must learn, for instance, how to hold and aim the club, and how to align yourself to the ball and the tar-

To feel the downswing properly, imagine the experience of being in a canoe as it is gradually drawn to a waterfall. You should feel that your legs and left arm are pulling the clubhead to the ball slowly, gradually increasing in speed until it flies over the edge at impact. (Artist: Stan Drake)

get. I will explain these mechanics to give you the basis you need for your swing. You can't master high school algebra if you never learned first grade math.

But the main thrust of this series will be to teach you to play by *feel*—the Toski "Touch System."

Mechanics will take you only so far. I strongly suspect that most people who read this series will have failed to reach their true potential as golfers because they have not gone beyond learning the mechanics of the swing. Most players get so wrapped up in mechanics—the so-called fundamental moves and key positions—that they never apply them with the freedom of movement and sensitivity of clubhead motion that allows a Chi Chi Rodriguez—or a Bob Toski—to hit drives 50 or 100 yards past men twice his size.

What we'll really be getting down to is making you aware of your God-given ability to *feel*. I'll tell you in many, many different ways how a super golf swing should *feel*; how your grip should *feel*; how your backswing should *feel*; how impact should *feel*; how your knees should *feel*. I will teach you how to visualize a successful shot before you address the ball, and then how to translate that visualization into the "feel," or sensitivity of "touch," needed to make the shot you've visualized actually take place.

Given a clear track, the human mind and nervous system can perform amazing feats of coordination. You don't need to "tell" your body what to do, where to move, into what position. In fact, this sort of mental direction merely clutters up the computer of your mind and keeps it from functioning smoothly. The golfer who stands over the ball for half a minute is merely feeding his mind a lot of extraneous information—"keep your head down," "hold on tight at the top," "hit with your left knee"—that it doesn't need. Ask almost any star golfer what he thinks about when he's over the ball and he'll tell you he's imagining how the shot will look, or feel. Or possibly he's thinking about one "key move" that will help create the feel he wants. He trusts his subconscious to take over from there.

We program ourselves to produce proper golf swings by experiencing, again and again, reactions to successful shots. When I strike a putt solidly and *feel* the ball coming off the face and see it rolling into the hole, I am, in fact, sending sensations of feel and sight into my computer. The next time I have a similar putt, my computer will recall for me these same sensations. I will imagine how the putt should feel and look. Then my mind and nervous system will make me move my muscles in a way that

> I'd bet the
> average 90-
> shooter could
> cut four or five
> shots from his
> score if he'd
> forget *distance*
> and stress
> *accuracy.*

produces a putt that actually looks and feels just like I'd intended it should.

Now I'd like to warn you about some tension-producing, distance-reducing factors so you'll guard against them as you learn to play golf by feel.

Ironically, perhaps the biggest cause of tension is the tremendous emphasis we put on distance itself. Sit around the 19th hole, and invariably you'll hear how far so-and-so drove on such-and-such hole. Joe may ask Sam what he used on his approach shot, but what Joe really wants to find out is who hit the longer tee shot, or who bangs his irons the farthest. Almost all of us have a distance fetish. That's why most people at a driving range or on a practice tee spend more time with the driver than all their other clubs combined. Power! In golf, as in baseball, everyone wants to hit home runs. And that's why most golfers "strike out."

I'm not all that impressed with power in golf. You shouldn't be either. I've seen very few golfers who know how to handle power. Nicklaus? Sure. But even he swings with only about 80 percent of his available power. And when you hear talk about the great players, how often is it mentioned how far they hit it off the tee? Hogan? I've never heard anyone talk about how far Hogan hit a golf ball. Nelson? Jones? Vardon? Hagen? Sarazen?

It soon hits home to these pupils, as it will to you, that, in golf, accuracy is vastly more important than distance. I'd bet that the average 90-shooter could cut four or five shots from his score—even sacrificing 15 yards per drive—if he'd forget *distance* and *stress accuracy.*

The fantastic thing is that once you quit trying to

slug the ball far—once you concentrate on merely making solid contact with a smooth rhythmical swing—you'll not only start keeping the ball in play, but you'll actually add many of the yards you were seeking when you were trying to slug the cover off the ball. You'll strike the ball squarely more often, and thus get more clubhead (more mass) behind the ball on more of your shots. You will also swing with far less tension and much better coordination, and this will give you greater clubhead speed (more velocity). As you read the later parts of this series and develop more control of your swing, you will learn to increase both distance and accuracy. But it's futile to go for distance before you have control.

If the pro has some great, mystical "secret" that the average golfer lacks, apart from a sound grip and address position, it is his ability to produce a golf swing that is *relatively free from tension and over-control.*

The pro understands the value of what I've told you in this article. He knows that he will produce maximum clubhead speed (velocity) and square contact (mass) only if he swings within his basic rhythm and avoids any tendency to over-control the club. He knows that if he tries for extra distance he risks losing the rhythm—and thus the proper timing—of his swing. He keeps at least 10 percent of his power in his pocket. He knows that fear of failure, or over-concern about various details of his swing, will produce over-controls that inhibit his clubhead speed and keep him from making square contact. The pro doesn't think much about how he will swing. He thinks more about *where* he wants the ball to go and *how it will look* going there.

greatest tips

Turn your shoulders until you feel tight tension
by Byron Nelson, October 1970

The goal of the backswing is simply to wind up fully and put yourself and the club in the position to strike the ball as squarely and as forcefully as possible. Some people are built in such a way that they accomplish this goal by swinging the club back to horizontal. Others—but not too many—must swing past horizontal. Many players make a full windup and reach good position before the club ever reaches horizontal. There simply is no one standard length of backswing that applies to everyone.

The length of your backswing depends a lot on how fully you can turn your shoulders and how far you can swing your arms without (1) loosening your grip, (2) moving your head, (3) relaxing your left arm, (4) overcocking your wrists or (5) going up on your left toe. If you swing back as fully as you can, without allowing any of these errors to occur, you will have reached the normal zenith of your swing. You will be wound up as fully as possible to hit the ball as far as you can. At this point, you should feel a slight tension across your back, up your left arm and down your left side.

Artist: A. Ravielli. (Courtesy of Historic Golf/Ron Watts Collection)

Swings of the Century

Jones, Hogan, Palmer, Wright, Nicklaus and Woods show us the way

by Mike Stachura

Much like an Escher drawing, there is an almost unquenchable, inscrutable seduction in swing sequence photography. The still photographs assembled in sequence seem to hold the secret of the golf swing, if only we will stare at them long enough and hard enough. Over the years, GOLF DIGEST photographers have captured the swings of hundreds of players and in each one there was a lesson or two or three that GOLF DIGEST instructors then provided for eager readers. The danger in reducing the motion of the full swing to a collection of images, of course, is that it tempts the novice and sometimes even the experienced golfer into

(continued)

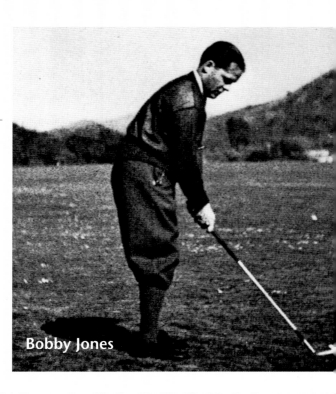

Bobby Jones

Ben Hogan

Arnold Palmer

forcing his body into certain positions in the hopes of mimicking the best swings. The fact is that often the positions are more an effect or result of the total motion of the swing, rather than a cause or an action specifically initiated by a player. But what matters is that they are still great fun to look at even when, as is the case here, some of the oldest sequences are incomplete. And what swings could be more fun or better for you than those of the great masters of the 20th century: Bobby Jones, Ben Hogan, Arnold Palmer, Jack Nicklaus, Mickey Wright and Tiger Woods. While each is different from the next (and, some would argue, each an improvement over its predecessor), there are three key similarities all share: a full shoulder turn on the backswing, club-head trailing the hands on the downswing and a balanced finish. The pictures make it all look so easy.

Pages 72–77:
Bobby Jones (Photos: Martin Davis/The American Golfer)
Ben Hogan (Photos: Golf Digest)
Arnold Palmer (Photos: Chuck Brenkus)
Mickey Wright (Photos: Golf Digest)
Jack Nicklaus (Photos: Golden Bear)
Tiger Woods (Photos: Dom Furore)

September 1997

Tiger Tips:
How and When to Chip with Your 3-Wood

A rarely used shot that's practically pressure proof

by Tiger Woods with Pete McDaniel

Chipping with a 3-wood may look difficult, but actually it is one of the safest and simplest shots in the game. My instructor, Butch Harmon, showed me how to play it during a practice round at the 1996 U.S. Open at Oakland Hills. The first time I tried the shot, at the 54th hole of the championship, I chipped in. Since then I've holed it out seven more times in competition, including three times at the Quad City last year.

The shot came in handy again a year later at the U.S. Open at Congressional. I chipped with my 3-wood twice during the championship, holing out one time and knocking it stiff the other.

The best time to chip with your 3-wood is when your ball lies no more than a foot into the first cut of rough. Hit down on the ball abruptly and let the loft of your 3-wood get the ball airborne enough to coast along the top of the grass. When it reaches the green, it will roll smoothly to the hole.

The 3-wood is a safer choice than your putter, which may snag in the grass behind the ball or drive the ball into the turf. And it's less risky than trying to blade the ball with your sand wedge.

Of course, you can't chip with your 3-wood every time. Here are some keys for playing the conventional chip with an iron as well as the specialty shot with the 3-wood. Practice them both, and you'll save a lot of pars.

Tiger Woods draws attention for his long drives, but his short game is as inventive as it is sound. (Photos: Jim Moriarty)

3-wood technique

Place forefinger and thumb on shaft for feel and control.

Move back of left hand down target line.

Use wrists to pop clubface into back of ball.

Conventional technique

Keep left arm fairly straight but relaxed.

Grip down on shaft for added control.

Open your stance and lean to the left.

April 1976

Shape Your Swing the Modern Way

Nelson recounts his discovery of "The Modern Swing"

by Byron Nelson with Larry Dennis

KEEP SHAFT ON LINE DURING TAKEAWAY

THE PROBLEM:

One of the major causes of the over-the-top move is getting the club laid off the clubhead too far behind the shaft—on the backswing. At the same time, the hands get separated too much from the body starting back.

THE CURE:

(1) Place a clubshaft against the ball of your right foot, parallel to the target line. Swing back to hip high and keep the clubhead outside the hands. At this point your clubshaft should be directly over and parallel to the shaft on the ground.

(2) Then feel the arms swing up, not around, to the top.

—Jim Flick,
June 1988

A Ravielli

All I was trying to do was find a better way to swing so I could make a living at the game. I found a better way and, as a result, I've been credited by most experts with developing the modern way to play golf. But I sure wasn't thinking about that at the time.

I started playing golf in 1925, when I was 13 years old and a caddie at Glen Garden Country Club in Fort Worth, Tex. I lived right out close to the golf course and I got to know another boy who caddied there. He lived across town and we went to different schools, so I never saw him except at the golf course—but I saw plenty of him there. His name was Ben Hogan.

Ben and I tied for the caddie championship at Glen Garden one year, when we were 14 or 15. We tied at 40 on the first nine holes, which was a par 37, and the members made us play another nine holes. I shot 39 and Ben shot 40.

I hadn't caddied more than a year or so when the golf pro took an interest in me and gave me a job in the shop cleaning clubs. We used to have to buff the clubs with an abrasive compound, because they didn't have chrome on them the way they do now.

When I was 16 and shooting in the 70s, the club gave me a junior membership. They gave Ben one at the same time. Years later, when we were both grown and had become champions—I was the U.S. Open champion by then—the club threw a big party for us and gave us both honorary lifetime memberships. But a lot had happened in the meantime.

Back in those early days I had the typical old caddie swing. The hickory shafts I used then in my iron clubs had a lot of torque, or twist, in them. So you had to roll the clubface open on the backswing, then roll it

closed coming through the shot. If you didn't, the force of your swing would leave the face open when you struck the ball. Naturally, you had to swing flatter, because you couldn't roll the clubface open and swing upright at the same time, the way we do today.

So the swing was loose and flat. "Turn in a barrel" we called it. There wasn't the foot-and-leg action you see today. The feet were kept pretty flat, and coming through we would hit against a straight left leg and side, kind of throwing the clubface into the ball to get it square again.

That swing worked pretty well with the irons. But all this time I was using steel-shafted woods and was hooking them something terrible. I never could figure

Artist: Anthony Ravielli. (Courtesy of Historic Golf/Ron Watts Collection)

out why. Then, about 1930, I got my first set of steel-shafted irons, and I began hooking with them as badly as I had with my woods.

I realized finally that the reason I was hooking was because the shaft didn't have as much torque, but my hands were still opening and closing as much as ever—pronating and supinating are the technical terms for this. I was rolling the steel-shafted club closed too quickly, and this was causing me to hook the ball.

When I discovered what was happening, I decided not to roll my hands so much. But I was still using that old caddie swing—low and around the shoulders. And I couldn't play as consistently. I'd play a 67 or 68, and all of a sudden I'd shoot 75 or 76 or 77. I didn't know where the clubhead was or what it was doing. I couldn't hit the ball as far, either, and I didn't like that at all.

Everybody else was in the same boat at the time, and nobody knew exactly what to do, but I kept on thinking. I decided that if I were going to take the club back without any pronation, then I'd have to start swinging more upright. So I began taking my hands back higher. But I was still using my feet and legs in the old way—which is to say not much at all—and that didn't work very well.

Then I decided I had to learn to take the club straight back. When I got to the top of the backswing, I felt as if I would just let it fall, with my feet and legs helping to carry it straight back through the ball and keeping it on line toward the target. This would eliminate the hook that was troubling me.

About that time I also developed the idea that I had to keep my head still, and with that discovery everything began to fall into place. Keep my head still—take the club right straight back through the ball—keep my feet and legs very active, leading the club and helping me carry it through the hitting area—keep the legs going straight through toward the target instead of doing any twisting—just back and through.

I started making this change in my swing in 1930, when I was 18 years old, but it sure didn't happen all at once. I hit a lot of golf balls trying to make it work. One thing that helped me was practicing against the Texas wind. Keeping the ball down against the wind helped me learn to take the club straight back and straight through. I also think my pronounced leg drive developed from trying to keep the ball low against the wind. I was trying to swing through the ball with as shallow an arc as possible at the bottom and keep the club going down the target line as long as I could. You need strong leg action to do this.

In fact, I received criticism for years from players who were still swinging the old way. They said I stayed down too low through the ball, that I had a dip in my swing, that my foot-and-leg action was too loose. In a way, they were right. I almost overdid it. My foot-and-leg action was even looser than what they use now. I don't think many people could play as loose-kneed as I did. But it worked for me; besides, all that criticism didn't worry me as long as I was cashing those checks regularly.

At any rate, I think I was the first player to make the complete change from the old way of swinging to the modern method we use today. Of course, the older players weren't making many changes, even with the steel shafts. They had played their way for so long that they probably were afraid to. As we get older, we tend to resist change.

But I feel the younger players did start to copy me. Most people, I guess, like to copy somebody who

> **One thing that helped me was practicing against the Texas wind. Keeping the ball down helped me learn to take the club straight back and straight through.**

greatest tips

Put your swing on the inside track
by Steve Dahlby, Director of Instruction, Troon North G.C., Scottsdale, Ariz., February 1998

If you've been struggling with your tee shots, you've probably been told you are swinging your club on an outside-to-in swing path. You may be wondering, outside of what? In to what?

The correct path is not a straight line; it's a curve. The clubhead should swing from inside the target line on the downswing, meet the ball with a square face, then return to the inside on the follow-through.

An effective bit of imagery is to think of your clubhead as a race car as it zooms around an oval track, as the larger-than-life PGA Tour pro David Berganio Jr. is demonstrating here.

The clubhead should travel along a path from inside the line of play, accelerate through the ball at the "top of the turn," then swing back to the inside to a balanced finish position. The ball will roar down the "straightaway" with a powerful draw.

(Racetrack Photo: ALLSPORT)

is successful, and after a while I began to have pretty good success with that swing.

I turned professional in November 1932, went to Texarkana, and played in a little $500 tournament there with Dick Metz, Ky Laffoon and people like that. I finished third and won $75. I was 20 years old by then.

The next spring they hired me as the pro at Texarkana Country Club. There was so little money in the tournaments back in those days that you had to make your living at a club. I stayed two years at Texarkana, was an assistant in 1935 and 1936 at Ridgewood (N.J.) Country Club, spent three years at Reading Country Club in Pennsylvania and was the pro at Inverness in Toledo from 1940 until 1946.

I began playing in tournaments right away, though. In 1933 I tried to play in two or three without any money and ended up hitch-hiking back home from California. I returned to the winter tour that fall, but in the summer of 1934 I played in only a few local tournaments. By then I had made enough of a reputation so that I was invited to the second Masters tournament. As it turned out, that was very fortunate for me.

Ed Dudley, who later became president of the Professional Golfers' Association, was the pro at Augusta National then. George Jacobus, the head pro at Ridgewood and president of the PGA at that time, told Ed that he was looking for a young man who had some promise to be his assistant. Ed referred my name to him and I went to work for George at Ridgewood in 1935.

My job was to work in the shop, play with the members some and teach. George developed an interest in me and was very helpful. He was a good teacher and taught me a lot of things about teaching. More important, he agreed to help me with my game. I had talked with George about the new method I was using, and, even though he was teaching the old way of playing, he agreed with me 100 percent that I was on the right track.

Often when I practiced, George would check several things in my swing that I felt were important. Was I keeping the club on line? Was I keeping my head still? Was I keeping my knees and legs moving

on the same plane that paralleled the one the club should be on?

At the time, I felt my lower body move was a simple lateral thrust toward the target. I didn't realize I was turning my hips as much as I was. Your hips must turn, of course, but because I had always turned mine against a straight left side, I now felt like my action had become all feet and legs.

I used my feet a great deal. When I came into the ball, it seemed as though I was driving off my right foot, and in the impact area I felt that I almost gave a shove off that foot. But I always made sure my weight stayed on the inside of the right foot on the backswing. I never let it get to the outside.

I started playing in local tournaments around that area. In 1936 I won the Metropolitan Open at Quaker Ridge in Scarsdale, N.Y. I played very well and very steady, which I hadn't been doing up to that time, and that gave me the confidence that what I was doing was right.

So I kept working on this theory of keeping the face of the club square with the back of the left hand, just as though I was trying to hit the ball with the back of that hand.

I felt I was controlling the swing from the left side. But I knew I was getting some power from the right side, not early in the swing, but late. That was something that just kind of happened. I wouldn't recommend that anyone deliberately try to hit with the right side, because if you do you'll be in trouble. Even though I felt I pushed off the right foot, I don't believe you should think about this, because you'll do it too much ahead of time. The right-side power builds up because of the proper use of the feet and legs. When you move to the right in the backswing and then back to the left, you automatically generate the proper use of the right side.

Finally, in 1937, I had developed this style of play to my satisfaction, and to George's, too. I also started winning consistently that year. I won the Masters and three other tournaments, and I played on the Ryder Cup team. I never tried to change anything in my swing from that time on.

greatest tips

Learn timing and rhythm first
by Dr. Cary Middlecoff, February 1968

To make a well-timed swing, you need to set up a rhythmic, unhurried pattern at the start. You don't hurry anything in the early stages. You don't need to. If you are fast and jerky at the start, you may yank yourself off balance before you can get the hands and the club back into hitting position.

Assuming you make a smooth, unhurried and full backswing, then your downswing should follow an orderly sequence of movements. While these appear to be made almost at the same time, they are in fact sepa-

rated by the barest fractions of seconds. The legs and hips move first, then the shoulders, and finally the hands and arms, with the club and clubhead trailing behind. If your swing moves in this sequence it is in good tempo, or timing. The clubhead will gradually accelerate into the impact zone, and you will get maximum distance. This will happen naturally if you think (1) legs, (2) shoulders, (3) hands and arms, and (4) clubhead on the downswing. Move your hands down first and you will lose timing—and distance.

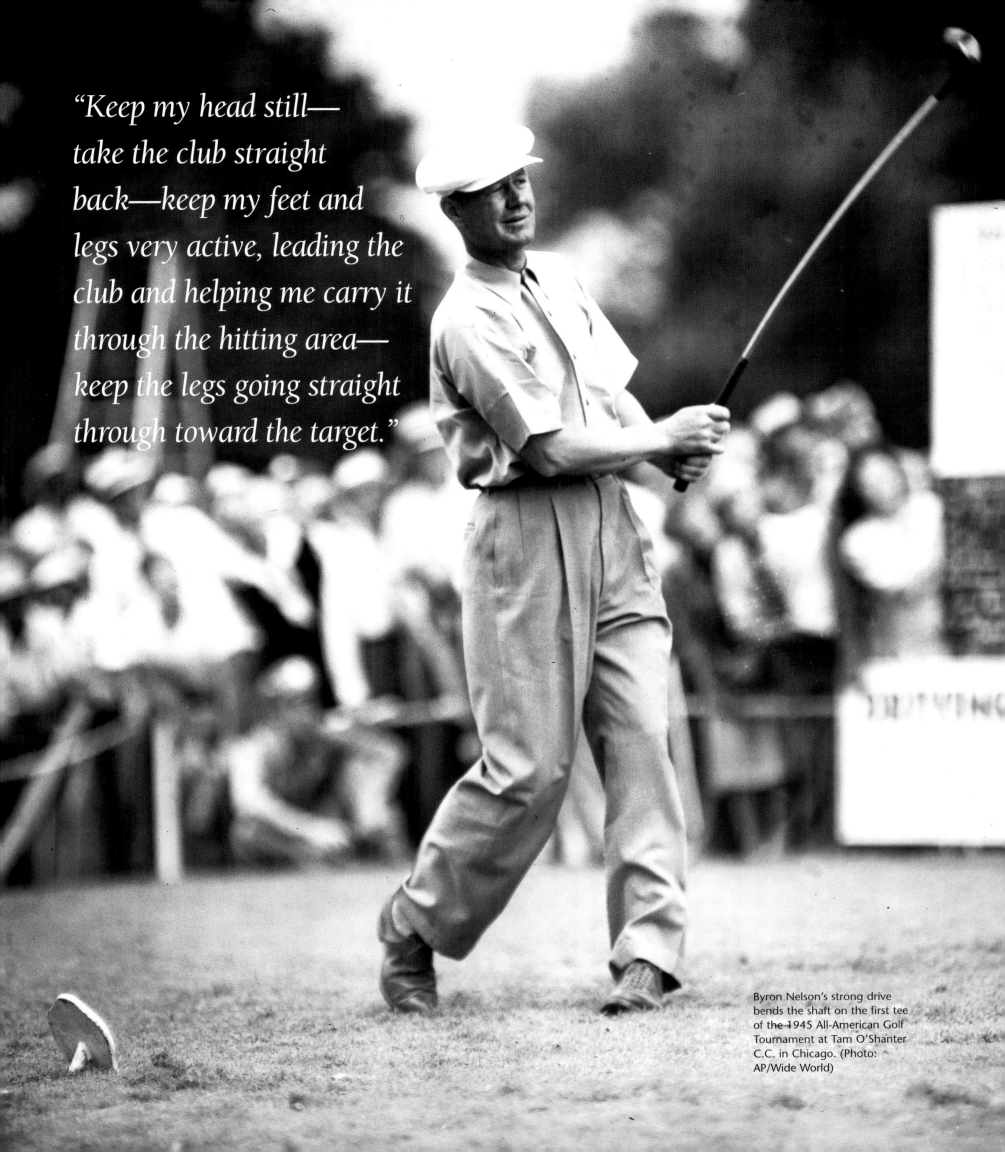

*"Keep my head still—
take the club straight
back—keep my feet and
legs very active, leading the
club and helping me carry it
through the hitting area—
keep the legs going straight
through toward the target."*

Byron Nelson's strong drive
bends the shaft on the first tee
of the 1945 All-American Golf
Tournament at Tam O'Shanter
C.C. in Chicago. (Photo:
AP/Wide World)

September 1972

I Can Get You Out of Sand with One Hand

Sound sand play requires surprisingly little physical effort

by Claude Harmon

Claude Harmon, then professional at Winged Foot, developed this innovative technique for getting out of the sand, and shared it with our readers in 1972.

Twenty-five years after his father Claude introduced the idea of bunker play made simple, Butch Harmon gave it a '90s spin.

Illustrations by Anthony Ravielli. (Courtesy of Historic Golf/Ron Watts Collection)

I don't know why any golfer would want to play sand shots with one hand—except perhaps occasionally to shake up an opponent—but the fact that you could do so once you mastered my system indicates, I think, its simplicity and effectiveness.

Obviously a system that allows you to move the clubhead through the sand with only one hand is a system that requires relatively little physical effort.

Because my system results in a thin cut of sand, it allows you to take a LONGER cut with minimal effort. Textbooks tell us to contact the sand only two inches

behind the ball. I insist that my pupils strike the sand AT LEAST four inches behind the ball. This requires both hands on the club, of course, but using my system I can actually enter the sand 10–11 inches behind the ball and still make a successful shot. Thus, my system, once mastered, all but guarantees that you'll no longer dig deeply into the sand and fail to get the ball out, nor catch it thin and skull it over the green.

Your shots from normal lies will fly high, settle gently and stop quickly. You'll find that those deep greenside bunkers are no problem.

Also, you'll find it possible to swing aggressively on those very short sand shots that otherwise would require an extremely delicate half-swing.

◀ The setup

Step up to the ball in the sand as you would for a normal wedge shot from the fairway, but with your right hand on the club. Choke down the shaft about an inch farther than normal with this hand and open the clubface so that it looks well to the right of target.

Then place your left hand on the shaft so that the thumb is on top of the cylinder and the back of the hand looks down the target line.

Open your stance by turning your entire body to the left until the clubface looks only slightly—a few degrees—to the right of target, and the back of the left hand now faces to the left of the target. Also, step back from the target so that the ball is well ahead of your left toe and your hands "trail" the clubhead.

Initially choking down on the club compensates for the general lowering of your body that will occur when you dig in your feet. Placing your left thumb on top of the club with the back of the hand facing down the target line prohibits any extensive closing of the face when you swing into the sand. Such closing would cause a deep cut into the sand.

Maintaining a slightly open clubface at address allows you to strike firmly with your right hand without fear of closing the face and taking too much sand. The face will merely return to a square position.

Playing the ball well forward lays back the clubface, increasing its loft and lowering the rudder. The result is a high shot with a shallow cut of sand.

▶ The swing

With your weight largely on the left side, pick up the clubhead quickly by immediately cocking your wrists. Your entire backswing is sharply upward.

Lead your downswing with a full weight shift to your left side. Throw the clubhead sharply downward, largely with your right hand, into the sand four or more inches behind the ball and straight forward toward the target. Try to clear a 10–12-inch rectangle of sand fore and aft of ball.

Weight to left at address and early wrist cock encourages a sharply ascending-descending swing pattern needed to get the clubhead under the ball.

Leading the downswing with a weight shift to the left side is vital to provide maximum length of cut through sand, thus avoiding skulled shots. This shifting also pulls the clubhead down and then under the ball while it is moving along rather than across the target line. On-line clubhead path allows ball to fly out readily on a forward-flying cushion of sand.

Throwing the club downward at least four inches behind the ball provides a safe margin against catching the ball first, assuring a sufficiently deep cut—despite the bounce factor—to clear under the bottom of the ball.

January 1992

I Can Cure Your Slice

With my figure-8 swing, you'll avoid that banana ball forever

by Lee Trevino with Guy Yocom

KILL THE HIPS FOR A BETTER TURN

For better players, make your takeaway with the hands, arms and shoulders. The hips are "dead." Take the club back at least one foot before the hips start to turn. This will produce a smoother, fuller shoulder turn.

—JoAnne Carner, September 1982

Teachers may not admit it, but to a man they dread taking on a slicer. If you want to know why, just look around you. Most of the people who sliced 20 years ago are still slicing. Everything they've been taught—the drills, the swing thoughts, the theories—haven't helped a damn. I hate to be blunt about it, but the slice-curing things teachers are telling golfers are all wrong, the dead opposite of what they should be telling them.

I don't blame the teachers necessarily. What happened was, a few teachers 100 years ago laid down some "basics" that for no good reason are still being taught today. They may be OK for some golfers, but for the most part they've created a nation of slicers. For instance, golfers in the early 1900s were told to set up in a closed stance, with the right foot drawn farther from the target line than the left. The closed stance enabled them to swing their arms and the club into the ball from inside the line of play, which discouraged a slice. The catch is, those players wore heavy coats that restricted their turns on the backswing, so the closed stance was necessary. But although the coats eventually went out of style, the closed stance didn't. A closed stance encourages a slice rather than preventing it.

That isn't all. Other expressions, such as "clear the left side," "pull down with your left arm," "lift the left heel" and "release the clubhead" are still being taught, and they've made everybody prisoners of the slice. I say it's time to take the ball and chain off these people, to tell them what really causes a slice and to teach them how to stop it.

I started teaching when I was 21 years old, right after I got out of the Marine Corps. I hadn't had a lot of lessons myself, so I had to rely on my own eyes and experience to stop my pupils from slicing. I learned to teach by trial and error, the students acting as guinea pigs. I got pretty good at helping these people. I never rebuilt somebody from the ground up, like guys do today. You don't have to change your entire swing. My feeling is, if you have

a leaky roof, you don't tear down the whole house. You replace some shingles. I'd make one or two little corrections, mold them like a piece of clay and they'd start working the ball from right to left.

Follow my suggestions. Some of them may sound a little unorthodox, but they're the keys I've used ever since I abandoned my fade and started hitting the ball with a little draw. They work, I guarantee it. Listen to old Lee Buck, and you'll get rid of that banana ball forever.

"I hate to be blunt about it," says Lee Trevino, "but the slice-curing things teachers are telling golfers are all wrong, the dead opposite of what they should be telling them." (Photos: Stephen Szurlej)

To draw the ball, make your swing a 'figure 8'

One reason a slice is so hard to cure is that your perspective of your own swing is warped. You may feel you're swinging along a draw-producing, inside-to-out swing path, when in fact you're cutting across the ball from outside to in. The solution to this is correct mental imagery, a conception of the correct swing path that translates easily into the real thing.

The best mental image to produce a draw is thinking of the swing as a figure 8. I've used this image throughout my career and more than anything else, it has helped me go from fading the ball to drawing it. My figure-8 swing is apparent in the large sequence photos below. I suggest you try to copy it.

First, note my address position (1). My stance is slightly open, with my feet aligned a little to the left of the target. You may have heard that a slightly open stance encourages a fade, but I've always believed it's easier to draw the ball from an open stance. The reason: If you close your stance, or draw your right foot away from the target line, you'll turn too far on the backswing. At the top, your body is pointed so far to the right that you'll instinctively come over the top, or spin your shoulders, in an effort to make the club travel down the target line on the downswing. With an open stance, you'll sense the necessity of swinging the clubhead into the ball from the inside.

Next comes the takeaway, which is the most critical element of the figure-8 swing. You must take the club back along a path parallel to your stance line (2). After you reach the top of the backswing (3), start the downswing by letting your arms draw down and inward so your right arm falls closer to your right hip (4). This allows you to swing the club into the ball from the inside (5), completing the bottom half of the "8." After impact, the club swings out to the right of the target (6), further defining the "8." The club travels up and around at the finish, completing the figure 8.

The swing of most slicers resembles a figure 8, but they run the race backward. The club traces the figure 8 in the wrong direction. Instead of taking the club back parallel to the target line, they whip it back excessively to the inside. Right there they are dead, for once they reach the top, there is no place for their arms and shoulders to go but "over the top". They cast the club out across the target line so the clubhead approaches the ball from outside the line of play. They usually hit a vicious slice, although they may also pull the ball to the left.

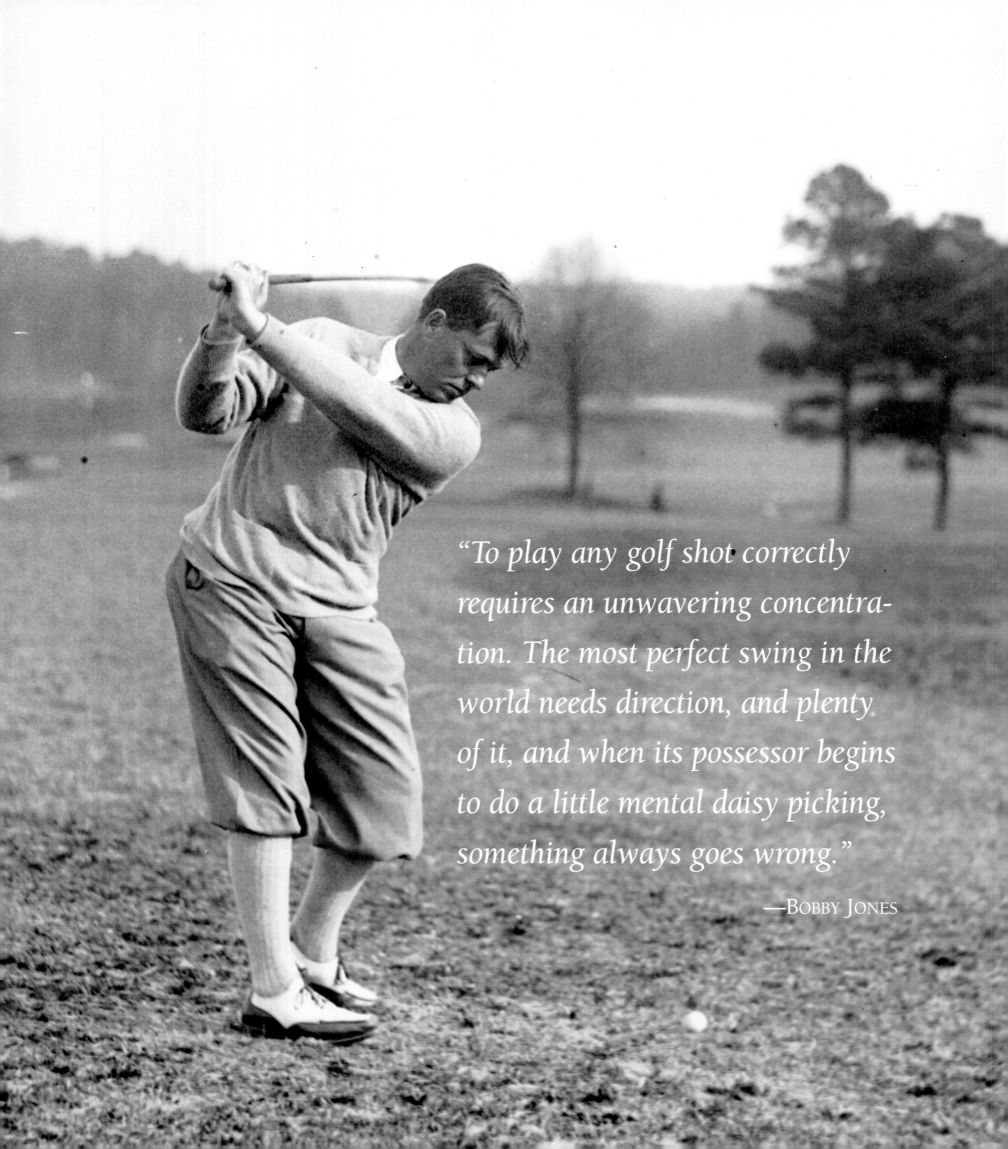

"To play any golf shot correctly requires an unwavering concentration. The most perfect swing in the world needs direction, and plenty of it, and when its possessor begins to do a little mental daisy picking, something always goes wrong."

—BOBBY JONES

POWER

February 1996

Bobby Jones on Power

Classic instruction: A new interpretation of a timeless work

by Bobby Jones

Jones wrote more than 300,000 words of instruction—more than any player in history. This story originally appeared as a newspaper article. He probably wrote it longhand on a yellow legal pad.

There are more than a few golfers in this land who wonder why, and how it is, that even when they connect sweetly with a drive, it never goes as far as an ordinary shot by a youth of much less physical power. Most of all, it puzzles athletes who still possess brawn and muscle far exceeding that of any first-class golfer in the game today. They cannot understand how a little 120-pound kid can stand up all day long and wallop drives far beyond the best efforts they could produce in a year.

Long driving, up to a certain point, may be explained by good timing. By this I mean that the increased length obtained by the whole rank of first-class players over that obtained by the second-class can be largely attributed to better timing. The dub suffers because he rarely expends his power where it will do the most good. But within the group of players we refer to as first class, there are a few who are able to drive a good bit farther than any of their fellows. This increase, I think, is not explainable on the basis of timing, for all the better players are good in this respect; these extra yards obtainable by the few are traceable to form and not timing.

Every now and then, even the average golfer will meet the ball exactly right—so far as timing and feel are concerned. When he does so, he reaches the ultimate for him; yet a more proficient player of much less physical strength has no difficulty in passing by many yards his longest drive. The things making this possible are to be found in the swing—the increased body turn, the hands high at the top of the backswing, the length and greater fullness of the arc.

The longest hitters in my day were Charles Lacey, Charlie Hall, Cyril Tolley, Bill Stout, and a Frenchman, Marcel Dallemagne. A noticeable feature of the style of each was a fast pivot or hip turn as the club approached the ball coming down. They made the best use of the most powerful muscles of the body, those of the back and hips, and by doing so, they gained over the rest of the field those few extra yards that made them stand out.

The average golfer uses his hips and body very little. He takes the club back mainly with his arms and he hits without making any effort with the muscles of his back. The player who is a little better, but still not expert, turns more; he may even turn back quite nicely, but an observer will note that his turn into the ball is retarded—he may even stop his pivot before he hits the ball. The expert employs a full turn, and continues his turn forward uninterrupted through the hitting area—and the long driver whips his hips around like a flash.

If this turn and twist are regarded just as the wristcock, as a source of power the problem is then to unwind in proper timing to deliver the maximum blow at the right instant. The expert golfer begins to unwind his hips at the beginning of his downswing. The turn back to the ball begins slowly, just as the downswing itself begins slowly, and the sudden powerful twist is reserved for hitting just as the wristcock is saved. It is important that the left hip should turn out of the way, but it is also important that the hips should not be twisted so quickly that the power of their unwinding will be used up in the first part of the downward stroke.

The action of the left knee almost exactly parallels the correct wrist action. This knee bends forward—to the player's front, not toward the hole—and swings to the right during the backswing. During the downstroke, it swings to the left, but does not straighten immediately; it actually becomes straight just before impact as the final powerful twist of the hips takes place. It is this twist that straightens the leg and throws the kneecap back and gives the impression, so often stated, that the player is "hitting against the left leg." I dislike this expression, because it suggests that a resistance is interposed by the left side. It is far better to "hit with the left leg."

When playing well, I have the feeling that during the first part of the downstroke I am pulling against something. There really is nothing to pull against except the tension in my own muscles—set up by the effort of the stroke. More or less rapidly this is overcome, and finally wrist, body, arms and legs all join to deliver their power simultaneously. The proper timing of these factors, with each one prepared to the limit, is the real secret of long driving.

Bobby Jones at the 1929 U.S. Open at Winged Foot, where he was victorious. (Photo: Golf World)

57 Keys to Distance

Powerful words from powerful players and teachers

February 1996

Steve Elkington: Power doesn't come from the arms, it comes from the pivot. Try to add more RPMs to your downswing pivot.

Tom Kite: Make sure your backswing is really slow so you can apply the power.

Ernie Els: My main thought is to finish the backswing. That makes it easier to release the club through the ball.

Billy Casper: Slow the swing down and be a little more precise.

Miller Barber: Make your swing as long as possible, extending through the ball.

Chip Beck: Play a draw. Swing your hands past your body on the downswing.

Hal Sutton: Wind up your shoulders as far as you can, then let it go.

Alex J. Morrison, *A New Way to Better Golf* (1932): Only by winding up the body to its fullest, then releasing the accumulated force in an expanding motion like the uncoiling of a spring, can a golf club be swung easily, naturally, accurately and with maximum power.

Justin Leonard: Make a little longer backswing, a little slower. Give it a little pause

Jay Sigel: Begin the downswing with your feet and knees and keep your head behind the ball at impact.

(Photo: Bob Ewell)

at the top so everything comes down together.

John Morse: Swing easier. It helps your timing.

Jim Gallagher Jr.: Focus on making a good turn—left knee behind the ball, left shoulder under the chin.

Woody Austin: Remain relaxed.

Dale Eggeling: Take it back a little longer, then go after it!

Colleen Walker: Wait a little longer at the top of the backswing and get everything started down together.

Cindy Rarick: Tee it higher, depending on where the wind is. Then swing harder.

Peter Senior: Don't get too quick on the takeaway. Keep it nice and smooth on the first half of the backswing. You can hit it as hard as you want from there.

Robert Allenby: Make a longer swing. Take it back straighter and wider—a big turn. Then give it a bit of a rip!

Vijay Singh: If you want to hit it farther, hit it harder.

Nick Price: Bigger shoulder turn.

Payne Stewart: I don't change my swing. I widen my stance a little.

Mark Calcavecchia: Make a nice, slow backswing to a good coil. Try to hit it solidly, not necessarily hard.

Phil Mickelson: Try to swing the clubhead faster through the ball.

Orville Moody: Make a wider arc. Turn quicker and drive your legs toward the target.

Percy Boomer, *On Learning Golf* (1946): Power is produced by the feet, calves and thighs—but it is gathered up and given the correct centrifugal golf direction by the hip brace and pivot.

Tom Lehman: Make your backswing slow and smooth and let everything gather fully to the top. You should feel like a coiled spring.

(Photo: Stephen Szurlej)

Calvin Peete: Use good timing to generate clubhead speed.

Larry Laoretti: Take it back slower and longer.

Bruce Lietzke: I normally swing at about 85 percent. To hit it farther, I swing harder, about 95 percent.

Davis Love III: Try to catch it solid. You'll get more distance if you swing at about 80 percent.

Duffy Waldorf: Your main thought should be making solid contact. Thinking of hitting the ball dead-center keeps you balanced.

D.A. Weibring: Check grip pressure and take the club back slowly. Jack Nicklaus says he takes it back slower when trying for the big tee shot. That's a great tip.

Juli Inkster: Tee it higher—about half an inch. Slow your backswing and

Background: Ben Hogan at Pinehurst. (Photo: Golf World)

> "Only by winding up the body to its fullest, then releasing the accumulated force in an expanding motion like the uncoiling of a spring, can a golf club be swung easily, naturally, accurately and with maximum power." —ALEX J. MORRISON

(Photo: Bob Ewell)

Laura Davies: If you want to hit long drives, hit them hard. Very hard.

(Photo: GOLF DIGEST)

Kris Tschetter: Concentrate on taking it back real slow and smooth. Then clear your left side through impact.

accelerate coming down, especially with your left side.

Barry Lane: Tee the ball half an inch higher, so you hit the shot more on the upswing. That way, you get less backspin and the ball runs farther.

Billy Mayfair: Tee the ball a little higher and play it off your front toe—maybe half an inch forward—to get more clubhead speed.

John Adams: Try not to hit from the top. Make sure your club starts accelerating halfway into the downswing.

Roger Maltbie: Widen your stance a little and lighten the pressure in your grip and forearms. Maintain both into the take-away. Then make a big turn "into" your right side.

Tommy Armour, *How to Play Your Best Golf All the Time* (1935): Hitting the ball a long way—depends on effective use of the hands, rather than on trying to throw the weight of the body into the shot—Hold

the club firmly with the last three fingers of the left hand, let the left arm and hand act as a guide and whack the hell out of the ball with the right hand.

Larry Mize: Get good and relaxed throughout the whole swing. Then try to make a full turn and generate a lot of clubhead speed.

Mark O'Meara: A wider stance gives you a more solid base, good balance and weight distribution. Then move a little slower off the ball, which generates width in your swing.

Bob Tway: The main thing is not trying to hit too hard. Making a slower and bigger turn really helps a lot.

Beth Daniel: Make your swing wider and slower and gather speed through impact.

David Duval: Make a bigger, fuller turn. Then hold the angle through impact as long as you can.

Bob Estes: Tee the ball higher and drop your right side, to catch it more on the upswing. Keeping the club low to the ground insures a wide arc.

Mark McCumber: Grip the club lightly. It allows you to make a bigger turn and get your hands set.

Tony Jacklin: Maintain the width of the swing.

Ben Hogan, *The Modern Fundamentals of Golf* (1957): The turning of the hips to the left releases the body, legs and arms in a cohesive movement to the left. As it enters the swing, each component adds

its contribution to the ever-increasing speed and power of the swing—As a result, the clubhead is simply tearing through the air at an incredible speed as the golfer hits through the ball.

Meg Mallon: Make a tighter turn, winding up like a coil. Keep your back to the target as long as you can on the downswing.

Kelly Robbins: Try to swing at 80 to 90 percent. It's easier on your body and produces more yardage.

Chi Chi Rodriguez: I just hit the hell out of it.

Jim Colbert: On the backswing, swing "into" a braced right leg. The more resistance, the greater the distance.

Walt Zembriski: Keep it as slow as possible on the backswing.

Bob Murphy: Tee it higher and play the ball farther forward in your stance with the club in its regular position. Aim down the right side, and release your hands to hit a hook.

Tracy Kerdyk: Drive your knees and legs through the ball, toward the target. Put some "pep in your step."

Becky Iverson: I put a two-inch plug in my driver and found 20 yards.

Julius Boros, *Swing Easy, Hit Hard* (1965): As my hands reach the hitting zone I can increase their speed to anything I choose within my capabilities. So here you have the secret: Turn with your shoulders, hit with your hands.

May 1993

Distance Through Resistance

Where and how you should feel it—from address to impact

by David Leadbetter with John Huggan

There must be, all through your swing, two forces working against each other, synchronizing your arm swing and body turn and maximizing power.

In every dynamic sport, motion combined with resistance produces power. Take tennis. The server winds up his upper body as his lower body resists, then he whips the racquet through impact.

The same is true with long-hitters of the golf ball. Their swings are a series of resisting forces working against each other to build up clubhead speed. It's a bit like your car accelerating as it moves up through the gears. Through the rotation of the upper body around a resisting lower body you build up leverage. Then, at the top of the swing, you—like the tennis player—are actually moving in two directions at once. As your arms reach the top, your body is already moving back toward the target. So the clubhead is lagging behind. That lag translates into speed, which is transmitted through your arms and hands into the clubhead as it catches up to your unwinding torso.

Having said that, only a tiny minority of players get the maximum from their swings in terms of clubhead speed and distance. Why? Simply, their swings have little resistance in them. The dictionary says resistance is "a force that tends to oppose motion." And that is the secret to hitting long drives. There must be, all through your swing, two forces working against each other, synchronizing your arm swing and body turn and maximizing power.

This article will show you where you should feel that resistance or push-pull effect all through your swing. For example, on the takeaway your left side is pushing against a resisting right side; at impact your right side is hitting against a resisting left side. And the drills will show you how to create those feels. Work on each stage separately. This is definitely a one-at-a-time learning process. Try to put them all together too early and you'll only get confused. And stay relaxed. You're creating resistance—not tension.

Pages 92-95: *(Photos: Dom Furore)*

Kick-start your swing

No doubt you've heard the line about "starting the swing with everything working away together." Like a lot of golf terms, that's incomplete. You certainly want your hands, arms and club to swing in sync, but your lower body has to resist to a certain extent.

The way to create that is to "kick-start" your swing. After waggling the club to reduce tension, subtly rotate your hips and shift your right knee toward the target. Remember, resistance is created by two opposing forces, so the top of the backswing isn't the only place you want to be moving in two directions at once.

Set up initial resistance in your thighs

To have resistance during the golf swing itself, you must establish it at address, which means you must create an athletic, "ready" position. And the keys to that are good posture and balance. Resistance at address is really a byproduct of proper posture and balance.

Stand as if you are going to address a shot. Pay particular attention to your legs. They must be flexed just the right amount. Bend forward until you have some sense of resistance in the front part of your thighs.

What does that feel like? It is an awareness, a feeling of pressure in your legs. You can have that and still have your legs be "alive" and prepared to enhance the backswing. It is neither tension nor tightness, both of which inhibit movement.

So the key is creating that resistance while staying relaxed and "ready."

Push on shaft to feel resistance

In any athletic address position, the position of the legs is crucial. Here's how to check how much resistance you have in them at address.

Set up as you would normally, then hold a shaft across your thighs and push down. You'll be aware of resistance if your legs are flexed correctly. If you feel it only by pulling the shaft with your arms, your legs are either too bent or too straight.

Maintain gap between knees

Once you reach a fully coiled top-of-the-backswing position, you should be feeling some resistance in your left knee. In other words, your right side—really your right shoulder—is now turning against the resistance of your left knee. That's vital. The last thing you want is to be in a position I see all too often; your knees all but touching, your arms collapsed, the club out of control, and the lack of windup or coil all too obvious. So the key is maintaining as much as possible the gap between your knees.

Continue to build early resistance

As you start into the backswing, focus the resistance on your right side. I see many players whose right sides turn away early, sending the clubhead too far inside the line and giving the appearance of a full turn prematurely. So, as your left shoulder begins to turn and the club swings away, your right knee and right shoulder must resist. It should feel as if your left side is pushing against your right. That makes it impossible for you to overturn early on.

Hit into your left side

The feeling you need through impact is one of your right side hitting as your left side resists. Your left leg needs to be firm as the clubhead strikes the ball. If the left side keeps going targetward (inset) you won't have anything to hit against, the clubhead will slow down and you'll lose distance.

The resistance of your left leg allows the right side, arm and hand to snap through impact. Think of it as slamming a door shut, your left side the door frame and your right the door itself.

Pull down against resistance of your right side

The most important aspect of the early part of the downswing is that it be "soft." There should be a smoothness to your transition, with no sudden movement or jerkiness. Your weight should be moving slowly to the left side—not rushing.

At this point the resistance should be in your right leg, specifically the knee. It must hold as the left side and arm pull the club down. Think about it. If you're going to pull on something, you must have something else to pull against. So, as the left side moves, the right side resists. If the right side moves too early, the resistance will be lost and you'll more than likely throw the clubhead to the outside and hit a slice or pull. Focusing on the pulling motion of the left side at this stage insures that the club starts down on plane, which maintains the radius of the swing and allows the club to approach the ball from the inside.

Legends tee off. Jugs McSpaden (1937 PGA winner), Sam Snead, Ben Hogan and Byron Nelson. (Photo: Kenneth Paik)

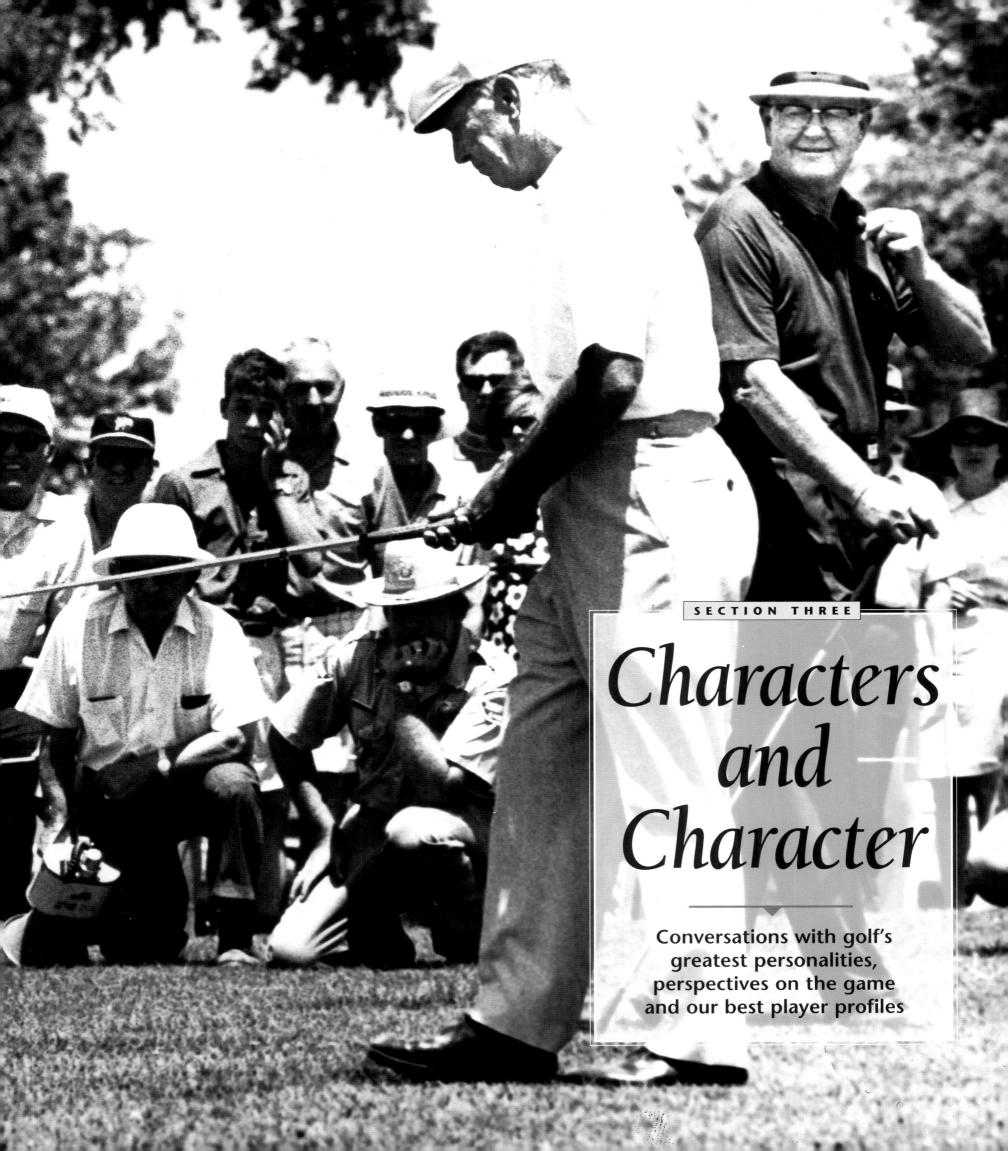

Characters and Character

Conversations with golf's greatest personalities, perspectives on the game and our best player profiles

by Scott Smith,
Senior Editor

Insights into the people who play golf have always been a part of GOLF DIGEST. Discovering where these golf personalities stand on issues not only makes for interesting reading but also provides us with a glimpse into their characters as golfers and people.

GOLF DIGEST has provided a sounding board for golfers since its early days, and through personal profiles and question-and-answer sessions, we have come to know some of our favorite players and other experts of the game a little better, adding a new dimension to our own golf perspective as well as bringing us closer to the individuals who contribute to making golf so special.

In the September 1970 issue, the famously reticent Ben Hogan told Nick Seitz, "Life's too short for me to go around explaining myself." But explain himself Hogan did, in his own words, and at length, in the pages of GOLF DIGEST. It was, as the cover proclaimed, "The most intimate story he has ever allowed."

Today, the Dialogue on Golf is a bulwark feature of the magazine. Each month golfers and other authorities sound off on all manner of topics, from pet peeves and past slights to issues of the day that affect all who play the game.

Though it's the voices of these men and women we tune in to hear, a "dialogue" is just that: a conversation between two people. And it is this give-and-take that often makes "in their own words" so memorable.

Exhibit No. 1: In 1997 Architecture Editor Ron Whitten sat down with eccentric architect Desmond Muirhead for a series of conversations that were ultimately published in the September issue of that year. Whitten not only brought his formidable, near-photographic recall of the architect's own work and design philosophy to the table, he also called on his previous experience as a prosecuting attorney. The result is a memorable exchange in which Muirhead defends his habit of creating fancifully shaped bunkers, including the anatomically correct "Marilyn Monroe" mounds on the 15th hole at Aberdeen. Whitten is not impressed with anatomical bunkers and, in shades of his lawyerly past, elicits a concession from Muirhead on the question of taste.

WHITTEN: That's not very subtle.
MUIRHEAD: OK, at Aberdeen, the symbols weren't always subtle. Not at all. Some were pretty crude.
WHITTEN: You once wrote, 'Crudity is a swimming pool shaped like a piano.'
MUIRHEAD: That's true.
WHITTEN: Then why isn't crudity also a bunker shaped like a fish?
MUIRHEAD: Good question . . .

At other times, the give-and-take has been more genial, but no less enlightening. In the July 1960 issue, readers listened in on a conversation between two of the greatest athletes of the 20th century, Ted Williams and Sam Snead. The two reflected on what would have happened if Williams had focused on golf and Snead had become, in Williams' words, "a king-size Yogi Berra." Mused Williams, "With all of his massive strength and fluid coordination, Snead would have terrorized pitchers for years."

More recently, GOLF DIGEST's Dialogues on Golf have succeeded in sparking discussions far beyond the pages of the magazine. In the September 1999 issue, GOLF DIGEST Senior Writer Bob Verdi got David Duval to take off his sunglasses and reveal sentiments that set off a worldwide debate over player compensation for—and perhaps even participation in—Ryder Cup Matches:

DUVAL: . . . The Ryder Cup is an exhibition. The whole thing has become a little overcooked, but it's probably going to stay that way until players choose not to play.
VERDI: Could that happen?
DUVAL: I think it could.
VERDI: Would you be among them?
DUVAL: I don't know. It's hard for me to say. But . . . where do you draw the line?

In a world of increasingly fractured—and fractious—sound bites, the luxury of hearing the musings, ramblings and thought processes of the players and people who shape the game is to be savored. So enjoy these conversations with some of our favorite people on the tour and from just outside the ropes talking about the same things we do on and off of the course.

Sam Snead's and Ted Williams' conversation, on switching hats and careers, is the cover story of the July 1960 issue.

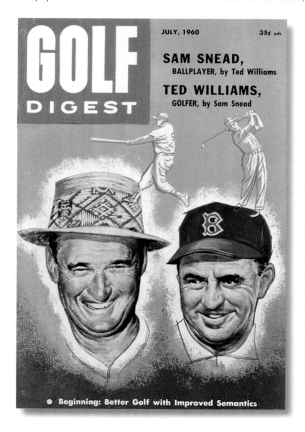

Starting out

Bob Rosburg, October 1996

Weren't you quite the child prodigy?

Well, I guess you could say that. When I was about 3 or 4, Fox Movietone [movie-house newsreels in the pre-TV age] found out I was playing golf. They came out to Harding Park [in San Francisco] and took a bunch of pictures. They set up all these elaborate camera angles; they dug all these big holes and shot up through glass while I was standing there swinging the golf club.

That then led to this thing with Admiral [Richard Evelyn] Byrd. My mother and I traveled, I guess for three months, on this tour of the country that he made when he came back from the North Pole. He was going around showing his pictures and lecturing, and I was his opening act.

They would show the Movietone bit, and then I would hit cotton golf balls out into the audience. I don't remember all that much about it. All I know is I was 5 years old, and we were in a hotel or on a train constantly. We went everywhere. We must have done 40 or 50 shows in different cities.

Tell us about the game you had at Olympic Club with Ty Cobb.

That was some match. I was 12 years old, and I guess I was an 8-, 9- or 10-handicap, something like that. I played Cobb in the final of our flight. I really had a pretty good day, and he didn't play too well; I beat him, 7 and 6. All his buddies started razzing him so bad—and you know he was a pretty hot-tempered guy—that he never came back to Olympic Club again. All the club members and his friends, they were saying stuff to him like, "How can a great athlete like you let a kid like this annihilate you? Not only beat you but

embarrass you?" He dropped his membership, went down to Menlo Park and played the rest of his days down there. Never came back.

He was tough, a fierce competitor even on the golf course. He got mad as hell at himself for some of the shots he hit. But I was never scared of him or anything like that. In fact, I've got a couple of baseballs in the safe that he signed. He signed them before the match [laughs]. I don't know if he would have signed them afterward or not. But he shook my hand after the match, that much I remember.

Parents

Jack Nicklaus, October 1991

Should your father have been tougher on you?

No. He was tough on me when he needed to be. When there were times when I didn't treat somebody right, I found out about it pretty quick. I remember getting knocked across the room a couple of times.

Why would you be reprimanded?

What any kid would get reprimanded for. I was insolent to my aunt one time when I was over at a friend's house and she wanted me to come home. I told her to go jump in the lake. I obviously didn't mean that. When my dad got home, I remember he hit me at the top of the driveway and I ended up on the cars in the garage. And you never forget that. But my dad also was a very kind and gentle man. He died of cancer in 1970.

Davis Love III, August 1998

With a father who was a teaching pro, did you ever feel forced into golf? Did you ever rebel against the environment he offered?

Surprisingly, not very much. But I did at certain points. In my own mind to get back at him: "Well, I'll just *never* play again, and *that* will show him." Which is just being a mad kid.

But it wasn't a problem, because he made it so much fun. That was the thing that was so great about him coming to me and saying, "What do you want to do? Do you want to play for fun or do you want to see how good you can get?"

He did the same thing with my brother. Mark took the other route. He said, "Just let me go, and help me when I ask." So my dad did. But he never tried to say to Mark, "Why don't you work harder?" Mark is about a scratch, still. He was probably better than that at some point. He doesn't play near enough.

I try to do the same with my kids. I don't ever say, "Here are some clubs. We need to go play." When Alexia asks for clubs, she gets them. If she wants to play, she plays. When she wants to go out and drive the cart, she goes out and drives the cart.

My 4-year-old, Dru, can't get enough of golf. But

Jack Nicklaus gets a congratulatory hug from his No. 1 fan, father Charlie, after winning the 1963 Masters. (Photo: AP/Wide World)

Davis Love III exults in his first major championship victory, the 1997 PGA at Winged Foot G.C. In a surreal touch that brought the champion's late father to mind, a rainbow arched across the sky as Love approached the 18th green. (Photo: Jim Moriarty)

when he says, like he did the other day, "I'm done," I say, "Fine." He said, "I want to go home and get some Oreos."

Learning
Peter Alliss, April 1997

Do you think any teachers are teaching anything new?

No. I don't think there is anything new. See, the game has changed very little. You tee the ball up, you start sideways on, you turn and you swing. That will always be the same. So what can you tell people? What would have happened if someone had got hold of Lee Trevino when he was a kid and said, "Listen, you can't stand like that, and you can't take it out there"? He may never have got better than a 5-handicap.

People don't want simplicity now. They go out and spend $100 or $200 or $500 on a lesson, and unless they are totally bamboozled, they don't feel they have had their money's worth. Look at Ian Baker-Finch, that poor chap can't play at all now. And that's ridiculous. Ballesteros at the moment is having a dreadful time. To tell him that he has got to alter his swing is totally ridiculous. He is completely befuddled.

We have always got to think of something new. I loved the remark of Ely Callaway, who really has been in the golf business for only five minutes. When he was asked how he did it, he said something like, "Smoke and mirrors." So it is all hype and nonsense and wonderful.

Heroes
Lee Trevino, September 1996

When you were growing up, did you have any heroes?

No. We had to survive. That's what a lot of people don't understand. When you go into the poor neighbor-

Lee Trevino lines up a putt on the final day of the 1971 U.S. Open at Merion. Trevino scored a victory over the field and his playing partner for the round—Jack Nicklaus. (Photo: Golf World)

hoods, you're trying to survive. You're wondering where the next meal's coming from. You're wondering if somebody's going to beat the hell out of you. You're wondering if you're going to have a warm bed or is it going to be dry. You don't have time to think about heroes.

People who have a nice house in a nice neighborhood and have got clean sheets every night, hell, they're the ones who are looking for heroes. Not kids that grow up and sleep five in a bed and there's no sheets on it, you're lucky you got a blanket to cover up with, and the cockroaches are eating the rats. The average person don't understand that. Heroes? You crazy? There's no such thing.

Competition
Lee Trevino, September 1996

At the 1974 World Series of Golf, you defeated Gary Player in a playoff. Wasn't that a time when you enjoyed your whisky?

Oh, I ran out of whisky there. Sundays you couldn't buy any whisky. We have to tee off at 7:30 the next morning. So the guy that ran the bar there, he called himself Elvis. So Albert Salinas [then Trevino's manager] was with me. We had to check back into the room. We were staying at the Ramada there or something.

I called Elvis up. "Elvis, I have got to have some whisky, man." I was into Scotch at the time. He said, "What do you want?" I said, "Bring me a bottle of Cutty Sark." Well, we sat in the room, and we were laughing and drinking and drinking. I drank about half of it already.

When I looked up to get another drink Albert had gone and locked the center door. He'd taken my

Greg Norman pondering quitting the game in his December 1992 GOLF DIGEST interview. (Photo: Peter Langone)

whisky with him. I'm beating on the door. I said, "Man, give me another drink."

He says, "Go to bed. You've got to get up early for a playoff."

I said, "Man, I don't care about no playoff."

I don't know what time I went to bed. I knew I was in trouble when I got my wake-up call. I look over, and there's still ice in the glass.

Frustration
Greg Norman, December 1992

Do you think you ever really could quit the game?

I was seriously considering it. Laura [his wife] said, "Why don't you just quit for 12 months?" But I couldn't do that. It was just, to me, either you stop or you fight your way through it. There's an old saying that I keep inside my head: I love to dig deep down inside myself when things aren't going my way.

That's why 1991 is by far the best year that ever happened to me. I learned so much from it. It's an easy cop-out to say you're gonna quit. Anybody can quit. I could if I wanted to. But here's what I did. I looked at myself in the mirror one day. I honestly stood there and stared at myself. And I spoke to myself.

You actually had a conversation with yourself?

Yeah. I do that a lot. You know why? Because you can't lie to yourself. Try it. Stare into your own eyes. It's the hardest thing in the world to do. Then keep doing it, and you ask yourself a question and you know what's coming out is the truth. You can't lie to yourself.

So, what was the conversation?

I just kept asking myself, "What do I want to do?" And finally I said, "I still want to be the best in the world. I miss it, I want it, I enjoyed it. I want to get back to practicing, because I love practicing. And, no, I don't want to stop."

That was enough. As soon as that happened, I went out and worked and worked and worked. I've kept working. And I know it's going to pay off. I've had a couple more conversations with myself since that. Once before the British Open. Once before the PGA Championship. I keep telling myself to focus, focus, focus.

Nick Faldo, January 1993

So it isn't good to bottle it up inside?

No, it isn't. The way [Craig] Stadler acts on the golf course is right: Get it out of your system. A lot of the Japanese scream. I don't know how you can hit a bad shot, when it's really important to hit a good shot, and say, "Oh, ho hum, I just bogeyed the hole," and walk off without reacting.

I'd be interested to know if Jack Nicklaus has ever come home and picked the clubs out of the back of

the car and just thrown them straight into the garage wall. I've done that. You've got to get it out of you or it makes you ill.

Surviving
Tommy Bolt, June 1993

What did you do when you got home from WW II?

Took up carpentry again and played golf. Mostly I played golf, at places like the Shreveport Country Club. There was only one big game in town and with everybody wanting strokes, it seemed like I had to shoot a course record every time I played. Every now and then a mullet would come to town with some money to spend and we'd pounce on him, boy. You know what a mullet is? It's a fish, about the easiest fish to catch there is. They'll bite at anything. That's what some of these guys were. Mullets.

I turned pro in 1946 and moved to Houston in 1947. I hung around Memorial Park hustling money in the golf games there. There were some characters. There was one guy we called Runt who loved to gamble and was easy pickings. One day we all teed off and when we got down the first fairway, Runt couldn't find his ball. It turned out he hadn't even teed off. We had him so flustered on the first tee he forgot to hit his ball. There was another guy named Red Nose Kennedy who worked as a garbageman. He was some intimidator. Once I asked him if he'd like to play a $5 nassau and he just snorted and handed a few fivers to his caddie. "Caddie, you handle Tommy's $5 nassau. Now who wants to play for some real money?" Right there, Red Nose Kennedy had me whipped. I learned from that.

> "We've got a society now looking for answers anywhere. They might go to a car wash to take a lesson."
>
> —FORMER MASTERS CHAMPION JACK BURKE JR., ON THE MODERN-DAY SEARCH FOR THE PERFECT SWING

The fans
Tom Watson, May 1993

Do you mind signing for fans?

When I was at the top of my game, I got my comeuppance about autographs. I was walking out of the locker room at Firestone with a bag over my shoulder. I was rushing to a plane and this little kid comes up to me and asks me for my autograph. I said, "No, son, can't you see my hands are full?" And his father was there and he calls me an a hole. I went face-to-face with him and said, "What did you call me?" He said, "You are an a--hole." I couldn't say anything to him. I just walked away.

But he was right. There was a little kid who wanted my autograph, who looked up at me with those eyes, and when I turned him down he looked at me with astonishment. I hurt him.

Did you sign his autograph?

No, I didn't. His dad said, "Come on, let's get out of here." That taught me something. That taught me a lesson that the first people on the priority list of getting autographs are kids. Then you get autograph dealers. Those are the lowest people on my list. People trying to make a buck off your autograph. That is terrible.

Jackie Burke, April 1992

Hogan was not known as a friendly guy to play with.

Listen. A person does whatever he can to cope with "The Struggle." People will pay big money to bear

witness to The Struggle. They will build a big yacht to watch a fish struggle on a line. And there are people, I'm telling you, who would pay money to watch people being executed. Just to see how they handle it, you see. Hogan had a hell of a struggle in life and he learned to deal with it the way he knew best, which was not talking to anybody. Trevino does it his way by talking. Chi Chi Rodriguez does his sword act. Hogan just said nothing. And he was a master at handling The Struggle.

People are funny. They can be bloodthirsty. When there are 30,000 people waiting for you at 2 p.m. at Augusta National on Sunday in the Masters, a lot of them are there to see if you vomit all the way down the first fairway. The player is very much aware of this. You've got a four-shot lead and they want to see if you're going to faint somewhere over the next five hours.

Effort
Tom Kite, September 1993

Then you're not a workaholic?

I have a problem with that term. I don't know who said this and I have repeated it a couple of times. I think it was supposedly attributed to Confucius and he said something like, "The man who finds a job that he truly loves never works another day the rest of his life." I have a job that I truly love. I don't feel like I work at that game.

If you want to call me a playaholic, then let's do that. Spending time on the practice tee for me is no more laborious than some 8-year-old kid shooting baskets all afternoon, or calling his dad and saying, "Dad, hit me some pop-ups. Let's play catch." Kids can play catch for hours. Kids can shoot baskets for hours. Kids can hit golf balls for hours. Just because you're 43, that doesn't mean you can't do it, too. When I was 11 years old or 13 years old, I did the same thing that I do now. Hit balls from morning till night. If a 13-year-old kid does that from sunup to sundown and all he is doing is having a good time, why is it any different for a 43-year-old kid?

Struggles
John Daly, February 1996

What was it like on the Hogan (now Nike) Tour?

I came back playing so good on the South African Tour, finished fourth on the Order of Merit. Then started playing the Hogan Tour and just didn't play good at all. Everybody knows I got put in the hospital in Maine in May of '90 for overdosing on Jack Daniels. My expectations were so high. I thought I was gonna come over here and win some tournaments, but it didn't happen.

I was really down. Me and a couple of buddies of mine—I ain't gonna say their names—we started

"When I was 11 years old or 13 years old, I did the same thing that I do now. Hit balls from morning till night."

—TOM KITE

Tom Kite speaking out on the job he loves. (Photo: Stephen Szurlej)

Class
Ken Venturi, May 1994

You toured with Nelson in a series of exhibitions, right?

But in that time, to sum up Byron Nelson—we would get on the first tee and Nelson would say, "What's the course record and who holds it?" Finally we got in the car one day and I said, "Byron, why do you always ask what is the course record and who holds it?" He said, "I want to tell you something, Ken. I want you to remember this as long as you work with me, and as long as you play golf. In tournaments it's different, but in exhibitions or rounds of golf, you find out the course record and who holds it. Because you never break the course record of the home pro. He lives there and you are only visiting." That's Byron Nelson.

Money
Gary Player, September 1995

You must have turned down money?

Never turned down $100,000 in my life. Whenever they offer me $100,000, I'm gone. Even now. Because when you've finished, nobody will hold a collection for you. The man in the street finds it impossible to believe that you would turn down $100,000 for a week's work, when he doesn't make that a year.

"Never turned down $100,000 in my life. Even now. Because when you've finished, nobody will hold a collection for you."

—GARY PLAYER

drinking about 5 o'clock at a pro-am party. I was drinking 'em so fast. We went to the racetrack and finally the lady told me she'd only give me one at a time. I was ordering 'em two at a time, triple Jack and Coke.

My buddy who was driving me back said he saw a bunch of saliva coming out of my mouth, and I wasn't moving. He had been drinking, too, and a cop pulled him over. He said to the cop, "Look, I have been drinkin', but my buddy needs to get to the hospital." The cop was cool, was what my friend said.

I don't remember any of that. All I remember is waking up with a bunch of black stuff in my nose and a bunch of tubes goin' up there. I played the next day and shot 75.

Integrity
Mickey Wright, July 1993

What was your most embarrassing moment on the golf course?

When I was 12 years old I cheated. I had been playing about a year and I was playing with Evelyn Braddock, another junior golfer from San Diego. She was older than I was and a better golfer. We were playing a little country club match and I hit a ball down into a canyon. I went down there and swung at it, I can't remember, maybe three times. Finally I get it up on the green, walked off the green and she asked what I had had. I said a 6. She said, "Run it through your mind again and tell me what you had." I said I had a 6. "No," she said and went back through it with me. Then she said, "You had a 7 and you're going to be too good to ever have to cheat." It was the finest lesson a 12-year-old could ever have. Never again in my life, in anything, have I ever cheated. Wasn't that a lovely way to tell a kid not to cheat?

Above: *John Daly singing about his struggles. (Photo: Dom Furore)*

Right: *Mickey Wright swinging from the blues in 1967.*

Gurus

David Leadbetter, September 1998

In a way, the role of teachers seems a lot more valued than it used to be.

Teaching these days is really the only expertise a golf professional can still have and call himself a professional. I mean, you don't have to be a golf pro to be a haberdasher or to run a club or run tournaments. Teaching is a specialized job. Now the PGA is starting to recognize this. I have been on them for years to get like a certified teaching program where people would come into the profession. The problem is there are a couple of these organizations now that advertise, "Come to us for a week and we will give you a diploma for teaching and then you can go out and make money teaching golf." So they have got dentists and plumbers and some guy who couldn't break 90 becoming certified golf instructors. I mean, how on earth can some guy, because he has read a couple of books and then gets a diploma in a week, be a legitimate teacher? I mean, what a joke. That's pathetic. That's a scam as far as I am concerned.

Jackie Burke, April 1992

Getting back to the club pro, what about modern teaching? Is the game being taught correctly?

As far as teaching goes, it's been taken out of the club pro's hands by the guru-type guys. The club pro can't afford to just teach any more than the history teacher at the high school can afford to do just that.

The demise of teaching is bad. At one time, the golfers would go to the club pro for lessons, and it made for a terrific relationship. The old pro would fix your club, get you a game, would give you his time and then charge you a very modest fee because you did business in his shop.

If he gives you a lesson now, you get a bill for it. There are discount shops all over town, see, and I have to make my money somehow else, from golf carts or from a salary. In the meantime, since I'm not teaching, the golfer becomes dubious as to whether I know anything about the golf swing because Mr. Know-it-all, the guru, is teaching exclusively and goes around town giving clinics and writing articles all the time. It's reduced the credibility of the pro.

Jack Nicklaus, October 1991

Are you at all critical of the modern players' reliance on this team concept?

I don't think it makes a lot of sense, frankly. Bobby Jones told me he used to run back to Stewart Maiden during those seven lean years of his career for lessons. He said that when he learned to be able to correct himself on the golf course, control his own game and do it himself, that's when he became a good player. Now, if you're going to continue to rely on somebody every time, you never end up doing it yourself. I sort of lived with what Jones did. I worked very hard—instead of running back to Jack Grout for everything—to learn to do it myself. Even though I would go back to Jack when I needed help, it was to assist me in my own judgment of what I thought was right and wrong.

The kids today, going through college programs with those college coaches, are so wrapped up in the psychology, the teaching and learning to play a certain way. The coaches are telling them how to play the holes. Let the kid *learn* to play. If he is going to be a good player, he has to learn himself. I have got to think that is one of the big reasons the European players are a little stronger right now. They didn't have all these fancy sports psychologists.

Bob Toski, December 1991

What was your approach to working with tour players or aspiring tour players?

I like to think I am a teacher of all players. I like to think I am a consummate teacher and that my empathy for the poorer player is even stronger than for the tour player. Because the poor player subsidizes the game. He would love to be able to swing the club like Bob Toski or hit the ball like Greg Norman and putt like Ben Crenshaw.

I never did particularly enjoy teaching tour pros for the sake of feeding my own ego. You don't get much credit for taking a 15-handicapper down to a 5. But give a good lesson to a tour pro and you can become famous. Teaching tour pros is bragging rights and PR—that's what it's all about.

In our interview with Tony Jacklin he was critical of today's pros for being too dependent on their gurus. What do you think of the phenomenon of these gurus now being on-site at all the majors to monitor their students' swings?

What has changed is this: Before, the doctor never went to see the patient; the patient always went to see the doctor. What's happened in golf is, now the doctor is going to visit the patient. And the patient will always let the doctor come to him if he doesn't have to go to the doctor. I don't care where you are. That's human nature. You aren't going to go to the doctor's office if he will come pay a house call. If [David] Leadbetter, Peter Kostis and these other gurus are going out to see those guys on tour and teach them, the obvious fact is they are creating that dependency, which I would never do. If I am a doctor of golf, you come see me. Besides, I'm not sure a major tournament is the time and place to be working on your golf swing.

You were the in-vogue guru 10 to 15 years ago. What was your approach?

I challenged them. I would say, "Let's go out and play. If you can get by me, if you can prove you can beat me, then I will be the judge of whether you can play out there."

> "Teaching these days is really the only expertise a golf professional can still have and call himself a professional."
>
> —DAVID LEADBETTER

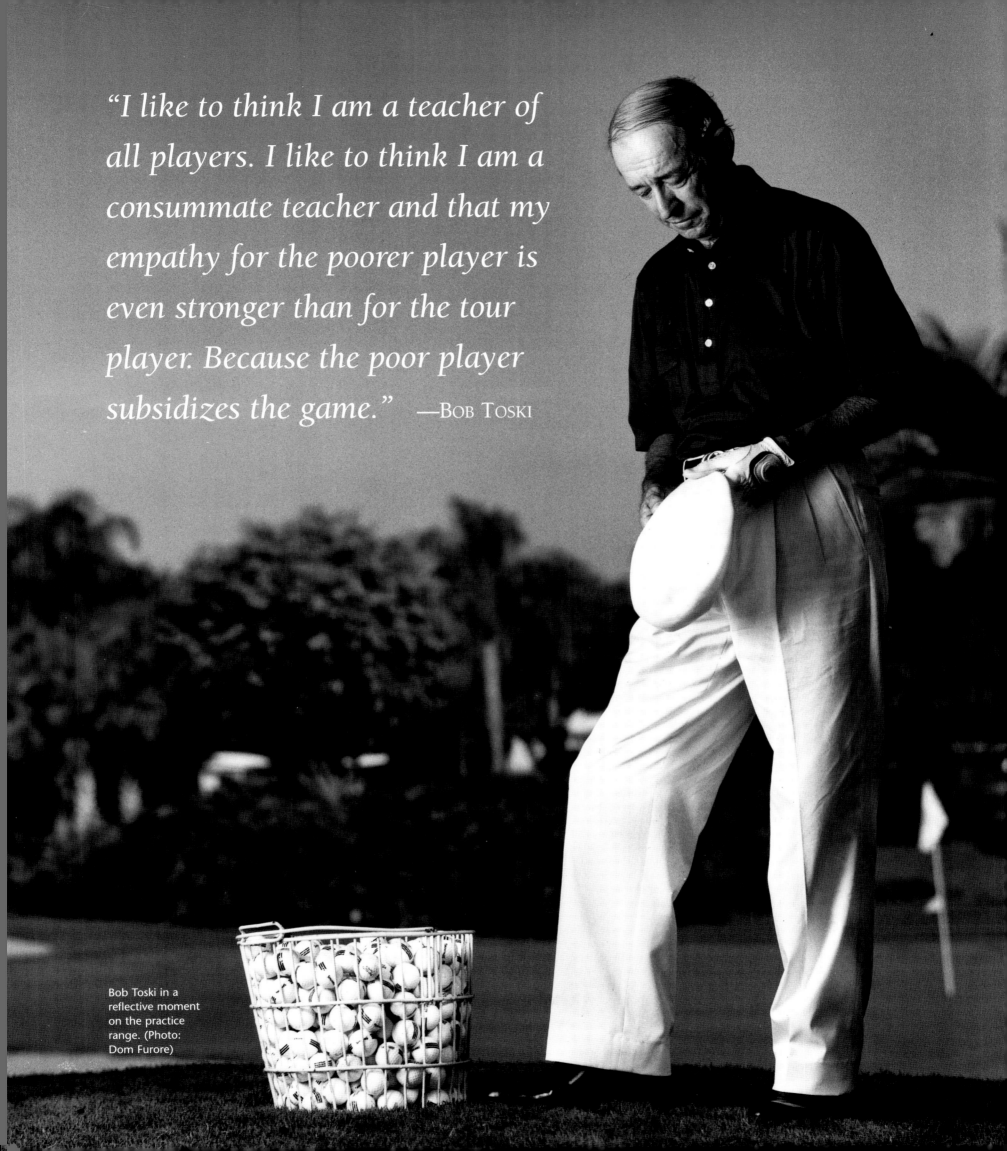

"I like to think I am a teacher of all players. I like to think I am a consummate teacher and that my empathy for the poorer player is even stronger than for the tour player. Because the poor player subsidizes the game." —BOB TOSKI

Bob Toski in a reflective moment on the practice range. (Photo: Dom Furore)

Joe Dey and Howard Cosell go back and forth during their April 1973 conversation. (Photos: Ernie Baxter and Hank Morgan)

> "That to me is true democracy, where a man's own merit determines whether he plays there."
>
> —JOE DEY

Equality
Tom Watson, May 1993

From a social and a legal standpoint, golf has put up a lot of barriers to women. Women more than other minorities have challenged them in court. What are your feelings about women's rights at clubs?

I think there is no question that the old rules where you cannot have women members at golf clubs are antiquated and archaic. I think there should not be any rules against women at a golf club, if they have a mixed membership. But on the other hand, I think it is perfectly all right to have all-men and all-women golf clubs. I don't think that's discrimination.

We are taking it way too far. Such as Augusta [National], because they have no women members. Women play there all the time. That rule right there, I

think, is an antiquated rule. But that's the way that club is. It shouldn't be a legal fight, but women are challenging the rules at clubs all over this country. And, rightfully, they are being given the privileges of membership.

You are saying that Augusta is a mixed club, so therefore women should be members?

I am not going to tell them whether they should have women as members of the club. That's their choice. But I think, on an average, the clubs that don't allow women in as full members are antiquated and archaic.

How do you think golf has handled Shoal Creek?

Cypress Point had to drop out because they didn't have a black member. They had Chinese members, women members and Jewish members. They didn't have a black member, but it wasn't any form of abject discrimination. No, not at all. How do you tell whether a club doesn't want somebody because of his race or his ethnic group or his religion? How can you really tell?

Joe Dey and Howard Cosell, April 1973

COSELL: Aren't you concerned that we haven't yet had a black man play in the Masters?

DEY: I would love to see a man who can qualify to play in the Masters play in the Masters, regardless of his color. That to me is true democracy, where a man's own merit determines whether he plays there.

COSELL: Don't you think the rules of eligibility for the Masters could have been amended, in good spirit, to allow a man like Sifford, who has won some tournaments, to have the opportunity to play?

DEY: If you were a cut below Charlie Sifford on the money list, and he were allowed to play for other reasons, you wouldn't like that, would you? That would be discrimination in reverse, would it not?

COSELL: As tour commissioner wouldn't you like to see some kind of organized program whereby, for a given day or two, Jack Nicklaus held a clinic for youngsters in Harlem, Arnold Palmer went into Bedford Stuyvesant, Dean Martin went into Watts and so on?

DEY: I agree. It would be a wonderful thing.

COSELL: What can you do? Have you done any thinking about it?

DEY: I must confess I have not.

COSELL: If I charge you with dereliction in this regard, Joe, will you accept the charge and plead guilty?

DEY: With a two-stroke penalty.

Versatility
Sam Snead and Ted Williams, July 1960

SNEAD: If Ted Williams had become a golfer I don't think the game would ever have seen a more

Slow players have been around for a long time. This gentle reminder was posted on a course in 1975.

positive player. I think Ted would have inclined to be a gambler, going for the pin with every shot.

WILLIAMS: How would you like to have a king-size Yogi Berra on your baseball team? That's what some lucky major-league team probably would have had if Sam had turned to baseball instead of golf. With all of his massive strength and fluid coordination, Snead would have terrorized pitchers for years.

Slow play
Mickey Wright, July 1993

What do you think about the slow pace of play on tour?

It's just disgusting. It's unconscionable that a threesome will take five hours to play a round of golf. It's horrible.

Well, what takes people so long?

I think we've had some examples from the men's tour that somehow made it OK. I don't buy it. I'm sorry. The arrogance of that disturbs me. I think it's just so terribly inconsiderate. I will hit into people. I did it the other evening. Somebody was in front of us and had either looked back and didn't care or didn't look back and was dawdling. I took it for two holes and that was it. I reared back and just flew it past him. I wasn't aiming at him, but he saw the ball go past, and with that he kindly stepped aside and waved us through. When it takes that to bring out decent golf etiquette, something's wrong.

Craig Stadler, May 1995

Would you agree to penalizing the slow guys with strokes?

You have to. They could care less if they get fined $200, $500, $750. That's pro-am money. You gotta start putting strokes on them, you gotta do it right away, not when the round ends. Don't threaten

them; just boom! If officials watch a group for two holes, they know who's holding things up. Boom!

I don't think that if I'm playing with some guy who's taking a God's age and we're two holes behind, that we should all get penalized. I mean, occasionally I'll say, "Come on, man, you gotta get going. Enough of this crap. Speed this thing up." It's gotten to the point—and I don't know how many guys would agree with me—but my only goal in life on Thursday and Friday is getting to Saturday, when you play twosomes. Thursday and Friday are just miserable. You take four hours and 40 minutes to play Waialae? I'm sorry, but there's no rough, the course is 6,500 yards, wide open, no tight OB, no nothing. It just takes forever.

Vanity
Jim Colbert, June 1997

How do you respond to those who make fun of your hairpiece?

The trouble with hairpieces is, in the business I do if you go out with me at night or something, my hairpiece looks really good. I've been out there in 100-degree weather practicing. If I take it off, it just looks terrible. I buy the best, have my own personally cut in, all that kind of stuff. But to wear it all day in the hot sun under a hat, it just looks terrible. I think mine are good enough that I'm not wearing a sign. But they're getting to be a pain in the neck. Bald would be a lot easier way to go. Just got to get by that first day.

Modern players vs. old timers
Tom Weiskopf, March 1991

But you keep hearing that there are more good players out there now . . .

Bull----. It's not possible. When I came out, low 70 and ties made the cut and the low 50 places paid off. You had to play your ass off. Now a guy can make the cut and earn $1,500 for just walking around. You tell me which system is going to produce great players.

Is that a reason the foreign players are so good?

Of course. They have to work harder at every level of the game. They don't have everything handed to them. Some guy interviewed Hogan once and asked him why he was so driven to improve. He said, "I had to. Nobody gave me anything. Either I improved or I went back to Fort Worth broke." And he did a few times. Look at kids today. Perfect courses, perfect equipment, coaches to hold their hands. They don't even walk anymore. They all ride carts. It's a lazy society and it's why we're getting our asses kicked. Hell, I know I sound like an old guy, but I don't care. Somebody's got to say these things.

Johnny Miller, May 1991

Why aren't today's players as good?

Nowadays they have top-10itis. I don't know who started this top-10 junk, but it gets me so upset. The guys will say, "How're you playing? How many top 10s did you have this year?" We never talked about a top 10 in a million years. The only thing that mattered was playing the best that we could and really shooting for the win.

I remember sitting on the stand with Jack Nicklaus at the Masters. I will never forget it. It was in 1971 and I should have won. Charlie Coody beat me, birdied two of the last three holes. I bogeyed 16 and 18, but 18 didn't matter at that point. I sat on the stand with Jack, and they announced that Nicklaus and Miller were tied for second. They called us up for the medal and as we were getting up, Nicklaus goes, "Big deal, right?" Now to me it was a big deal. But his thinking was "Big deal, second-place medal."

Nowadays, our tour doesn't have a player like Nicklaus who will say that winning is the only thing that matters. To win, you have got to say, "Am I willing to do the things the other guys are not willing to do that week?"

I am going to get myself in trouble, but right now I see the U.S. players like thoroughbred sheep.

Likeability
Ben Hogan, September 1970

Does your reputation as a grim, machine-like person bother you?

I couldn't care less. I get along with everybody I know. I know who started those stories and why, and he's sorry, and that's enough. Too many people hear or read something written from uneducated preconceptions, and it takes off. There's a great difference between intelligence and wisdom. You might have a college sheepskin; that doesn't make you educated. Life's too short for me to go around explaining myself. A lot of people don't understand modesty. Not everybody wants publicity, you know.

Modern equipment
Tom Weiskopf, March 1991

What about the long putters used by guys like Orville Moody?

I've never used one, but it doesn't look like golf to me. Why doesn't the USGA adopt this for a rule? You can't have a club in your bag that's longer than your driver. That's fair.

Do you think the USGA has abdicated its responsibility in controlling how far the ball goes?

The ball is ruining the game. Period. I don't give a damn what the USGA says; I know the ball goes substantially farther. Look, I'm 48 years old and I hit the ball longer than I did in my prime. I'll give you a perfect example. I've played thousands of rounds on the Scarlet Course at Ohio State. Today I hit one club less on all the par 3s. There's a par 5 there that I never reached in school. This summer, on watered fairways, I hit it easily with a driver and a 1-iron. Now you tell me the ball doesn't go longer. Bull----. And it goes straighter. That doesn't bother me as much as the distance, though. The ball is making the great courses obsolete. How can that be good? How about Merion? Do you mean to tell me that the Open can never go back to Merion, but we shouldn't roll back the ball?

The yips
Bernhard Langer, April 1994

What about your yips. Were they caused by fear?

I was scared every day. Every time you gave me the putter, I was scared. Even when you gave me an iron, or my caddie gave me an iron, I was scared I would hit it too far away from the hole and three- or four-putt.

Can you remember when your yips first happened?

I can't recall what it felt like the very first time, but I've had it for so long. The first time lasted four years, then it came back two more times, so I know very well what it feels like.

Can you describe it?

It's an uncontrollable movement of the muscles. It can go anywhere from a twitch, to a freeze where you can't move at all, to a sudden explosion.

What's it like mentally?

It's very confusing. Everything is totally out of whack, out of sequence, out of control. It's like your hands and arms are not part of you, not part of your body.

What were your symptoms?

I really didn't have much of a mental picture. I just . . . I did everything. I left them way short, I hit them way past, I could hit them way left and way right. Just anywhere but good.

And how many times have you had it officially?

Well, I had it from 1976 to 1979 most of the time; well, some days were a little better than others. Then it came back in 1982 and again in 1988. Like Trevino says . . . when someone asks him, "Why did you take three putts?" he says, "I enjoy putting so much."

> "The ball is ruining the game. Period. . . . The ball is making the good courses obsolete."
> —Tom Weiskopf

Tom Weiskopf, possessor of one of the game's strongest swings, has equally strong opinions. He came down hard on modern equipment in his 1991 interview. (Photo: Bob Ewell)

"A real golf course should look natural. It's got to have a little bit of untidiness to it, like nature itself, a bit of chaos."

—PETER THOMSON

Television
Dave Marr, September 1997

How would you describe your style as a TV announcer, your approach?

I never want to be real critical of a player in missing a shot or something. If it was behavior, that's something else. I like to do it just as if I'd be here sitting and talking to you and we were watching a telecast of the Masters together. Just be informational in a quiet way and shut up when they hit a shot—just as if you were gallerying, we would stop and let the guy hit and then say whatever it is that jumps in your mind. I have always liked announcers, say, like Pat Summerall. They are calm, they are not yelling at you. I don't like to be yelled at or pointed at.

Beth Daniel, November 1994

What do you think about the LPGA's relative lack of network exposure?

I don't think the commentators treat the women the same way they treat the men. When you watch a men's golf event on TV, the commentators talk about the shot the guy has and what they think he's going to do with it or what he should do with it. In women's golf, when a woman comes on TV it's, "Well, there's so-and-so, she just found out this week she's pregnant and, oh, there's her shot." It's a different telecast.

It's like my mom once said, watching women's professional golf on TV is like watching a gossip show. If I watch LPGA golf, I turn the sound off and I do it sometimes on men's golf, too. I want to watch golf and I want to see golf shots. I don't want to hear all this other junk.

Architecture
Peter Thomson, July 1994

There's a trend toward pristine conditioning, particularly in America. Clearly it's not something you approve of.

It's artificial. A real golf course should look natural. It's got to have a little bit of untidiness to it, like nature itself, a bit of chaos. There's none of that at Augusta. A course needs a little touch of absurdity here and there.

You've said that in a great golf course there should be respect, joy and humor versus just difficulty.

Yes, evermore so. I've always said if your grandmother can't enjoy it, it's not a great golf course. I have begun to rate courses by the number of balls you need. For instance, if a course is a one-ball course, assuming it has all the usual features, I think it's a great course. But a 12-ball course I think is rubbish. There are plenty of those around. That's my basic criticism of Jack Nicklaus' courses. They are very much like the man himself, very serious and lacking in humor.

Desmond Muirhead, November 1997

Would you agree, 10 years after Aberdeen, that maybe your symbolic forms weren't necessarily subtle? After all, the 15th hole there, which you called "Marilyn Monroe," has two huge mounds emulating breasts.

That was loused up. The mounds had a couple of nipples on them to start with. It looked really fabulous, but they were removed when women objected to them.

What's the point of nipples? Were you trying to arouse people?

No, I wasn't trying to arouse anyone. Breasts have nipples.

That's not very subtle.

OK, at Aberdeen, the symbols weren't always subtle. Not at all. Some were pretty crude.

You once wrote, "Crudity is a swimming pool shaped like a piano."

That's true.

Then why isn't crudity also a bunker shaped like a fish?

Good question. With a swimming pool, you are trying to find the essence of water. You are not trying to find the essence of music, in the way you are with a piano. A piano swimming pool is kitsch.

What's kitsch?

It's false art. It's lowbrow. It's embarrassing. A Mickey Mouse ears bunker is kitsch. An island green shaped like an apple is kitsch.

Desmond Muirhead's controversial 15th hole at Aberdeen G. & C.C., known as "Marilyn Monroe," has since been modified.

So why isn't a fish bunker kitsch?

That fish bunker is on a hole shaped like a mermaid. I think it's perfectly valid. I was following a theme. The whole thing smacks of consistency: Mermaid, fish, water. But a piano and a swimming pool are widely divorced.

I'm not perfect. I never pretend to be. Remember, Stone Harbor and Aberdeen were very experimental. There are holes at both that make me wince. I don't think they were crude in conception. I'd say about half were crude in their execution.

Jan Stephenson, November 1991

Let's talk a little bit about course design. Is it something you are interested in?

I would like to do it, but I have to fight people all the way to let me. I have always been observant on the course and I have strong opinions about architecture. The tough part is convincing some people that I can do more than just consult. When I designed my own golf course in Japan, they thought I was going to just stick my name on it. I drove them nuts, sending in blueprints, sending them pictures, saying this is the way I want it. That's how you have to be.

People are still afraid of letting a girl design a golf course. What they don't understand is that I can identify more with the average golfer than a Jack Nicklaus can. Jack and all the men who design golf courses play from the championship tees. Well, I play from the men's tees when I play. And I hit the ball about as far as the average man hits it.

People say they want a man to design the course and they want me to design the ladies' tees. Well, I never play from them. The few times I have played from the ladies' tees I was struck by how bad the condition and the thinking behind them were. They are afterthoughts.

Robert Trent Jones Jr., March 1993

Where do you stand on the environmental impact of golf courses?

I am an environmentalist. What architect isn't? We are involved in the game because we like its beauty and the environment it provides. I speak at the public hearings about the positives of golf courses because there are others who will speak against them. I speak of courses as being the lungs of the city. Fly over cities such as Bangkok, Los Angeles, Chicago, Miami, any city, and you'll see that most of the green spaces are parks and golf courses. The courses are self-financing. Golfers pay their own way. They are bird sanctuaries and animal habitats.

We are building a golf course at Squaw Valley, Calif. You would think by reactions in the community that we're the worst violators of the land. Doctors have said at public hearings that we are going to hurt unborn fetuses because chemicals will leach into the groundwater and get into the fisheries. There's so much misinformation out there.

David Feherty, November 1992

Your newest outlet for creativity is golf course design. We imagine you have some strong feelings there.

To me, the game has disappeared. I really don't think we're building courses right now. First, they're taking walking out of the game. You can't walk golf courses in America. Kiawah Island had three-quarters of a mile between the ninth green and the 10th tee, and there are so many beautiful things to see out there when you're walking that you'd miss in a cart. The only way you'll see a wild fowl or whatever is if you happen to flatten it in your cart.

It really depresses me. I fear for the future of traditional golf, where people get out, have a bit of a stretch, hit a few shots and walk around a nice place. That is the first thing a golf course should be: a nice place to walk. Most of the courses we play these days, you might as well be walking around the parking lot at Piggly Wiggly. There would be no pleasure in this game at all if it wasn't for walking.

Number 11 at Aberdeen is Desmond Muirhead's mermaid hole—complete with fish-shaped bunkers. (Photo: Paul Barton)

"That fish bunker is on a hole shaped like a mermaid. I think it's perfectly valid. I was following a theme. The whole thing smacks of consistency."

—DESMOND MUIRHEAD

Champions Gene Sarazen and Sam Snead walk the hallowed fairways of Augusta National at the 1984 Masters—35 years after Snead won his first of three, and 49 years after Sarazen's "shot heard around the world." (Photo: Stephen Szurlej)

VOICES

by Jerry Tarde,
Editor

There is a certain timbre to the voice of golf. You have to be a player to hear it. Baseball shouts. Football rumbles. Basketball bellows. Even tennis, the other country club sport, shrieks. Maybe that's the way our game should be, too, in this new century. But golf's voice has always risen above the others. When you want to be heard, they say, whisper.

The whisperers of GOLF DIGEST are the magazine's columnists. They are charged with explaining the game and the players while keeping it all in perspective. Humor and empathy come easy to them; after all, they're golfers.

One who wrote more words, traveled more miles and took more X's in pursuit of golf was the great British columnist, Peter Dobereiner, who was distinguished from the rest also by having an ego the size of a ballmarker. He viewed every other writer as his superior. He described himself as "a dust-bin collector next to Charley Price," "not good enough to carry Dan Jenkins' 7-wood," and "an abject failure compared with Henry Longhurst." Of course, it was all hogwash.

Dobereiner, much to the good fortune of his readers, was a Zelig-like character who always seemed to be standing inconspicuously beside the golfer making history. Nicklaus and Palmer considered him a trusted friend. Ballesteros said he could make him laugh and cry in the same sentence. Who else but Dobers would have stumbled into Greg Norman in the Augusta National locker room on the eve of his final round in the 1996 Masters, with a six-shot lead and a green coat within his grasp. Dobereiner gave his old mate a bear hug and uttered the now-infamous refrain, "Greg, even you can't muck this one up."

Peter was one of a stable of star writers who ushered GOLF DIGEST into a new era of reporting and interpretation of the game. Sometime beginning in the mid-1970s, the magazine stepped up its feature writing and commentary with the addition one by one of these wonderful eccentrics who had no equal as writers on golf. Occasionally a Herbert Warren Wind or

Alastair Cooke or John Updike would join their ranks, but every month the magazine published the ruminations of this murderer's row: Longhurst, Dobereiner, Price, Jenkins, Frank Beard, Dave Marr, Peter Thomson, Peter Andrews, Nick Seitz, Frank Hannigan and, in later years, Tom Callahan, Dave Kindred and David Owen.

That stretch through the 1980s into the 1990s was a Golden Age of Golf Writing. Readers who took GOLF DIGEST in that period were as lucky as the golfers of Fort Worth in the 1920s who found Byron Nelson and Ben Hogan in the same caddie yard.

Longhurst was elected to Parliament with Churchill. Price lived with Walter Hagen. Dave Marr was the pro from 52nd Street. Jenkins was the son Hogan never had. Thomson won five British Opens in the morning and wrote his own newspaper accounts in the afternoon. Hannigan officiated at national championships for 20 years. These were rollicking writers with widely diverse backgrounds sharing one common trait: they knew golf.

The traditional job description of a columnist is to hunker down on the sidelines until the battle is over, then go out and bayonet the wounded. But these writers prided themselves only to pick on the giants, the commissioners, the superstars, the Augusta Nationals and Greg Normans—it was Jenkins who wrote of Greg, "He looks like the guy they always hired to kill James Bond." How were we to know it was Norman's fate to fall off the funicular at the end of every major?

Some columnists never left any blood on the victim. Whenever I as editor would get a call of complaint about a Callahan column, I would listen sympathetically and explain: "Oh, no, I'm sure he meant it as a compliment." With Jenkins, that line never worked. Dan could offend everyone with such versimilitude and wit that only a tour pro could take umbrage.

Some writers put their future at risk by never compromising an opinion. The column by Frank Beard chosen for this chapter criticized the Masters sufficiently that it cost him a career as a network television broadcaster.

Others were simply great raconteurs. Who else but Dave Marr would recall that a syphon used to steal gasoline in the early days of the tour was known as "an Oklahoma credit card"?

But for sheer elegance, the style of Charles Price belonged on a Paris runway in an earlier time. He believed in never using a metaphor or analogy that wasn't at least 50 years old. "I want my stuff read for generations," he'd say. "The latest Spielberg flick might not be around so long."

Contributing Editors (left to right) Dave Anderson, Charles Price, Peter Dobereiner and Dan Jenkins. (Photo: Jim Moriarty)

Henry Longhurst

There's no time to smell the roses today

Henry Longhurst (Photo: Leonard Kamsler)

As I survey the modern golfing scene and read continually of the super-colossal amounts of money involved, I sometimes wonder whether the very size of the operation has not in many ways tended to spoil it, both for the players and those who go to watch—for all, indeed, except those who sit at home with the television.

There was a time when you could actually walk around with the giants of the day, and even touch the hem of their garment, instead of surveying them with field glasses from beyond distant ropes. You could stay in the same hotel and sit up and swap yarns with them in the evening. Newspapermen came to know the players in a manner impossible today for their more numerous brethren who have to rely on the official "press interview," after which perhaps 150 typewriters may be heard, all pounding out the same story.

The golden age of golf to me always will be associated with the names of Hagen, Sarazen and Jones, especially Hagen, who probably *spent* as much money as anyone in the history of golf. I believe him to have been the original of "I never wanted to be a millionaire. I only wanted to live like one."

Hagen's famous motto was "Never hurry. Never worry. Never forget to stop and smell the flowers along the way." It so impressed the late Duke of Windsor when Fred Corcoran quoted it that he scribbled it down on the back of an envelope and hurried in to read it to the Duchess. The motto would cut no ice today. Nearly all of the players seem to be hurrying and worrying all the time.

It took Hagen about five leisurely weeks to win the British Open, which was in those days *the* one to win. In 1929 his traveling companion was the great Tommy Armour (due to win it himself two years later). After a voyage of seven days on the Aquitania they checked in at the Savoy. Following a bath and shave Armour dropped by Hagen's suite to find installed a case of whisky, a case of gin, and a case (not a bottle) of champagne. When reprimanded for this extravagance, Hagen opened his hands and smiled. "But we are bound to be having people in and out," he said.

> *The golden age of golf to me always will be associated with the names of Hagen, Sarazen and Jones, especially Hagen.*

Having made $2,800 from an exhibition match with Archie Compston (you could certainly add a zero to that figure today), Hagen went on to win the Open. He and Armour then crossed to France, where Hagen picked up one tournament and two exhibition fees. And at the end of it all Armour had to fork out $200 to get his free-spending companion off the ship in New York—where the Haig at once set about recouping his fortunes on the strength of winning the British Open.

Life on the ocean waves in these big ships is now merely a memory. My mind goes back to 1949 when I had the good fortune to travel home from the U.S. in company with the American Ryder Cup team. It was captained by Ben Hogan, who less than a year previously had been left for dead beside the road after a head-on collision with a bus.

I often met the great man in the Queen Elizabeth's admirable Turkish bath and felt privileged, and still do, to be able to sit and talk with him. Still pale and gaunt, he had one leg encased in a stocking and could stand for no more than a half hour at a time. When I referred to him jocularly as the non-playing captain, his mouth shut like a trap and his eyes narrowed. Then with sudden venom he said, "This life is driving me *crazy*. I want to *compete* again. I'm no good unless I'm *competing*."

I remember thinking, "You'll be lucky if you ever play again, much less compete." We had many talks together and they increased my knowledge of, and of course my respect for, this remarkable man, in circumstances that would be impossible in our airplane age of today.

That was in September and as I think of his "comeback" early in the following year, I still find it difficult to believe that it was the same man. Could this emaciated, almost immobilized figure be the same as the one who only a few months later was to shoot 73, 69, 69, 69 in the Los Angeles Open—only to be beaten, naturally enough, by Sam Snead in a playoff? Or could it be the same as the one we were to see striding down the last fairway at Carnoustie to add the British Open to the Masters and U.S. Open titles he'd won earlier in the year.

I count myself lucky indeed to have been part of the scene when there was no mad rush for the airport and there always seemed time to stop and smell the flowers.

Frank Beard

Augusta's a nice place but it's not heaven

Frank Beard (Photo: Maggie Roctberts)

If you want to be traditional, then preserving a great golf course is a good place to start.

Before Cliff Roberts or Bill Lane or whoever is running the Masters these days gets all up in arms, I want to preface this column by saying I like the Masters Tournament. I also like Augusta National. It's always been one of my favorite courses. But I think it's time things were put in perspective.

The mystique of the Masters captures the fancy of golf fans every year. It has become a springtime rite, almost a sacred observance. In a way, that's good, because anything that stimulates the public's interest in golf is beneficial. But I don't think any mystique should keep the public from seeing and hearing about a tournament the way it really is.

What brings this to mind is that the Masters people apparently don't want any professional golfers doing television commentary, as some of us do at other tournaments. I've always felt that having an articulate pro on a telecast is a good idea, because he can provide some insight the fans might not get otherwise. I'm happy the networks are starting to agree. But the Masters folks obviously feel differently.

I can only assume this is because we golfers are sometimes more outspoken than the regular commentators, and the Masters doesn't want anyone marring the picture of perfection it is trying to create, even unintentionally.

An example of this attitude occurred a few years ago when a well-known commentator, one of the best in the business, referred to an excited crowd at Augusta as a "mob." He was invited not to come back, although he has since returned.

That, it seems to me, is a bit much. It's a good golf tournament and a nice place, but we shouldn't have to get reverent about it.

As a matter of fact, the crowds at the Masters, while knowledgeable and sophisticated on the whole, aren't any better than those at a lot of other tournaments. They make noise and kids run up and down drinking beer. Augusta needs marshals to keep order, just like anyplace else. The fans there are interested in golf, sure, but they're also just folks out having a good time in the spring sun.

How much mystique would the Masters have if it were played in August, or late October, instead of in early April when the entire northern half of the country is just getting its appetite whetted for golf? The tournament might not be a "rite" at any other time of year.

We all know that, because of the invitation restrictions, the Masters has the worst field of any tournament we play all year. The top stars are always there, but there are fewer good players at Augusta than at Quad Cities.

What boggles my mind is that the people who run the Masters make such a fetish about the tournament being a living memorial to Bobby Jones—as well they should—yet turn around and keep making changes in the golf course that Bobby Jones and Alister Mackenzie built!

Some of the changes have been for the worse, in my opinion. They moved the tee back and put big humps in the fairway on the par-5 No. 15 and completely changed the character of the hole. It was designed as a hole where you could gamble on getting home in two shots, and if you mis-hit your second you risked going into the water in front of the green. Now you have to be a very long hitter to start with, and then catch two super shots to get there, and it's really not as exciting a hole.

They put in a large bunker on the left side of the driving area on 18. On the face of it, this was a good change, because it certainly makes the tee shot with a driver more exciting. Except that most players now lay up with a 3-wood to avoid going into the bunker. Then they have to go with a long-iron shot. The green is about half the size of a small room, and the top half of the putting surface is so severe it's almost impossible to putt.

They've made many other changes over the years, adding bunkers, lengthening holes. Most of the changes have been good, but I don't agree with the idea of making them. In the first place, Augusta National was designed as a putter's course and a second-shot course, which means that if you're going to have a chance to putt well on the treacherous greens, you must put your ball in certain places on those greens. So I don't feel that longer holes and extra bunkers are really needed.

More important, the course was conceived by Bobby Jones, and his ideas, his dreams, his whole being went into it. When it was done and the first shot was fired, that was the course he wanted. I'm not in favor of changing a great old course, particularly one that Bobby Jones created. His stature in the game makes that course hallowed ground, as far as I'm concerned, and I can't imagine anyone being presumptuous enough to change it just because the players' equipment and skills have improved over the years.

If you want a different golf course, go build one, longer and tougher. But don't make Augusta National into Augusta National Jr. If you want to be traditional—and nobody is more of a traditionalist than I am—then preserving a great golf course is a good place to start.

November 1980

Dave Marr

Missing old friends and good times

Dave Marr (Photo: Dom Furore)

Even though I still make my living from golf, it's not the same as when I was a young guy struggling to survive on the pro tour. And frankly, although I'm making more money now than I ever dreamed I could make, I miss those old days.

Maybe we all have this problem as we grow older, but it seems we never see enough of the good friends we made when we were younger. I used to spend a lot of time on the tour with Johnny Pott, Tommy Jacobs, Jim Ferree and Mason Rudolph, and I miss them. They are friends I feel I will have for life, and yet we never seem to get together.

Everybody seems to be in such a hurry now and maybe that's why I even miss the time I used to spend driving between tournaments. I loved driving to Los Angeles for the first tournament and wondering what kind of year I was going to have. I used to leave Houston the day after Christmas and I'd stop at the snake farms and alligator farms and at Judge Roy Bean's place in west Texas—I really enjoy seeing the country. Now I fly everywhere and no longer seem to have time to reflect on things.

After Los Angeles we always drove up to the Monterey Peninsula for the Bing Crosby tournament, and that was nice. I really miss Bing and the way his tournament used to be. There was a place at the lodge called the "Snake Pit" where we would go to play cards or just kibitz. Bing might drop in and you would see guys like Don Drysdale, Don Cherry, Fred MacMurray, Phil Harris. Harris was the ringleader and there was always action when he was around. But the tournament has got so big and seems to have lost a lot of its informality. Or maybe it's just that I've got older and there's a bunch of new guys there that I don't know.

The bigness and the loss of informality remind me of a point I've wanted to make for a long time. People talk about today's pros being so serious because of the huge amounts of money they play for, but I think it should work the other way. Today, with all the money that's available, the players ought to be more relaxed.

In any case, it seems to me we were more relaxed than today's players. Also, the tour veterans used to take more time to help the struggling young guys. I can remember when I was just a rookie, listening to Pete Cooper and Doug Ford talk about life on the tour and what a young player should do to take care of himself. I don't believe that much of this goes on now. Nobody takes the time.

> *Some days I felt like Superman and other days I found I was made of Jell-O.*

One man who always took the time was Jimmy Demaret, who would kind of take me under his wing at the Texas Open when it was at Brackenridge Park in San Antonio. That's where Mike Souchak set the record of 257 in 1955, and I really miss that old course. Another guy who was nice to me was Lloyd Mangrum. He used to call me "Cuz," because Jack Burke was my cousin and Lloyd and Jack were good friends.

I also miss the competition quite a bit. I love to compete and I always liked finding out what I was made of. Some days I felt like Superman and other days I found I was made of Jell-O, which was a little discouraging, but at least I learned something about myself. I was on my own from the beginning, with no sponsor, and I had to find out quickly whether I could play.

Believe it or not, I miss qualifying for the U.S. Open. I miss the major championships, and to me the 36 holes of qualifying for the Open was the most exciting day of the year. That's the most nervous I have ever been, because it was so important to me to play in the Open. I've harped on this theme before, but I really can't understand those good players who don't enter the Open. Some people accuse Nicklaus of putting too much importance on the majors, but that's nothing new. I'm sure Harry Vardon felt it was pretty important when he won the British Open around the turn of the century, too.

There are certain pairings I miss, too. One of the greatest days I ever had in golf was playing the last round of the 1964 Masters with Arnold Palmer. He was only 34 then, and who would have thought it was the last major he was going to win? I miss the fun of playing practice rounds with Arnold or going to Augusta and playing a practice round with Ben Hogan, who was still competing then.

I guess what I miss most of all is how nice a lot of people were to me. In 1960, my first year on the tour, my daughter Elizabeth was born prematurely and we had to rent an apartment in Los Angeles for the six weeks she was in the hospital. The people at Riviera and Bel-Air were kind enough to let me play their courses as often as I wanted even though I was just a rabbit on the tour.

During that time we got to be good friends with James Garner, who was out of work because of a contract dispute with his studio. We played a lot of golf together and he used to come over to our house in the evening for potluck dinner. When we finally got Elizabeth home, we opened the door one morning and there was a little stuffed animal Garner had sent to her.

Twenty years isn't so long, but sometimes those days seem far away—and I miss them.

Peter Dobereiner

Will Greg Norman reach superstardom?

Peter Dobereiner (Photo: Dom Furore)

I have only once seen him in total command of his swing.

According to the statistics of foreign prejudice, the average Australian is a potbellied drunk with bad teeth. According to the view that Australians hold of themselves, the average Australian is seven feet tall, stomach hard and flat as a spade, built like a brick outhouse with muscles abulge, dazzling white grain against mahogany complexion and clipped, flaxen hair. Furthermore, he is a two-fisted, spit-in-your-eye, down-to-earth cove with none of our effete English intellectual pretensions, and the sheila has not been born who can resist his vibrant sexual magnetism for more than seven seconds.

The mythology of this Australian stereotype is sustained by a tiny fraction of the population, of which Greg Norman is a Class A member. He is a slight disappointment because he does not have the essential Australian coarseness of a Jack Newton, who tends to order his steak with the instruction: "Just cut off its horns, wash it off and serve it up." And Norman does not stay up until 2 every morning drinking 20 pints of ice-cold lager and emphasizing his points of view with lusty punches to the face of anyone who voices a contrary opinion.

Otherwise., Norman is an Aussie's ideal of an ideal Aussie, 6-1, hair the color of whipped cream (inherited from his Nordic mother) and shoulders so wide that he has to edge sideways through the average doorway.

He is deeply religious, which in Australian terms means that he is a sports freak. As a boy growing up near Moreton Bay on the eastern coast of Australia he played them all: tennis, cricket, soccer, rugby and that curious amalgamation of the two football games plus a liberal seasoning of kung fu, Australian Rules. He also boxed and swam and surfed and it was a reluctant 16-year-old who was pressed into service to caddie for his 3-handicap mother in a competition. He thought golf a sissy game and it was only curiosity after the round that prompted him to try a few shots for himself on the range. He nailed one shot and that is all it takes.

In less than two years he was down to scratch and facing a quandary. His ambition was to be a fighter pilot, a properly macho occupation, and he had passed his examinations for flying training. His father went with him for the enrollment formalities into the Royal Australian Air Force. A squadron leader had the enlistment papers prepared and Norman had his hand poised to sign when he tossed down the pen and announced: "No, I am going to be a pro golfer." For better or worse the choice was made and he became an assistant, winning his fifth tournament as a pro (better) and then blowing sky high when he was paired with his idol, Jack Nicklaus, in the Australian Open (worse).

On balance it was a highly promising start to his career, and it was at this time he established the origins of his nickname The Great White Shark. Like Nicklaus, he relaxed from golf by deep-sea fishing and there are few better waters than off the Brisbane coast.

It annoyed Norman that, having hooked into a big one, his catch would be devoured by a passing shark just as he was reeling it to the surface. He bought a government army surplus rifle. Almost every male over the age of 55 within the British Commonwealth is familiar with the Short Lee Enfield rifle, the standard infantry weapon for half a century or so. (Even today I swear I could dismantle and reassemble it blindfolded, naming each part down to the rear spring retaining pawl. My left palm still tingles at the mention of the Short Lee Enfield because as a young cadet I was detailed for the ceremonial party for the funeral of a Lord of the Admiralty. We must have slapped those magazines a thousand times in rehearsing our "Present Arms" because the admiral inconsiderately took two weeks to die.) Norman's association with the Short Lee Enfield was less formal. When he saw a shark gliding into the vicinity of his boat as he was hauling in a catch he would give the creature five rounds of .303, rapid fire, and that way he began to land more than dismembered fish heads.

In his first full year as a tournament pro Norman made the top five of the Australian order of merit table and that qualified him to compete on the European circuit. He arrived in Britain in 1977, having won a Japanese tournament en route, and immediately established himself as one of the most exciting young players on the tour. His attitude was modest and mature. "I am in no hurry," he told me. "I regard Europe as my apprenticeship as a golfer. Once I have learned to win here there will be time enough to start thinking about major championships."

For the next five years professional golf in Europe provided fascinating competition. The fledgling European circuit was raw in many ways, compared with the richly endowed and efficient U.S. Tour. There was no great depth of playing quality, but the annual battle for supremacy was intense—and the golf, I insist, was often the best being played on any circuit in the world. As well as Norman there were the emerging Severiano Ballesteros, Nick Faldo, Sandy Lyle and Bernhard Langer, with classy but veteran players such as Neil Coles and Christy O'Connor to pit experience against youthful zeal. Norman regularly won two or three tournaments a year, although only once, in 1982, did he take the title of European No. I. His international reputation, founded on two victories in the World Match-Play championship, was enhanced by successes in his increasing world travels, with wins in Fiji and Hong Kong and dominance of his home circuit (Australian Open, 1980; Australian Masters, 1981, 1983).

Norman is a streak player, as he again demonstrated with his winning the Kemper, finishing second in the U.S. Open and winning the Canadian Open in successive outings. He is no slouch at any time, with his booming drives (averaging 274.4 yards on the PGA Tour stats), but when every department of his game clicks into place he is unbeatable. I have only once seen him in total command of his swing, when he walked away with the 1980 French Open at St. Cloud and made nonsense of the par 5s with driver and 9-iron.

I will wager my Scottish castle that Norman will win at least one major championship. Beyond that I would prefer to hedge my bets.

You could have put Vardon, Jones, Hagen, Nelson, Hogan, Nicklaus and Watson against him that week and they would have been powerless to match his sublime play. Last year he decided that he was ready for America and had already taken unto himself an American wife and sired a daughter. He made a leisurely journey to the United States, winning four successive overseas tournaments on the way to Bay Hill, Fla., where he has a house on Arnold Palmer's up-market development. Norman was a revelation to the cloistered world of American golf that tends to believe foreigners are incapable of playing golf until the ritual laying on of hands by Commissioner Deane Beman and the awarding of a PGA Tour card.

At the Bay Hill Classic Norman tied for first and was beaten, by an absurdly rash putt and Mike Nicolette, in the sudden-death playoff. It is always a matter of some delicacy knowing what to say to a friend who has just blown a winning chance, and a long friendship with Ben Crenshaw has not taught me a diplomatic turn of phrase for the occasion. My trepidation was groundless. Norman sought me out and said, "Come and look at something." The something was a blood-red Ferrari that had just been delivered, an event of much greater importance in Norman's mind than losing a playoff. He is an unabashed car perv, in his phrase, and his stable contains two Rolls Royces plus sundry high-performance beasts. On this occasion my envy was expressed in a caustic question about what shall it profit a man to own a Ferrari in a country with a 55 mile-per-hour speed limit, not counting a reasonable tolerance on the part of the highway patrol.

Norman completely ruined my day by saying that

he had an arrangement with a racetrack and could give his hairy monsters their head anytime he liked. My guess is that he will soon start flying lessons.

A few more guesses are in order at this stage of his career as, at the age of 29, he is poised at the crossroads. Will he take the Pilgrim's Progress path to greatness and spiritual fulfillment? Or will he be diverted into the lush byways of winning millions of dollars without causing a flutter among the record books? Well, I will wager my Scottish castle, my Black Forest shooting estate and 20 of my most attentive handmaidens that he will win at least one major championship. Beyond that I would prefer to hedge my bets. It all depends on that core of ambition and determination residing so deeply within him that even he cannot unravel its secrets.

Those who know him best are equally ambivalent about his potential. Every golfer respects his ability, but, in the rarified level that we are discussing, technique is 10 percent of the game, at most. Australians are notoriously reluctant to find a good word about their fellow countrymen. Peter Thomson, five times the British Open champion, has serious reservations about Greg Norman's capacity to go all the way in golf. Jack Newton refers to him as "The Great White Fish Finger." Graham Marsh, on the other hand, believes that Norman will improve further and become a truly dominant figure. It is, of course, best that we do not know, because life would be arid without the mystery. It is enough to know of the rich rewards to be had from watching Norman's progress, win or lose.

The young Norman in 1983, his first year on the PGA Tour. (Photo: Stephen Szurlej)

February 1987

Peter Thomson

Looking for golf courses my grandma would love

Peter Thomson (Photo: Stephen Szurlej)

You don't have to be a weatherman to notice a change in the climate. Just read Jack Renner's quote about the U.S. Open course at Shinnecock Hills last year.

"I'll tell you what's great about Shinnecock," he said. "No railroad ties and no greens in the middle of lakes. There are choices here, options. The modern golf course removes strategy and options from the game of golf. It's a defensive game. You just try to keep away from trouble. Here there are three or four ways to play most holes."

Does this mean what I think it does? Have railroad ties and greens in lakes had their day? Passed out of fashion like Bermuda shorts and fins on Cadillacs? Are the cold, gray skies of depressing winter giving way to warmer days of celebration and good fun?

I, for one, hope so.

The truth is, the TPC at Sawgrass and courses of that ilk are hell to play. Such courses were designed and built for the amusement of spectators, not for the pleasure of playing.

They were born in commercialism as part of Commissioner Deane Beman's bold plan to make the PGA Tour self-sufficient by the staging of tour events in its own stadiums. Built into these arenas are the features that make for colorful television—the horror stretches of water and wilderness, railroad ties and savage sawgrass, areas wherein it might be hoped a front-runner will come to grief to the sniggers of the multitudes watching from the high mounds. The mixture of these patterns makes for the photogenic aspect that magazines and calendars lap up, the reflection of green grass and trees in calm blue water. (Out West you can even have snowcapped mountains mirrored in the hazards.) It sells a load of real estate but has little to do with golf and, more often than not, gets in the way.

What we are seeing in these courses are not practical innovations, but distortions of dimensions—not works of art but caricatures.

The whole sorry business stems on the one hand from the silly attempt to keep winning scores up at around par for four rounds, about 288. Winning scores in the early 1900s were near the 300 mark, but they steadily declined with the advancement in clubs and balls and the tremendous improvement in course maintenance.

Winners of major championships, in this day and age, should crack the 270 mark, but for some nonsensical reason the game's authorities decided that scores should hold at the par mark. To counter low scores came the mucking about with the course, distorting its length and width, and the conversion of non-hazard areas into "penalty zones." The result of this misguided policy is the present-day competition for the most outrageous and bizarre.

On the other hand is the modern axiom that a golf course will sell real estate, and that the more notorious the course the higher the surrounding land prices. The trick for the developer, as devised through his architect, is to build something that is photogenically stunning, however impractical, extravagant or absurd. Never mind the golfer, that most gullible of all citizens. "Just get us into the color magazines" seems to be the working theory.

The effect of this kind of marketing is to lead the game of golf down the garden path. By pounding out the message endlessly that golf is a gambit of tortures, and that it is somehow plebeian to play an entire round of golf with one ball, commercialism is doing a great harm to a noble sport.

These trends have been raging now for two decades or more. The consumer has had precious little say in the matter. The free market has not been in effect, he has been caught up in a mad competition of propaganda.

Yet there is a ray of hope. There are signs of a change of season as a few brave professionals like Jack Renner are beginning to speak their minds. But the little man should be heard from, too. Not the land speculator or investor, but the golfer who loves the game.

As for me, when I first took to journalism, my kind but stern mentor laid down the principle that if my grandmother couldn't understand what I was writing about, it was a lousy piece of composition. I've come to carry this along into golf architecture. If my grandma can't play it, it has to be a lousy course.

> *The message that golf is a gambit of tortures is doing a great harm to a noble sport.*

No. 17 at TPC Sawgrass—easy on the eyes and tough on the scores. (Photo: Stephen Szurlej)

Charles Price

The last days of Bobby Jones

Charles Price

By 1968 Bobby Jones' health had slipped from the terrible to the abysmal. His eyes were bloodshot from the spinal disease he had endured for 20 years, his arms atrophied to the size of a schoolgirl's, his ankles so swollen by body fluids they spilled over the edges of his shoes. This was a man who could once effortlessly drive a golf ball a sixth of a mile.

Still, he had not lost the humor with which he viewed so many things, often at his own expense. Confined to a wheelchair all day, he had to be put into and taken out of bed by a male nurse, who was the size of a linebacker. "He handles me like a flapjack," Bob said by way of complimenting the man when he introduced us. Then he chuckled. Bob laughed a lot, although never out loud, and he laughed during his last days mostly to put people at their ease, especially strangers. Meeting him then for the first time could be a shock, and Bob knew it. But he insisted on shaking hands with everybody, painful as it had to be, excruciating if his hand were squeezed. But it was part of the price he insisted on paying for having been Bobby Jones, the one and only.

Having covered the Masters for 20 years, I had become his companion during it by a choice that was as much his as mine. Those years became the most fulfilling of the 44 I have been writing about golf. I've never written about them, and I don't know why. In looking back, that period in his life seems as towering as the Grand Slam.

For 10 years we had been collaborating on a number of writing chores. Since I then covered the tournament for Newsweek and wrote a column elsewhere that appeared only monthly, I had the time to act as his legman. He had long been unable to watch the Masters even from a golf cart, and his son, Bob III, was on the course most of the day as an official. I became somebody who could bring younger players and foreign writers to him, someone with whom he could pass off a casual observation about the tournament on TV without fear of explaining himself, someone he could share lunch with now that he no longer would eat where people could watch him.

We would sit at a card table next to a window in his cottage that overlooked the 10th tee. A curtain prevented spectators from looking in but allowed Bob to peer out. He had the same thing for lunch almost every day. First there'd be a couple of dry martinis, which he drank with relish but scolded himself for. "I shouldn't be drinking these," he said to me one day. "They don't mix with my medicine." The martinis would be followed by a hamburger, in part because he liked hamburgers but mainly because he could no longer cut meat and disliked anyone cutting it for him, so gnarled had his fingers become.

Bob smoked more than two packs of cigarettes a day, sometimes in chain fashion, and they were lined on the card table in neat rows for him, each in a holder so he would not accidentally burn himself. An elegant lighter, covered in leather, sat ready. All he had to do was push down a lever that any child could. But even that was becoming an effort. So, with as much nonchalance as I could devise, I'd pull out a cigarette of my own, thereby giving me the excuse to light his.

He had been a man who never looked as though he needed help, even when he was dying, and it was part of Bob's magnificence that his disablement evoked admiration more than pity. Those cigarettes were actually a token of his will to live, not the other way around. One day he left me speechless after I lighted one for him. "I've got to give these things up," he said. "They're bad for me."

I had long known what was wrong with Bob, and he asked me not to write about it while he was still alive. "People think I've got arthritis," he said. "Let's let it go at that."

Actually, he had what is known as syringomyelia—pronounced *sir-ringgo-my-ale-ee-ah*—an extremely rare disease of the central nervous system. It took eight years to diagnose. Researching it, I found neurosurgeons who had never even seen a case. "And I guess," one told me, "that I've treated 20 cases of amyotrophic lateral sclerosis, or Lou Gehrig's disease."

Syringomyelia is a disease you are born with, although it is not hereditary and does not manifest itself until much later in life. Bob had been 46 when his symptoms first appeared. His right leg began to pain him, then the right arm. Eventually, he lost the use of both legs. For a while he got around on elbow crutches, then a "walker" and finally a wheelchair. Then his whole body began to waste away.

Even in that condition he went to his law offices in Atlanta every day he could, chiefly to keep from vegetating. The disease had no effect on his mind.

Indeed, the complex nature of it is such that it doesn't kill you, as it didn't Bob. Clinically, he died from an aneurysm, but actually from the exhaustion of

> *He never looked as though he needed help, and it was part of Bob's magnificence that his disablement evoked admiration more than pity.*

just trying to stay alive. "If I'd known it was going to be this easy," he told Jean Marshall, his secretary, days before he died, "I'd have gone a long time ago."

Bob and I first collaborated in 1959, when he agreed to rewrite some old instructional articles for Golf Magazine, of which I was the first editor. Three years later he wrote the introduction to a history I had written with his help, which by itself has been widely quoted, especially his line about golfers sometimes being "the dogged victims of inexorable fate."

A few years later another book of mine had been dedicated to him, and we had talked about golf at such length and in such detail that I suggested he put together a book from his old newspaper columns and magazine articles. He had written hundreds, not a word of them ghosted. Bob was reluctant, what with his flagging energies, but I convinced him it had to be done. People would be interested in what he had to say about golf a century after he was gone, or long after every other golfer's thoughts had left the public yawning. His ideas were so eloquent, so down to earth, so free of technicalisms. He agreed when I volunteered to collect them, cut out what was dated, and dovetail the rest into logical order. These were words Bob himself hadn't read for 30 years or more.

Like a lot of people who are good at it, Bob did not like to write, only to have written. Notwithstanding, he threw himself into the project. My manuscript was retyped by Mrs. Marshall into triple-spaced pages so Bob could mark between the lines any changes he wanted, which he did with a ballpoint pen inserted into a rubber ball he could grip with his crippled fingers.

Sitting with me across from his desk in Atlanta, he'd study every word, pushing each page aside only after he was sure of what he wanted to leave to posterity. I'd note the changes, all the while finding excuses to light his cigarettes. When he was finished, I'd take the changes back to New York, where I lived, while he pondered what was still to be done. The whole process took almost a year. Bob was the most honestly modest golf champion ever. But he was well aware of, and conscientious about, his unique role in the game's history.

The book became *Bobby Jones on Golf* (Doubleday & Co., 1966) and I was pleased to learn from Mrs. Marshall that work on it had given Bob a new purpose in life. For the first time in years he was doing something creative and constructive, something only he could do. That's what Bobby Jones was all about. He did things in golf only he could do, of which the Grand Slam is just a monument.

At this stage in our friendship, it had become apparent that Bob was passing some sort of torch to me.

I was a writer and I represented the generation immediately after his. He wanted to leave somebody behind who could straighten out the facts of his life if they had to be, as O.B. Keeler did when Bob was at the peak of his career. There was no other explanation for all he told me about that career. Bob not only seldom reminisced, he disliked to.

We were joined once in his cottage by two former U.S. Open champions from his era. Bob did all the listening, and I could see he was getting restless. Finally, he made an announcement. "I wonder if you fellows would excuse us," he said. "Charley and I have something to discuss that can't wait." Minutes went by after they left. I had to come out and ask him what it was he wanted to discuss. "Oh, nothing," he said. "I just can't stand sitting around talking about ancient history."

Yet he would with me, all day long, with the Masters Tournament taking place just outside his window. Armed with his confidence in me, I approached him about doing a film on his life, concentrating on the Grand Slam, the drama of which had never been explained to my satisfaction. He was reluctant, as I knew he would be. But I pointed out the inevitable. If he didn't do the film, somebody else would eventually, disarticulating it with the sort of hyperbole he hated and which he made such an effort to avoid in his own accounts.

So he agreed. Somehow word got out before we had hardly begun and we were approached by potential producers, one of whom conferred with us in Atlanta. But the project never got much further. Bob became too exhausted to continue. He never came back to the Masters and died in December 1971.

I was abroad at the time. When I got home, there was a package from Bob's office for me. In it was that lighter with which I had lit so many of his cigarettes, trying to circumvent his pride. There was a note from him, typed by Mrs. Marshall but signed by Bob in his scrawl. "You weren't fooling me a bit," it said.

> Bob was the most honestly modest golf champion ever. But he was well aware of, and conscientious about, his unique role in the game's history.

Bobby Jones presiding at the head of the table at Augusta National with a young Jack Nicklaus. (Photo: Morgan Fitz)

December 1994

Dan Jenkins

Why I hate family golf

Dan Jenkins (Photo: Jim Moriarty)

Not long ago I had the unforgettable experience of trying to play 18 holes behind one of those foursomes known as a plague on earth when it is not known as the Family That Golfs Together.

I don't believe I've ever taken vacations that long, frankly.

Upon finishing the round, I limped into the men's grill and asked the bartender for a pen and notepad. While trying to calm my rage with a few cocktails, I thought it would be therapeutic to make a list of things I would rather do in this lifetime than play another round of golf directly behind such lovers of the game.

I decided I would rather:

1. Eat a veggie burger.
2. Lift heavy furniture.
3. Attend a political rally.
4. Drive across country without smoking.
5. Watch a game show on TV.
6. Listen to accordion music.
7. Discuss wine.
8. Read Proust.
9. Go to a rock concert.
10. Try to deal with "frozen cursor syndrome" on my word processor.

I play fast, of course. I don't line up putts from four sides, three sides or even two sides in most cases. I don't "sweep" the line, figuring that any object the ball may hit along the way will give it a better chance of going in the cup than my putting stroke.

The only time I walk around with a towel is after I've showered. I might add that the only time I plumb-bob is when I'm conducting a symphony.

My club selection never causes any delays. I know what I'm going to hit before I get to my ball, because I've been there many times before, or in a location just like it.

(Art: Gahan Wilson)

What's more, I can hit two mulligans while my companions are improving their lies.

I am among those who firmly believe that a round of golf should not take more than 3 ½ hours, four at the most. Anything longer than that is not a round of golf, it's life in Albania.

So now I'm out there behind the Family That Golfs Together, all of whom are wearing shorts and anklets, naturally.

Macho Dad has a five-piece swing that strongly suggests he can't possibly play below a 22-handicap, but he insists on hitting from the tips, from so far back his takeaway runs a serious risk of getting caught in the crape myrtle.

Never-ready Mom wears a wide-brimmed straw hat and her golf glove features a handy little wrist compartment for her wooden tee.

Idiot Teenage Son has his baseball cap on backward and grips the driver as he would a sledgehammer. He is here at gunpoint. He wanted to be at the beach today with his pals, drinking beer, doing drugs and falling madly in love with the third runner-up in the Miss Cerebral contest.

Sullen Teenage Daughter is also here at gunpoint. She would rather be locked in her room at home, chain-smoking cigarettes and listening to gangster rap.

I will only describe one hole.

Macho Dad stripes it down the middle, about 167, bringing it in from left to right. He struts to the cart, puts the big furry-animal head cover back on his driver.

From the blues, Idiot Teenage Son swings for the centerfield fence but hits a trickling 30-yard bunt. He trots after the ball, brings it back, tees it up again. Macho Dad goes over to give him a lesson. He points the V's, firms up the left side, adjusts the stance. This time Idiot Teenage Son swings for the rightfield wall but hits a toe-job pop-up shot that barely clears the ball washer. He's not happy to learn he'll have to play that one.

Sullen Teenage Daughter goes first at the reds. After four whiffs and a yard of turf plowed up, she hits one 10 yards, although the club sails 15 yards. She retires to the cart with a shrug. Never-ready Mom takes six tedious practice swings, then smother-tops it into the rough, where they all enjoy an Easter egg hunt.

After what seems like an hour later, the Family That Golfs Together is finally on the green where Never-ready Mom stands over a one-foot putt, forever. Members of my group are now hollering such things as, "Pull the trigger, Mom!"

Myself, I'm playing Scarlett O'Hara, except I'm holding a golf ball instead of a turnip. But my fist is raised to the sky, and I'm saying, "As God is my witness, I'll never play golf on Sunday again!"

123

Tom Callahan

We know who they are

Tom Callahan

> *On the amateur level, the club level, the muny level, any level, "We know who they are" is the truest fact of golf, and maybe the only conforming law.*

Nothing has been said this year in golf or in sports that rings with a sharper truth than the five words: "We know who they are."

To a leading question in a dinner setting, Tom Watson acknowledged in late winter that there were cheaters on the PGA Tour. "The game is a game of integrity," he told an Australian interviewer in Melbourne, "but you are talking about money and you're talking about livelihoods."

Invited to name names, Watson said icily, "We know who they are."

As if candor were calumny, Tom was slammed in the U.S. for once again sticking his blue nose where it wasn't wanted. But the slammers lost momentum when Nick Price told The Fort Lauderdale Sun-Sentinel, "There are two [players] I know of for sure on tour who cheat, and many others who I have come across in my travels. But once you do it, the guys all know who you are. Forever."

While PGA patriots were extolling Jeff Sluman's honesty at Bay Hill, Ben Crenshaw, of all gentle people, was saying, "Cheating is the absolute worst thing on tour, period. It's like the people who play golf are one big family, and once you get cast out of the family, there's no way to get back in."

If that were literally so, Watson and Gary Player, Greg Norman and Mark McCumber, Nick Faldo and Sandy Lyle, Seve Ballesteros and Paul Azinger—and all the other jousters who have tilted bloodily over honor—would never know peace in each other's company. (A few never will.) But time is a funny thing.

Many U.S. Opens ago, a large Californian named Lon Hinkle seemed to hang over young Ballesteros like a gargoyle at every green. Asked about it afterward, Hinkle said in a measured tone: "He is a great young player, but he is going to have to learn to mark his ball like a professional." Evidently, he did.

There's an American star on tour who, long ago, in the crucible of the Q school, left a birdie putt on the lip and angrily whiffed the tap-in. With a face whiter than Gold Medal flour, he proceeded to the next tee and drove off as if it were still his honor.

His two playing partners were so stunned that they said nothing. He won his card by more than a shot; all three qualified. But, late that night, the other two got to talking, and drinking, and one went to the telephone. "I just want you to know," he said in the alcoholic mist, "that I saw what happened out there today and you'll have to live with it the rest of your life." Only one word came back in rebuttal, softly: "OK."

Maybe a higher sense of obligation, some extra quality of effort, comes out of such a lonely start. Because, through the years, the player in question has gained the respect of the industry. But there are still whispers. Perhaps that's what Watson, Price and Crenshaw mean.

On the amateur level, the club level, the muny level, any level, "We know who they are" is the truest fact of golf, and maybe the only conforming law.

An old Kentucky newsman, Mike Barry, used to announce on the first tee, "You fellows go ahead and play whatever game you want. I'll be playing golf." In other words, he wouldn't be hitting a mulligan at No. 1, bumping his ball in the fairway or moving his coin to avoid an abrasion ("teeing it up on the green," as Jim Colbert calls that popular practice).

By the average hacker's code, none of these qualify as cheating, but they set a tone. Barry, who almost never broke 100, had a theory about amateur cheaters that is passed along here not for moralizing purposes but as practical advice.

Mike was convinced the cheaters weren't after his $2; they just wanted to shoot 88 instead of 93. But their machinations actually cost them strokes, and not just because teeing up a ball to miss a 3-wood is a ridiculous alternative to an honest 8-iron!

Besides defaulting on their own confidence, they were throwing away golf's most mysterious benefit, the springboard disguised as setback.

Jack Nicklaus will testify that he may never have won the 1986 Masters without a spike mark that popped up in his path at 12. That bogey meant more than any par to his round. It was what propelled him on.

Barry lived a rich life and died well, surrounded by family. In a bonus of timing, he narrowly outlived his archrival, the well-known governor, baseball commissioner and scoundrel, Happy Chandler.

When someone at Barry's bedside recalled Ol' Hap had "lied in state" at the Capitol, Mike came to for just an instant to say, "He lied in every state he ever went into." Then he settled back to sleep, the blissful sleep of those who always played the ball down.

Jerry Tarde

The man who stood up to Arnie and Jack

Jerry Tarde

Hardin stood steadfast against it all. He once famously warned that his members would never allow a Pizza Hut Masters; "We'll shut her down first," he said.

The late Hord Hardin was known to the world for those endless minutes he spent, green jacketed and glassy-eyed, interviewing the Masters winner on television each year as the Augusta National Golf Club chairman.

"Seve, let me ask you," he started, in 1980. "A lot of people have asked me . . . how tall are you?"

"Six foot," replied Ballesteros.

"Even six foot?" Hord followed up.

"Yes," said Seve, squinting now.

Hord leaned in. "What do you weigh?" he asked.

The scene was out of a Monty Python movie, but only years later did I realize the full extent of Hardin's panic. "I knew Seve was a handsome fellow," Hord said. "I was building up to asking him about girls. But I got halfway through asking about height and weight when I realized maybe he'd say, 'I don't like girls. I like guys.' So I sort of froze up. I always realized how terrible I was at those things."

Despite his stone-faced demeanor, Hardin had a wry, self-deprecating sense of humor. And only Sam Snead was his equal for telling jokes unsuitable for mixed company.

I always thought, in fact, that Sam was his spiritual kin. Hord had been an extraordinary athlete, too. Besides qualifying four times for the U.S. Amateur and once, in 1952, for the U.S. Open, he captained the baseball team and quarterbacked the football team at Washington University in St. Louis (where he earned his law degree).

Like Sam, he loved a wager and was an absolute thief with the handicap system—a delicate irony for a president of the U.S. Golf Association. In one celebrated incident, he qualified for the U.S. Amateur, which requires a 3-handicap or better, while entering a calcutta tournament in Pennsylvania with an 8-handicap. In recent years as an 18-handicapper in the AT&T Pebble Beach National Pro-Am, he was still making the USGA squirm.

Hardin was a tough old bird who knew golf as both a competitor and an administrator. Into his late 70s he could knock it to the bottom of the hill at Augusta's No. 9, and he had a lawyer's command of the rule book (although his business actually was banking). He was known as a fast golfer who prided himself on playing through his fellow members at a gallop; "I part 'em like the Red Sea," he liked to say.

As chairman from 1980 to 1991, he was totally dedicated to the Masters and Augusta National and not once flinched from his principles. Sometimes unpopular among members or staff or tour pros, he ruled the club with a stern efficiency and never backed down from a fight.

His battles with Deane Beman were legend as the PGA Tour commissioner annually contrived to expand the small Masters field. In Hardin's USGA days, he once even went toe to toe with Arnold Palmer when Palmer advocated changing the rules to allow 16 clubs. Arnie said, "Look in every member's bag; they've got more than 14." Hord replied, "Arnold, if you want to start running the game by what your members do, we'll be smoothing out footprints, tamping down spike marks and rolling the ball out of divot holes." And the argument died.

But my favorite Hord exchange involved an interview Jack Nicklaus did that was carried by CNN on the Tuesday prior to that fateful 1986 Masters he was to win so dramatically as a near-senior. Disgusted with his putting in the practice rounds, Nicklaus told the reporter he couldn't believe they had verticut the greens during Masters week. This was the equivalent of accusing a barber of cutting your hair with pinking shears.

The Masters committee was so upset by Nicklaus' comments that several members asked Hardin to speak to Jack. "No," replied Hord. "He's playing lousy and he'll just blame it on us."

The following month, Hord, who was a captain of Nicklaus' Memorial Tournament, skipped the event as an unspoken rebuff to Jack. The next time they met was at the British Open in the lobby of the Turnberry Hotel. Nicklaus asked why he hadn't come to the Memorial. "I'll tell you, but not in public," Hardin said. So they went to Nicklaus' hotel room, where Hord confronted him. Nicklaus denied making the comments.

"We got tapes to prove it," Hardin said, bluffing. "Jack, you may be the finest golfer ever to play the game, you are a great father and a real gentleman," he said, "but you are the most egotistical sonofabitch I ever met."

Last April, Hardin sat in the modest suite that bears his name at Augusta National and remembered this conversation from a decade ago with his typical unswerving certainty. At age 84 he recalled, "I sort of waited, figuring he might come at me. I was ready. But Jack said, 'Hord, you're right. I apologize.' "

(continued on next page)

(Jerry Tarde continued)

Hardin was the hero of all his own stories, but in your obituary, you are entitled to be. He died last August as one of the game's great men. He ran the Masters during Wall Street's decade of greed when corporate sponsors discovered pro golf and sent the tour down a commercial-interrupted path from which it has not recovered.

Golf pros used to arrive in cabs and wear neckties; now they drive Ferraris but don't own a suit. A quiet game that Palmer played hatless in a plain, white shirt now is typified by Corey Pavin sporting five different logos: left sleeve, left breast, right breast, right sleeve and hat.

Hardin stood steadfast against it all. He once famously warned that his members would never allow a Pizza Hut Masters, "We'll shut her down first," he said.

It was one thing to be anticommercial when there wasn't any money at stake in the days of Cliff Roberts. It was quite another to say no when the decimal point kept moving right. As the USGA and the PGA Tour

gave way, Hardin alone kept the barbarians at the gate on Washington Road.

He may be remembered for a few of the innovations he brought, most notably Augusta's bold switch to bent-grass greens, but the game is indebted to Hord Hardin for drawing a single line in the sand. Golf may be for sale everywhere, he said, but not at the Masters.

Hord Hardin in his office at Augusta National. (Photo: Stephen Szurlej)

October 1998

David Owen

Golf and discipline

David Owen

My driver had been misbehaving, so I put it in time-out. I didn't make it sit on the stairs, the way I used to do with my kids, but I moved it to the back of my bag and pulled the head cover down tight. "I know you don't like holes with out-of-bounds on the right," I said in the calmest voice I could manage, "but you and I both need to think about what just happened." Some guys will abuse a driver that has launched a ball into an adjacent county, but, believe me, the short-fuse approach doesn't work with golf clubs any better than it does with children. You can't straighten a slice with violence and fear.

I don't yell at my ball when it's hooking into a hazard. I don't shout "Hit a frog!" or "Get right!" or anything else that golfers shout when their shots are bound for the bottom of the pond. I just stand quietly on the tee with a shattered look on my face, to show that I'm disappointed. If I find my ball in the water, I silently lift it out and dry it off. There is nothing I could say that would change the fact that I am now hitting 3 from

the drop zone, so why say anything at all? Throwing a tantrum would only make matters worse.

Rather than scream at my equipment when it lets me down, I try to praise it when it does something right. As is also true with children, positive reinforcement is a vastly more powerful instrument than shame or humiliation. Most golfers will curse a shank yet stand smugly silent when their 7-iron stripes a ball straight at the pin. How would you like it if your boss took credit for all your best efforts and never spoke to you except to pick on your mistakes? Even when a shot of mine goes wrong, I try to find something encouraging to say: "Wasn't that a little draw I noticed just before you bounced into the parking lot?" "I don't believe you've ever driven it farther into the pond."

The most sensitive issue of all is probably the addition of a new club to the bag. I bought a 60-degree wedge recently and was excited to try it, but I left it parked next to my driver for a couple of rounds, to reassure my old wedges that they were still as important to me as they had always been. Intra-bag rivalry can play havoc with a short game. You need to break in a new club slowly and with unglamorous assignments, such as retrieving balls from creeks or measuring the distance for free drops. By the time I used my new wedge for a real shot, my other irons had long since ceased to feel threatened. As a matter of fact, I'd almost be willing to bet that my sand wedge was relieved. The soft lob over trouble has never been its favorite shot.

The short-fuse approach doesn't work with golf clubs any better than with children. You can't straighten a slice with violence and fear.

November 1998

Dave Kindred

A sudden end to a love story

Dave Kindred (Photo: Stephen Szurlej)

Stuart Appleby
(Photo: ALLSPORT)

All love stories should include a moment when the heroine sends out her 2-iron for repairs. This one does.

Renay White's 2-iron shots flew on a line not much higher than a wallaby's belly. So the Australian teenager decided the stick needed a new shaft. Her coach delivered it to another young player, Stuart Appleby, a country boy off an outback dairy farm who made ends meet by doing the odd club repair.

As it happens, Appleby earlier had admired a small, strong, smiling woman striding with wonderful cockiness through his field of vision. He asked, "Who's that?"

"Renay White," said Ross Herbert, her coach.

"Does she have a boyfriend?"

"No."

So in the summer of 1992, Appleby came to know White as smart, funny, cute—and altogether too much the flirt. She returned the favor by declaring him drop-dead gorgeous with those blue eyes—and what a snob.

Ah, young love, sweet love. She was 19, he was 21, they were confused.

He knew certainly that he wanted to put his hands on her 2-iron. Within minutes, Appleby gave the club back to the coach, who later said, "Stuart was very keen to do a good job on it. Even then he and Renay were using golf to communicate."

Words had failed when they mistook voice for character. She was loud, laughing and sassy. He was quiet, reserved and serious.

But soon enough they understood each other. No flirt, she had been born vivacious. No snob, he came to work focused. They filled in the gaps of each other's personality. On the Australians' tour of U.S. college teams that fall, it was only natural Renay and Stuart were mixed-twosome partners.

And from then on they were always partners, first friends and lovers, then husband and wife who lived by one of life's coolest rules: *Dance as if no one's watching, love as if it's never going to hurt.*

THE STORY REALLY BEGINS ON A BEACH.

After the American matches, Appleby knew he wanted golf and Renay. He had the one but not the other. Then she asked, "Why don't you come visit my place?"

It's a five-hour drive from his home to hers on Australia's southeast coast. Appleby made it in, oh, five minutes. They spent a day together before he went home. His mother soon said, "Stuart, you're moping, you're useless. Go back to Renay's."

This time around, Stuart and Renay swam, took the sun and sat on the beach, where by the end of a week he said words that came so easily they seemed inevitable.

He said, "I've always wanted to meet someone like you. I want to spend the rest of my life with you." She said, "I want to be with you." And she thought, *"Oh, my God, this is it."*

She told her sister, Duean, she had met this guy, she adored him, they spoke each other's thoughts, he made her laugh and he laughed with her.

Renay had been a promising golfer since age 12, a contemporary of Karrie Webb, who became a sensation on the American tour. But, however talented Renay might have been, she no longer cared. She knew her passion for golf ran a distant second to her passion for Stuart.

She would rather be with him than put in the work demanded of a Webb or an Appleby. She sat for hours on practice ranges from Melbourne to Orlando, watching her guy, waiting, talking, sometimes even curling up to sleep on the night's-coming grass. She often caddied for him.

They had great dreams together, and there came a day when he said, "These dreams were fulfilled to a very high extent right up to the time she left us."

From the road, she wrote letters to her parents. She carried a laptop computer and filled cyberspace with laughing e-mail. Any happenings, any new jokes, any sudden realizations would put her on the phone to Duean, determined to keep her sister within five seconds of all the news.

THE NEW YORK TIMES, WEDNESDAY, AUGUST 12, 1998

GOLF

Death Leaves Golfer All Alone on the Course

By CLIFTON BROWN

REDMOND, Wash., Aug. 11 — It is difficult to imagine the grief Stuart Appleby will feel as he competes in the P.G.A. Championship this week.

Appleby's wife, Renay, was killed on July 23 in an accident outside a train station in London.

As Stuart and Renay were unload[ing] ... from a taxi, Renay was ... taxi and an- ... mistaken- ... instead ...

had a huge impact on a lot of people."

Her death has saddened the atmosphere of the year's final major championship, with Appleby's peers determined to help him through his ordeal. Renay was an outstanding golfer and she made many friends among the players when she spent several months as Stuart's caddie during the 1996 season.

Until the accident, Appleby was having the most successful year of his career, with $678,562 in winnings, four top 10 finishes, and a victory at the Kemper Open in June. Appleby's [frien]ds are glad he is back on tour.

... said he would rather be busy ... at home thinking about ... [Ro]bert Allenby, a fellow ... who has known ... [the]y were teen-agers ... [majo]r tournaments. ... him

127

When Stuart drove to the golf course, Renay told him where to turn.

When he dawdled, she said, "Stuey, move your ass," and he did, laughing all the way, a two-hour tiff for some couples, for them two seconds.

When he groused, "I'm putting so bad," she brought light to his eyes by saying, "Bad? Bad? You're putting bloody terrible And, by the way, I love you."

When Stuart played, she walked along by the gallery ropes, wearing a schoolgirl's shorts, T-shirt, sneakers, a funny little cap and a backpack.

When he missed seven cuts in nine tournaments early in 1998, she wrote an e-mail to his coach. Steve Bann, saying, "Stuart's playing so very well. He's about to win." And he won the Kemper Open.

He had become a star at age 27. Through 2½ seasons on the PGA Tour, he had won twice and earned about $2 million. He and Renay bought a house in Isleworth, the Orlando development that is home to Tiger Woods, Mark O'Meara and tennis pro Todd Woodbridge, whose wife Natasha had become Renay's best friend.

Renay won Tash with laughter. Such a happy woman. Todd Woodbridge thought to teach the golfer tennis and heard Renay shout, "Why is it the ball's NOT STILL?"

One evening Tash needed a glass for red wine.

"The crystal," Renay said.

But we're going out in the boat. "So?"

So crystal stemware awarded to the winner of the 1997 Honda Classic found itself in use at a backyard picnic.

This June, Renay sat on her veranda. She had played golf with the Australian pro Jody Adams. Renay's first round in months, a 75, had been so remarkable Adams encouraged her to try the tour.

"No need, Jody," Renay said. "I couldn't possibly be happier with my life."

She and Stuart painted bedrooms, finished a television room and installed a 12-seat dining-room table made of Australian wood. They hung aboriginal art and set out bowls carved from Australian trees. In the kitchen, after workmen cracked a kitchen countertop, Renay re-ordered it. She loved its look, loved to move her hand across its face. It is black Italian marble.

They wanted children. "She'd have been an amazing mother, so loving, so patient," Stuart said.

Tash Woodbridge once whispered to Renay, "I might be pregnant," and Renay punched her arm. "No. No. You can't be. We're getting pregnant at the *same time!*" When the pregnancy test came back negative, Tash said, "We jumped around together like 2-year-olds," so happy were they to still have a chance at simultaneous maternity.

The last time they spoke, Tash heard happiness. Renay and Stuart were on a second honeymoon. From London they would take the next day's train to Paris. So Renay called to ask about Paris. Where to eat, which churches, which museums.

They spoke across the Atlantic for 45 minutes. Then Tash's husband said the girls should get off the phone. He said they could talk another day.

The next day, she died. Struck by a car backing up as she waited with Stuart to leave their taxi at London's hectic Waterloo train station, Renay Appleby died before reaching a hospital. The watch she wore that day, Stuart carries in his pocket today, still on London time.

She wore a chain around her neck with her name on it. He wears it now. On his golf visor is her PGA Tour wife's badge. He touches her pajamas. He looks at the train tickets, London to Paris, and says, "They're the end of the story. Full stop."

The light of joy disappears, emptiness rushes in with its darkness. Stuart Appleby, empty, came to the PGA Championship four days after last taking flowers to Renay's grave. He asked to do a press conference. He came to the dais a haunted man, unshaven, stricken, weeping and brave as hell.

He called Renay "first prize of a raffle in life." He talked about her laughter, her friends. He'll mention her name, he'll talk about the memories. One day when he needs her, she'll be there, a force of belief working for him. It's the little things you miss, a kiss good night, orange juice in the morning, a half-hour's conversation. "They make up someone's life," he said.

Stuart asked that Renay's headstone be carved from the black Italian marble she loved in her kitchen. Her family and Stuart agreed on an epitaph, leaving the last lines to him . . .

In Happiest, Loving Memory of Renay Appleby

We can only hope to pass on your qualities to those we meet

We are blessed to have you in our lives

The memories you have given us will always remain

Adored wife of Stuart

"My best friend forever."

And from then on they were always partners, who lived by one of life's coolest rules: Dance as if no one's watching, love as if it's never going to hurt.

Renay was often seen caddieing for her husband. (Photo: ALLSPORT)

January 1999

Nick Seitz

Legend on the loose

Nick Seitz (Photo: Dom Furore)

> *Snead is golf's rejoinder to John Glenn.*

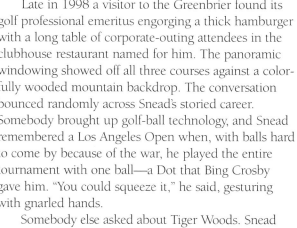

The Slammer today in his namesake golf shop at the Greenbrier Resort. (Photo courtesy of the Greenbrier Resort)

Samuel Jackson Snead was on his way to do a clinic for a group of executives, which would earn him a fast $8,000. But he was waylaid by an eager tourist who proposed a game. Snead's eyes widened and his homey mountain twang went up an octave with interest. All his pigeons are dead, he has lamented, but a live one had just landed.

"How about a hundred dollars?" the old gamester began.

"I need strokes," the pigeon pained.

"I'm 86," said Snead. "We'll play even."

As they headed for the first tee, Robert Harris, the Greenbrier resort's director of golf, interceded to steer Snead back toward the clinic. "He can't resist a game," Harris says. "It's not the money. He was going to forget an $8,000 clinic to play for $100. He just loves a match."

Snead is golf's rejoinder to John Glenn. The Greenbrier, his five-star employer in West Virginia, is a National Historic Landmark. Snead deserves the same designation. This year, like most years, marks a cornucopia of anniversaries that dramatize his career. Fifty years ago, in 1949, he won the first of his three Masters titles, donning the first green coat the tournament presented, previous winner Claude Harmon helping him into it. Forty-five years ago he won his seventh and last major, beating Ben Hogan in a classic Masters playoff. Forty years ago he shot the first 59 in competition. Twenty-five years ago he finished third in the PGA Championship at age 62. Twenty years ago he shot his age in a PGA Tour event. Ten years ago he came out No. 1 in an all-time ranking by the tour. Pause for breath and perspective.

Late in 1998 a visitor to the Greenbrier found its golf professional emeritus engorging a thick hamburger with a long table of corporate-outing attendees in the clubhouse restaurant named for him. The panoramic windowing showed off all three courses against a colorfully wooded mountain backdrop. The conversation bounced randomly across Snead's storied career. Somebody brought up golf-ball technology, and Snead remembered a Los Angeles Open when, with balls hard to come by because of the war, he played the entire tournament with one ball—a Dot that Bing Crosby gave him. "You could squeeze it," he said, gesturing with gnarled hands.

Somebody else asked about Tiger Woods. Snead marveled that Woods won the Masters without three-putting, as he considers Augusta National's greens the most difficult in the world. He is not a fan of recent changes Woods has made in his full swing.

"I don't like the way he's shortened it. He doesn't give himself enough time now, and he moves on it a little, rushing to catch up. He comes with a fast swing. I remember playing with him when he was 6. His swing was whoosh-whoosh then."

The lunch disbanded, and on the way out Snead passed a comely young woman with striking red hair. "Don't see many redheads," he said appraisingly.

She seemed flattered.

The next morning the visitor stopped by the tasteful, wood-paneled shop that carries Snead's name in the main hotel building. A fascinating crossroads of the commemorative and the commercial, the place fairly bursts with Snead-endorsed products and memorabilia, from clothing to prints to miscellanea such as duck decoys carved from wooden clubheads. One day a week Snead sinks into a cushy leather chair and signs everything that will hold still, including the decoys.

A replica of his outsized first book *Sam Snead's Quick Way to Better Golf* sold for a dollar in 1938. In the shop it's $29, or $54 if Sam signs it for you.

The typical customer appears delighted to buy something and exchange a few words with the legend as he signs it.

SNEAD: "How you playing?"

CUSTOMER: "I can't get out of the sand."

SNEAD: "Keep your weight on your left foot."

Another man recalls watching Snead play a Shell's match in Atlanta decades ago.

SNEAD: "At Peachtree?"

CUSTOMER: "Yes."

SNEAD: "Against Boros?"

CUSTOMER: "That's right."

Snead went on to recap the match.

"This is just great," the man said as he left, thrilled. "A living slice of history." A large slice.

by Roger Schiffman,
Executive Editor

Golf for as long as it's been played has been replete with characters, some colorful, some colorless, and some enticingly enigmatic. GOLF DIGEST for the past 50 years has been blessed with writers of character, stylish wordsmiths who captured on paper the personalities we hardly knew on screen or inside the gallery ropes. What a winning combination.

Whether it was Nick Seitz hanging out for a week with the reclusive Ben Hogan and surviving, esteem intact, to document it and philosophize about it, or Dan Jenkins His Own Self giving us the real story about Arnold Palmer's meteoric rise to capture the imagination and hearts of the American public, or British wordmaster Peter Dobereiner analyzing the zodiacal psyche of the Black Knight, Gary Player, the GOLF DIGEST reader each month has been treated to a special kind of insight not found anywhere else.

The powerful combination of, say, Tom Callahan (who wrote 25 cover stories for Time magazine before joining the GOLF DIGEST cadre of writers) with, say, Ernie Els, always proved memorable, the reading juicy. Tom doesn't just give you a profile of the golfer; he gives you a profile of the golfer as related to his country, then puts it in perspective with baseball, boxing and the Cleveland Browns. And, as in the case of the Els piece, "Out of Africa," Tom is often ahead of the curve, his sense of time and place so perspicacious that we sometimes wish we'd run his articles nine months later, not earlier. For sure, Els won the first of his two U.S. Opens a year after Tom's article appeared.

But what a good problem to have.

GOLF DIGEST's profiles have come in all shapes and sizes and styles.

In 1979 Brennan Quinn composed a delightful short piece summarizing the plight of Japanese professional Tommy Nakajima using the unique setting of the Road Bunker fronting the putting surface of the 17th hole at St. Andrews. That was where the young pro, while in contention in the '78 British Open, and having made a horrendous 13 in that year's Masters, hit the green, only to putt his ball into the bunker and proceed to make a 9. Quinn's masterful weaving of Haiku poems into the piece

brought laughter and tears to readers' faces—we felt a sense of sympathy for the hapless pro, for we've all been there on our own course, in our own hellish bunker.

Or what about the compelling story of Mac O'Grady, as told by writer Kevin Cook, who held little back in revealing why O'Grady is such a tortured genius? Anybody else with a childhood like Mac's would either not be alive today or would be in one kind of institution or another.

Or consider Marino Parascenzo's inside look at the downfall of the '70s can't-miss kid, Bobby Clampett, the pro who looked like Harpo Marx and for a while played golf like Chico played the piano—flawlessly. That is, until the third round of the '82 British Open at Troon.

And leave it to the Grand Master, Peter Andrews, to find a way to make us admire Ken Green, the surly tour pro who managed to pick separate fights with Deane Beman and Seve Ballesteros. In a photo-essay treatment, Andrews compelled us to reconsider the luckless but talented Green and give him yet another chance.

And, of course, who can forget the fictitious profile subject, maybe the grandest character of all, Slamming Suki Sukiyuki, from the imagination of one of the magazine's early writers. This spoof proved to be so popular among readers, many of whom believed the wild tales of 400-yard drives and dozens of broken course records by the ambidextrous Samurai pro, the son of well-to-do peasants who perfected a double-hit technique, that the magazine reprinted the original feature more than once.

It was all in fun.

Since the magazine's beginning, however, there was a distinct desire among the GOLF DIGEST editors to find out what made the legitimate characters tick. The editors didn't want readers to only know how the subjects acted and played the game. They wanted readers to understand why. What early influences shaped their lives? Who were the people integral to their makeup, both physical and mental?

In the case of the cocky Johnny Miller, Nick Seitz found it to be an unselfishly supportive wife. In the case of the once-stuttering Ken Venturi, Tom Callahan discovered a warm-hearted mother. In the case of the charismatic Nancy Lopez, Dwayne Netland revealed a blindly devoted father. In the case of the "hated" J.C. Snead, Texas writer Mickey Herskowitz unveiled a connection to Sam Snead's dad (J.C.'s great uncle). And the list goes on.

But like a pure golf swing, too much analysis only ruins it. So enough talking about these articles. Herewith is a sampling of the more memorable profiles that have graced the magazine's pages for the past 50 years. You can judge their character for yourself.

Nick Seitz on Ben Hogan was the cover story of the September 1970 issue.

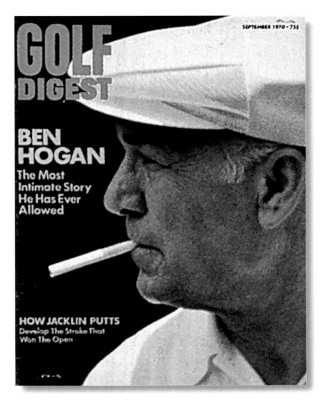

September 1970

Ben Hogan Today

A wonderful week with the Wee Ice Mon from Fort Worth

by Nick Seitz

For millions of golf followers it will matter not a shred if Arnold Palmer wins the rest of the schedule, or Raquel Welch becomes a touring caddie, or the price of a hot dog on the course dives to a nickel. The year 1970 was made when 57-year-old William Benjamin Hogan, his swollen left knee squeezed into an elastic brace, limped intently out of retirement to finish ninth in the Houston Champions International and challenge briefly in the Colonial, which he has won five times.

Imagine Joe DiMaggio donning his old uniform and coming off the bench to rip a grand-slam home run before a capacity crowd in Yankee Stadium and you have some idea of the drama that drenched Hogan's performances on two of the most arduous courses in the sport.

The short return to professional golf of the man widely considered the greatest player ever, a winner of all four major championships, a national hero after he overcame the near-fatal effects of a 1949 car-bus crash, gives rise to fascinating questions. Why did he do it? What is his life like today? Has he, as some reports suggest, "mellowed?" What achievements mean the most to him? Hogan long has been the least understood of great athletes, often summarily characterized as "cold" and "aloof," and the years since he reached his playing zenith in the late 1940s and early 1950s have brought disappointingly little insight into his lifestyle and outlooks.

Hogan permitted me to follow him for a week in Fort Worth, observing and questioning. I took up with him during the Colonial and spent two days with him afterward, as he reverted to his customary activities, which seldom include complete rounds of golf, let alone tour play. In that time, I think I came to know somewhat a Ben Hogan only remotely related to the single-dimensional, distant figure I had been led to expect.

The thing that surprised me most about Hogan was his sense of humor: droll, flavored with an earthy Southwestern spice, often evident. I remember my unsuspecting introduction to it. I accompanied him to Shady Oaks Country Club for lunch—he is the Fort Worth club's most esteemed member—and he introduced me to the manager, who personally attends him. "This guy has 15 kids," Hogan said. Expressionless, he added, *"Bleeped* himself right out of a seat in the car." I had heard dozens of stories about Hogan's dourness, and in no way was prepared for this. I nodded innocuously. After a lengthy silence, I suddenly became aware of what he had said, and burst out laughing. Hogan, who had been watching me closely, joined in the laughter. He was amused not at his own line but at my delayed response. His probing blue-gray eyes suggested: "Didn't expect that from the austere Ben Hogan, eh?"

Of his friend, Jimmy Demaret, who does not have to be coaxed hard to sing, Hogan says, "I love Jimmy's voice . . . but I don't think I can stand 'Deep Purple' again."

Hogan is no raconteur, but he enjoys hearing a good story. Golf temper stories featuring Tommy Bolt and Lefty Stackhouse are his favorites. And he enjoys, even more, spontaneous humor. Paired with Bob Goalby in Houston, Hogan burned a long drive into the wind. "Who do you think you are?" Goalby asked, "Ben Hogan?" Hogan liked that.

During the Colonial, Hogan did his warming up at Shady Oaks, 15 minutes away. The practice area at Colonial Country Club is not large, and he always has preferred to practice by himself anyway ("You don't get in anybody's way, and nobody gets in yours, and you can have your own thoughts"). At Shady Oaks he hits balls from a spot between the 14th and 15th holes, across the 14th, 13th and 17th fairways. One morning,

Ben Hogan is as much a gallery favorite coming briefly out of retirement, at the 1970 Colonial, as he was at the height of his tour career. (Photo: Al Panzera)

some writers covering the Colonial were playing at Shady Oaks, and "played through" Hogan's practice area. Hogan chatted with them and asked one, Kaye Kessler from Columbus, Ohio, about his swing. "It's kind of disjointed," Kessler said. "My boss told me I shouldn't take it out of town because if it broke down I couldn't get parts." Hogan chuckled delightedly. There is plenty of Irish in him.

Hogan spends several hours a day and an occasional evening at Shady Oaks, the club built by his close friend and early backer on the tour, Marvin Leonard. He is comfortable there. It is the poshest club in Fort Worth, but the members treat one another with a congenial irreverence, Hogan included. "Ben gets tired of people getting' down on their knees when he walks into a room," Tommy Bolt says. "I've had some great name-callin' arguments with him, and he loved it."

Early every afternoon, his leg and the weather permitting, he will empty an old shag bag and hit balls for 40 to 90 minutes, starting with a 9-iron and working through the set. With each club he will hit basic shots, then before putting it away will hit two different types of shots, moving the ball to the right or left, or hitting it low or high. "The basics of the swing remain the same," he says. "But I'm always experimenting, looking for better ways to hit finesse shots. I never hit a shot on the course I haven't practiced." His clear voice, neutral at first, takes on more of the drawling intonations of Texas as he warms to talking. "I'm a curious person. *Experimenting is my enjoyment.* I won't accept anything until I've worked with it for a week or two, or longer. I bring out new clubs from the plant and try them out, and I get ahold of clubs that we've sold to check them.

If something doesn't work, some part of my swing or a club, I throw it out."

The scientific method. Hogan is the Linus Pauling of his field, subjecting any hypothesis to rigorous, impartial testing. If it works, he keeps it, generalizes from it. If it doesn't, into the garbage can it goes. Gardner Dickinson worked for Hogan when Hogan had a club job in Palm Springs in his younger years. Dickinson majored in clinical psychology in college, with a minor in psychometrics—mental testing. Intrigued by Hogan's personality, he would slip IQ test questions into conversations with him. "I knew I'd never get them all past him, so I'd give him only the toughest ones from each section, knowing if he could answer those he could get the others." Dickinson says, "I calculated that his IQ was in excess of 175. Genius level is about 160. Ben didn't go to college, he regrets that, but he's a brilliant person."

One reason Hogan practices where he does at Shady Oaks is to hit into the prevailing wind. When the wind moves, so does Hogan. "If the wind is at your back, it destroys your game. You tend to try to pull the ball, swinging from the outside in, which is bad. If the temperature is below 60 degrees, you lose me. You can wreck your swing playing in cold weather, bundling all up." Each shot is aimed at a target: a small nursery building near the 18th fairway. He uses no glove. "I never could feel anything wearing a glove." Traffic is light at Shady Oaks. Such is Hogan's eminence, when strangers playing the course interrupt his practice, they often apologize.

Shady Oaks, not as long or difficult as Colonial, where Hogan formerly belonged, is nonetheless

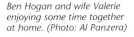

Ben Hogan and wife Valerie enjoying some time together at home. (Photo: Al Panzera)

Hogan still has the swing of a champion 11 years after his last of over 60 victories—including nine majors. (Photo: Corbis-Bettman)

a course. The greens have to be large to provide multiple pin placements and prevent their wearing out. You have to have heavy play or you're going to lose money. You give the greens character in the contouring. I like a clean course. You could grow rough for a tournament. Champions Golf Club in Houston is my idea of a tremendous course for the locale."

Hogan probably will build his course in or near sprawling, wealthy Houston. The course is sure to place a premium on driving, which Hogan deems the most important area of play. Expect the par 4s to bend slightly left or right (an equal number each way). The par 3s will call for iron shots, even short-iron shots, precisely placed. "I won't design it," Hogan says, inhaling hard on a cigarette. "I'm no architect. A person can have just so much knowledge, and there isn't enough time in the day to absorb very much and be proficient. I'll work with the architect, but not in detail. Everything takes a professional."

Hogan will build only one course.

It is common for a legendary athlete, no longer very active competitively, to sell his name—to let it be used for promotional purposes or to open doors, as the saying has it. Ben Hogan does not play the game of business that way. "I don't consider myself a businessman," he says crisply. "Once you consider yourself something, you fall flat on your face, you see." He is behind the wide wooden desk in his spacious office in front of two framed full-color maps. Several neat foothills of mail have accumulated while he was playing the two tournaments.

A high-salaried executive in the employ of AMF, with stock options and the rest, he is in full command of the Ben Hogan Company, a firm which is doing so well it can't produce golf equipment fast enough to fill the orders. He does not play golf with customers. He plays company golf once a year, at the principal sales meeting. He makes a few speeches, although he is a captivating speaker. "Some people love that sort of thing. I don't like it. If I accept a speaking engagement, I do the best I can, but I'm not comfortable."

The plant and offices are in a nondescript, outlying warehouse district. Fronted by a perfectly kept expanse of putting grass, they stand out. A visitor is asked to sign in with a receptionist, then is led to Hogan's office by Claribel Kelly, his trusted executive secretary. There are no slick public relations people around Hogan. He is not easy to see, but Claribel is his only visible shield. She went to grammar school with Hogan, and remembers him and his mother, who still lives in Fort Worth, attending a music recital she had a part in. She has worked for him for 18 years. She calls him "Mr. Hogan" as often as "Ben."

She opens his mail, but does not screen it. He reads it all, scrawling terse notes across the tops of letters for her to amplify. Hogan is sterner in his office. Trying to reach a businessman on the phone, Claribel enters his office to report that he is in a meeting and will call back. "When?" Hogan asks. Gene Sheely, the man who puts together the models for Hogan clubs, comes in with a

challenging and pretty, if that term may be applied to a golf course. Hogan designed most of the bunkers. They are numerous and imaginatively and variously shaped. They are not difficult to shoot from; they are not deep and do not have high lips. "Bunkers serve two purposes," Hogan says. "They are for framing a green—to give it definition and to give the player an idea of the distance he has in hitting to the green. And for beauty. They are *not* for trapping *people*."

Hogan holds decided views on what a golf course should be, and no one knows more about shot values. It is his ambition to build The Perfect Golf Course, a project he has contemplated since his touring days. "I'm very close to buying the property now. The market research looks favorable. You have to know where you'll wind up before you start—otherwise you'll go broke. You have to have the right piece of land. I'm in hopes of getting a nice, rolling site with a lot of trees. That means it won't be in the Fort Worth area. I want a course that both the club member and the pro can play.

"Length isn't necessarily the key. Length has to do with climate. Where it's humid, you can't have too long

Emphasizing his belief that a driver—especially one with his name on it—is the most important club, Ben Hogan gives the photographer a close-up opportunity. A week before turning 53, Hogan was warming up for the 1965 Philadelphia Golf Classic. (Photo: Corbis-Bettman)

wedge special-ordered by a tour star. Hogan puts on the glasses he wears for close work. "I found out playing in the Colonial I'm gonna need 'em to play golf, too. I couldn't see the pins. I had to ask the caddie." Hogan asks a couple of pointed questions, soles the club on the carpet. Sheely wonders if the player should be charged for the club. "Well, heck yes," Hogan answers softly but firmly. The player endorses the clubs of another company. "That's one reason we don't have playing pros on our staff," says Hogan. "Just me."

In the Hogan company's early, struggling years, Ben worked 14 and 16 hours a day to set up a system that was just as he wanted it. Walking through the plant, nodding at employees, occasionally stopping to inspect work at a particular station, he says, "I've done all these jobs myself. I like to work with my hands."

Dealing with his help, Hogan relies on direct communication. He does not phone them or send them memoranda, he has them summoned to his office and talks to them. Directly.

Today, Hogan usually will work only in the morning, and is perhaps the only executive in the country

who consistently can take off at noon for his golf club and not be second-guessed. He cannot understand modern golfers—or executives—who say they do not have time for golf. "I have other business interests that I find time for. I piddle around in the oil business. I fool around with the stock market quite a bit. I'm in the process of looking for a cattle ranch. I'll find what I want. I want it within 150 miles of Fort Worth. I keep hearing there's no money in it, but if that were true you couldn't buy a steak."

Each year Hogan is offered well-paying peripheral jobs, such as commentating on golf telecasts. Each year he declines. "Television is a different business entirely," he says. "It takes a professional to do a professional job. And I'm fed up with traveling."

He has been approached many times about involving himself in a tour event that would carry his name, but always has refused, in part because he is wary of lending his name to an undertaking if he does not have complete control over the quality, and in part, probably, because he has had it in mind to build his own course, the natural site for a "Ben Hogan Classic."

Hogan is considering writing an exhaustive instruction book. "It would be this thick," he says with thumb and forefinger as far apart as they will stretch. "It would confuse a lot of people, but I can't help that. I get so darn tired of these bromides that don't mean anything. Explain to me the expression 'Coming off the ball.' What does that mean? What *caused* it, that's what I want to know. I never see that explained. Or 'Stay behind the ball.' What does *that* mean?"

Gardner Dickinson says he has seen Hogan turn down $500 for a five-minute lesson. Why doesn't Hogan teach? "You can't find anybody who wants to learn." A silence. "I did teach at one time."

Hearing Hogan speak about the formative years of the tour is a remarkable experience. "I'll tell you how the tour got started, and I've never read this anywhere," he said one noon as we ate *chalupas*, a zestful Mexican dish that is perfect by Fort Worth criteria—hot enough to make your eyes water but not hot enough to make you choke. "The wives of a handful of club professionals in the East—Bob Cruickshank, Al Espinosa, Tommy Armour, I believe—took it on themselves to book a tour in the 1930s. Their husbands were off work in the winter. Before that you just had a smattering of tournaments across the country. The wives wrote to chambers of commerce and so forth in California, and convinced several cities to have tournaments. Some of the purses were only a few hundred dollars, and we'd go to civic-club lunches to promote ourselves. The wives kept up all the correspondence and handled the books. Then the manufacturers saw what a great promotional vehicle the tour could be and hired Bob Harlow, Walter Hagen's manager, to conduct it. Later the PGA got in on it. That's how this $7 million business began.

"We'd play five exhibitions apiece to pay our Ryder Cup expenses. We got no money from the PGA. If somebody on the tour died or had troubles, we'd work out an exhibition schedule to help out. I never did make money playing the tour. It cost me more, total, than my purse winnings. I had to do other things.

"We traveled together and ate together and sat around hotel rooms and talked at night. We were a smaller group, and invariably more closely knit. It seems to me like we used to have a more *gracious* life playing tournaments in those days. In many places we dressed for dinner, in dinner jackets. I cringe when I see fellas today walking into nice restaurants in golf clothes."

I asked Hogan which of his 60-some victories, including nine of the modern major championships, an unequalled three in the same year (1953), means the most to him. The 1950 United States Open at Merion was his answer, because there he proved to himself, in a tense, wearing, 36-hole final only a year after that horrendous car-bus accident, that he could be the best in spite of his injuries.

The past and the present were joined this spring when Hogan, away from tournament golf for nearly three years, his last victory 11 years ago, played back-to-back tournaments, and made them quite special. Each time he walked slowly onto a green with that rolling, purposeful stride, his younger playing partners often lagging respectfully behind, he was met with an ovation, an ovation very different from the usual. There was none of the raucous shouting that welcomes Arnold Palmer. This was loud, prolonged, sincere applause with an added depth. Bearing himself with customary dignity, Hogan nonetheless was moved. He frequently tipped the white cap he special-orders by the dozen. "I'm very grateful," he said in the locker room after one round. "These people are just wonderful, and I wish there was some way I could thank them."

He was, of course, thanking them merely by his presence. His huge galleries were heavily peopled with fathers in their 40s and 50s who had brought youthful sons to see a man who was the best at his profession, who elevated it to the level of aesthetics. But there were, not entirely expectedly, thousands of teenagers on their own and young couples in their 20s. Yes, there were even a few dozen hippie types, protesting nothing except that it was damned difficult to get a look at Hogan.

Bob Goalby counted 31 of his fellow pros following Hogan on a hot afternoon in Houston, and said they were impressed. The deeply tanned Hogan's swing appeared superb. His putting stroke, once a shambles, was smoother. His yogic concentration, a striking amalgam of intensity and composure that suggests utter transcendence, seemed not to have been impaired by the long layoff; Herb Wind's description of Hogan competing "with the burning frigidity of dry ice" came to mind.

Hogan always has said he would not compete unless he believed he could win. Possibly he has softened that stance. Why did he play at Champions and Colonial? "I don't know what in the world he is trying to prove," Byron Nelson had said. Claude Harmon said he didn't know if Ben was trying to inspire business for the Ben Hogan Company, but that Winged Foot, where Harmon is the head professional, is selling a lot of Hogan balls to guys who never bought them before.

Hogan says he expects a business residual from his tournament appearances, but that isn't why he played. "I couldn't play until I got better," he says. "Plus I was overweight, and this is a good way to lose it. I used to run in place a lot and exercise. I like to hunt, but had to quit. I was up to 175. Now I'm about 165. In the 1940s I weighed 130 to 135, then after my accident it was 145 to 150. I was curious—I wanted to see if I could walk for four days. I wanted to see if I could play some kinda decent golf hitting off my back foot. The fact it was the 25th anniversary of the Colonial had something to do with it. I've played a lot, but I've missed a lot of years. I missed three years in the service. I missed a year after the wreck. I missed two years because of my shoulder and two years because of my knee. Time's runnin' pretty short if I don't play now. I *enjoy* practicing and playing in tournaments. Besides, I haven't really done what I wanted to do."

"What is that?" someone asked.

"I haven't won enough tournaments."

"Like Joe Louis and Walter Hagen, he'll never quit until they carry him out. They may be able to beat this boy in muscle, but not in the mind."

—TOMMY ARMOUR
ON BEN HOGAN

April 1986

How Hard It Is to Be Ken Venturi

TV's favorite commentator makes his annual bittersweet return to the tournament he should have won

by Tom Callahan

Consider how life was laid out for Ken Venturi, a dreamer on the wharf drawn not to the sea and the common ports but to the lushest dry land and the most elegant game. Figuratively and literally, Venturi was born a left-hander in a right-hander's world, and being forced to convert took his breath away at the age of 9. He stuttered to the point of loneliness and the edge of silence. "Golf was easy for me," Venturi says now, "because it was easy to be alone."

Venturi was the choker who turned into a national champion, the stammerer who ended up a national communicator. And, as if he needed another poignant affliction, Venturi's hands began peeling away on the back side of his career. But he kept his grip.

His father was a San Francisco ship chandler, whose wares of net and twine were available to all fishermen on credit. Those who made it big and now have their own chowder houses today still regard Venturi as "the kid." At 54, he is unable to pick up a tab for a drink or a dinner on the waterfront. His father also collected green fees at a municipal golf course, but Ken

Ken Venturi, here working at the 1985 Masters, was voted the No. 1 golf color commentator in GOLF DIGEST's 1984 reader poll. He speaks about golf in the language of ordinary people, with grace. (Photo: Jim Moriarty)

had to make his own way there. He remembers borrowing "a few hickory clubs from the garage across the street and walking three miles to hit a ball."

Ken felt an early affection for baseball, but only if he could man the most remote position, center field. And he must have been a pretty fair player, too, because Lefty O'Doul came along one time with a contract from the New York Yankees organization. But ball playing requires a modicum of conversation, and imagining those boisterous bus rides around the minor leagues, Venturi figured there was a more serene way to go.

While hitting golf balls as a teenager, he taught himself how to talk by giving out with a halting patter of play-by-play. On two counts, this amounted to a prophesy. Occasionally, a passerby crept up from behind to inquire sheepishly, "Whom are you talking to?" but he would only blush and wait for solitude to return so he could resume announcing, "Ladies and gentlemen, Venturi needs just this last tricky approach shot and two solid putts to w-w-win the United States Open."

The memory still touches him. "Isn't it funny? Always the U.S. Open. I thought I'd win the Open someday, I really did. But I never thought I'd be able to speak a whole sentence."

At age 14 he lost a tournament match 7 and 5 to a "cup hunter" who blatantly belonged in a lower flight. When Ken did not return home, his mother went out to the course and found him still at the 13th hole in tears. "She put her arm around me and said, 'You may cry in victory, but don't ever cry in defeat again.'"

When Venturi won his first San Francisco City Championship at 18, his father mused, "You've gone and done it now." Ken laughed jauntily, "What do you mean? I won." Looking at him squarely, the ship chandler said, "That's the problem."

"When you're as good as you are now, you might as well tell everyone," his father observed one day in that singular way the old man had of reaching back for the other shoe. "But if you ever get really good, they will tell you."

A number of people were telling him how great he was in 1956 when, just out of the Army at 24, Venturi was forgiven Augusta's usual qualifying procedures and summoned to the Masters by his fellow players. Fresh from trimming U.S. Amateur champion Harvie Ward in San Francisco, Venturi was annoyed by the absence of his name on the scoreboard beside

the first tee. He briskly birdied the opening four holes, stepped back momentarily and grinned. Applying the lessons of stroke and temperament he had been taking formally from Byron Nelson and vicariously from Ben Hogan—"I was taught by Michelangelo and shown by da Vinci"—Venturi led the tournament after three rounds by four shots.

In those days, tradition paired the Sunday leader with Nelson, but Clifford Roberts worried about the propriety of coupling Venturi and Ken's mentor. The Massa of the Plantation, later the custodian of Bobby Jones' relics, had nothing against amateurs, far from it—"We expect and hope that you will become our youngest champion," Roberts told Venturi. That Saturday evening when Venturi was summoned before the council and given his pick of any other playing companion, he thought, "Why not Snead?" Ken, who had never jousted with Sam, announced, "If I'm going to win, I want to walk up the 18th fairway with someone like that." Though Roberts gently warned, "Snead's a tough man to play with," Venturi quickly rejoined, "So am I." The edge in this new voice bothered Mr. Cliff.

Come the next morning, a billowing wind arose with the sun and turned the baked greens into crackling skillets. Never having experienced such an advanced stage of treachery, Venturi took three putts six times. While his amateur nerves may have twitched under the conditions, the fact remains that only two players broke par that day—Snead and Jackie Burke, who made up eight strokes to win. Ken shot 80 and lost to Burke by one. Contrary to a few words carelessly uttered by Venturi and callously reported by a wire service, he had neither been chilled

by Snead nor abused by Roberts. Oddly, what most intruded on Venturi's concentration was the word "millionaire." He says now, "I kept thinking of the house I'd buy my mother and father when I became the richest golfer in the world." At the Metropolitan (N.Y.) Golf Writers Association banquet following his U.S. Open win eight summers later, Venturi greeted Snead from the dais with a message that must have perplexed a number of the guests in the audience: "Sam, if I had it to do over, I'd still choose you."

From 1957 to 1961, the dashing young Venturi was either the favorite or co-favorite in almost every tournament he entered, depending largely on the whereabouts of Arnold Palmer. In 1960 Palmer and Venturi finished one-two on the money list. In the 1958 Masters they dueled down the stretch for possession of the game. Over Venturi's protests at the par-3 12th, Palmer played out both his original tee ball, which had been "partially" imbedded behind the green, and a provisional one, so they moved on to the par-5 13th either tied for the lead or two strokes apart. "They're going to give me a 5 back there, aren't they?" Venturi recalls Palmer wondering aloud as Arnie contemplated risking the creek, to reach the green in two.

"You're damn right they are," Ken muttered. But Palmer not only bagged the eagle he gambled for, he also cashed in on that retroactive 3. Fuming, Venturi fumbled to fourth place.

"Two Masters later, Palmer strung three 3s over the final three holes to catch me and won by one stroke. At the ceremonies, he turned to me and whispered, 'I'm sorry it had to be you.' I looked away and said, 'Two years too late.' " Beyond that, Venturi voices no unpleasantness for the record, though there was to be plenty of it ahead.

Tormented by back spasms and also misgivings, the runner-up in the Palmer Sweepstakes misplaced his game in 1962 and almost lost himself in 1963 as his winnings plummeted first to $6,951 and then $3,848. He began to drink beyond his usual requirements. Invitations to tournaments started drying up. Finally, the 1964 Masters, the grail he expected to pursue forever, went on without him. Reaching down for another wordless resolve, Venturi returned to a hard style of work, and when he could feel his touch coming back even before his scores improved, Ken bit his proud tongue and begged his way back into several fields. As always, his eye was to the Open. Venturi likes the phrase, "Fate has a way of bending a twig and fashioning a man to his better instincts." Meaning, loosely translated: the wonderful way a man wins one Open can be worth all the ways he ever lost the Masters.

Twenty-two years afterward, Venturi still remains in sharp focus at Congressional Country Club bearing up under his white linen cap and Washington's worst summer heat and humidity, trudging 36 delirious holes in the company of young Ray Floyd, old Joe Dey and destiny. "It could be fatal," a physician warned the dehydrated fighter between rounds. "I'm already dying," Venturi told the doctor. "I have no place else to go."

After Venturi holed his last putt of that finish he had rehearsed as a boy—speechlessness overtook him again. Not only that, he could barely put a pencil to his scorecard, for the numbers were all a blur. Dey leaned over his shoulder and said softly, "Sign it, Ken, it's correct."

Venturi sighs still, "If it hadn't been for Joe, I might still be sitting there. I handed Raymond his card and it was completely blank. All the time he had been keeping my scores so carefully, I hadn't put down even a single number for him." Floyd turned his back discreetly and scribbled everything in.

Venturi was the choker who turned into a national champion, the stammerer who ended up a national communicator.

After 36 delirious holes on Sunday of the 1964 U.S. Open at Congressional, and fighting severe dehydration, Ken Venturi is finally overwhelmed, in victory. (Photo: Corbis-Bettman)

Venturi's game would leave him again within months, but his drama would continue for years through hand operations for a circulatory disorder diagnosed as Raynaud's phenomenon that threatened his flaking fingers with gangrene. "Was it really my hand or is it in my head?" he asked the surgeons, who scraped scars from the nerves and tendons of his right hand to ease the pressure on the median nerve. "It was your hand," one answered. "It's the worst hand I ever saw."

At one dark point Venturi blurted out to his father, "Dad, I'm scared to death. I don't know what I'd do if I can't play golf." But then his father dropped the last and most important shoe. "It doesn't matter if you never hit another golf ball. You were the best I ever saw."

In 1966, Venturi scored his final tournament victory, back at Harding Park in San Francisco, the site of his first round of golf. And he beat Arnold Palmer. "I guarantee you," Venturi says, "I wrote that acceptance speech when I was 14 years old."

His game is a private preserve now; besides a few impersonal lessons, what endures of his art is private. He'll go off by himself and hit golf balls, suitable shots for the senior tour, but not for him. "I'm not sharp, I'm not toughened," he says. "It's like I know the way to make a three-footer, but I've forgotten how to do it. The respectable seniors are the ones who really never left the game: Don January, Miller Barber, Gene Littler, Arnold Palmer. To be decent, I'd need to practice competition. But how do you practice competition?"

Eagle Creek, in Naples, Fla., a handsome golf course originally designed by Larry Packard, has been turned over to Venturi. "I had to be allowed to put my 'signature' on it," says the author who writes with a sweeping hand. Every detail from the tilt of the cart building to the layout of the bar is smudged with his fingerprints.

Venturi personally drew the floor plan for a clubhouse on a swatch of tablecloth. Capping his tour de force, even the photo landscapes in the golf shop were snapped by him. Interestingly, the most prominent photograph in the shop, centered over the door frame, is not of Venturi at Congressional but of Hogan winning the 1950 U.S. Open at Merion.

For 18 years Venturi has been a television commentator of many sentences and little syntax. "I've been knocked around for my grammar," he agrees with a laugh. "I have to tell you, I write 'chipping' and 'putting,' but golfers say 'chippin'' and 'puttin'.' " Maybe I should say, 'He has an insufficient amount of iron to accomplish the green in such an environment,' but I find myself just saying, 'He has no chance with that club.' I speak emotionally and I cry a lot—almost as much as Pat Summerall does. Both of us are capable of crying at groundbreakings."

The generosity of Summerall and other broadcasters—Jack Whitaker, now with ABC, for another—can make him misty too.

So can the memory of the original chance that Frank Chirkinian took on him at CBS. "I told him, 'Frank, you don't want to hire me. Hell, I'll embarrass us

Leading the charge down the stretch at the 1964 Open. (Photo: Ken Regan)

both.' But he said, 'Just talk about what you know best,' and I think I've done it."

Venturi seldom finishes a sentence. At the '84 Masters, when a suspended few holes had to be completed on the next day, Venturi's word bank became overloaded to the point of burlesque: "Mark [Lye], who bogeyed the 12th hole after hitting it on the green yesterday, and going back out this morning three-putted the 12th; he made double bogey at 16, as he did at nine—which was yesterday—and now faced with another double bogey, has made three double bogeys and not put the ball in the water."

Summerall: "That's amazing."

The joke doesn't need pointing up. "But," Venturi plunged on, "of all places that he had to miss it—of course, he missed the shot in the bunker—but he was only maybe three feet from absolutely playing a perfect shot, but that's the gamble you have to take if you expect to win."

However, although Venturi may not parse, he does communicate. Ordinary men feel he speaks their language. And he instructs with grace. When he flubs a shot on a TV tip, that protective pride Venturi keeps for his game does not prevent him from smiling at himself. Some of his most exquisite duffs make it on the air and humanize him all the more. Which may be why he was ranked the No. 1 color commentator in a GOLF DIGEST reader poll in March 1984. While he is not in the Brent Musberger income bracket, his TV earnings keep the shag bag full. Venturi's total salary package from CBS is in the neighborhood of $200,000 a year.

Describing Venturi as a journalist would be an exaggeration. Consider his feigned "spontaneous" interview with Hogan at Colonial in 1983. Venturi

introduced the segment as if he had run into his "old friend Ben Hogan" at Shady Oaks, just by chance, with a video crew in tow. In fact, Hogan's advertising agency arranged for the interview as a promotion of his company's 25th anniversary. Still, it should not be forgotten that Venturi managed, only for an instant, to penetrate an emotional fortress and let his audience see inside the most elusive figure in golf.

Many of the hard days show in Venturi's words. On the air he is inclined to mention money and seems to relate especially to peripheral struggles that others might consider inconsequential—matters of modest scores and moderate paychecks. "I think he'll take his par here," Venturi is forever saying, "and walk away quietly." At the same time, if Curtis Strange is about to let go of himself and the Masters and everything else but the money, Venturi is quick both to see it and say it. "Now Curtis has brought the hole into a new dimension, a possible 6," he forecasts precisely before Strange is even a third of the way to that horror.

Venturi thinks like a golfer.

"It's amazing," he gets to musing sometimes, "how many people don't know me as a golfer anymore, just as a talker. My own kids never saw me play the way I could play."

But he conveys no sense of sadness, or trace of envy. "I admire these young players and I think it shows in my telecasts. I hope it does."

In his clubhouse or on his tower, Venturi can look back from a long distance and say, "I'm glad to be where I am. If I'd won the Masters, maybe I wouldn't have been sitting here. Maybe a lot of things. But right now I like my position."

Ken Venturi will take his place where he is and talk away gladly.

June 1978

Nancy Lopez: Almost Too Good to Be True

A star is born, a tour revived

by Dwayne Netland

The trouble with Nancy Lopez is she's too good to be true. We are accustomed these days to our sporting superstars having a few rough edges—an iconoclastic zeal, perhaps, a self-centered outlook or at least the trace of an irritable temperament. But here is this smiling and pleasant product of a modest background who has burst upon the LPGA Tour with a talent so luminous that she is already one of its leading players at the age of 21. And nobody can find a critical word to say about her—not even the people she's beating.

The most intriguing thing about Lopez is that, in an environment where petty jealousies and even smolder-ing hostilities frequently flourish, everyone seems to like her. "She's a real asset to the tour," says Kathy Whitworth. "I've seldom seen anyone out here handle herself with such grace."

The timing could hardly be better. Just when the women's tour was crying for a new personality with a combination of looks and ability—*marketability*, as they say in show business—Nancy arrived with all her credentials in order. She placed second in the U.S. Women's Open last July in her first professional start and then finished second in her very next two tourna-ments to win GOLF DIGEST's LPGA Rookie of the Year Award. Earlier this season she won two straight tour-naments and shared first in the next one before losing a playoff to Sally Little.

If the veteran tour players were impressed, they were not totally surprised, having known something of her fine amateur record. What they didn't expect was how quickly she would adjust to the level of competition.

"Nancy is a great driver and putter," observes Jane Blalock, an astute judge of young talent. "When you have those clubs going for you, the other parts of the game tend to take care of themselves."

Adds Donna Caponi Young, "She hits her iron shots with two clubs less than almost anyone else out here. That's a tremendous advantage. She is a strong player with a good, functional swing. The only thing she lacks right now is tour experience."

The rapid maturing of Nancy's game may have been best expressed by the ebullient Debbie Austin, a five-time winner in 1977 who finished a stroke behind Lopez in the Sunstar Classic at Los Angeles in March. "Last year on Long Island I went head-to-head with Nancy on Sunday and beat her," Debbie says. "She seemed nervous and unsure of herself. This time she came after me and won. I don't think there's a player out here who doesn't regard Nancy right now as a star."

In the midst of snowballing acclaim, Nancy Lopez proceeds serenely along toward her private goals of (1) earning $100,000 in prize money this season and (2) ultimately becoming the tour's best player.

"I was hoping I could win a tournament this year, so I wouldn't have that pressure hanging over me like it has hung over others," she says, referring to Laura Baugh. "That's out of the way now. I know I'll have to work hard. My game needs constant practice, and there are times when I get tired and lose my concen-tration. But I've seen enough of the tour now to realize what I can accomplish."

Nancy Lopez won several tourna-ments, placed second in the U.S. Women's Open and won GOLF DIGEST's LPGA Rookie of the Year Award with the basic swing her father taught her—and a few refinements. (Photo: Stephen Szurlej)

Lopez reviewing another winning scorecard with fans Nos. 1, 2 and 3: her father, Domingo, sister, Delma, and Delma's husband, Bernie. Lopez's mother died in 1977. (Photo: Lester Nehamkin)

Just when the women's tour was crying for a new personality with a combination of looks and ability—*marketability*, as they say in show business—Nancy arrived with all her credentials in order.

Lopez is winning with pretty much the basic swing she learned from her father, Domingo, in Roswell, N.M. She has refined it slightly in the last year, curtailing a loop at the top and slowing her tempo almost to a crawl. But she still starts the swing with a distinctive forward press with the hands and completes it with a big, sweeping follow-through.

It is a muscular swing, tailored nicely to her sturdy body. Nancy is 5-4¼ and weighs 155 pounds. "I'd like to lose 15 pounds," she says, patting her tummy.

Nancy averages 235 yards off the tee, about 15 yards longer than most LPGA players. She hits a 5-iron 170 yards, which is remarkable for a woman.

Susie Berning, the three-time U.S. Women's Open champion, referred to Nancy's short game in this way: "She hits it all over the ball park, but she can get it up and down out of a garbage can. I'll bet she chips in once a round. Youth, it's wonderful."

Perhaps that ability to score is one reason Nancy has never got involved in theories of the swing.

"I don't know a lot about swing techniques," she says. "And I don't want to. I have a swing that I trust. Lee Trevino once told me to keep it as long as it worked. That's something I've always remembered."

Nancy remembers what her father taught her, too. One of his bits of advice was never to think about the money involved on a shot. "I violated that advice just once," Nancy admits. "It was at Long Island last August, my third tournament as a professional and my second after getting my LPGA card. Debbie Austin had it won. I needed a two-foot putt on the 72nd hole to tie Kathy Whitworth for second. I started figuring what a missed putt there would cost me. I froze. The more I looked at the putt the longer it got. Finally I just jammed the ball into the hole. I haven't thought about the prize money since."

Money was a critical subject in Nancy's childhood, because there was never an abundance of it in the family. Domingo Lopez, now 64, runs an auto body repair shop in Roswell. His wife Marina, who died at 52 last year of complications following an appendectomy, was a diabetic. They raised two daughters. The oldest, Delma, 32, never got involved in golf. She and husband Bernie, who also runs an auto body repair shop, live with their three children in Harbour City, Calif. The sisters are close friends.

Nancy began playing golf at 8 with her parents at the Cahoon Park municipal course. It has 18 holes today, but at that time had only nine. Domingo was then a 4-handicap player (his game has deteriorated since Nancy left home).

"He knew a lot about the golf swing and he could play," Nancy says. "I couldn't beat him until I was 12." By then she had won the first of her three straight New Mexico Women's Amateur championships. At 15 she won the 1972 U.S. Girls Junior in her first try, won it again in 1974 and was Western Junior Girls champion in 1972, '73 and '74.

Domingo financed his daughter's amateur golf career by watching his dollars carefully, saving small amounts each month. The only vacations he took were to Nancy's tournaments. To say this selfless little man sacrificed for Nancy is inadequate; he virtually devoted his life to her. Domingo Lopez saw in his youngest daughter's talent an opportunity for her to rise above the toil he had known as a farm laborer and auto body repairman and savor a life rarely accorded Mexican-Americans in the Southwest.

"I hear a lot of athletes crediting their success to their parents," Nancy says. "In my case I mean it. They gave up so many things for me. Mom put off buying a dishwasher for years because of my golf expenses. She wanted to live in a bigger house, but instead my folks bought me a car so I could drive to the course. They were always doing things like that for me."

Six weeks after her graduation from high school in 1975, Nancy finished second in the U.S. Women's Open at Atlantic City. It was the first time most of the LPGA pros had seen her play. Nancy indicated her intention at that time of eventually joining the tour, but she wanted to attend college for at least two years to gain maturity. Scholarship offers were pouring in.

She accepted a $10,000 Colgate scholarship, and the announcement was to be made in August at the Collegiate All-American dinner, honoring the top men's college players, at the Waldorf-Astoria Hotel in New York City.

On the day of the award, Nancy was competing in the Women's Western Amateur at Tanglewood, near

Winston-Salem, N.C. It was arranged for her to fly late that afternoon into Newark and be met by a Fugazy Continental Corp. limousine. William Fugazy is the founder of the All-American Collegiate Golf foundation and a close friend of Bob Hope, who was master of ceremonies at the dinner.

A mix-up in communications resulted in there being no limousine. As she pondered whether to take a cab or return to Winston-Salem, the limo showed up and whisked Nancy to the formal dinner at the Waldorf. She appeared on the podium just in time for the presentation, still wearing her golf shorts and sweater.

"Congratulations, Nancy," beamed Hope. "But after hearing your story, I'm not sure if I want to book one of Bill's limos again."

With the Colgate scholarship, Nancy decided to enroll at the University of Tulsa, where a seven-time Oklahoma Women's Amateur champion named Dale McNamara had established one of the country's best golf programs for women.

Lopez was destined for greatness in golf from her first days on the LPGA. During her first year Lopez already felt "very much at home on the tour." (Photo: Stephen Szurlej)

College golf was a walk in the park for Nancy. She entered 18 tournaments in two years and won 14, plus the Women's Intercollegiate championship as a freshman.

Having conquered all the challenges of college golf, Lopez was anxious to get out on tour and relieve her parents of additional financial responsibility. She signed with Mark McCormack's International Golf Group and turned pro shortly before the 1977 Women's Open at Hazeltine.

Hollis Stacy methodically won that tournament, but Nancy was in contention until she took a double bogey on the 12th hole the final round and finished second, two strokes back. Her parents were in the gallery, walking every hole.

After gaining her LPGA card the next week, she finished second again in a Colgate tournament at Sunningdale in England and shared second in her next start, at Long Island.

Shortly afterward Nancy's mother died, a shattering experience for the closely knit family. "I promised Dad I'd dedicate my first LPGA win to Mom," Nancy says. "But I had to wait until this year to do it."

The occasion was the Bent Tree Classic in Sarasota, Fla., played in frigid weather. Sharing the lead late in the final round with Jo Ann Washam, one of her playing partners, Nancy rolled in a 15-foot downhill birdie putt on the 71st hole to take a one-stroke margin into the final hole, a par 5.

"She played that hole like a veteran," says Washam. "Knowing I had to gamble for a birdie, she hit a 2-iron off the tee and a 4-iron second. I hit my second into a greenside bunker and took three to get down. Nancy just threw a nice little pitch onto the green, two-putted and that was it."

Rushing to a phone in the press room, Nancy called her father. "I won, Daddy," she said softly. As Nancy broke into tears, Domingo Lopez replied from his garage, "Mom would have been proud of you, honey."

She followed with another win in the next tournament, the Sunstar Classic, and, going for three straight, Nancy shot 68 in the final round of the Kathryn Crosby/Honda Civic Classic. But Sally Little finished with a blistering 65 and won the playoff on the first extra hole.

It was disappointing to Nancy, but hardly cataclysmic. There would be other weeks and other victories. She has found, somewhat to her surprise, a rich enjoyment of the tour routine. "I wasn't sure how I'd like all the travel," she says. "But so far it's been fine. I feel very much at home on the tour."

She is also making sure that her family shares in her success. Nancy bought a lovely fur jacket in Australia for her sister, and took her father along to tournaments in Japan and Australia. Domingo loved it.

"I'm not going with Nancy to Japan this year, though," he says. "I don't like those shots."

Domingo was referring to the mandatory vaccinations, not the delightful kind pouring out of his daughter's golf clubs.

August 1975

How Bob Drum and I Invented Arnold Palmer

Johnson had Boswell, Arnie had Drum

by Dan Jenkins

The first time any of us ever actually noticed a guy named Arnold Palmer it was on the veranda at Augusta around 1957 and we wondered who that vacationing longshoreman was talking to Bob Drum, the writer.

Later, Drum said, "That's Arnold D. Palmer of Latrobe, Pa., the next great golfer."

"Yeah, sure," one of us said. "And I'm the next Steinbeck. But first I got to get me some of those maroon pants with the cuffs turned up, and a green shirt, and an orange alpaca, like your pal over there. Arnold who?"

There were only two golfers then, we liked to joke. Hogan and Snead. Well, maybe there was a Middlecoff occasionally. Writers are very strict about touring pros having familiar names. Editors make writers take laps and do pushups when Jack Fleck or Orville Moody wins a U.S. Open.

In any case, I was convinced our next hero of the era would be Ken Venturi. Others fancied Gene Littler.

"Venturi perhaps," Drum would say. "But there's no such guy as Littler. He mails in his scores. Arnold D. Palmer of Latrobe, Pa., is the next great chin. He makes 4,567 birdies a day."

Usually, when Drum spoke, you were forced to listen. He was larger than all of the rest of us put together, he could outdrink the British army without showing it, and he was one of the more entertaining writers on the golf circuit. At least he was to those of us who were familiar with The Pittsburgh Press, or who would read over his shoulder as he sat typing in the press rooms roaring with laughter at his own words.

I should point out right here, I think, that it is impossible to reminisce about Arnold Palmer without continually thinking of Bob Drum, of whom an army captain once said, when Drum was defending our country by teaching Nazi prisoners how to play softball in Italy and North Africa: "You're aptly named, Drum. Big, loud and empty."

That was wrong. Drum was big, loud and *hilarious*, and he merely introduced most of us to half of the people in the world that we know. As I have said over many a cocktail through the years, "Bob Drum *invented* Arnold Palmer."

That statement will of course ring with accuracy only to anyone in the profession of journalism. No one really invented Arnold Palmer, naturally, except Mr. and Mrs. Palmer. But if ever an athlete had an unofficial publicity and public relations director who could do a job for him—purely out of friendship, admiration and no doubt a little hero worship—Arnold had such a man in Bob Drum. And Arnold had him in the days when it mattered the most—when Arnold was *becoming* the Arnold of "Whooo, haaaa, go get 'em, Arnie."

Writers have golfers, you know. And golfers have writers. In a way, I suppose, a lot of us thought of ourselves as a modern-day version of O.B. Keeler, who had Bobby Jones.

Ben Hogan belonged to everyone, to be sure, but I certainly felt he belonged mostly to me. I was from The Fort Worth Press, and Ben was the reason I started going to the big tournaments. My assignment in those days, therefore, was to follow Hogan, shot-by-shot, quote-by-quote, and, secondarily, to cover the tournament proper.

In so doing I became a sort of Hogan walking bibliography, which is what our old friend, the late Walter Stewart of The Memphis Commercial-Appeal, became with Cary Middlecoff. It is what Kaye Kessler has become in Columbus with Jack Nicklaus, and what Art Spander has become in San Francisco with Johnny Miller. And it is what Bob Drum was in Pittsburgh with Arnold Palmer.

Drum and I became friends back in 1951. We

According to Dan Jenkins, "It is impossible to reminisce about Arnold Palmer without continually thinking of Bob Drum." Arnold Palmer and Drum have been linked for many years, shown here together circa 1960. (Photo courtesy of Mrs. Bob Drum)

Palmer taking a breather at the 1970 Tournament of Champions. (Photo: Lester Nehamkin)

"Arnie has more people watching him park the car than we do on the course."

—LEE TREVINO
ON THE ETERNAL
DRAWING POWER OF
ARNOLD PALMER

first met trying to avoid a drink check on the Masters veranda. (When I think that I will be going to my 25th anniversary Masters with him next spring, I entertain the idea of decorating myself with a medal.) Possibly, we became friends because I could supply him with Hogan quotes and he could give me Snead quotes. I didn't know Snead well. He was the enemy.

Drum would say to me, "Hey, Texas," as he typed on deadline. "Gimme a Hogan quote."

If I didn't have any yet, I would invent one. If Drum didn't like it, he would yell, "I read that in Herbert Warren Wind's *book*, you rotten son of a bitch. Gimme something fresh."

Ultimately, together, Drum and I would come dangerously close to making Ben Hogan out to be a standup comedian in The Pittsburgh Press and The Fort Worth Press.

I recite all this only to prepare the world for the confession that Drum and I, over the years, did as much for Arnold Palmer. As Drum was saying recently, "He thinks he *said* all those things."

An example of *all those things* would be this: The brilliant journalists are on deadline, Arnold has won the Masters again, and it's time for a human voice to appear in our copy, but we haven't spoken to Palmer yet.

Let's say this is 1960, as Drum and I are blazing away on the typewriters. Couldn't anyone tell by the smoke? Faster. The stories are eating away at the cocktail hour.

"What did he say?" I would ask.

"He said Augusta's a par 68," Drum would babble, typing it. "He said he's going to the British Open. He said the modern professional Grand Slam is the Masters, the U.S. Open, the PGA and the British Open."

"Arnold Palmer said that?" I asked.

"Who the hell are we talking about?" Drum said. "Laurie Auchterlonie?"

Thus, *Arnold Palmer* would read in The Pittsburgh Press that he would go to the British Open. He would also learn what the Grand Slam was. In a roundabout way, it was Bob Drum who rejuvenated the British Open, for when Arnold started going, everybody else did who mattered.

Much has been written about Palmer at Cherry Hills in 1960, of what he said in the locker room before going out for the final round of that U.S. Open when he shot the 65—and shot down the field. Arnold never actually made a serious prediction that day. He was too far back; practically out of the tournament.

Drum and I found Arnold sitting on a bench in the locker room. He was sitting there with Venturi and Bob Rosburg. They were eating hamburgers and drinking ice tea. We stumbled across them, in fact. We had been looking for Mike Souchak, the leader.

The three of them were joking around, as players do who are out of contention. We simply sat down to listen. Eventually, Arnold got around to talking about how much Cherry Hills' first hole "bugged" him, as he put it.

"You ought to be able to drive that thing," Arnold said. "With the right bounce over the rough, you could get it on there."

It was a par 4.

"Sure," Drum said. "If you're George Bayer in a limousine."

"I've almost been on it," Palmer said.

"I've almost been on it in two," said Venturi.

It went along like this for a few more minutes, or until it was time for Arnold to tee off for the last 18.

He stood up and smiled at Drum.

"You coming?" he said.

Drum said, "I'm tired of watching duck hooks. There's a guy named Souchak leading the tournament. He's from Pittsburgh, too."

"If I drive the first hole I might shoot 65," Arnold said.

"Good," said Drum. "You'll finish 14th."

"That would be 280," Arnold said. "Doesn't 280 always win the Open?"

I said, "Yeah. When Hogan shoots it."

Arnold laughed and left.

He had driven the first green and birdied the first four holes before Drum and I caught him and climbed, sweaty and out of breath, under the gallery ropes, as our armbands permitted.

As we loitered on the fifth tee, Arnold took the Coke in a paper cup out of my hand and sipped on it. He took a pack of cigarettes out of my shirt pocket and lit one.

He did say, at that point, and with a grin, "Fancy seeing you here."

But he didn't say, "Who's winning the Open?" He said that a few holes later, after he had birdied six of the first seven, and had noticed that *he* was leading the Open.

As much as I would like to give Drum the credit, Bob did not originate "Arnie's Army." A young fellow named Johnny Hendrix did, in The Augusta Chronicle.

Drum immediately recognized the historical importance of it, however.

As we were reading the paper one morning during the Masters in the old Bon Air Hotel coffee shop, Drum said, mostly to himself, "I'll be a son of a bitch. Here's a mush mouth from the South like you who's just made himself immortal."

There was a pause, and Drum said:

"Arnie's Army, comma."

I was fortunate to get to know Arnold early, me being the guy who was always with Drum. When he captured his first Masters, in 1958, I got to be with Arnold and Winnie that evening, as Drum and I earnestly sought our "Monday follow-ups."

When he took the British Open at Troon in 1962, Arnold celebrated by having a reasonably quiet dinner with Winnie, Drum and I in the dining room of the Marine Hotel. I remember the staff sending over a cake to the table with an inscription in icing: "Open Champion." Arnold sliced the cake, took a piece, stood up, smiled at the room, and sat down.

Whereupon he turned to us and asked:

"Do you suppose I have to eat it?"

I can still see him in the parking lot at Oakmont in 1962 after he had lost the U.S. Open playoff to Nicklaus. He's angry. He's slamming the clubs in the trunk of the car.

"You three-putted 12 greens in the tournament," I said. "He only three-putted once."

"Screw statistics," said Drum. "The fat kid can play golf."

The competitor came out in Arnold.

"I can beat the fat kid the best day he ever had," Arnold said.

On our way back to the press tent, I said, "That was a hell of a quote."

Drum laughed, agreeing.

"And we didn't make it up," he said.

We were in Arnold's home in 1966 not too long

after he had blown the Open to Billy Casper. Nobody could blow seven shots in the last nine holes to anybody, but Arnold had.

"I could have played safe," Arnold said, "but that wouldn't have been me. That's not how I got where I am. He kept playing safe even when he was catching up. I couldn't believe it."

Drum said, "If you'd played safe and won, we'd have said you were a dirty, rotten coward."

Arnold roared laughing. It helped.

As late as 1959 I was still not convinced that this guy from Latrobe, who so far had only taken one Masters, was going to be The Man. And just as I was about to be convinced, on that Sunday in Augusta, as Arnold was leading going to the 12th tee, on the verge of winning the Masters two years in a row, catastrophe struck—and almost took Drum with it.

We were up on the press tower that overlooks the 11th green, and all of the par-3 No. 12. It is not an exaggeration that when Arnold hit his shot into Rae's Creek at the 12th hole—he would take a double bogey and blow the whole thing—Drum lost his balance in an emotional struggle to hurry the ball over the water.

I recall hearing, "Aaada . . . got . . . son of a . . . eeeiiiiiii . . . ," as all 260 pounds of Bob Drum fell off the tower.

In his glory days Arnold Palmer was probably the most gracious and friendly of any superstar, ever. He was forever helpful and had time for any writer, whether the writer's name was Drum or not.

I never saw him refuse to sign an autograph for a fan, no matter how inconvenient it might be, no matter how obtuse the person.

One of the reasons was because Arnold was just naturally a good-natured individual. But another reason, after he became Arnold Palmer, was because Bob Drum frequently schooled him on how to handle himself. Or teased him into doing the proper thing. Or joked him into it. Or provoked him into it.

There was the year when we were all in Las Vegas, at the Tournament of Champions, when Arnold wanted to go home. He wanted to skip Colonial, an event to which I was obviously partial, it being in my old home town of Fort Worth.

"You've got to play Colonial," said Drum. "It's in our friend's town." He meant mine.

"I'm worn out," Arnold said.

After a while, Drum said, "You don't want to go because you can't play the golf course. It's too tough. You can't play a tough, narrow course."

You could almost hear Arnold growling. He went on to Colonial, and, incidentally, won the tournament.

Not too many seasons ago, during the Los Angeles Open, I was expected to do a rather lengthy television interview with Arnold for a show that was cosponsored by the magazine I work for, Sports Illustrated. I explained to Arnold that he would be doing it for free, and that it would probably require an hour. It was being set up for the next day, after he completed his round.

"I'll have to clear it with Mark," he said, meaning

A passing of the torch: young Palmer and Ben Hogan warming up on the practice green. (Photo: Golf World)

Mark McCormack, through whom he had been clearing his empire for years.

It was a doubly uninviting thing for Arnold to do, because we would be talking about why he wasn't winning anymore.

The following day when I approached him, he said, "I talked to Mark and I'm afraid I can't do it. There's a complication with another network, and some other reasons you're aware of."

I said, "Forgetting business, why don't we just look at it as a personal favor to me?"

Arnold fidgeted with that thought for a while, as we had a drink, and finally he said:

"Aw, hell. Let's do it, anyway, and not tell Mark."

In the great years when he seemed to win whenever he was in the mood, or whenever it was important, he earned a sort of underground nickname among a few of us. Bubba.

I think it must have been around 1962, and, again, at Augusta, when it happened. More things have happened to Palmer at Augusta than have happened to Bob Drum on side streets.

Anyhow, neither Drum nor I will soon forget

Arnold lining up a birdie putt on the fourth green at Augusta during the playoff with Gary Player and Dow Finsterwald. Near us behind the ropes, among the hordes, was your basic southern golf fan, all decked out in cap, cleats, hotdog, binoculars, sunburn and accent.

Quietly, the fan said:

"You make this one, Bubba, and you da leader of da tribe."

Bob Drum and his trusty sidekick, me, and a few others in our drinking and typing club, have been calling him "Bubba" ever since.

But Arnold Palmer, whose wife calls him Arn, and whose army calls him Arnie, has never known why.

Now that all of us mostly deal in memories, since Drum no longer writes for a paper and Arnold seems unable to win the big ones, we will have to tell him that one of these days.

"You were the best, Bubba," Bob Drum will conclude, raising a glass of vodka. "There was no such sport before you came along."

And I will agree, smiling at them both with immense pleasure and fondness.

September 1984

J.C. Snead: Bad Guy or Good Ol' Boy?

Digging for a soft center inside a hard crust

by Mickey Herskowitz

*The misunderstood J.C. on tour
(Photo: Larry Petrillo)*

Once you have said that J.C. Snead is a real live nephew of his Uncle Sam, the connection kind of breaks down. Sam Snead is part of the glory of golf, an original, a name that ranks with Hagen, Hogan and Nelson among the Old Masters.

J.C. (for Jesse Carlyle) Snead may or may not be the least-popular player on the tour today, one of the 10 toughest interviews, or one of the five most in need of a Dale Carnegie course. It is troubling enough that some people think so, and these conclusions have appeared in a distinguished national magazine (this one). I mean, has the media ever lied to you?

Of course, a lot of athletes would have taken that rap and run with it. That is, they would have advertised themselves as "The Golfer You Love to Hate," and hired Howard Cosell's PR man, and affected a scowl that would have made Mr. T look sweeter than Michael Jackson.

Do you know what would have happened? People would have started to write and talk about what a stand-up guy J.C. is, a rugged individualist. They would have dug around for the soft center under the hard crust. He might have published a book and become an analyst on golf telecasts and starred in a Lite Beer commercial.

It's the American way.

But none of this, and less, has happened to J.C. Snead. During a period of what he sees as bad press and bad karma, his game and health and purse have all suffered. In the past 12 months he has earned almost nothing in fringe monies. "I have gotten a reputation for being a hard-ass," he says, "and I think it is undeserved."

That sentence is pure J.C. Snead: direct, earthy, a little wistful. It is almost as if he had been taking a test ever since he turned pro in 1964. And now, at 42, after $1.5 million in winnings, and seven titles, and competing on three Ryder Cup teams, he had been told he was to be graded only on neatness and personality.

He had been a late-starter, coming to golf at 27, as Sam's nephew, and as a failed ex-baseball player, out of a Grizzly Adams kind of childhood. Whatever else one thinks of him, a background so distinctive should have made J.C. an unending source of what is loosely called "good copy." We can only wonder what combination of his shyness, or stubbornness, and the critical judgments of press and fans, relegated him to a lesser universe.

His wife, the former Sue Bryant, is a city girl, a product of the Florida suburbs, bright and strikingly pretty. She has her own theory about her husband's reputation. "Jesse isn't very good at game-playing," she says, "and he isn't always tactful. It all goes back to how he was raised. You're raised in this country, and if you step in mud or dirt or whatever, you say so, you don't call it banana pudding. It's sad, but on the tour it seems there have to be good guys and bad guys. And he's been labeled a bad guy."

The question is, why? What did he do, to whom and where? Even if he didn't, how does he deal with his problem? If you don't think you are the least-liked player on tour, what can you do? To paraphrase a former president of the United States, it is hardly the most effective form of public relations to cry out to the world, "I AM NOT A HARD-ASS."

Yet a small irony is at work here. He openly admires the kind of sportsman whose label he doesn't want. Ted Williams, George Blanda and Bobby Knight never were afflicted with terminal niceness. Says J.C.: "Williams was the only idol I ever had. I thought he was a god." Knight is "a great coach whose players learn about life." Blanda is "another one who had to keep proving himself."

Sam Snead did not always have a saintly image, but he disarmed his critics with a quip or a story or sometimes a grin. Sam defends his nephew, although—given that famous Snead honesty, that no-bull's-wool reflex—the issue seems briefly in doubt. "The boy is his own worst enemy," says Sam. "He takes after my dad. He was a haughty sort of man. Never said a bad word to anybody. Never said much of anything.

"J.C. is a person who is kind of hard to make friends with. He doesn't want to bother people. He

147

Above left: *Talking with his wife, Sue, and Uncle Sam in downtown Hot Springs, Va. (Photo: Jim Moriarty)*

Middle: *Ready to chop down a tree on his 900-acre farm. (Photo: Jim Moriarty)*

Right: *Showing the form that enabled Snead to hit the ball so far "it was a joke." (Photo: Stephen Szurlej)*

thinks he does the right thing by staying out of their way. I've told him, some people want to be bothered. If they applaud a shot, he ought to tip his hat or wave or smile or say hi. Don't just walk off."

The J.C. Snead story is an interesting one not only for the local color and the family connection. It is interesting because it brushes the line between writers and the people they cover, and goes to the heart of the contract that exists between the writer and you, the reader. Have we treated these people fairly and without favor, and as fully dimensional figures? Do we owe them more sympathy, or none?

Nothing has haunted and disturbed J.C. Snead quite so much as the Case of the Phantom Pro-Am. It is a tale that seems to rank right up there with the story of The Vanishing Hitchhiker. The story travels.

It has been reported as having occurred at four or five courses, but the details are fairly consistent. The money involved is described as between $600 and $750, the putt of the amateur partner between two feet and six. The pro (J.C. Snead) has ignored his partners or grouched at them for 17 holes. Then, at 18, it dawned on him that they needed this dinky putt for a birdie to win it all. Suddenly, he was Mr. Goodwrench, friendly and helpful, lining up the putt and reminding everyone: "Now, pards, if you make that, we'll win the pro-am and I'll win $750."

Given that encouragement, the high handicapper back-handed the ball across the green and into a bunker. Up yours.

The only flaw in the story is the fact that Snead swears it never happened and no living soul has ever come forward to verify it. First reported in the fall of 1983, the anecdote has followed him from Orlando to Canada to Doral to San Diego. Not a week goes by that he isn't asked or kidded about it.

Many of his fellow golfers found the story amusing. Arnold Palmer thought it was harmless and advised J.C. to go along with it. "But, Arnold," said Snead, "it

never happened. And if you were the head of a big corporation, and you wanted 15 pros to play in a clinic with your best customers, would you invite me after reading that?"

Palmer said, "I see what you mean."

J.C. Snead just misses—by about a quarter of a mile—finding any humor in the story or the corner it has boxed him in. "I figure it cost me at least $100,000 this past year," he says, "maybe more. The only pro-ams I got invited to were Amana and the three or four I've always done. Not a single new one. Last summer at Westchester they had five pro-ams going at the same time on Monday, and I was in my motel room. They had guys playing who couldn't qualify for a tournament. And I wasn't invited. It comes from that story."

Snead knows he should shrug it off with a casual French phrase and concentrate on his game. But the story spreads like some kind of fungus. "It hurts," he says. "I haven't even admitted that to my wife. But it really hurts to feel you're not wanted. Since this crap really started, I think I would have quit if I had something else to do. It got to the point where it was embarrassing to show up, to hear people make their little snob remarks."

Uncle Sam chips in: "When those things get going they just seem to build. It's too bad, because common sense tells you it didn't happen. That would be stupid, a man knocking off a ball when his team has a chance to win. No matter how he hates the pro, I never heard of any club golfer blowing a chance to win like that."

J.C. has a better reputation among his fellow pros on tour, many of whom seek his advice on the practice tee. "Some of the tour players such as J.C. who the public thinks are awful are the ones the players like the most," says tour veteran Andy North. "He's a devoted family man who loves his time away from the tour and enjoys the basic things of life. To me, he's one of the most likable guys out here."

Adds Joe Inman: "What he says most of the time is the truth, but he talks sometimes when he shouldn't say anything. In our world today there are a lot of false people, but J.C.'s not one of them. If they have a war and line everybody up, I want to be on his side. He's a good person—he just never learned how to politic."

But one of J.C.'s appealing qualities is his willingness to lower his guard, and to describe a moment that may not reflect to his own advantage. "I'm sure I struck people as temperamental," he says. "In pro-ams, it was a case of wanting to win but not feeling real easy with people I didn't know. The last eight to 10 years, I always made it a point on the first green to offer my help in lining up putts or club selection or yardage. After four or five holes you generally can tell who needs help and who will accept it. If a guy takes a suggestion and seems eager for more, I'll help him every swing I can the rest of the way.

"Then you run into guys who feel they know more about golf than you do. I corrected a banker once and he argued with me. I told him, look, if I came to you for a loan, I wouldn't expect to tell you how to determine your interest rates.'

"Another time I had a run-in with John Y. Brown, before he became governor of Kentucky. He probably thinks I'm the biggest horse's ass in the world. We were playing in a pro-am in Kentucky. He's a pretty good player, a 5- or 6-handicapper, but he hit one in the rough on a par 5. No way he could hit it out of there. I couldn't hit it out of there. The grass is up to your ankles. He gets in there with a 3-wood. I said, in what I thought was a nice way, 'Now, wait a minute. Take a 7-iron or something and hit down the fairway. You can get on the green in three.'

"He said, 'No, I want to hit a 3-wood.' I said he couldn't and he said, 'The hell I can't.' That kind of got me going. I bet him $10 he couldn't hit it 20 yards. His face turned red and I thought he was going to explode. He got in there and took a cut and the ball went about five feet. I mean, Jack Nicklaus or Ben Hogan couldn't have hit a 3-wood out of there. It was like trying to hit a 3-wood out of six inches of water. Can't be done. The next two par 5s John Y. put it back in the rough and he was going to show me he could hit that damned 3-wood out of there. Never did. Took himself right out of the hole each time. And I never got invited back."

At first blush, the alleged incident of the rude pro and the tanked putt might seem of only passing interest, hardly worth taking sides over. But J.C. feels he can't ignore it, believing the story to be at the bottom of his selection as The Least Favorite PGA Tour Player in a poll of 20,000 GOLF DIGEST readers (March 1984). It wasn't the kind of cause that would send people pouring into the streets, waving their "Free J.C. Snead" placards. But he welcomed the expressions of support that came from friends and even some amateurs who had gone to the firing line with him.

One such letter went to GOLF DIGEST from Thomas R. Devlin, the president of Rent-A-Center Inc. in Wichita, Kan., who was in Snead's foursome the first round of the Disney World Classic in Orlando.

"I wasn't expecting to enjoy the day," Devlin wrote.

"However, Mr. Snead was friendly and warm. One member of the group was very nervous. Mr. Snead went out of his way to work with him and help him to relax and feel comfortable. I was very impressed with his manner.

"The next morning, on my way to breakfast, I ran into J.C. He recognized me and invited me to go to the club with him for breakfast and introduced me to some of the other pros. He was very gracious. I suspect that many people are misinformed, as I was, about him."

A congressman from Illinois, Marty Russo, also took issue with the results of the survey. Wrote Russo: "I find it hard to believe that anyone who has talked to him and gotten to know him could rank J.C. as anything but first-rate, on any scale." All of which recalls a story told by a onetime Illinois congressman named Abe Lincoln about a man being tarred and feathered and run out of town on a rail, who said: "If it wasn't for the honor, I'd just as soon walk."

To know or to understand the Snead who isn't Sam, it is necessary to examine the soil from which he sprang. The town of Hot Springs, Va., sits in a scenic valley surrounded by majestic mountain ranges on three sides. The names echo and soar and clap with thunder: Allegheny, Appalachia, The Shenandoah. It is a town that grew up around a field of mineral wells and a hotel called The Homestead.

On a clear and balmy summer day, J.C. climbed behind the wheel of a Chevrolet and headed through the hills to the airport at Roanoke, 35 miles away. He turned into downtown Hot Springs on a street with no sign. ("It's the only street we got," he said. "Must be Main Street. They built a new post office and a new bank and added a wing to the hotel. That's the only things that have changed since I was a little kid.")

At 8 in the morning the town was stirring. That is, a man in a straw hat was talking to a burly fellow outside the office of the Exxon station.

"There's Sam, now." said J.C., swinging into the driveway.

Sure enough, it was.

Sam walked over, put his elbow on the passenger-side window and said, "Thought you were leaving."

J.C.: "Running late. I'm on my way."

Sam: "All right. Did you hit some yesterday? Hit 'em better?"

J.C.: "Pretty good, but I was still turning the short iron. Right to left."

Sam: "Well, dammit, follow it along the line a little more and they won't close up as fast." He backed off a step and gave the rented Chevy a curious look, "This your car?" Assured that it was not, he nodded and said, "Well, don't get your ass up over the dashboard, as they say."

J.C.: "I won't. Thanks."

You had to see the look on the nephew's face to appreciate the meaning of the phrase "hero worship." It was the kind of awe and affection you have seen on the faces of small boys looking up at an all-star first baseman, a look without doubts.

The fact is, J.C. barely knew his Uncle Sam when

> "I have had people tell me lately how much they enjoyed playing with me. They tell me I'm really a nice guy, a credit to my profession. I tell them, 'Don't tell anybody; you'll screw up my image.' "
>
> —J.C. SNEAD

he was a youngster. He was on closer terms with his uncles Pete and Homer. But what he really knew was the land, these roads, that bridge. He knew them inch by inch. Hot Springs was a company town and the company was The Homestead, where his father retired as chief engineer after more than 50 years on the job.

No more than 5,000 people live in all of Bath County, which includes Hot Springs, and a crime wave is when someone steals a chicken. The man talking to Sam Snead at the gas station was the brother of the fellow who manages J.C.'s farm, just outside of town. "Now that guy right there," J.C. was saying, "comes from a family of 11. That bunch was raised like somebody was raised in the 1880s. They didn't have any running water, no electricity, they hunted for most of their food, they raised a big garden and their mother canned everything."

With his golf earnings, J.C. and Sue bought two parcels of land, the Patterson place and the Jenkins place, for a total of 900 acres. They completely restored and doubled the size of a farmhouse first built in 1901, adding a second story and a master bedroom with a bathroom bigger than some of the clubhouses J.C. once changed in. It has a Jacuzzi.

A trip through those hills with J.C. turns into a travelogue. George Washington passed through town. Robert E. Lee spent the night in a house where the Cascades Hotel now stands. One of the fiercest battles of the Civil War was fought a few ridges away.

He points out his father's house, and Sam's, and the red-brick building where he attended grade school. A groundhog, an odd-looking creature, skitters across the road. A hundred yards away the leaves rustle as a fawn leaps deeper into the woods. All nature seems to call.

Over there he shot his first deer, and two mountains over he killed a bear. Through those trees you can see the path where the Cherokees once came to take the mineral waters, 110 degrees, right out of the ground.

"I appreciate nature and what a good friend it is," says J.C. "I notice when we're playing golf, the guys I play with, they walk around the course and they only notice three things: the grass, the greens and their ball. That's it. They don't see frogs or snakes or squirrels or turtles. I'm always looking for something. My eyes are always working."

There have been Sneads in that valley since the 1700s, hard by the West Virginia line. They are mountain folk—you may even call them hillbillies—and proud of it. They are governed by a code that J.C. describes in this way: If you've done anything wrong and you're asked a direct question, you admit it, even if you were one of many. But you volunteer nothing.

Once he worked as a lifeguard at The Homestead and, to save his job, on the advice of his superior, he denied an act of mischief to the lady who ran the place. "You know what?" he says. "It still bothers me today, that I stood there and looked that woman in the eye and denied something I had done." He paused, then added: "That was nearly 30 years ago."

It is part of J.C.'s natural honesty, that belongs with

the natural athlete and the natural outdoorsman, to not sugarcoat or nudge the myth of family fidelity.

His love and respect for Sam need no embellishment here. Just try to suggest to him that Ben Hogan had more shots or Byron Nelson more style. But into his early 20s he was never quite sure how to take him.

"When I was a kid," he says, "Sam never really made me feel comfortable. He always said something to hurt my feelings. Like, I'd slip out to one of the courses to watch him play in a tournament, and I knew he was a famous golfer and all that. I was always shy. I'd want to say hello as much as anything. He was family, and he was supposed to be the best.

"He'd see me. He'd cut a look out the corner of his eye and see me standing over there and he wouldn't say a word. And maybe a hole or two would go along and then he'd come by and he'd say something, and it would always hurt my feelings. Just the way he was. Like, 'Boy, what are you doing out here? Why the hell aren't you out caddieing and making some money?'

"I know now he didn't mean anything by it. If nobody had been around it would have been all right. But there was always a crowd around and he'd say it in front of other people and it always made me feel like a jerk, or so out of place."

As time went on, Sam realized that his brother Jess' boy was the one most like him. At 6-2 and 205, J.C. was bigger than his illustrious uncle. Both had been brilliant all-around athletes in high school and shared a love of baseball. Sam briefly played Class D ball and was once a partner with Ted Williams in a sporting-goods store.

J.C. has been described as one of the finest athletes the state of Virginia ever produced. He was born in 1941, two years after Sam Snead had already blown the best chance he would ever have at winning the U.S. Open. J.C. was a triple threat: in football, in basketball he averaged 26 points a game and led the team to the only state championship in the school's history, in baseball he batted .400.

He played junior college football—the first Snead ever to attend college—and signed a contract in 1961 with baseball's Washington Senators. In three minor league seasons he hit a high of .318, but broke an ankle and clashed with a manager and gave it up.

The final conflict was over a stolen glove. A gang of kids ripped off his team's clubhouse and J.C. lost a new glove. The insurance covered the cost of a new one, $40, but when the old ones were found a few weeks later buried in the ground near the ball park, the manager told J.C. he ought to reimburse the club. J.C. told him to take the old glove and put it where the sun don't shine. The manager filed a report citing J.C. for having a bad attitude.

Even after he had quit the team, the act of doing so was painful enough that he stayed in his motel room three days before he left for home. There he faced a disappointed Uncle Sam, whose first words were: "Boy, why'd you quit?"

"I told him," says J.C., "that in baseball until someone told you that you could play, you didn't play. I

It is part of J.C.'s natural honesty, that belongs with the natural athlete and the natural outdoorsman, to not sugarcoat or nudge the myth of family fidelity.

Hot Springs, Va., is a company town and the company is The Homestead. The beautiful resort is where J.C.'s father worked for more than 50 years and J.C. was once a lifeguard. (Photo: Jim Moriarty)

decided to try golf. After playing baseball, and swinging that heavy bat, I could hit it so far it was a joke."

Three weeks after he put away his baseball glove, J.C. had an assistant's job at Purchase, N.Y., working for a pro named Charlie Beverage, another Hot Springs product who had apprenticed under Sam.

The first time Beverage asked Sam to check out his nephew, Sam declined. First, he had to be convinced that J.C. was serious about the game and, second, that he wasn't looking for a handout.

"When Sam first started out," says J.C., "a few guys hustled him out of some bucks. And some of the family —not mine—hit on him a few times. When you get out there and scratch from absolutely nothing, and you get something, and along the way people take some of it away, you learn the hard way and you learn quick. Sam may have a reputation for being tightfisted. He's really not. He does a lot for people that nobody hears about. That's the way people are around here.

"I had already joined the tour [in 1968] before I finally got to play a round with Sam. He was the pro at Boca Raton and I'll tell you, I was scared to death. That was just about as nervous as I've ever been in golf, the first time I played with Sam. After he found out I was really dedicated he did everything he could to help me. Our relationship has just gotten better and better. We're not only uncle and nephew, we're friends."

A few weeks later, the Sneads played golf in Hot Springs and Uncle Sam birdied seven of the last eight holes and had his nephew down four strokes with four to play. "He's his own worst enemy," said Sam, candid as ever at 72. "Hard-headed as a damned mule. We were riding in the cart and I said, 'Just because you're mad, you follow a bad shot with another. You have to stop that.' J.C. has got ability out of this world, but it flashes on and off. Palmer told me, 'He doesn't know how good he is. He doesn't take advantage of it.' I think a lot of people on the tour envy the talent J.C. has."

They may not envy him his reputation, or temper, or a recent siege with low blood sugar that sapped his strength and weakened his game. And no doubt he could use a little of his Uncle Sam's showmanship.

But there is no pretense about him, and he needs no polls—good or bad—to tell him who he is or where he came from. He is J.C. Snead, who is never going to be Sam, who is 42 and playing for his wife and his son Jason, 5, and his own pride. He is battling to get back his health and his game and his reputation. Well, he isn't so sure about the reputation.

"I have had people tell me lately how much they enjoyed playing with me," says J.C. "They tell me I'm really a nice guy, a credit to my profession. I tell them, 'Don't tell anybody; you'll screw up my image.' "

The Old Course at St. Andrews, unfurled in all its glory for the 1990 Open Championship. (Photo: Stephen Szurlej)

119th OPEN GOLF CHAMPIONSHIP

LEADER BOARD UNISYS

HOLES	+PAR	PLAYER	SCORE
70	-11	FALDO	
71	-14	STEWART	
70	-13	McNULTY	275
70	-12	BAKER-FINCH	
72	-12	WOOSNAM	276
71	-12	MUDD	276
72	-11	NORMAN	277
72	-9	PAVIN	279
72	-9	GRAHAM	279
72	-9	PATE	279
72	-9	HAMMOND	279

PLAYER

GAME NO. 35
PARRY
STEWART
GAME NO. 36
B'FINCH
FALDO

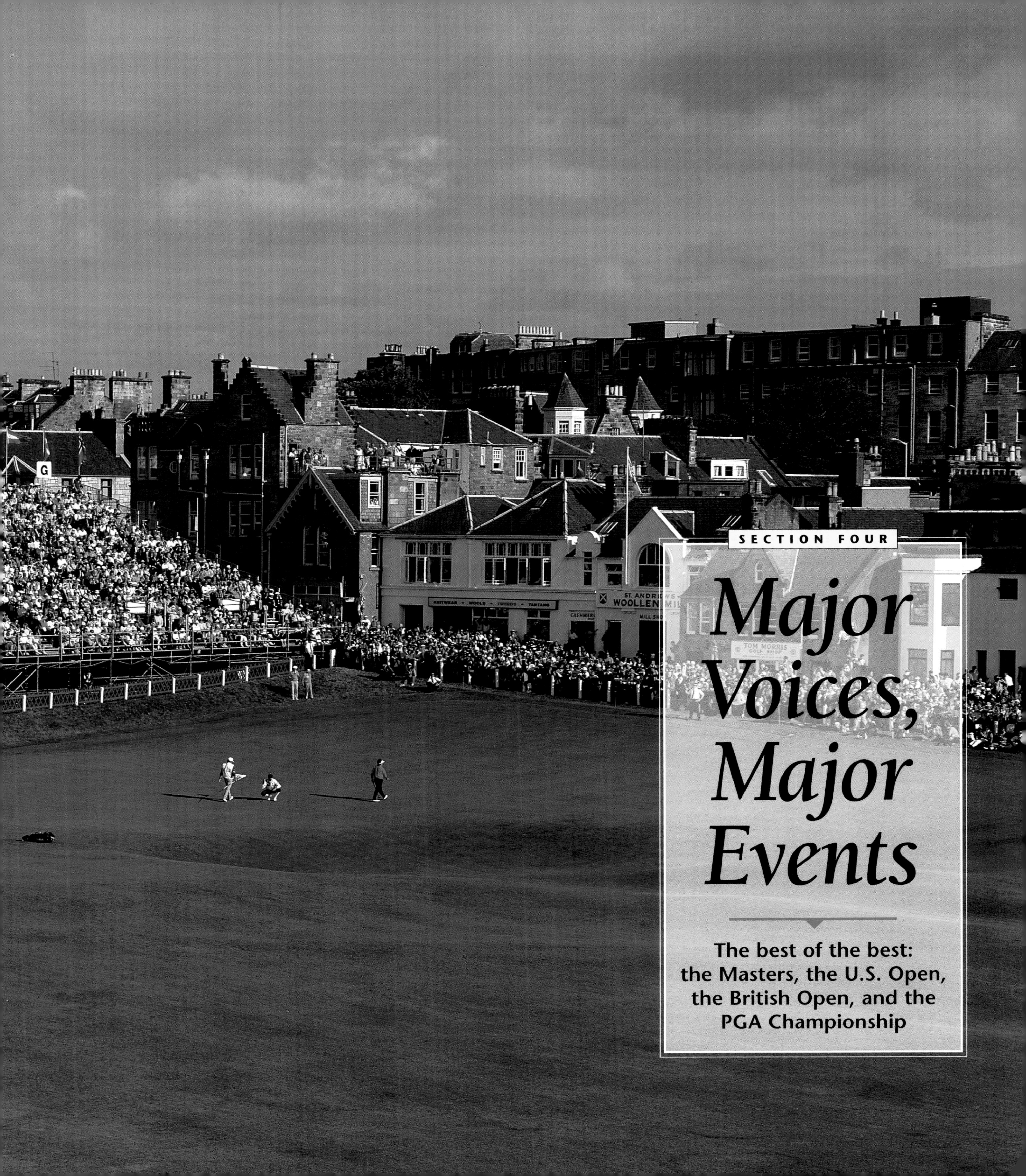

SECTION FOUR

Major Voices, Major Events

The best of the best: the Masters, the U.S. Open, the British Open, and the PGA Championship

BEST OF THE BEST

by Peter McCleery,
Senior Editor

Just as the players point toward and ultimately have their careers judged by their performances in golf's major championships, so do writers and editors try to "get up" for the big occasions. Jack Nicklaus elevated winning majors to an art form, and GOLF DIGEST has tried to do the same with extensive previews and reviews of the events in its pages.

As the game exploded in recent years, the GOLF DIGEST previews of the Masters and U.S. Opens expanded to as many as 50 pages. As a monthly magazine coming out well ahead of these events, the angles have to be timeless and varied so as not to be susceptible to becoming outdated. Unlike the weeklies or dailies, speculation about players and their "form" is practically useless as the magazine's preview goes to bed two months before each major is played. Thus, picking winners proved particularly nettlesome; during a 20-year period, the magazine's "form chart" endured a drought of not getting a single major winner correct in its early forecast. Hard to imagine, with Nicklaus in his prime, that we wouldn't get a few right just by picking Jack every time. But more often than not, we went with quirky or somewhat "surprising" picks, and none came through between Nicklaus in the 1972 U.S. Open at Pebble Beach and Fred Couples in the 1992 Masters. It all goes to show you, as Bobby Jones once scolded a fellow writer, "The game of golf does not lend itself to pontification."

However, this strategy of going for the unusual or surprising angle has served us well with the preview stories. There are some pieces that are so obvious they can't be avoided, and topics like the course, the host club and historic tie-ins to each major have been recurring themes over the years. But while the TV networks covering the majors pretty much stick to what's happening inside the ropes in their coverage (the Masters is famous for never showing anything outside the gates of Augusta National Golf Club), GOLF DIGEST went far and wide in its search for the off-beat and sometimes controversial angles. There was a photo essay about the local caddies kicked out of the Masters, a hard-hitting look at how the U.S. Golf Association sets up its Open courses and an opinion piece on

why the PGA Championship had become a "fourth-rate major," to name three that would be quickly censored by TV. We even once wrote about O.J. Simpson and what "clues" to his wife's murder he might have left behind at Riviera Country Club, where he was a member, ahead of the 1995 PGA Championship. That one was too far off the cartpath for many readers—and Riviera members—who complained about it.

Perhaps the best description of what makes the majors different from your workaday PGA Tour stop came from Charles Price, himself a fine player and longtime GOLF DIGEST columnist. "It's been said that there are three types of golf: golf, tournament golf and championship golf," he wrote in 1984 before the U.S. Open at Winged Foot. "All of them can be likened in my experience to walking a tightrope.

"Ordinary golf is the type where we roll the ball over, ignore some of the rules, concede each other putts 'inside the leather.' It's like walking the rope when it's just off the ground. Tournament golf is when they raise the rope to 60 feet. Championship golf is when they take the net away."

Because it arrives first, in early April just as winter is giving way to springtime for much of the country, the Masters is probably the most eagerly anticipated of all the majors—for fans as well as players. Peter Dobereiner, the elegant British voice of the magazine for much of its existence, captured the essence of it this way: "Over the last 50 years, golf has settled into a rhythm as inexorable as the seasons. The golfing year does not start until Azalea Day, the pagan festival when players and golf lovers from all over the world congregate in Augusta, Ga. The ritual includes Saluting the Geriatrics, Assumption of the Cloak of Legends and the Parade of the Golfers.

"Nothing that happens before the Masters is worth a button. January, February and March are for tuning up the instruments; the overture starts in April."

Two months separate the Masters and the U.S. Open, but then the majors come fast and furious with the U.S. Open in June, the British Open in July and the PGA Championship in August. Each has its own distinctive flavor. The U.S. Open, played on tight, tree-lined courses bordered by punishing rough, relishes its image as the world's toughest championship. It is the ultimate physical and mental examination, so much so that the organizing body has been accused of playing mind games with the players. A former executive of the USGA admitted as much to GOLF DIGEST once when he said he refused to cut a swath of shorter grass between the rough and the fairways, routinely done on tour, because "I like to see them get their socks wet."

The British is characterized more by the capricious-

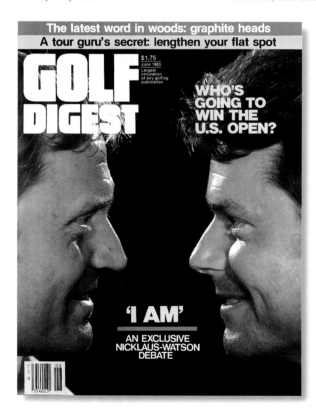

The June 1983 U.S. Open preview featured a head-to-head interview with co-favorites Jack Nicklaus and Tom Watson. The event was won by Larry Nelson.

"As the tour itself grows more and more commercial, the Masters and U.S. Open keep looking more and more important and more honest. Let the Kmart Invitationals have their fun, but if you care about the glories of this game or have any sense of history or, in fact, have any taste, relish the majors and cradle them in your arms."

—DAN JENKINS

ness of the wind and weather that often buffets its magnificent links courses. It is the world's oldest championship, dating back to 1860, and features the most international of fields and the best name for a trophy in the game—the claret jug.

The PGA Championship underwent an identity change when it switched from match to stroke play, and has suffered since from the heat and humidity that often suffocate its August dates. However, the PGA of America in recent years has been compensated by a consolation prize of sorts. It now has what many consider the "fifth major," the Ryder Cup Matches, a biennial match played between teams from Europe and America that has developed into the most dramatically compelling contest of all.

GOLF DIGEST previews were handled by a variety of different editors and writers over the years. But the reviews of majors have been handled since 1985 by a singular force: Dan Jenkins, a much decorated and imitated sportswriter for more than 50 years. Only the Texas born and bred Jenkins, lured to the magazine after a long stint at Sports Illustrated, could bring a fresh wit and perspective to these events so they wouldn't be moldy when readers got the magazine a month or more after they happened. The emphasis on the majors has only increased during his tenure.

We dedicate this chapter to His Ownself, the Dean of the Press Tent, Dan Jenkins, who has done for our profession as much as Nicklaus did for his in elevating the status of the majors.

Payne Stewart pumps his fist in triumph after winning the 1991 U.S. Open at Hazeltine in an 18-hole playoff for his second major championship. Tragically, Stewart was killed in a plane crash in 1999, just months after his second U.S. Open title. (Photo: Jim Moriarty)

April 1995

Is It Heaven . . .

by Dave Kindred

Our writer and his evil twin unmask the two faces of Augusta

Every April, on the most beautiful piece of land on this planet, the Masters happens again. God is good.

So every April we do the pilgrimage to Augusta, there to see the ghosts and prophets, to see Gene Sarazen, who was born before airplanes, and to see Ernie Els, the coming of the 21st century. There we see the shadow of Ben Hogan falling across the practice tee.

We see Arnold Palmer's grin and Eisenhower's cabin. We feel the presence of Bobby Jones.

We think of those three men, American icons in every decade of this century except the first. Robert Tyre Jones Jr., Dwight David Eisenhower and Arnold Daniel Palmer came together at Augusta, drawn there somehow, smiling creations of inexorable fate.

Is this Augusta? This is heaven.

Here we see Jack Nicklaus, golden in the April

. . . or Is It Hell?

The Masters is dead. It just doesn't know it yet. It's still walking around, but it's dead. Or as Gary McCord would report the news: "RUN FOR YOUR LIVES! ZOMBIES IN AMEN CORNER! CARRYING BODY BAGS!"

The death was caused by Dixiecrat panjandrums who threatened to horsewhip anyone bringing the 20th century down Magnolia Lane.

For decades now, the Masters has had the weakest field of the four major championships and has made only the slightest attempts to invite everyone with a chance to win.

Once bold in its invitations to rising stars not yet recognized in the United States—it was the first glimpse we had of Gary Player, Seve Ballesteros and Greg Norman—the Masters is now slow to identify up-and-comers. Only last year did an invitation go to Ernie Els, the South African who became 1994's sensation.

Without the full complement of the PGA Tour's top 50 money-winners, the Masters always leaves a potential winner on the outside looking in.

The weakness of the field is not the lone problem caused by Augusta's invitation-only policy. Suddenly, the world is crowded with such invitational events. Unless Augusta does something to strengthen its field, it runs the risk of losing the aura of exclusivity that made its invitation a player's lifelong dream.

The Masters perennially small field looks only marginally different from the fields in Jamaica and, for crying out loud, Braselton, Ga. Instead of creating a breath of fresh air with the addition of, say, 15 more possible winners from the PGA Tour and 15 more

Only Bobby Jones could make a tournament, the Masters, more meaningful than the national championships of the United States and Great Britain.

light. We hear the soft echo of Ben Crenshaw's words on the day when joy moved him to tears, telling fans at his victory ceremony, "If I could cut out a piece of my heart and give it to you, I would."

Have we mentioned the azaleas? Monet on a hot streak never painted pinks so pink as those we see in the parade of blossoms along the 13th fairway at Augusta National Golf Club.

Of the countless ways the Masters is the finest sporting event in the world, first is mystique.

Only Bobby Jones could have said a golfer's grip on the club "should be no firmer than it would be while shaking hands with a lady." Who else but an English literature major from Harvard would have borrowed the name of a Walter Scott heroine and called his driver "Jeanie Deans"?

Only Bobby Jones. . . .

A thousand paragraphs could begin with that phrase, for only Bobby Jones among all athletes in all sports came to be the highest example of his game's highest skills and highest principles.

And it was Jones who caused Augusta National to be built. He invited there the masters of the game in 1934. He sanctified the cathedral in the pines. Only Bobby Jones could make a tournament, the Masters, more meaningful than the national championships of the United States and Great Britain.

To stand on ground where Jones stood is to become part of something larger than victory.

Have we mentioned the azaleas lately?

Alistair Cooke once said the Masters is as much Edwardian garden party as golf tournament. He saw patrons in pastels engaged in airy conversation, transported by attitude from the world's hurly-burly to a kinder, gentler place among azaleas where at any moment a croquet game might break out.

The Scots would have it otherwise. They gave us golf with a Calvinist's understanding that pleasure comes at the cost of an equal amount of suffering. So at Carnoustie we fall into combat with a hairy beast. Muirfield is a slog in a storm. Royal Troon is a Russian haircut.

We prefer Augusta, where azaleas are as wild as it gets.

Cypress Point has the Pacific. It needs the Pacific. Augusta National needs only itself.

It is a perfect test of skill and will, demanding a thinker's sophistication and a hero's daring. Great ones win here more than once: Hogan, Snead and Nelson. Palmer, Player and Nicklaus. Watson, Ballesteros and Faldo.

The winner must drive it long. He must approach high and soft. He must be accurate with every club, because the greens are (1) devilishly contoured, (2) devilishly fast and (3) devilish in their possibilities for hole locations.

It has been said that if the Masters were called the Pizza Hut Screen-Door Open, men might shoot daily

---

Augusta is on public record preferring death to today's marketplace. These killjoys want nothing to do with the real world.

international players on the rise, the Masters chooses the suffocation of the status quo.

No more proof of that regressive attitude is necessary than Augusta's refusal to capitalize on its product.

Television would pay millions to carry the Masters all four days, all 72 holes. But Augusta sniffs in contempt at any suggestion of selling more than the last nine holes the last two days. If TV doesn't want what we offer, the reasoning goes, we won't sell a thing.

Augusta is on public record preferring death to today's marketplace complexities. In 1988 Chairman Hord Hardin sneered at the idea of a corporate title sponsor: "We're not going to be the Pizza Hut Masters."

Hell, no, Augusta would rather keep the money itself than develop a partnership with a corporation willing to donate $3 million-plus to charity for the opportunity to be associated with the Masters. Alone of the major championships, alone of the PGA Tour events, Augusta donates only what it terms "modest" amounts of its tournament proceeds to charity. The rest, presumably, goes to defray club expenses for Augusta's members.

Hardin went so far as to suggest the Masters would close down rather than submit to the indignity of corporate sponsorship, a suggestion at once typical, shortsighted and suicidal.

These Augusta killjoys want nothing to do

with the real world. They should have put a sign over Magnolia Lane: "Abandon Cheer All Ye Who Enter Here."

They give TV a list of acceptable nouns and adjectives, insisting on no mention of the purse. They force the broadcast of the Butler Cabin winner's interview, during which Hardin once began, "Seve, let me ask you . . . how tall are you?"

Pinkertons monitor the walking speed of customers. (No "running.") No periscopes allowed, no standing on chairs, no cheering misfortune. (Well, if misfortune occurs to a foreigner about to win, it becomes obligatory to make the sound of a feline in heat, also known as a "rebel yell.")

The Masters bosses are so intent on bending reality to their wishes in a strong-arm attempt at creating their version of perfection, whatever the cost in individual freedom, that it can properly be said: If Augusta were a country, it would be Singapore.

And its golf course would be just another 18 holes of no particular distinction. After 60 years of the Masters, Augusta National is a Bobby Jones heirloom, not a championship test.

Look at the great players who've never won: Greg Norman and Lee Trevino, Johnny Miller and Curtis Strange, Nick Price and Julius Boros, Hale Irwin and Paul Azinger. Even worse is who will win: John Daly. Yikes.

So the Masters is a poem to golf. Only Augusta National has refused to allow its event to be transmuted from poetry to commerce.

64s. We beg to differ. The course is mighty. Its par 3s are an architect's masterpieces. And if mystique adds to the test by running 64s into 74s, all the better.

Augusta National's questions have one answer only. If the second shot at the 14th calls for a 6-iron 184 yards, no other answer works. Five yards less can mean four putts; five yards more means a chip shot as frightening as they come.

A player usually faces such a risk-reward dilemma five times a round. At Masters it may be 30 times.

The weight of such work is cumulative and erosive. Thursday's second shot to 13th may be easy, but Sunday's shot for the same spot will be treacherous, and the smallest mistake is painful, magnified by Augusta's shaved embankments at the edge of all water.

As for the greens, a putter with no courage nor wisdom is better suited to lesser tasks, such as winning the U.S. Open.

The Masters is heaven at 13 on a Stimpmeter.

It's heaven largely because the Masters people know exactly who they are.

Augusta National's members, chosen by the club from all parts of the world, are nominated not for their social cachet or business connections but for their undoubted commitment to the game itself. So the Masters is a poem to golf. And for 60 years, alone in the world of grab-a-buck sports events, only Augusta National has refused to allow its event to be transmuted from poetry to commerce.

Augusta sells no corporate tents, no wall-to-wall TV coverage, no on-site advertising. Masters-logo merchandise is sold only through the club in this country. Rather than squeeze its television partner, Augusta trades money for control.

The Masters broadcasts are model golf telecasts with few commercials, no network promotions and

Long removed from the Jones idea of a bounce-and-roll course, Augusta in the mid-1950s rewarded disproportionately those players longest off the tees. Nowadays improved equipment conspired with Augusta's refusal to grow rough to make everyone long enough to win, especially since the back-side 5s are basically toothless par 4s.

Left with two options to defend—icy-fast greens, holes cut into impossible spots—Augusta uses both tricks in a desperate and unfair attempt to hide the truth that the course lives on a reputation it no longer deserves. The wearers of green-coats also cause embankments at water edges to be shaved to the ground so any shot mis-hit even a little bit rolls into the water.

Such gimmickry isn't golf. It's chip and putt. It's usually played on cow paths decorated with windmills and clown faces. When people laugh at a

course, as people laugh at putt-putt courses, you are d-e-a-d dead.

The Masters is dead and gone to hell because its bosses believed time stood still.

Hardly an hour passes from New Year's Day to the second Sunday in April without someone advising us about the heavenly virtues of—golly gee—"the cathedral in the pines."

By that he means the dirt under Jack Nicklaus' feet on those four days when the golf world's attention falls on red clay that in 200 years has been diminished from Indian homelands to a plantation nursery to a golf course reserved for the private pleasure of white men with lots of money. The current membership's profile is that of 30-handicap CEOs who can't break 100 with Ben Crenshaw reading greens for them.

The zealot who speaks in religious metaphors about Augusta National knows nothing about golf.

restrained announcers. The club allows no mention of prize money, and only once would the Masters suffer the air pollution of a Gary McCord speaking of "bikini wax" and "body bags."

Paying customers get a good deal, too. A four-day ticket costs $100; a Super Bowl ticket now goes for $200. Concession prices are so reasonable that even sportswriters stop by if hungry for another pimento-cheese sandwich.

These are fruits of benevolent dictatorship. Clifford Roberts, once a Wall Street investment banker, and Bobby Jones had the last call on all decisions.

Today's chairman, Jack Stephens, demonstrated Augusta's respect for tradition in 1993. No attendance figures would be released, he said, because "Mr. Roberts didn't think it was a good idea. I'm scared to change. He might come back." At the time, Roberts had been dead 16 years.

After all, everyone else comes back. Every April, they come to the Masters, to the same spot under the same tree, to watch scores still posted by hand, to see the Hogan shadow and to see Sarazen in knickers.

A man will say, "Momma got me tickets and I'm keeping 'em till they take 'em away from me. One year Billy Casper pulled it left at 15, right under my Momma's chair. Casper came over, everybody got to bending over looking for the ball, and my Momma bumped butts with Billy Casper, knocked him off balance. Momma was a good-size woman."

They know Billy Joe Patton on sight, and they'll tell you he damn well did the right thing going for it that time in '54. No telling what Hogan was doing, so Billy Joe had to go for it at 13, water or no water.

They can tell you about the azaleas, too. They'll tell you how beautiful the azaleas were last year. My, my. Pretty as a picture.

Then they'll tell you that as pretty as the azaleas were last year, this year's bunch looks the best ever.

Death came to the Masters the way death comes to all those high and mighty who believe they can forestall the future.

What he knows about life in the 20th century he learned the night he heard the Abe Lincoln joke.

First man: "So ol' Abe Lincoln got to drinking one night. Next morning he wakes up with this big hang-over. And y'know what he said, don'cha?"

Zealot: "Nope."

First man: "Ol' Abe rubbed his head and said, 'I freed the *what*?' "

Death came to the Masters the way death comes to all those high and mighty who believe they can forestall the future by imposing the past on the present. Augusta National remained the plantation reborn, an elitist's concept executed by elitists for the pleasure of elitists. No institution so created can long endure.

The first time a black player seemed about to qualify for a Masters invitation—Charlie Sifford waited in vain, good enough for the PGA Tour, but not for Augusta—the dictator Clifford Roberts said he would be happy to greet Lee Elder. He expressed this happi-ness by calling blacks his "dark-complected friends."

For the first 50 years or so, an entire Masters field of white players would stroll the heavenly cathedral grounds while behind them, carrying the golf bags, came an equal number of black men. The same relationship existed from dining room to locker room: black men serving white men.

The dying of the Masters has been a steep decline from robust health to preparations for embalming to be followed promptly by mummification.

Of course, the men who run the Masters have no idea they now are zombies, the living dead. Nor do most people know of their deaths. Truth is, their decades of life have been so spiritless that one is reminded of Dorothy Parker's question when she heard of Calvin Coolidge's death. She asked, "How can they tell?"

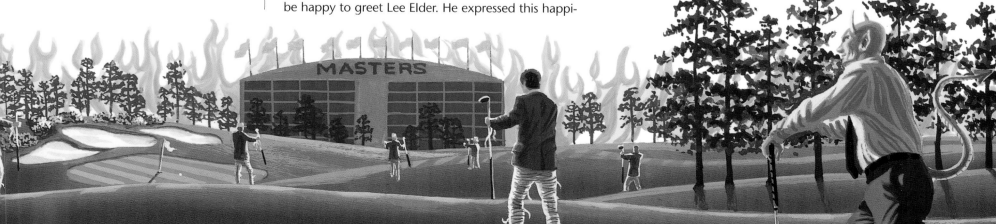

"The magnolias that line Magnolia Lane are a metaphor for everything the Masters stands for. Unstudied beauty—the way the flowers frame the course rather than the other way around. A hint of history—can you think of any truly great golfer since it began who hasn't won the Masters?"—CHARLES PRICE

Seve Ballesteros of Spain, the 1980 and 1983 Masters champion, finds himself in one of the most beautiful-awful places at Augusta National, after pull-hooking a long approach to the par-5 13th. (Photo: Jim Moriarty)

April 1984

Let Us Now Praise Amen Corner

In spectacular paintings by Donald Moss and a first-time account of how it was named

by Herbert Warren Wind

Herbert Warren Wind, the game's preeminent historian, is a writer for The New Yorker and a frequent contributor to GOLF DIGEST. We asked him to explain how he came to name that fearsome stretch of holes at Augusta National, "Amen Corner."

As one of the older folks in the press tent, I am approached from time to time at the major championships by writers who have taken to covering golf in relatively recent years and who wonder if I might be able to provide some information on an earlier champion or championship. It is a pleasant role to be put in, especially when you can supply the particulars your colleagues are after. However, at the 1981 Masters, I found myself in an extremely embarrassing position. Two young writers came up to me, separately, and asked if I knew how the Amen Corner—which is composed of the second half of the 11th hole, the short 12th, and the first half of the 13th—came to be called the Amen Corner. First, I found it exceedingly awkward

the era of the typewriter hadn't quite arrived. In high school, one wrote his themes and other homework in longhand. In college a small minority had moved on to the typewriter, but I continued to write in longhand. When I wrote for the college newspaper or, later on, for the newspaper in my hometown, after finishing my piece, I copied it neatly in the very legible hand I had acquired, and then handed it in. Even when I moved on to the typewriter, I found that, except for letters and other informal chaff, I preferred to do my first draft by hand and then, after amending things, to type it up. As a result, I was anything but a speed merchant, but since I wanted to be a magazine writer, this wasn't all that critical until 1954 when I went with the newly founded weekly, Sports Illustrated, as its golf editor. On most pieces, I had sufficient time to proceed at the semi-reflective pace I had become accustomed to, but there was one considerable problem: If a major championship finished on a Sunday, the coverage of the tournament had to be in early on Monday.

For writers habituated to meeting a fast deadline— a considerable talent—this would have been no trouble at all. For me it presented a problem. I felt that I could not begin the article until the tournament was completed. Only then would I know what had been the significant shots. My regular regimen at the Masters, for example, was to retreat quickly to my motel room, work till about two in the morning getting the piece in shape, rise at six, reread the piece, type it, and take it to the Western Union office. In an effort to find a less strenuous process, one year I asked the editor if I could do a day-by-day diary-type account of the tournament. The result was that I spent each night of that Masters working in my room, and missed all the fun of getting together with old friends. In 1958 I asked the editor if it would be OK if the magazine ran a block of text along with a photograph of the winner in the issue directly after the tournament and then follow this up in the next issue with a long, detailed piece on the tournament. He was kind enough to agree to try this.

That 1958 Masters was a memorable one. It hinged on how Arnold Palmer, paired with Ken Venturi, played the 12th and 13th on the final day. Since the course had been thoroughly soaked by rains the night before and during the morning, a local rule had been invoked: a player whose ball was embedded in the fairway or rough was allowed to lift and drop it without penalty. On the 12th, a 155-yard par 3 across Rae's Creek, Palmer's iron carried over the green and embedded itself in the steep bank of rough behind it. The official on the hole evidently was not aware of the local rule, and he instructed Palmer to play the ball as it lay. When Palmer did this, he holed out in 5, after missing a short putt. Then, politely but pertinaciously, Palmer went back to the pitch mark of his tee shot. He obviously felt that the official's ruling was not correct, and elected to play an "alternate" ball. After dropping the ball over his shoulder, he ran a delicate chip three feet from the cup and made the putt for a 3.

At this point, no one knew whether Palmer's score

to tell them that I thought that I had given that famous stretch of course its appellation. And second, neither of the young writers was especially taken with my explanation, since the key to it was the title of an old Southern shout that I had first heard on an obscure recording back in my college days.

Later on at that Masters, I ran into Ross Goodner, one of my best and oldest friends in golf. We share—as do many people—an enthusiastic interest in sports and popular music. Ross, I think, is the only person I had previously told about coming up with the name of the Amen Corner. I thought he would get a kick out of it, which he did. During our conversation at the 1981 Masters—where else but on that marvelous press stand that juts out on the right side of the 12th fairway—I told him about being asked about Amen Corner by the young writers and how my explanation had clearly disappointed both of them. "Well, I suppose that's to be expected," Ross said comfortingly. "Outside of Hugues Panassie, how many people have heard of the number?"

Let me go back a little. When I was growing up,

The classic risk-reward 485-yard 13th hole is where many Masters are won and lost. As a par 5, it's reachable in two for even medium-length modern professionals, but the penalty for an errant shot is swift and painful.

on the 12th was a 3 or a 5. Palmer, however, didn't let it bother him. On the 13th, a 485-yard dogleg left, he followed a solid drive with a great 3-wood from a side-hill lie that carried the arm of Rae's Creek that wraps itself around the green, and then canned his 18-foot downhill putt for an eagle 3. When he was playing the 15th, he was informed that his official score on the 12th was a 3. That, in effect, won him the tournament. Incidentally, it was Palmer's first victory in a major professional championship.

With plenty of time to think out the article, I felt that I should try to come up with some appropriate name for that far corner of the course where the critical action had taken place—some colorful tag like those that Grantland Rice and his contemporaries loved to devise: the Four Horsemen, the Manassa Mauler, the House that Ruth Built, the Georgia Peach, and so on. The only phrase with the word *corner* I could think of (outside of football's "coffin corner" and baseball's "hot corner") was the title of a song on an old Bluebird record. (Bluebird was RCA's label for its cheaper disks. Its prestige label was Victor.) On one side, a band under the direction of Milton (Mezz) Mezzrow, a Chicago

clarinetist, had recorded "35th and Calumet"—most likely the site of a jazz joint in Chicago. The reverse side was "Shouting in the Amen Corner." There was nothing unusual about the song but apparently the title was catchy enough to stick in my mind.

The more I thought about it, the more suitable I thought the Amen Corner was for that bend of the course where the decisive action in that Masters had taken place (as indeed it had in some past Masters and would in several in the future). My article, in the issue dated April 21, was called "The Fateful Corner," and the opening sentence went like this: "On the afternoon before the start of the recent Masters golf tournament, a wonderfully evocative ceremony took place at the farthest reach of the Augusta National course—down in the Amen Corner where Rae's Creek intersects the 13th fairway near the tee, then parallels the front edge of the green on the short 12th and finally swirls alongside the 11th green . . ."

I have no idea how the name caught on. To be candid, I am delighted that it did. To be connected even in the flimsiest way with a course like Augusta National and an institution like the Masters is good for the soul.

Open-Minded Geniuses

The peculiarities of the course setup have identified a select group of conquerors

by Frank Hannigan

Above: *In 1995 GOLF DIGEST commissioned a special illustration of all the Open champions in connection with the centennial of the championship. The three players named by the author as the Open's all-time best are in the foreground (from left), Hogan, Jones and Nicklaus. (Artist: John Monteleone)*

Below: *Open sightings: periscopes help provide less obstructed views of history. (Photo: Jim Moriarty)*

The U.S. Open Championship, bolstered by a century's worth of history, exemplifies a particular form of golf: grim and merciless. These qualities are a consequence of the meticulous preparation of the courses—what has come to be known as the "U.S. Open setup."

The U.S. Golf Association philosophy presents the good people as those who drive accurately, if not for great distance, who hit a high percentage of greens in regulation figures, and whose nerve endings can deal with abnormally fast and firm greens. The bad people spray the ball off the tee, attempt to make amends with a variety of garbage shots around the greens, and get out of sorts after suffering a double bogey.

Open courses, once prepared for the championship, are not fun. The USGA says a 10-handicap golfer should expect to shoot 91 on its creations. But that is only a mechanical estimate not taking into account the dejection that goes with endless searches for balls in high rough, not to mention the shock of stroking a 25-foot putt 15 feet past the hole. I make the novice 10-handicapper's Open score nearer 100.

The Open setup can be expressed numerically. Fairways will average just over 30 yards wide at Shinnecock Hills. They will be bordered by a six-foot-wide layer of two-inch "intermediate" rough. Beyond that is the real stuff, about five inches and lush from the rains of spring. The USGA calls it "primary" rough.

The greens, starved and on a life-support system for the week, will never reveal a ball mark. In Stimpmeter terms, they are an honest 11. They may be juiced up to 12 at Shinnecock, where the greens are relatively flat. Historically, the primary rough has been brought in menacingly close to the greens.

Originally there was no such thing as a U.S. Open setup. Between 1895 and World War I the courses were whatever the host clubs had in mind. Fairways were much wider than now; the greens were slow by our standards. But the primary rough may not have been mowed for a full season and was therefore brutal.

The USGA began to make fitful attempts to influence course conditioning during the 1920s. By the '30s, clubs were receiving written instructions from USGA headquarters. The instructions were sometimes ignored by the locals, whose members equated high scores with manhood. Oakmont, in particular, gave the USGA fits in an attempt to come up with a course on which nobody could break 300 over 72 holes.

Open courses were also prepared inconsistently after World War II. Riviera was too easy in 1948 and yielded record scores. But the USGA was more dismayed with the celebrated renovation of Oakland Hills in 1951 by architect Robert Trent Jones. There were

Ben Hogan's tightly controlled game and temperament were ideally suited to the demands of the Open, resulting in four victories in five attempts between 1949 and 1953. (Photo: Golf World)

"Those nerves jump and frolic like grasshoppers on a spree when the Open rolls around. The thought of it sends chills tap dancing along your spine. Your hands grow cold. Your heart thuds with the mocking beat of a jungle dream. Food is tasteless and sleep seldom arrives."

—GENE SARAZEN

only two scores under 70. One was Ben Hogan's epic 67 in the final round.

There was a similar aberration in 1955 at the Olympic Club, where the rough was absurd—the equivalent of the one-shot penalty for driving into a lateral water hazard.

The components for a definitive U.S. Open arrangement were then settled upon permanently by Richard Tufts, the most effective of USGA presidents, and Joe Dey, the USGA executive director and therefore head of its staff.

Tufts and Dey called for rough that would be the equivalent of a half-stroke penalty, one that would allow the player to advance the ball purposefully but without being able to stop it on the greens.

Today the USGA tracks what it calls "cost of rough" with an index calculated from breaking down all the scores on the 14 non-par-3 holes into those made from the fairways and from outside the fairway.

Last year the USGA got just about what it wanted at Oakmont with a "cost of rough" index of .47 per hole. Indeed, the USGA purred when it was learned that its champion, Ernie Els, hit five more greens over 72 holes (54 of 72) than anyone else in the field.

By 1960, with an improved financial situation, the USGA was able to exercise complete control over Open courses by assigning staff members to take up residence months in advance to make sure the host clubs did not do anything bizarre.

The challenge of the Open then has been remarkably static over the past 35 years. Shinnecock Hills,

aside from vagaries of weather, will be much as it was for the 1986 Open, just as the Oakmont of 1994 was recognizable as the Oakmont of the 1983, 1973 and 1962 Opens.

The length of Open courses crept up gradually from little more than 5,000 yards in the gutta-percha-ball 1890s to more than 6,500 yards in the '20s. It settled in at about 7,000 yards in the 1960s.

There has been no appreciable change in distance in more than 30 years. The average score declines because of a general improvement in the breed; that is, there are many more excellent players today than there were in the '60s.

There is one notable recent innovation in the Open setup: "Chipping areas" have been installed to the rear and sides of some greens. These are zones 12 to 15 feet long, cut at fairway height. Essentially, they enlarge the size of the targets.

The number of "chipping areas" has been expanded to nine for this year's Open. The USGA says this innovation is an appropriate reaction to the common criticism that chipping, a vital part of the game, was eliminated at the Opens.

Personally, I find the USGA misguided in its attempt to be all things to all people. The "chipping areas" are as out of place at an Open as occasional patches of five-inch rough would be near some greens at the Masters.

Course preparation is a matter of personal preference reflecting the facets of the game the organizers want to emphasize. The Masters rewards power and

Bobby Jones, seen here after his 1929 triumph, left the competitive arena early at age 28, after his 1930 Grand Slam. Had he continued into his 30s, he would likely have won more Opens than anyone else. (Photo: Golf World)

exquisite work around the greens. Its fairways are some 15 yards wider than those at an Open, and the Masters rough is hardly worthy of the name. In 1994 the top-24 finishers in the Masters hit, on average, 47 fairways out of 56. By comparison, the top 24 in the 1994 Open at Oakmont hit only 35 fairways.

It's no accident then that Curtis Strange has won two Opens while Seve Ballesteros has prevailed twice in the Masters.

But course preparation, no matter how calculated, can only tilt to favor varied styles of play. It is not necessarily decisive. Nick Faldo, the most precise of modern players, seemed more likely to win two U.S. Opens than two Masters. Meanwhile Andy North, by any standard a wild driver, won two Opens. (I attribute North's Open record to a rare capacity for final-round resolution that far exceeded his ball-striking abilities.)

Over the years and under these conditions, a select group of players emerged who consistently excelled in the national championship. Since we live

in the age of quantification and this is the Open's 100th anniversary, it is fitting to reflect on the most successful U.S. Open players and to confect a list of the best.

A list of the Open's best follows, but with two quirks. It consists of 11 players, rather than the customary 10, and they are divided into three clusters presented alphabetically, with no attempt to separate them internally, on the grounds that a genius is a genius.

The methodology is necessarily subjective and reflects the following credos:

■ Winning, if not the only thing, matters more than any other factor.

■ Credit must be given for finishing near the top consistently.

■ Longevity matters. No consideration is given to anyone who played in fewer than 10 Opens.

■ Even though no man can do better than beat his contemporaries, I am influenced by the knowledge that it's harder to win now than it used to be.

Here then are the U.S. Open all-time best, and why they are the best:

Group A
The three all-time conquerors

BEN HOGAN won four Opens in five attempts between 1948 and 1953. He missed 1949 while convalescing from an automobile accident in which his car was hit by a bus. He finished in the top 10 on 15 consecutive occasions; was a late bloomer who did not win his first Open until age 35. He was held in such reverence by the USGA that they modeled their setup, dating from the 1950s, on the way Hogan played the game—fairways and greens. Because of World War II, Hogan missed out on four other Opens as he was reaching his prime.

Hoganophiles insist their man won a fifth U.S. Open, the fifth being an event titled the Hale America National Open, played in 1942. They point to the USGA gold medal Hogan received as its winner. Once and for all, that was *not* a U.S. Open Championship. The USGA announced suspension of its championships for the duration of the war immediately after Pearl Harbor. The USGA did lend its name as a co-sponsor (along with the PGA of America and the Chicago District Golf Association) to the Hale America event run for war-related charities. And the USGA threw in a medal. It was played on the short and easy Ridgemoor Country Club in Chicago, where Hogan shot 271, a score still not

achieved in real U.S. Opens. The week was jazzed up with non-U.S. Open sideshows such as a long-driving contest.

BOBBY JONES played in his first Open in 1920, as an 18-year-old prodigy, when he tied for eighth. He played in only 10 more before he gave up competitive golf after his Grand Slam of 1930. Between 1923 and 1930, Jones won four Opens and was second three times—twice in playoffs. He put more space between himself and his contemporaries than any golfer ever: Walter Hagen and Gene Sarazen were without argument great players, but they were miles behind Jones, who finished ahead of them during his 11 Open years 18 of 22 times. His Open scoring average of 73.1 was a shot and a half better per round than Sarazen's and Hagen's. Tommy Armour, himself winner of both the U.S. and British Opens, said unashamedly that in casual rounds of golf he received a handicap from Jones of one hole (not one stroke) per nine. Suppose Jones did not pull back from golf at age 28, but went on playing through his 30s, the prime decade for most golfers: He would probably have won at least two more Opens during the 1930s and settled forever any discussion as to who was the best Open golfer.

JACK NICKLAUS is unique in that he stayed at the peak of the game longer than any other golfer, which is to say he could stand the heat better. He had his first chance to win as a 20-year-old amateur in 1960, when he finished second to Arnold Palmer. His four wins were spread over 19 years between 1962 and 1980 and he might have won an unprecedented fifth but for Tom Watson's miraculous birdie-birdie finish in 1982 at Pebble Beach. While Nicklaus has continued to play, and his nature is such that he always imagines he has a chance, the reality is that he has not been a presence in any fourth round of an Open since 1982.

Group B
More multiple winners

WILLIE ANDERSON won four Opens between 1901 and 1905, three of them in succession, but he still had to depend on club jobs to earn a living. A troubled man who held 10 different club jobs between 1894 and 1910, Anderson died at the age of 32—alcohol was likely a factor. I have relegated Anderson in the group below the top, despite his four victories, because his competition was not the equivalent of what was to come. In Anderson's years, there were never more than 91 entries for the Open.

JULIUS BOROS had the primary Open attributes. He was imperturbable and a magnificent driver. He was unique in his capacity to get the ball close to the hole from the snarly greenside rough, something he accomplished with a long and languid swing. From 1950 to 1965, he had 10 top-10 finishes in the event, including victories

Opposite page: *Gene Sarazen (left) and Walter Hagen were showmen as well as outstanding players in the first part of the 20th century, winning two Opens apiece. (Photo: Golf World)*

Left: *The laconic Julius Boros won Opens 11 years apart and was still a contender 10 years later at age 53.*

Right: *Sam Snead was the most famous Open failure—shown here after losing to Cary Middlecoff in 1949—and still met everyone's historical definition of greatness. (Photo: Golf World)*

The Open, like all of golf, has to be dealt with on two levels. The mechanics are useless if the emotions run amok. And while there might be something like the ideal way to grip a club, there is no one state of mind guaranteed to survive an Open fourth round.

in 1952 and 1963. At 53, in 1973, Boros was still very much in the Open until the final holes.

WALTER HAGEN was second only to Nicklaus in number of top-10 finishes, with 16 to Jack's 18. He is the only one of the elite 11 who was not a straight driver. He coined the classic put-down of freak winners by saying, "Anybody can win the Open—once." (He waited to say that until he'd won it a second time in 1919.)

HALE IRWIN is the only three-time U.S. Open champion. The Open plays right to his strong suits— driving accuracy and a tough mental approach to the game. Irwin has conquered the Open's famously long, hard par-4 holes with a series of magnificent long-iron shots. His first victory, at Winged Foot in 1974, came on the harshest Open course of modern times. He won with seven over par.

GENE SARAZEN comes closest to Nicklaus in terms of longevity. He entered the scene with a victory in 1922 at Skokie (the first year tickets were sold, mostly to a gallery dying to see Jones) and he was still at the top in 1940 when he lost a playoff to Lawson Little. Happily, he has prevailed as well in mortal longevity as the Open's oldest living champion. He is now 93. *(Editor's note: Sarazen died four years later in 1999.)*

Group C
Exceptions to the rules

ARNOLD PALMER is the only one in the hierarchy of 11 who did not win at least two Opens. He had the

misfortune to lose three Open playoffs in a five-year span between 1962 and 1966. A superb driver of the ball in the sense of being both straight and long, Arnold continued to be a threat to win the Open years after he was no longer a factor in the other majors. He was near the lead in the final round of every Open from 1972 to 1975.

ALEX SMITH was one of the five brothers from Carnoustie who emigrated to the United States. His younger brother Willie won the 1899 Open by the record margin of 11 strokes; Macdonald Smith appears on all lists of the best players who did not win an Open. One of Alex Smith's two Open wins came in a three-man playoff with brother Mac and Johnnie McDermott. Alex was a constant threat with a total of eight finishes in the top three starting in 1898. He won despite his celebrated putting woes, which inspired his classic advice: "Miss 'em quick."

LEE TREVINO was an obscure Texas player when he qualified for the 1967 Open. Trevino finished fifth and, with his Open prize of $6,000 as a stake, joined the tour. A year later he won at Oak Hill. He won a classic Open at Merion in 1971 by beating Nicklaus in a playoff. He derided the common criticism that the Open "takes the driver out of their hands" by pointing out that the narrow fairways didn't scare *him* out of using his driver.

This list illustrates just how influential the Open has been. Only one American, Sam Snead, did not win the Open but still managed to meet everyone's historical definition of greatness. Snead was undoubtedly poisoned for the Open by making an 8

Lee Trevino (left, in 1971) and Hale Irwin (in 1990) won multiple Opens with contrasting styles and mental approaches to the occasion. (Photos: Golf World [left] and Jim Moriarty)

Below: *Arnold Palmer is the only player to earn a spot in the Open pantheon with just one victory. He had many other near-misses, the most infamous coming in his 1966 playoff loss to Billy Casper shown here.*

on its 72nd hole in 1939 when 5 would have won him the title.

Snead's Open horrors reveal that the Open, like all of golf, has to be dealt with on two levels. The mechanics are useless if the emotions run amok. And while there might be something like the ideal way to grip a club, there is no one state of mind guaranteed to survive an Open fourth round. The mental states of the Open's three great conquerors could not have been more diverse.

Jones had a fierce battle internally. He wrote that, prior to a round, he "had that hollow feeling in the pit of my stomach, and my concern was to get the agony over, rather than to have the conflict started." He had a terrible time retaining big leads. Later, two other supreme players would leave the game early. They were Byron Nelson and Mickey Wright, both of whom said that golf had become intolerable.

For Nicklaus, the Open's final day was what he lived for. He actually used the words "relish" and "pleasure" to describe the prospect. Nicklaus concocted a strategic approach based on the notion that if he could just stay anywhere near the lead for three rounds, the fourth was his.

Hogan set out, and apparently succeeded, in making the Open nothing more than the most important of his rituals. He was paired with the amateur Bill Campbell in the first two rounds of the 1954 Open at Baltusrol. On the 16th hole of the second round, within a shot of the lead, Hogan told Campbell he was ready to go home. He said he had put so much effort into preparing and planning that he found the championship itself an anticlimax. Hogan's exact words, according to Campbell: "I am bored."

July 1985

Maurice Flitcroft: The Open's Don Quixote

How a hapless hacker harassed the Royal &Ancient

by Peter Dobereiner

One year the golf course went up in flames, and the British Open was brought to a halt while fire engines raced along the fairways. Another time a gale flattened the tented village. Then there was the occasion when vandals invaded the course at dead of night and dug up one of the greens. Calamity is endemic to the Open Championship, which is why the Royal and Ancient Golf Club takes extreme care in selecting the members of the championship committee. You need chaps who can be relied upon to retain absolute inflexibility in a crisis.

During those aforementioned catastrophes, not so much as the tinkle of an ice cube in the gin and tonics betrayed a nervous tremor in the hands that administer the Open. However, there is one contingency that throws those stalwarts into a state approaching panic. Whisper the word "Flitcroft" within hearing of an R&A man, and he degenerates into a passable imitation of Chief Inspector Dreyfuss in the "Pink Panther" movies when confronted by Inspector Clouseau. The uncontrolled facial twitch, the blush of embarrassment and stammered gibberish into the telephone betray the classical whammies.

The cause of this deep neurosis, Maurice Flitcroft, looks harmless enough. He is age 55, a trim figure of 5-foot-7 in his spiked shoes. He lives on social security, and the work he is currently out of is that of a crane driver, having previously pursued the callings of stuntman, laborer, railway porter, ice-cream salesman and bus driver. The reason the R&A committeemen quiver at the mention of his name is because Maurice believes, on the flimsiest of evidence, that he is a golfer. Many of us labor under the same delusion, but Maurice pursues his obsession to the point of regularly entering the British Open, with hilarious results for everyone except his bewildered playing companions and the flustered championship officials.

It started in 1976 when Flitcroft sent in an entry form, describing himself with a certain literary license to be a professional golfer. In those days of blissful innocence, the R&A had no reason to doubt his status, and he managed to compete in the qualifying competition at Formby.

His fellow competitors soon had their suspicions aroused as Maurice happily hacked his way to a 61 on the front nine, where he revealed a deep understanding of the game by remarking that he would have to improve on the back if he were going to make the qualifying mark. And he did. He was back in 60, and the R&A informed him with icy insistence that his presence was not required for the next round. Maurice departed, to the consternation of the press corps, which was awaiting details back at championship headquarters.

Telephone communication was established with his mother, who, on hearing that the call concerned Maurice's performance at the Open, asked: "Oh, has he won?" When it was explained to her that such was far from the case, she took the news philosophically: "Oh, well, everybody has to start somewhere."

It transpired that Flitcroft's score of 121 at Formby, under the circumstances, was not too shabby, the circumstances being that this had been the first round of golf that Maurice had played in his life. All his preparation for a tilt at the Open Championship had been made on the sports field of a school near his home, with the long-jump pit as his bunker. To hone a sharp edge to his putting touch he sank two coffee tins into the back lawn at home.

That score of 121 relieved a Milwaukee postal sorter of the ignominy of having put up the most inept performance in the history of the Open. Walter Danecki was another self-appointed professional golfer who lost patience with the U.S. Professional Golfers' Association for its narrow-minded insistence on a five-year apprenticeship as well as evidence of a certain competence. His plan, as he explained, was to win

Maurice Flitcroft's semi-serious attempts to qualify for the British Open added to the unique flavor and character of the world's oldest championship. (Photo: Lawrence Levy)

one of the big ones. "Then they'll have to let me in."

In the summer of 1965, Walter took a vacation in Britain without telling friends at work and his municipal golf course that he proposed to play in the Open. Danecki sent in his entry, his conscience insisting that he describe himself as a professional because "I wanted that crock of golf." That Open was also to be played at Royal Birkdale, and Walter was drawn to qualify on the neighboring Hillside course. He went around in 108, and the R&A officials were so confident that he would not return for the second round that they failed to make arrangements to intercept him. The next day he shot a score of 113 for a two-round tally of 221, which was 70 strokes too many to get him a place in the championship field. He took his failure with philosophical composure, remarking as he departed: "I want to say that your small ball is right for this sort of course. If I had been playing our bigger ball, I would have been all over the place."

The Danecki incident alerted the R&A to the need to screen the entries, no easy task with the numbers of participants rising every year. Keith Mackenzie, who was then championship secretary, had some doubts about the credentials of an unfamiliar Japanese pro one year

and made a special trip to the qualifying course to watch him in action. The pro hit a screamer off the first tee, long and straight, and a relieved Mackenzie returned to his duties. He was doubly annoyed, therefore, to receive a report of a Japanese golfer who was creating mayhem in the qualifying round because of his ineptitude. It transpired that the man really was a pro—the pro at a driving range—and that he had never before tried to hit a ball with an iron club off grass. Neither he nor Walter Danecki attempted a second crack at the Open, but Maurice Flitcroft, true to the spirit of the championship rules laid down in 1861 that the competition be open to all the world, came back for more.

Flitcroft used various pseudonyms and on occasion had his entry posted from the country of his chosen nom de guerre. Four more times he has had his entry accepted, his spurious status of "professional" giving him exemption into the final qualifying rounds. In 1978, he managed to play nine holes before an R&A official invited him to withdraw on the grounds that he had already blown any chance of qualifying. Maurice agreed, on condition that his entry fee be refunded.

In 1980 he pulled out of the qualifying competition without hitting a shot because he felt that his game was

Scenic overview of the long and treacherous 18th hole at Carnoustie—just ask Jean Van de Velde, who made an infamous triple bogey here on the last hole to force a playoff in which he lost the 1999 British Open, how demanding it can be. (Photo: Stephen Szurlej)

not sharp enough for a sustained challenge. The next year he had no such misgivings, but his confidence was not shared by the officials at South Herts Golf Club, who called a halt to his antics after nine holes.

Under the guise of Monsieur Gerard Hoppy, professeur de golf, registered out of Switzerland, he was back in the qualifying competition for the 1983 Open, blowing his cover with every swing of the club. The R&A was not amused and saw him off the premises of Pleasington Golf Club.

Something had to be done about this Scarlet Pimpernel of golf whose blundering incompetence caused such havoc to the chances of those unfortunate enough to be drawn to play with him. A sophisticated

screening system was put into operation by the R&A to scrutinize the annual crop of more than 2,000 entries. Her name is Joyce Scott, a secretary in the championship office with a gift for detecting forgeries. In 1984 she spotted the telltale characteristics of Flitcroft's handwriting, disguised though it was.

This year [1985] Flitcroft applied for an entry form, as usual, and the R&A, as usual, sent him one, together with the standard letter outlining the qualification categories. For his part, Flitcroft is determined to get into the qualifying contest, at the very least, again this year. Only the sharp eye of Scott stands between Maurice Flitcroft and his date with destiny, or another grotesque Don Quixote tilt at a windmill.

Top right: *The Honourable Company of Edinburgh Golfers, whose home club is Muirfield in Scotland, has been a host for a century's worth of Opens, from 1892 (won by Harold Hilton) to 1992 (Nick Faldo). It returns as the Open's venue again in 2002. (Photo: Stephen Szurlej)*

Bottom right: *Zimbabwe's Nick Price jumps for joy after making a monstrous putt on the 17th hole at Turnberry in 1994, the decisive blow in his come-from-behind Open victory. (Photo: Phil Sheldon Golf Photo Library)*

July 1987

The Grand Slam That Almost Was

Fifteen years ago, Trevino hit a shot that stopped Nicklaus' impossible dream and ended Tony Jacklin's career

by Dave Anderson

In two days, the 1972 British Open would begin. Beyond the heather and the gorse, a chilly wind had put a froth on the Firth of Forth in a niche of Scotland's northeast coast. On the Muirfield moors, Scots in tweeds and turtlenecks swarmed over the linksland as Jack Nicklaus moved through a practice round. Near the 14th green, a ruddy-faced Scot watched the 32-year-old American float an iron to within 15 feet of the cup on the 447-yard hole.

"Aye," the Scot said, "he's something to beat."

Something indeed. In winning the Masters and the U.S. Open at Pebble Beach that year, Nicklaus had either led or shared the lead in every round. He had won the 1966 British Open at Muirfield and now, his blond sideburns thick in the style of the time, he had returned to pursue the modern Grand Slam—winning the Masters, the U.S. Open, the British Open and the PGA Championship in the same year.

Greg Norman discovered in 1986 that the Grand Slam could be so close and yet so far. And this year at the Masters he appeared to have one leg up before Larry Mize chipped in. But 15 years ago Jack Nicklaus had two legs up.

"Take a good look," another Scot was saying now to his small son as Nicklaus approached the 15th green. "There's one of the 10 most famous men in the world."

All week the local newspapers would call it The Grand Slam Open, but what only a few knew was that Nicklaus had awakened with a crick in his neck the previous morning at Greywalls, the small stone hotel near the ninth green. He has never used it as an alibi, then or now. "But my neck wasn't very good," he recalls today, "until halfway through the third round." By then he appeared to be all but out of contention for the title he had won at St. Andrews two years earlier. Despite decent scores of 70, 72 and 71, he was six strokes behind Lee Trevino, breezy and bold at the high noon of his career and the winner of both the U.S. Open at Merion and the British Open at Royal Birkdale the year before. And he was five strokes behind the 28-year-old Tony Jacklin, the elegant Englishman who had won the U.S. Open in 1970 at Hazeltine and the British Open in 1969 at Royal Lytham and St. Annes.

But by sunset the next day, these three golfers would place the 101st British Open on a pedestal in history. And put the slippery struggle of the Grand Slam in focus.

ROUND 1: TUPLING TAKES THE LEAD

In the 1966 British Open, the last time the championship was held at Muirfield, Nicklaus had been cautious, hitting his driver off the tee a total of only 17 times throughout the tournament. And now, in the opening round in 1972, he was almost as cautious. Off the tee he used his driver only five times, his 3-wood six times, his 1-iron once, his 2-iron twice. But of those 14 tee shots, six sailed

The three principals in the historic 1972 British Open at Muirfield, Scotland: Home favorite Tony Jacklin faces off against Lee Trevino with Grand Slam-seeking Jack Nicklaus in the middle. (Photo: Al Satterwhite)

into the rough, one into a bunker. "I hit some good shots too," he said after the round."

Although some Americans were hitting the 1.68-inch American ball at Muirfield, Nicklaus was using the 1.62-inch British ball, then popular in many tournaments throughout the world. "I've never used the big ball in a small-ball tournament," he explained. "If you really get the small ball going, you can shoot nothing. By using the American ball, you're giving away too much to the rest of the field." His 70 was only two shots behind the first-round leader, Peter Tupling, a 22-year-old Englishman who had won only $700 in prize money that year. Asked if he thought he could win the British Open, the young pro laughed.

"Oh, God, no," he said.

Nicklaus, meanwhile, was thinking only of winning. No golfer had won the Masters and the U.S. Open in the same year since Arnold Palmer in 1960, but Palmer lost the British Open to Kel Nagle by a stroke at St. Andrews. And no golfer had won the Masters and the U.S. Open and the British Open in the same year since Ben Hogan in 1953, but Hogan could not enter the PGA due to conflicting dates with the British Open.

Others also were thinking only of winning, especially Jacklin, just one stroke behind at 69, and Trevino three strokes back at 71. The possibility of Nicklaus getting the Grand Slam had challenged Trevino.

"If anybody can stop Jack," he told friends, "I can."

To prepare to defend his title, Trevino had gone to Killeen, Tex., to visit his friend Orville Moody, the 1969 U.S. Open champion. Each morning Trevino played 18 holes, jogging between shots. After lunch, he hit balls for two to three hours, then went fishing with his family. Fit and eager, when his jetliner landed in Scotland he looked around the airport for the driver who was to meet the defending champion. No driver. Trevino phoned a London contact.

"Where are you?" his friend asked.

"I'm in the Prestwick airport," Trevino said.

"Your driver is in Edinburgh."

Rather than take another flight to Edinburgh, Trevino hired a minibus and driver for the trip to the refurbished castle near Muirfield where he and his friends would be lodged.

"When I wound up at the wrong airport," he later said with a laugh, "I was sure I was going to win."

ROUND II: TREVINO AND JACKLIN SET THE HALFWAY PACE

After 36 holes, Trevino was growing more sure of himself. With a 70 in the second round, he tied Jacklin for the lead at 141. Johnny Miller, who holed a 3-wood at the 558-yard fifth hole for a double eagle, was a stroke back with Doug Sanders, who butchered the 18th for a triple-bogey 7, and Nicklaus, who had a 72 in the unseasonably warm sun.

"What kind of temperature is this?" Nicklaus said on the third hole, tugging at the collar of his white cashmere turtleneck. "I've got the wrong clothes."

The temperature was on its way to 70 degrees. After putting out on the ninth for a two-over-par 38, Nicklaus hurried into nearby Greywalls hotel where his wife, Barbara, was waiting with a white golf shirt and a salmon-pink cardigan.

"I made up my mind after three-putting the seventh that I was going to change shirts," Nicklaus said later. "I was hot out there. Just plain hot."

Another bogey at the 10th kept him hot under his open collar. He birdied the next three holes and ended his round with a bogey on the 18th. Still cautious with his driver, he had put six tee shots in the rough—four with his driver, two with his 1-iron.

"It's hard to line up your tee shots here," Nicklaus said. "There are no trees, no big bunkers like on the American courses. The bunkers look flat."

ROUND III: NICKLAUS FALLS FARTHER BEHIND
Nicklaus now needed a good score on Friday to position himself for Saturday's final round (the Open finished on Saturday in those days). But even with birdies on the 16th and 17th, he shot a par 71. Not good enough. "I played as disappointing a round as I have in a long time," he said afterward. "I made some swings I'm not familiar with. If I got a few in, I could have shot 65."

Through the 13th that day Jacklin was leading and he finished with a 67 for 208, but Trevino closed with five consecutive birdies. The day before, Trevino had used an old dimpled Helen Hicks sand wedge to chip in from the rough alongside the second green, about 40 feet away. He had found the club in a grab-barrel.

"Only cost me $200," he boasted.

"For that?" a friend jeered. "You paid $200 for that?"

"It'll make me more than that."

Now, late in Friday's round, Trevino grabbed that old sand wedge after having pushed a 6-iron into the back of a bunker on the short 16th, about 60 feet from the cup. Exploding out of the sand, his ball landed about six feet short of the pin and bounced into the cup. With a whoop, Trevino bounced his light-blue cap on the grass. Then, after another birdie at the 17th, he was walking off the 18th tee after his drive when he turned to his caddie.

"I'd like to make a birdie here," Trevino said. "I have never made five birdies in a row in Great Britain—I mean Scotland."

His 6-iron into the wind rolled over the green onto brownish grass trampled smooth by golfers on their way to the R&A scorer's shed. Using a 9-iron from about 85 feet, Trevino chipped. Into the cup. Another birdie for a 66 and 207, snatching the lead from Jacklin and dropping Nicklaus six strokes behind. Six strokes.

Some of the Scots couldn't understand it. On the 12th hole, Nicklaus had plopped a pitch shot about 30 feet short of the cup.

"That is one of the worst shots I've ever seen him play," a Scot snapped. "Good grief! Damnation, indeed."

These three golfers would place the 101st British Open on a pedestal in history. And put the slippery struggle of the Grand Slam in focus.

"It was the kind of thing that might not ever happen again. But it doesn't have to happen again. It happened once."

—TONY JACKLIN

ROUND IV: JACK MAKES HIS RUN

Desperate, no longer willing to be cautious, Nicklaus was center stage Saturday in a yellow shirt and chocolate-brown slacks. On the second tee, after having used a 3-wood in each of the previous three rounds, he hit a driver that rolled to the fringe of the green on the 349-yard hole. He pitched to six feet and dropped the putt. Birdie. At the 379-yard third, his wedge stopped six feet away. Birdie. At the 558-yard fifth, a 3-wood to the green and two putts produced another birdie. At the 495-yard ninth, his chip to three feet set up another for 32, four under par for the front nine.

"Ask Barbara to stop after nine and get me a cold lemonade," he had asked a friend on the seventh hole. "Tell her no lime juice. It's dry enough out here without any lime juice."

Dry as electricity. The tournament was on. At the 473-yard 10th, a four-foot putt disappeared for another birdie. Five under. "Jack might catch one of us," Trevino had told Jacklin on the first tee, "but he won't catch both of us."

But he had caught and passed both. Trevino and Jacklin were on the ninth tee when they glanced at a leader board. Through 64 holes, Nicklaus suddenly was five under par. Through 62 holes, Trevino, distracted by a startled hare a moment before he missed an eight-foot par putt at the seventh, had slipped to four under, Jacklin to three under.

It was then that Trevino, who had used a 3-wood on the ninth tee in previous rounds, turned to his caddie, Willie Aitchison. "Gimme a driver," Trevino snapped. "We've got to make something happen."

Up ahead, the Scots were making something else happen. When the thousands gathered along the 11th hole saw Nicklaus appear at the crest of the fairway, the cheers resounded. After winning the 1986 Masters, Nicklaus would remember that moment at Muirfield as the first time his eyes ever welled with tears on a golf course.

What soon developed everyone there would remember. Nicklaus was hunched over a five-foot birdie putt on the 11th when a roar rumbled across the moors from the ninth green. Trevino had rolled in an 18-footer for an eagle to go six under. Nicklaus stepped away, then settled over his putt again. Another roar from the ninth. Jacklin had dropped a 10-footer for an eagle to go five under. Walking to the 10th tee, Trevino glanced at Jacklin.

"That'll give Jack something to think about," Trevino said.

Hearing the second roar, Nicklaus had straightened, smiled and stepped away from his putt again. Now he settled over his ball for several long, Nicklausian moments, then stroked it. Birdie. Another roar.

Back on the 10th tee, Trevino turned to Jacklin. "I think the man just gave us something to think about," Trevino said.

Up ahead, Nicklaus was unable to hole birdie putts of 12, 15, 20 and eight feet, but when he arrived at the tee of the 188-yard 16th hole, he remembered his 1966 victory. "That year," he recalled, "I thought that if I finished 3-4-4, par-birdie-par, I'd more than likely win the tournament. That's what I did and I won. And if I could do that now, I'd more than likely win this tournament. I still had my destiny in my own hands. The difference was that in 1966, the short 16th and the long 17th were downwind. This time they were into the wind."

Perhaps too conscious of the wind, Nicklaus pulled a 6-iron into the light rough to the left of the 16th green.

He pitched to within six feet, but now had a downhill putt that would break to the left. Stroking it gently, he watched his ball slip past the left side of the cup. Bogey. Into the wind on the 542-yard 17th, he couldn't get home in two and settled for a par. Another par on the 18th completed a 66 for 279, one stroke behind. But back out on the 17th tee Trevino had been distracted by two photographers.

"One cameraman with a tripod ran in front of me and I backed away," Trevino now recalls. "Then here comes another one with cans of film. I backed away again, then I pulled my tee shot into one of those bunkers on the left."

Stalking off the tee, Trevino was grumbling. From the bunker, all he could do was pitch it out onto the fairway. Then he pulled a 3-wood into the left rough about 30 yards short of the green and about 10 yards short of where Jacklin's ball had stopped in the neck of the narrowed fairway. Even more annoyed than before, Trevino flipped his 3-wood.

"I had the impression that Lee had given up," Jacklin remembers. "Lee never hooks the ball, but he had pulled his tee shot and his third shot. To me, that was an indication he was losing his concentration."

Trevino's 7-iron chip scooted across the green and up into heavy grass on the back slope. There in four, he would be lucky to salvage a bogey. Jacklin then chipped to within 16 feet, a possible birdie, and presumably, a sure par. And in the R&A shed, Nicklaus was checking his scorecard as Trevino's troubles were being shown on television sets near the 18th green.

"Trevino's blown!" somebody yelled.

On the slope behind the 17th green, Trevino stabbed at his ball with a 9-iron. "I think I might have given up," he said later. "I felt like I had. My heart wasn't really in that chip shot." But his ball hopped onto the green and rolled toward the cup. And into it. Another roar, the loudest of the day.

Behind the 18th green, somebody yelled, "Trevino holed his chip!" Nicklaus' caddie, Jimmy Dickinson, flung down his yellow caddie vest in disgust just as Jack emerged from the scorer's shed.

"He holed a chip shot for a 5!" Dickinson yelled.

"What?" Nicklaus said, his voice shrill in shock.

Trevino had stayed one stroke ahead of Nicklaus, but if Jacklin could make his 16-foot birdie putt, the Englishman would take the lead. The headlines in many of the Scottish and British papers that morning had rooted for "Jacko" to win, as he had three years earlier, the first British golfer to win the British Open since Max Faulkner in 1951. And now even Princess Margaret had come to see if Jacko could do it again.

"There was no Seve Ballesteros then, no Sandy Lyle, no Nick Faldo," Jacklin says now. "I was in the pressure cooker. Going into that last day, I told myself, 'Keep your head and hold steady,' I felt like I'd done that all the way through, but when Lee's chip ran in, I ran out of patience. I could have run the ball up close, but my immediate reaction was, 'He's not going to beat me like that.'"

Jacklin stroked his putt firmly. The ball hurried past the left side of the cup and stopped about 2½ feet away.

"I wasn't jumpy on that first putt," Jacklin says. "I still felt in control. I wanted to make it so badly. In those circumstances, 2½ feet was too much."

Jacklin missed that 2½-footer. Instead of a birdie, he had a bogey, which dropped him one stroke behind Trevino.

"Once I three-putted, it was all over," Jacklin recalls. "After that I won a tournament every year to 1982 when I stopped playing, but I never really challenged in the major tournaments again. That finish in '72 kind of knocked the stuffing out of me. I lost a lot of confidence. It was the kind of thing that might not ever happen again. But it doesn't have to happen again. It happened once."

THE FINISHING HOLE

Watching from behind the 17th green, Trevino knew he needed only a par at the 18th to stay ahead of Nicklaus, to win.

"Instead of leading, Tony was out of it," Trevino recalls. "And by the time he finished putting, I had my composure."

Trevino's caddie turned to hurry to the 18th tee, but Lee grabbed his arm. "No, not yet," Trevino said, "let's wait for Tony before we walk back there." As much as Trevino wanted to hit quickly, he knew that if he hurried to the tee, he would be forced to wait until Jacklin walked back there inside the gallery ropes. Instead, he walked back with Jacklin, but as they neared the tee, he turned to his caddie.

"I told Willie to get out of my way because I was going to hit quick," Trevino says. "I grabbed my driver, teed it up, took one look, did my little left-foot shuffle and hit it."

By now, Nicklaus was watching television in an R&A trailer. His arms were folded, his legs crossed as Trevino's ball soared against the blue sky.

"Hit a long drive, didn't he?" Nicklaus said. Long enough for Trevino to float an 8-iron about seven feet behind the cup on the 447-yard finishing hole. "At long last," Henry Longhurst intoned on the BBC, "we have seen the shot that has won the Open." Nicklaus scratched his head and departed. Behind the bleachers he was being escorted to the press tent when he saw his wife, Barbara.

"Hi there," she said softly.

Without a word he kissed her and held her for a moment, then he heard the roar that saluted Trevino's par for 71 and 278—one stroke ahead of him, two ahead of Jacklin, who had bogeyed the 18th after pulling his approach into the left bunker.

"I was there and I let it get away," Nicklaus told his wife. "I felt a 65 would do it. I had a 65 and let it get away."

ODDS ON THE SLAM

If he had finished 3-4-4, as he did in 1966, Nicklaus would have won this British Open, too, but he finished 4-5-4—a two-stroke difference that was all the difference. Suddenly the PGA at Oakland Hills outside Detroit in two weeks would be just another PGA, not the summit of a Grand Slam. (Nicklaus would finish six shots behind the winner, Gary Player.) When Jack sat behind a microphone in the press tent, the golf writers were trying to phrase a gentle first question when he looked down at Norman Mair of The Scotsman.

"Well, Norman," he said, smiling, "I guess I cost you a trip to Detroit."

The writers laughed, then the questions and answers flowed. Asked about the odds on his producing a Grand Slam in the future, Nicklaus grinned. "They're pretty high right now," he said. "I shot 279, and 19 out of 20 times that'll probably win. But it didn't. That's what you're fighting. That somebody will beat you. For 16 rounds, to put it together, that's difficult. I'm disappointed, because I felt I could put it together, but I didn't. I got beat. That's why everybody enters and plays. You don't want to give it to one guy." In those few words he had defined the difficulty of the modern Grand Slam that perhaps no golfer will complete. Then he stood up to go to the presentation ceremony.

"Lee Trevino is some good player," he said. "If I had to lose, I'm glad it was to him."

Maybe if Nicklaus hadn't been quite so cautious in the early rounds, he would have won. But then and now, he has never publicly second-guessed his strategy. "I'll always believe I played the course the right way and just didn't play well," he said that day. "What can I do about a guy who holes it out of bunkers and across greens?" Four times Trevino had holed it from off the putting surface, twice with his 9-iron, twice with his Helen Hicks sand wedge that he presented to British friends who auctioned it for charity. But every so often Jack Nicklaus thinks about how close he came to going to the PGA that year with an opportunity to complete the Grand Slam, how maybe it would have happened if he hadn't awakened with that crick in his neck.

"Not winning that British Open was a very big disappointment then," he says today. "And it seems to have become bigger as the years go by. But that's why the Slam is so tough. You've got to win those four tournaments over a span of four months. When you wake up every day, you never know how you're going to feel."

> "At long last," Henry Longhurst intoned on the BBC, "we have seen the shot that has won the Open."

August 1973

How I Won One PGA and Lived Royally Ever After

No one squeezed more from a single major victory

by Dave Marr

The author was a successful player, TV commentator for three networks (ABC, BBC and NBC) and captain of what is widely considered the greatest American Ryder Cup team in history (1981). But he carried for life the title of "former PGA champion."

Those were four magical days in the summer of 1965. I scored an upset victory in the PGA Championship at Laurel Valley Country Club, practically on Arnold Palmer's lawn, and virtually in an instant my golf career was made.

I doubt that any golfer ever squeezed more rewards from a single triumph. Many winners of major championships haven't found such financial success. For me the PGA title was the seed . . . I did most of my own cultivating. But once the crack was open in corporate doors I made the most of my opportunity.

I was 31 then and it seemed certain to me that the PGA Championship would be only the beginning of a marvelous string of victories. But it just hasn't happened. My golf game hasn't been as productive as I hoped and several physical problems have harpooned my efforts along the road. I have not won a tournament since that 1965 PGA, but nobody can ever steal that descriptive tag "former PGA champion" from me. It's my lifetime meal ticket.

If I had not won the PGA, chances are that ABC-TV would have overlooked me as a prospective commentator. But, with that everlovin' title, I got my chance and hopefully have found a home as the "voice from the 15th green."

When I won the PGA, it would have been simple enough to pick up a few extra dollars for endorsements over the following months, maybe a dozen $2,000 exhibitions and some $300 appearances at sporting goods stores. I wasn't ready to settle for that.

At the time, I lived in the New York area. That gave me several vehicles to market myself. I hung around with a lot of influential people. I drank with writers at Toots Shor's and broke bread with corporation higher-ups at Manuche's. I kept some late hours and spent a great deal of money, but all the time I pounded my name and my image into some important heads.

Since the ABC job developed, my market has mushroomed. I have a contract with Allied Chemical and some other small companies to do VIP-customer relations chores. That is, if you call flying to a resort and playing golf with congenial, influential people a "chore," I spend a couple of days teeing it up and chatting with clients and they pay me several thousand dollars. Not bad, eh?

Now don't get the idea I'm a salesman. Allied Chemical would hit the ceiling if I started talking about its business. The most advanced formula they trust me with is H_2O, which everyone knows goes best with scotch.

I've kept plugging away on tour, missing more 36-hole cuts than I've made of late, knowing that the touch will someday return. I can feel it coming, but it's

Key moment: Marr birdies the 15th hole during his final round of the '65 PGA. His 280 total was good for a two-stroke victory over two of the game's reigning heavyweights, Jack Nicklaus and Billy Casper. (Photo: AP/Wide World)

I have not won a tournament since that 1965 PGA, but nobody can ever steal that descriptive tag "former PGA champion" from me. It's my lifetime meal ticket.

been torture at times waiting for my golf production to get back on even terms with my outside work.

Last year I won only $13,000 on the tour. That's about like being a pro football coach and going 0-13-1. The first half of 1973, with the exception of a fourth-place finish in the Bing Crosby, was more of the same. Still, in my heart I know my golf can again reach the heights it hit at the 1965 PGA. I'm an honest 39, and it's not too late.

My reasoning in ranking the Masters No. 2 is its position on the calendar. It is first among the major events and the champion at Augusta National has a clear field to stack up a lot of side business before the Open arrives in June.

To most American players a victory in the British Open would not mean as much as winning one of the other three. The exceptions are men like Nicklaus, Palmer, Gay Brewer, Doug Sanders and Trevino who have business interests around the globe.

Now to the PGA. This one unquestionably has the toughest field to beat. There are no amateurs clogging up the field, no special invitees from overseas and no weekend players who might have got hot and qualified like you can for the Open. It's a tournament dominated by the touring professionals. There are some club pros in the field, but the only ones to reckon with are fellows who were tour guys and gave it up for the stability of a stay-at-home job.

For 40 years the PGA Championship was decided at match play, head-to-head eliminations. That ended in 1957 when Lionel Hebert edged Dow Finsterwald, 2 and 1, at Miami Valley Club in Dayton, Ohio. There have been 15 stroke-play PGAs since then and it'll stay that way despite annual cries for at least one match-play championship among the Big Four.

The problems with match-play stem mainly from television coverage. TV has meant a great deal to the financial well-being of American tour golf and the networks aren't too excited about having two colorless, unknown pros squaring off in the 36-hole finals. And, to almost any fan, the interest will decline if there isn't a glamorous final such as Nicklaus against Trevino or Palmer versus Player. You've got to have the names.

I think the match-play format and its uncertainties helped make the PGA No. 4 among the majors with most golf followers. In stroke play, you know a Nicklaus or a Trevino can wipe out a seven-shot deficit on Sunday and win it all despite so-so rounds the first three days. In match play one bad day knocks out a man for good. There's no coming back from a 77 to win. You can also shoot a 68 and be eliminated. For those reasons I favor keeping the PGA and the other majors on a stroke-play basis.

Another thing that detracted from the PGA Championship for many years was the selection of courses. Politics played an important part in picking subpar sites such as Columbine near Denver in 1967 and Pecan Valley at San Antonio the next year. Those are not championship courses of U.S. Open caliber.

To be a great event, the PGA has to play on marvelous courses such as Merion, Oakland Hills, Firestone, Olympic, Pebble Beach, Winged Foot and Southern Hills. There has been a definite and appealing swing in this direction over the last few years.

When I won the PGA in 1965, there was an extra incentive to the tour players. At that time the champion received a lifetime exemption from qualifying for all regular tour events. As long as I can walk and swing a club I can tee it up without ever enduring those terrible Monday morning qualifying rounds.

Currently, the PGA winner gets a 10-year exemption to all tour tournaments. It's just not quite as much to shoot for. If I didn't have the lifetime free pass, I would be qualifying with the kids every Monday. It might make me quit the tour at a time when I know there's still plenty of gas in my tank and it's just a matter of getting it flowing into my engine.

The tour is still great fun for me. It's somewhat of a college environment where you enjoy every type of personality from Big Fat Sam the caddie to the president of General Motors. And I admit I still get a charge being around golfers the caliber of Nicklaus and Palmer. Things happen when Jack and Arnie are on the scene and I love being in on the action.

I hope you can see what winning the PGA Championship, or any one of the Big Four, can do for a golfer. When you see somebody scratching for a first major victory at Canterbury, maybe you'll have an idea what it can mean to the fellow. My only advice to the winner, if he's never won a big one before, is to push that title for everything it's worth. For him, as for me, opportunity may knock only once.

Seve Ballesteros and Jose Maria Olazabal, the Spanish Armada that was the spiritual core of the European Ryder Cup team, shown in action at Kiawah Island in 1991. Together, the duo won more matches than any partnership in history, helping elevate the biennial contest against the United States into a thrillingly competitive spectacle. (Photo: Jim Moriarty)

1985 – 1999

Major Dan: Our Man Jenkins on the Scene

Highlights of his GOLF DIGEST tournament reports

1999 BRITISH OPEN

On Jean van de Velde: When a double bogey wins a major, you don't turn yourself into a martyr with a triple. But that's what Jean of Argh did on Carnoustie's 487-yard par 4, where the Barry Burn winds around and around, yearning for any mis-hit shot. You can only wonder why the Frenchman didn't play it with, say, 4-iron, wedge, wedge, and even three putts. That would have been a 6, but good enough. But instead he Van-de-Velde-ed it, or Clouseau-ed it, take your pick. He played it driver, 2-iron/grandstand/wall of burn/rough, burn, drop, bunker, blast, putt—which actually turned out to be a somewhat miraculous 7, when you think about it. How bad was it? There was a rumor in the press tent that Van de Velde was French for Greg Norman. But not even Norman's suitcase flew quite so open quite so quickly during any of his major collapses.

1998 MASTERS

Thursday really belonged to two other people, neither of whom was eventual champion, Mark O'Meara. One was only a month away from his 86th birthday, Sam Snead, and the other was the amateur with a name like a ski jumper, Matt Kuchar.

Snead had suffered what was first thought to be a mild stroke on Tuesday, but after being hospitalized in Augusta and undergoing tests, it was diagnosed as a blood vessel in the back of the neck that chose to act up. By Thursday morning, he was on the first tee.

Yeah, there he was, the strokeless Slammer, out there on the first tee in the immortal-est threesome that exists in golf today: Snead, Byron Nelson and Gene Sarazen. So, natty as ever in gray slacks, navy sweater and straw hat, all Sam did with that still-sweet swing was take the club back to a position that most codgers can only dream of and pound a drive straight down the middle of the fairway, about 230 yards, slight draw, after which the old show-off kicked his leg up in the air like a Radio City Rockette.

It was a moment to take away from the '98 Masters that was better than any souvenir.

1998 PGA CHAMPIONSHIP

The first duty in Seattle was to learn what Sahalee means. It seemed there was a choice. It was either a Chinook word for "high, heavenly ground" or the name of a Chinook's second wife.

1997 MASTERS

As you no doubt know by now, Tiger Woods' overwhelming performance in the Masters this April made it the tournament that changed golf forever, changed golf-course design forever, and may have changed society forever. So the main question that begs to be answered, after watching him reduce everyone else in the game to a bit player, if not set decoration, is what can be done to stop him, or at least slow him down before he makes some of us forget that we ever saw Ben Hogan, Byron Nelson, Sam Snead, Arnold Palmer and Jack Nicklaus swing a club?

Fortunately, I've given it considerable thought—much more time than it took the Masters field to give up—and I hereby present 10 Steps to Stop or Slow Down Tiger Woods:

1. Make him wear Harry Vardon's tweed suit.
2. Make him wear Greg Norman's planter's hat.
3. Make him read a David Leadbetter instruction article.
4. Make him use Phil Mickelson's clubs.
5. Make him play the gutty.
6. Make him wear Tom Kite's glasses.
7. Make him read every word of the new Jack Nicklaus autobiography.
8. Make him go to dinner with Mark Rolfing.
9. Make him attend the annual golf writers' dinner.
10. Make him get married and have to go to Ace Hardware a lot.

Tiger Woods' 12-stroke victory in the 1997 Masters announced, with exclamation points, the arrival of a new era in the professional game. (Photo: Stephen Szurlej)

At their best, Jack Fate and Arnold Destiny never put on a better show than Ben Crenshaw at the Augusta National Golf and Predestination Club.

1996 MASTERS

Any golfer could understand what Norman had gone through. Hell, even Harvey Penick's four volumes can't tell you how to stop the bleeding in the middle of a round. It's the hardest thing in the world to do. Greg couldn't even run over the demons in one of his six or seven Ferraris. Future historians won't know what really happened any more than most of us eyewitnesses. They'll read his daily scores: 63-69-71—78! And after they gasp, what will they think? I'll tell you what they'll think:

1. Boy, the wind must have howled that day.
2. Boy, I hope I never get food poisoning that bad.
3. Boy, Greg Norman must have gotten some terrible news that morning about one of his nine private jets, 14 yachts, or 75 or 80 Ferraris.

1996 BRITISH OPEN

Listen, anybody who doesn't like Blackpool just doesn't have a sense of humor. Blackpool is a combination of Coney Island times 10, with 50 more tattoo parlors and fortune-tellers, and a Jurassic Park where most of the visitors are fatter and scarier than the dinosaurs. In Blackpool if you don't find Britain's oldest tram system, one of the world's tallest, steepest and most terrifying roller coasters, or the world's silliest replica of the Eiffel Tower, you have no fewer than three pleasure piers stretching out over mud-caked beaches in desperate search of the Irish Sea.

1995 MASTERS

Did Ben Crenshaw really win the Masters in April or did everybody spend the week watching him star in the remake of a couple of old movies, "Angel on My Shoulder" and "God Is My Co-Putter"? Co-Pilot. Sorry. At their best, Jack Fate and Arnold Destiny never put on a better show than Crenshaw at the Augusta National Golf and Predestination Club.

1995 U.S. OPEN

You could call it another shot heard round the Greg Norman household, but it was more than that. Corey Pavin's magnificent 4-wood to the 72nd green at Shinnecock Hills not only sealed the result of the U.S. Open in the merry month of June, but it offered further proof that when the championship goes to a long, rugged, bewildering golf course, a gritty, short-hitting shotmaker will win it almost every time.

1995 BRITISH OPEN

While more than one immortal lost his touch, patience and composure under the old-fashioned conditions of a flag-bending wind, and while certain people like Costantino Rocca managed to play underneath it, Daly simply threw his chocolate-croissant-fed frame into the gales, overwhelmed the stockpile of par-4 holes and demonstrating that a gravy-eating lout can chip and putt like any of the game's stylists, though not necessarily hair stylists.

1995 RYDER CUP

Here's what these thrilling Ryder Cup Matches are proving now: Talent hits great shots as always, a Higher Power hits lucky shots, and fat tournament purses that reward mediocre play on both tours are responsible for the dumbbell shots and hideous displays of the choking-dog variety.

1994 U.S. OPEN

This Ernie Els person, a big strapping blond dude from Johannesburg—he's got a chance to be Greg Norman without the arrogance, someone mentioned—hit so many wild tee shots into so many bizarre places to prolong the 94th Open, you'd have sworn he was looking for the missing letters in his name.

1993 U.S. OPEN

The United States Greed Association—er, golf, I mean—and the Baltusrol Automobile Club—golf, I mean—got better than they deserved on a hot and humid mid-June week when a guy dressed like a 1908 Cincinnati Red beat a guy dressed like a waiter on a golf cruise in a thrilling finish to become the surprising National Open champion. Lee Janzen was the one in the pinstripe shirt and the baseball cap that advertised a nonalcoholic beer. Payne Stewart, the runner-up, was the guy in the plus fours, long socks and snappy little cap, the attire he usually wears when he brings you the lunch menu before he hits long irons off the promenade deck.

1993 BRITISH OPEN

Welcome to Masterpiece Golf starring—finally—Greg Norman. In this episode at Sandwich along a gray, damp, blustery coast of Kent in the game's oldest professional championship, Norman on the final day of the 1993 British Open did what has long been expected of him. Under gripping conditions against the best players in the world he fired a round of golf that was suitable for framing. His closing 64 not only left Nick Faldo scratching his head in defeat, it was the lowest finishing round for a winner in that ancient competition. The best thing was, he did it with authority, hole after hole. The second best thing was, he did it without wearing a hat.

1993 RYDER CUP

Ever since 1983, when the Europeans gained equality—give or take a wedge shot—the event has been loaded with drama, comedy, suspense, surprises, shock, tension, mystery, controversy, what have you. A putt here, a chip there, and it could go either way. Then came this last one in late September that was played in the gray, breezy bowels of England, and it topped them all where brilliant golf shots were concerned. There is no reason to suspect that the Matches won't continue to be just as close, just as thrilling, in the future, as the international competition goes to Rochester, N.Y., in '95, to Spain in '97, to Inverness or Winged Foot in '99, and no doubt back to the Belfry in 2001, a date that sounds so

Paired together and tied for the lead at 12 under par, Faldo stared a hole through Greg's brain on the first tee and then conducted a clinic with a near-flawless 67 while Norman thrashed around with a woeful 76.

alarming in certain respects that a geezer-codger like myself might fully expect it to be decided by holograms on computer screens.

1992 U.S. OPEN

Tom Kite walks around today as living proof that if you work hard enough at golf, even though your ability is limited, a day will come along when the cups on the greens at a major championship will expand and swallow up your golf ball at a precise moment in history and all past disappointments will become a quaint memory. When Kite withstood the wind and the rough and the pressure of the final round to capture the U.S. Open at Pebble Beach in June, particularly on a brutal day that turned talented players into comic figures, more than anything else it called to mind the words of Cary Middlecoff from many years ago: Nobody wins the Open, it wins you.

1991 BRITISH OPEN

Ian Baker-Finch had spent his career being low hyphen in the clubhouse, but today the handsome Australian dude is the only hyphenated name ever to appear on a major championship trophy, unless, of course, you want to count Ben Immortal-Hogan or Lord Byron Nelson-Streak.

1991 PGA CHAMPIONSHIP

Hasta la vista, Greg Norman and all you so-called long hitters. I have seen the future of golf and it comes from Dardanelle, Ark. It's got a baby face and a blond wig but when it drives the ball, it makes everybody else look like an interior decorator. John Daly, who in August became the greatest unknown since Jack Fleck to win a major, is far more than his previous nicknames of Wild Thing, Macho Man, Killer and Long John. He's Terminator 3, 4, 5 and 6. He's alien golf. Golf in the cosmos.

1990 MASTERS

The fact that Nick Faldo seems to have a habit of picking up majors that Americans drop makes one wonder if the U.S. has been as kind to England since the days of FDR and lend-lease. Raymond Floyd, Scott Hoch and Paul Azinger are now members of an exclusive philanthropic society. They have bequeathed three majors to Faldo in the last four years.

1990 BRITISH OPEN

Saturday, July 21, will be remembered as the day Nick Faldo undressed Greg Norman in front of 45,000 fans and millions more on TV and left him with a new nickname: Crocodile Gerbil. Paired together and tied for the lead at 12 under par, Faldo stared a hole through Greg's brain on the first tee and then conducted a clinic with a near-flawless 67 while Norman thrashed around with a woeful 76, which happened to be the third-worst score of the day. Simultaneously, it was both an astounding sight and a pitiful sight. One man confident, dominant, executing his shots with studied

perfection; the other trying to figure out which end of the club to take a grip on.

1990 PGA CHAMPIONSHIP

The 1990 PGA being rife with controversy and subsequent TV advertiser pullout and enormous media attention on the issue of human rights rather than golf drama, it may well be remembered that Wayne Grady won something called the Milford Plaza/Gold Bond Medicated Powder Classic—those seemed to be the only sponsors left.

1989 U.S. OPEN

All U.S. Opens are a little bit goofy, some more so than others, but the one at Oak Hill Country Club in soggy old Rochester, N.Y., would surely be remembered as a Strange one, and not just because Curtis won it. Among other things, it was a championship in which holes-in-one for a while looked cheaper than junk food, a championship in which the casual water was deeper than Lake Ontario, and a championship in which Tom Kite demonstrated the proper way to take the wheels off a car and drive it into a ditch.

1989 PGA CHAMPIONSHIP

No matter how hard they sometimes may seem to try to de-major it with some of the sites, history refuses to let the PGA ruin the championship. How can we forget those great old match-play tournaments that Walter Hagen and Gene Sarazen won, that Ben Hogan, Byron Nelson and Sam Snead won, and all of the stroke-play championships that Jack Nicklaus won and Arnold Palmer didn't. But wave a substantial amount of cash in front of the PGA and you, too, can have a PGA Championship on your very own golf course that will live on in the annals of cornfields or condos or insurance compounds. Classy golf courses are not named after insurance executives. Trust me on this one. I didn't make it up. Nowhere in the lore of golf is there talk of Kemper Beach, Kemper Valley, St. Kemper, Royal Kemper, Kemperhurst No. 2, Kempercock Hills, Winged Kemper, Cypress Kemper. Classy golf courses are named for oaks, rivers, creeks, forests, monts and rols.

1988 U.S. OPEN

Those who think an 18-hole playoff to decide the U.S. Open Championship is anticlimactic have fallen prey to television. For some, their only reality is what they see on television. Happily, the U.S. Golf Association has another view. It believes that its trophy is so important, so prestigious, that it would be a shame to have the Open decided at sudden death, purely for the sake of a network. May it ever be so. Moreover, anyone who disagrees with this is ignorant of U.S. Open history. Most of the playoffs have been thrilling and suspenseful, regardless of what the final figures show. A good example was the battle between Curtis Strange and Nick Faldo at The Country Club in Brookline, Mass., earlier this

From top, major memories:
Nicklaus' magical run to a sixth green jacket in the 1986 Masters (Photo: Jim Moriarty); Europe's Ian Woosnam celebrating yet another improbable Ryder Cup victory in 1995 (Photo: Stephen Szurlej); Nick Faldo and winner Curtis Strange showing again why 18-hole playoffs aren't anti-climactic in the 1988 U.S. Open (Photo: Jim Moriarty); and John Daly's out-of-nowhere victory in the 1991 PGA Championship, chosen the most memorable in the event's 83-year history. (Photo: Stephen Szurlej)

summer. Curtis finally brushed his way into pro golf's elite by winning a major, and he would be the first to tell you it wasn't easy even though his even-par 71 against Faldo's four-over 75 makes it now look like a stroll through a boutique.

1988 BRITISH OPEN

It seemed more than appropriate that on a golf course that has become a graveyard for American pros, the greatest golfer in the world today, Severiano Ballesteros, played the greatest round of his life—and career—to win the British Open, his fifth major, and strongly insinuate that he is the player of the '80s. Years ago, like 62 years to be exact, when Bobby Jones became the only American ever to win at Royal Lytham and St. Annes, they put a plaque next to a bunker at the 17th hole to commemorate the shot Jones hit on his way to that victory. But it might not be possible to commemorate Seve's final-round 65 with plaques, for it would render the course unplayable.

1988 PGA CHAMPIONSHIP

When Jeff Sluman scooped up the PGA Championship out there on the Oklahoma plains in August, he prompted a question: What does Jeff Sluman have in common with Jack Nicklaus, Lee Trevino, Jerry Pate, Orville Moody and Jack Fleck? Answer: A major was his first victory in pro golf.

1987 MASTERS

In the end, that first week in April, it came down to Greg Norman looking at another 10-million-to-one shot. If he continues to be in the right place at the right time, he can lose the most spectacular Grand Slam in history.

1987 U.S. OPEN

Of all the enduring traditions in golf, the one at the Olympic Club in San Francisco is certainly becoming the hardest to reckon with. Hold a U.S. Open there and the wrong guy will win it every time. Olympic is now three for three. Fleck over Hogan. Casper over Palmer. And now Scott Simpson, your basic journeyman pro, takes Nob Hill and turns it into an urban renewal project. Simpson over Watson. God over the press again.

1987 RYDER CUP

The myth that was finally exploded at the 1987 Ryder Cup Matches was that America's Bubba Joe Grooves, known for his dashing 16th-place finishes on our PGA Tour, can go out on any old golf course any time he feels like it and whip up on any old European hacker, who would be a lot better off if he stuck to soccer or cricket or drinking warm beer. Well, old Bubba Joe got exactly what he deserved out there in Dublin, Ohio, in late September—and so did our PGA, and so did Commissioner Deane Beman and the PGA Tour. It's the PGA of America that has a qualifying system that leaves so many stars off the U.S. team. And it's Beman and his

policy board who try to insure that every touring pro gets rich though he may not know any more about golf than how to hit a mediocre iron into a soft green, drive a courtesy car, wear a visor with a silly logo on it and smile only at people who look like they might be executives from Nabisco.

1986 "THE GREATEST" MASTERS

If you want to put golf back on the front pages and you don't have a Bobby Jones or a Francis Ouimet handy, here's what you do: You send an aging Jack Nicklaus out in the last round of the Masters and let him kill more foreigners than a general named Eisenhower.

On that final afternoon of the Masters Tournament, Nicklaus' deeds were so unexpectedly heroic, dramatic and historic, the taking of the sixth green jacket would certainly rank as the biggest golf story since Jones' Grand Slam of 1930. That Sunday night, writers from all corners of the globe were last seen sitting limply at their machines, muttering: "It's too big for me."

What indeed could be said? That it was one for the ages? That Jack Nicklaus saved golf from the nobodies who populate the PGA Tour these days? That surely this was Jack's finest hour, his 20th major? As much was said back in 1980 when he surprisingly won the U.S. Open and PGA. But here he comes again, six years later, now a creaking 46, hopelessly trailing a group of younger stars, most of them glamorous foreigners like Seve Ballesteros, Greg Norman, Bernhard Langer, Tommy Nakajima, Nick Price and Sandy Lyle, and what he does is suddenly catch fire over the last 10 holes of the tournament, shoot a seven-under 65 (with two bogeys), knock all the invaders into a killer funk and win a sixth Masters by filling the Augusta National's pine-shadowed corridors with roars unlike any before them.

1986 PGA CHAMPIONSHIP

Since Toledo, Ohio, is one of those fun towns where you go to buy a Jeep or get your spark plugs changed, it was probably fitting that Greg Norman finally leaked enough oil at the Inverness Club to let Bob Tway become the PGA champion of 1986.

1985 U.S. OPEN

The events at Oakland Hills Country Club in mid-June bring to mind a mystery novel: The Man Who Only Wins Opens, by Elmore Dashiell Andrew North. True enough, but the coldest Open ever, certainly the oddest, set in an elegant suburb of Detroit, belonged to a little man named Tze-Chung Chen the whole week, and the only reason the championship isn't his today is because he played a single hole in the final round as if it were made in Taiwan. Sam Snead once lost an Open by making an 8. That was at Spring Mill in Philadelphia back in '39. Snead's 8 lives on. So will Mr. Chen's and, if anything, his was far more bizarre. Mr. Chen carried three wedges in his bag at Oakland Hills: one for sand, one for pitch shots, and now we know what the third one was for—hitting a golf ball twice in one swing.

Nothing like the cheers of a gallery to make a golf tournament—or a golf magazine—come alive. (Photo: Dom Furore)

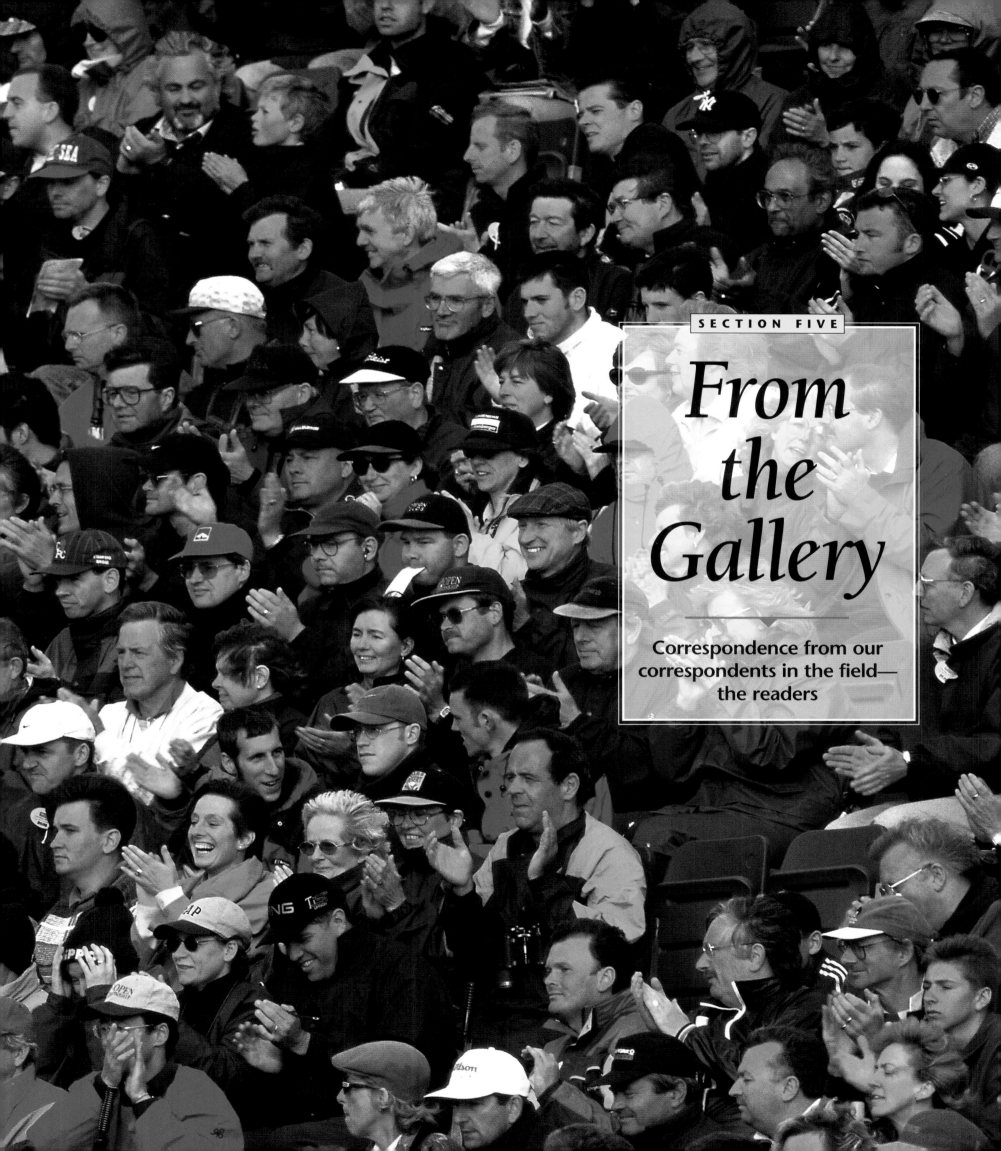

SECTION FIVE

From the Gallery

Correspondence from our
correspondents in the field—
the readers

IT'S YOUR TURN

by Mike O'Malley,
Managing Editor

GOLF DIGEST learned very early that there could be no magazine without a gallery—and that the gallery should be heard.

We've been fortunate to have an army of knowledgeable consultants on hand to offer advice and share good story ideas: They're the magazine's readers, and they're as passionate about GOLF DIGEST as they are about their own games.

Readers' letters in "From the Gallery" became our version of a 19th-hole grillroom, where one correspondent might relate a rich anecdote ("*In Babe Ruth's heyday, his left-handed drives ranged from 240 to 275 yards, but he had trouble keeping the ball in the fairway*"), another might offer delicately worded constructive criticism ("*Cancel my subscription!*"), and yet another might brag about an unusual feat from Anytown, U.S.A. ("*Three members of our foursome all made eagle on the same hole. The last player, Mr. Smith, quit golf for the day*"). Sometimes we all fumed together when the plug was pulled on yet another late-running golf telecast.

In the early days, a staple of the letters section included proud papas sending in photos of their daughters as candidates for the magazine's politically incorrect "Most Beautiful Golfer" award (long since abandoned, but come to think of it, isn't that where we introduced readers to Laura Baugh?).

Celebrities, pros and golf enthusiasts all took a place at the monthly roundtable. March might bring a tongue-in-cheek reaction from Bing Crosby to an analysis of his swing; May might include former U.S. Open champion Jack Fleck setting everyone straight on exactly who was the first to pace off yardages. (Hint: It wasn't Jack Nicklaus.) When Tom Watson was suffering from putting problems, you overwhelmed him, and us, with advice. And when Roberto De Vicenzo missed making a playoff in the 1968 Masters because of a scoring error, it elicited a record number of letters. You felt his pain.

The letters have borne an air of civility ("*President Ford asked me to thank you for your thoughtfulness, and now understands why he is being invited to so many tournaments!*"), occasionally replaced by a more shrill tone that perhaps reflects society today. You've scolded us when you've felt we've strayed (perhaps we should have pleaded no contest after devoting 11 pages to O.J. Simpson); you've breathed fire when you've been aggrieved (a wounded but eloquent Mac O'Grady scorched us with this: "*The system cannibalized me over a decade ago. There's no more flesh to eat.*"); and you've agonized with us about overcoming the game's challenges, from slow play and exclusion to the environment and skyrocketing costs (annual dues at Olympic Club in 1974: $331).

The common denominator is that we, like you, are fanatics. The letters section is just one part of the relationship we share. When we challenged you to become "Armchair Architects," more than 22,000 of you took part, showcasing talent, imagination—and, in some cases, masochistic tendencies that would send Pete Dye screaming into the night.

That's the kind of enthusiasm that bubbled up when we asked you to help identify America's Worst Avid Golfer. After witnessing 257 strokes at Sawgrass by one Angelo Spagnolo—including 66 whacks at the par-3 17th, where "the wheels came off a little" we were confident we had our man.

When nothing seems to help, a little humor goes a long way. In September of 1988 we published broadcaster John Madden's essay on his experiences with this most maddening game. "Golf's a game like no other," wrote Madden. "You never get golf. Golf gets you." Madden won hearts and minds with that one. "Finally one of us has been heard from in your magazine," one of you wrote. "I enjoyed every word and paragraph." Sometimes our attempts at empathy fail. An article entitled "Golf in Hell" did not amuse many. "I assure you there will be no golf in hell," declared one letter.

Point taken. We make more of our on-course struggles than is necessary at times. But then, like everyone else, we're trying to get over the hump, too. That's why it's not unusual to walk through our offices and see editors trying out the latest tips as articles are in the working stages. Then imagine the gratification when letters arrive from you with tales of your newfound success: "*David Leadbetter's simple instruction to move my left shoulder and arm away from my chin really works. Now, David, do you have any good tips on how to eliminate three-putting?*"

What's next? As the information age takes us to new places, we'll be exchanging instantaneous feedback. We'd like to think we'll be on the same page more often than not, but as a wise old boss once said, sometimes wise people agree to disagree.

This selection of 50 years worth of letters reflects our time, and yours. Enjoy it. You may well recognize yourself. And let the dialogue continue.

The first "Armchair Architect" article ran in 1972 and spawned two contests, one in 1988 and one in 1991.

75¢
November 1972
Largest audience of any golfing publication

GOLF DIGEST

HOW TO BE AN ARMCHAIR GOLF ARCHITECT

Jack Nicklaus on chipping

Most Beautiful Golfer of 1972

Behind Bruce Devlin's comeback

Jane Blalock's swing analyzed

Would you accept a golf bet from this man? Beware Bob Hope (here at the 1987 Crosby Pro-Am)—or so said Bing Crosby. (Photo: Julian Graham)

CROSBY UNMASKS HOPE

Thank you for the highly informative and deeply constructive article involving the golf swings of Mr. Hope and myself ("Hope and Crosby: What to Learn From Their Swings," December 1969).

Of course, Bob Hope's golf swing has nothing to do with his golf game. His biggest play is on the first tee—that's where all his matches are won. After his lengthy negotiations, anything that happens thereafter is routine. All he has to do is finish on his feet to win.

I'm sorry that the pictures depicting my golf swing showed me wearing a sports coat, which failed to disclose the full play of the massive muscles of my shoulders and back.

Honestly though, it's a very good story, and I enjoyed it immensely. I hope your readers do, also.

—BING CROSBY, BEVERLY HILLS, CALIF.
MARCH 1970

THE WAIT IN WEIGHT SHIFT

My wife just caught me in the bathroom (sans apparel) with one foot on her scale and one foot on mine, swinging a golf club. Seriously, wouldn't it be interesting to your venerable readers to get statistics on players on the senior tour who were featured in the first tests? Perhaps there could be some dramatic changes in weight distribution for older players that could correlate with loss of distance for example.

—MARVIN POSNER
KINGSMILL, VA.
JUNE 1989

MIND OVER MATTER

During the 1930s George Lake was in charge of "everything" at the Huntington Beach, Calif., public course. He had a golf shop, but the Depression was on and he could not afford to carry a line of clubs. Lake did club-repair work, though. One day a man brought in a new set of woods which he said were too heavy, and asked Lake to take some weight out of them. After the man left, George saw that the clubs had a new type of screw in them. In trying unsuccessfully to remove the screws, George scratched the clubheads slightly. Later the man returned when Lake wasn't in the shop. He saw the scratches, assumed the clubs had been fixed and took them out for a round. The man came back and told George they were too light now, so put back half of what you took out. Lake couldn't take out half of nothing, so he didn't touch them and later gave them back to his customer. The man played another round, came back and threw the clubs on the floor with the comment that "now none of them weigh the same." This goes to show just how much the mind plays a part in the game of golf.

—BURT BROOKS, YORBA LINDA, CALIF.
NOVEMBER 1963

IN THE GROOVE

How much would a pro make who shot par in every tournament? I contend he would make about $10,000—am I right?

—C.W. RONNETTE, PITTSBURGH
APRIL 1958

Not quite. A par-shooter in 1958 would have won both the U.S. Open and Colonial National Invitation and $23,924 in prize money.
—Ed.

CLUB ACCESS

In 1966, I was a young Marine stationed in Vietnam. While there I wrote to Bobby Jones asking him if I could play Augusta National Golf Club when I got home. I was rather naïve at the time, not realizing it was a very private club. All I knew was that Mr. Jones *was* the Augusta National Golf Club as far as I was concerned.

Within days, I received a letter from Mr. Jones indicating he would try to arrange for me to play the course when I returned. I was but a lowly Marine Corps corporal, but Mr. Jones treated me as if I were a king.

I remember every shot I hit that beautiful day in January of 1968. But what remains with me most is that I was the guest of Mr. Robert T. Jones. He had made it clear to the staff that I was to be treated as a special guest and, believe me, I was.

—CPL. GERALD JUSTINE, USMC (RET.)
PALM BEACH GARDENS, FLA.
APRIL 1994

At least Jesper Parnevik's uniform doesn't come with a number on the back. (Photo: Bob Ewell)

NOT A FAN OF LOGO-MANIA

I thoroughly enjoyed the article "The Latest, and Least, of Fashion Wear" by Charles Price (November 1988). It is a damn disgrace to see the logos these pros attach to themselves and their equipment that has nothing to do with the "grand game" itself. They do not possess the class or the shots of Hagen, Jones and Hogan, to name only a few. I remember very well when Ben Hogan refused to play in a George S. May tournament because the players were required to wear numbers on their backs.

— J. STUART CARSWELL, RUTLAND, VT.
FEBRUARY 1989

MAC'S KNACK WITH WORDS

If everything written in this article ("Golf's Tortured Genius," Kevin Cook, July 1998) were factual and true, perhaps I really do need to see a psychotherapist. Is Sigmund Freud still alive?

I didn't know I was that important to so many people and such "Hard Copy" for a golf periodical that is sycophantic and parasitical in nature. Sadly enough, GOLF DIGEST caught another wave of Jerry Springer tabloid sensationalism that is sweeping across American journalism, too—all in the name of what? Ratings? Not only was a social autopsy performed on my professional career, but my private life as well. They quoted every slimy, sleazy, upright, walking scumbag invertebrate life and the game of golf, unfortunately, exposed me to throughout my 47 years on earth. Each of these fly-by-nights went on the record to capture their 15 seconds of Tonya Harding fame, which GOLF DIGEST provided earnestly with pleasure. How pitiful. I, like others, who have at least a half-brain, was appalled by the overkill nature of the story. What reasons justify publishing such trash? If it's open season on me, who is at the bottom of the food chain of exempt status on the PGA Tour and profes-

sional sports, what's in store for others? Fuzzy Zoeller's character was overtly targeted and assassinated. Who is next? Why are they coming after me for the one-millionth time? The system cannibalized me over a decade ago. There's no more flesh to eat. A fossilized carcass is all that remains. Don't they realize I'm ancient history? My bones and career petrified long ago, DNA too, but never my spirit!

The article was fraught with blatant, premeditated inaccuracies, inflammatory lies and other misnomers. It almost took on a World Wrestling Federation personality of playful, jovial, jocose behavior. They delightfully called me every illicit name in the book except a liar, a cheat, or that I was gay. So maybe, just maybe, the publishers, editors and writers of GOLF DIGEST are not absent of moral reasoning and a conscience after all. They didn't say I was Dennis Rodman's half-brother or a predatorial pedophile.

—MAC O'GRADY, PALM SPRINGS, CALIF.
SEPTEMBER 1998

TAKE THAT

During my tour of duty in Vietnam, I have received GOLF DIGEST every month. I especially enjoyed the articles by Tony Jacklin and Dave Marr in the September 1968 issue. Several of us in the battalion try to keep our golf swings intact by hitting old golf balls (mailed to me by my wife) out into the valley where "Charlie" (the Viet Cong) lives. So far we've recorded no known hits but we've often wondered what enemy soldiers would think should a golf ball land nearby.

—JOHN A. MCDONALD
BATTALION CHAPLAIN, VIETNAM
DECEMBER 1968

SEVEN MORE SINS

I read your cover article in the January issue entitled "How to Cure 7 Deadly Sins." I am a daughter of an avid golfer and have come up with "Golf's 7 Deadly Sins, According to a Non-Golfer."
1. Staying home on a Saturday and Sunday morning.
1. Not teeing off by 8 a.m.
2. Actually relaxing while on vacation, instead of playing.
3. Not buying a new golf bag every other week.
4. Not informing anyone who will listen about every hole you played, in detail.
5. Not getting everyone in the family golf lessons.
6. Not making golf the center of my life.

—STEFANIE FAXON, BAY VILLAGE, OHIO
MARCH 1987

A reader hoped to take advantage of Billy Casper's neglected food groups. (Photo: Lester Nehamkin)

BILLY CASPER C/O GOLF DIGEST

Dear Mr. Casper,

I have read that you are a Mormon and that you don't smoke or drink.

Statistics show that the average American male smokes 37½ cartons of cigarettes and drinks 42 gallons of liquor a year.

I would appreciate your sending me your unused 37½ cartons of cigarettes and 42 gallons of liquor, because I do drink and smoke.

AUGUST 1968

JUST WONDERING

I noticed Gene Sarazen listed only nine players on his top 10 players of all time. I couldn't help but wonder if the Squire miscounted or if he considered his signature number 10.

—JIM STODDARD, WEST WINDSOR, N.J.
FEBRUARY 1995

CALIFORNIA BEAUTY

Please accept my entry of Laura Baugh in your 1971 Most Beautiful Golfer contest. Laura is 16 and plays to a handicap of 5 at Recreation Golf Course, Long Beach, Calif. She has been a skilled golf competitor for many years, dating from 1961 when she won the National Pee Wee championship for her age (6) group. Presently she is the Los Angeles and Long Beach women's champion. In 1970, she reached the quarterfinals of both the USGA Junior Girls and Women's Amateur.

—ERNEST J. DE TOURNILLON
LONG BEACH, CALIF.
OCTOBER 1971

FANS WANT ARNIE IN OPEN

It's not often GOLF DIGEST readers react with unanimity, but they were vehement in their contempt for Contributing Editor Frank Hannigan's position against Arnold Palmer's Open exemption (June 1994). Robert Solorio of La Habra, Calif., expressed the majority opinion when he penned, "To the dungeon with the knave! Long reign King Arnold."

Terry Ketner, a longtime subscriber from Las Vegas, felt compelled to speak out: "Who cares that a young amateur doesn't play in the Open? Who cares that a touring pro might have missed out qualifying and doesn't play? They certainly have not come close to what Arnold Palmer has done for golf."

It's Arnie's humanness that many find so irresistible. Ed Love of Amherst, Mass., wrote, "Yes Arnie became rich and famous, but no other athlete has exposed his own frailties and aging skills as he has. Arnie is the man who took the 'elite' out of the country club atmosphere and proved golf was a sport for all of us. Golf became interesting to me when I watched this common man with a great heart give his all."

Wendell Choy, speaking for the regulars at his driving range in Honolulu added, "Seeing Arnie at Oakmont gives the TV audience warm smiles. That's good for golf."

Even readers from outside the United States expressed indignation. "Try to imagine what would happen in my country if Roberto De Vicenzo is invited to play the Argentinian Open and someone would object to that. Pretty foolish, isn't it?" wrote Alejandro Navas from Buenos Aires.

AUGUST 1994

CHALLENGE FROM BOLT

Who is this guy Doug Sanders who is trying to steal my "Best Dressed Golfer" title? He doesn't even keep his shoes well-creased. I'll challenge him to a style show on a runway anywhere in America.

—TOMMY BOLT, SARASOTA, FLA.
MARCH 1966

DIRTY OLD MAN?

I read the results of the TV poll with interest. I'm called a "dirty old man who looks like a heavy drinker who doesn't play golf."
I play golf.

—BOB DRUM, PINEHURST, N.C.
MARCH 1988

LAWRENCE WELK'S SWING

I couldn't resist ordering a copy of your new book, *The Square-to-Square Golf Swing*. I was wondering if you got the title from my *Square-to-Square Music*, or perhaps from the image with which I've been associated.

I'm rather surprised that you didn't send me "ah-one or ah-two" copies as a promotional gimmick! Of course, I'm only kidding. I'm more than happy to pay for anything with such an appropriate title.

—LAWRENCE WELK, SANTA MONICA, CALIF.
AUGUST 1970

JENKINS BIRDIES HIS BYPASS

Dear Folks,

Yeah, the record shows I played it one under. I was scheduled for a quadruple bypass, but after they took that heavy divot out of my chest and went in there to hit practice balls for a few hours, they decided I only needed a triple. I didn't even use my mulligan.

I must confess that the worst part was being dragged kicking and screaming to the electric chair, like James Cagney. Of course, I tried to act nonchalant for the family and hummed "Every Street is a Boulevard in Old New York" as they wheeled me away. That's how I wanted to be remembered if I never came out of the operating room to find out who won the TCU-Kansas game.

I can only report to all of you future bypass people that if a gutless coward like me can do it, *anybody* can.

Thanks for the notes, cards and prayers. See you soon among the living, where I will be asking the burning question, "New heart, new teeth—*now* what?"

—HIS OWNSELF, DAN JENKINS
PONTE VEDRA BEACH, FLA.
DECEMBER 1994

PACING THE GAME

Regarding the statement on Jack Nicklaus' being the first professional or amateur to use yardage books ("But Is It True?" March 1991), he may have been the first to use a yardage book, but I was the first to use yardages, by pacing off and making notes on each hole on the scorecard.

In 1946 I watched Ben Hogan playing alone in practice rounds on the winter tour. I observed him hitting two or three balls to the greens, and after hitting certain clubs, he looked to each side of the fairway, maybe memorizing a tree or bunker location to make sure of actual yardage. I decided if I ever were to become a tournament professional, I would need to know more accurate yardage. I practiced pacing in the snow in Iowa and measuring the steps for a one-yard pace. In 1946 I used my pacing of yardage in Iowa tournaments. In the 1955 U.S. Open at Olympic Club in San Francisco, I was the only one pacing yardage. A number of pros said, "That will do you no good." After I won, many pros started to pace.

—JACK FLECK, MAGAZINE, ARK.
MAY 1991

Bob Drum set the record straight on whether he was a "dirty old man who looks like a heavy drinker who doesn't play golf." (Photo: Jim Moriarty)

A rather cool introduction to Muirfield turned into a heartwarming experience. (Photo: Stephen Szurlej)

HONOURING MUIRFIELD

The excellent article written by Senior Editor Dwayne Netland, "Honourable Muirfield: A Lusty Challenge" (July 1980), returned fond memories of that great golf course and particularly an experience with the same Captain Paddy Hanmer, referred to in the story.

My wife and I were golf touring in Scotland with two other couples and were booked into the Greywalls Hotel a mere week before the British Open. Being so close to Muirfield we quite naturally wanted to tackle it. Hanmer's response to our query was at best condescending, and paraphrased amounted to, "Don't you know that the Open is next week, that the course has been closed for a month and that preparations are still in progress?" Further entreaty was futile.

As we turned to withdraw, I reached into my Navy background and asked the good captain if he might have served in Scapa Flow during WWII at the time I was there with an American squadron. The thumb came out of the dike! He most certainly was on the HMS Anson. More sea stories followed and then the question, what was it we sought? What a turn

of events—we six Americans had the Muirfield course to ourselves on June 28, 1972.

—Capt. Asbury Coward III
Whispering Pines, N.C.
September 1980

RESULTS OF HIS OWN DOING

That was an interesting article on Mark Brooks ("Another Texas Gusher" June 1993). He is an interesting young man with a golf game to match. I thought his comment about the USGA setup of Pebble Beach for the last round of the U.S. Open was off base. I do understand that someone who shoots 84 in the last round of the Open, especially when he starts the round with a solid chance to win, is not likely to think kindly about the conditions that he failed to handle. Nonetheless, his criticism reflects the continuing disposition of some tour players who fail to handle the requirements of winning an Open to impute both the USGA's judgment and motives.

If anyone is interested in assessing who or what was responsible for Brooks' awful final round, account should be taken of the following. Having parred No. 1 and birdied No. 2, Brooks hit his second shot about 25 feet past

the hole on No. 3. He then was tied for the lead. He hit a lousy first putt, leaving it about 2 1/2 feet short. His next putt, struck with a stroke with some yip in it, missed the hole by about three inches on the left and left him with a two-footer coming back, which he also missed on the left. He did not look like a player in control of his game. Pebble Beach was not a place where someone not in control of his game should be.

I believe that the results on that last day at least in part reflect how the game is developing for tour players. Virtually every week they are playing on some carefully manicured golf course with yielding greens, comfortingly and consistently paced. The result has been the development of a sort of computerized game played largely from point to point in the air. They were called upon to play a very different game in that last round in Pebble Beach, and they simply could not manage it.

—Frank D. (Sandy) Tatum Jr.
Former USGA President,
San Francisco, August 1993

VIN'S SWING OF THE DAY

Many thanks for the article, "Toski Weighs Anchors" (January 1988), and Bob Toski's analysis of that swing of mine. I have 50 others that wait to be used like brooms in a closet. One correction: I made both of my aces at Bel-Air Country Club, including the one described in the article when I was waved to play through by the pros.

Now if you'll excuse me, I'll go back to practicing and burning incense at the altar of my patron saint, Bob Charles—like me, a left-hander.

—Vin Scully, Pacific Palisades, Calif.
March 1988

REMEMBERING BOB AND BING

Bob Hope's reminiscent article, "Bing and Me" (February 1985), brought back fond memories. Sometime in the 1940s I was lucky enough to caddie in Bob's and Bing's foursome in a hospital charity tournament.

The humor started on the first tee when Hope, arriving late, placed his clubs at Bing's feet with the words, "Take this bag, son!"

On the first green, Bing was to putt first and he proceeded to take an eternity lining up his putt. After taking a final look, he asked me if the greens had been cut that day. I nodded affirmatively. Not to be outclassed, Bob then went through identical maneuvers and finally, kneeling for a final look, stared toward me and asked, "What time?"

—Cliff Miller, Bayport, N.Y.
April 1985

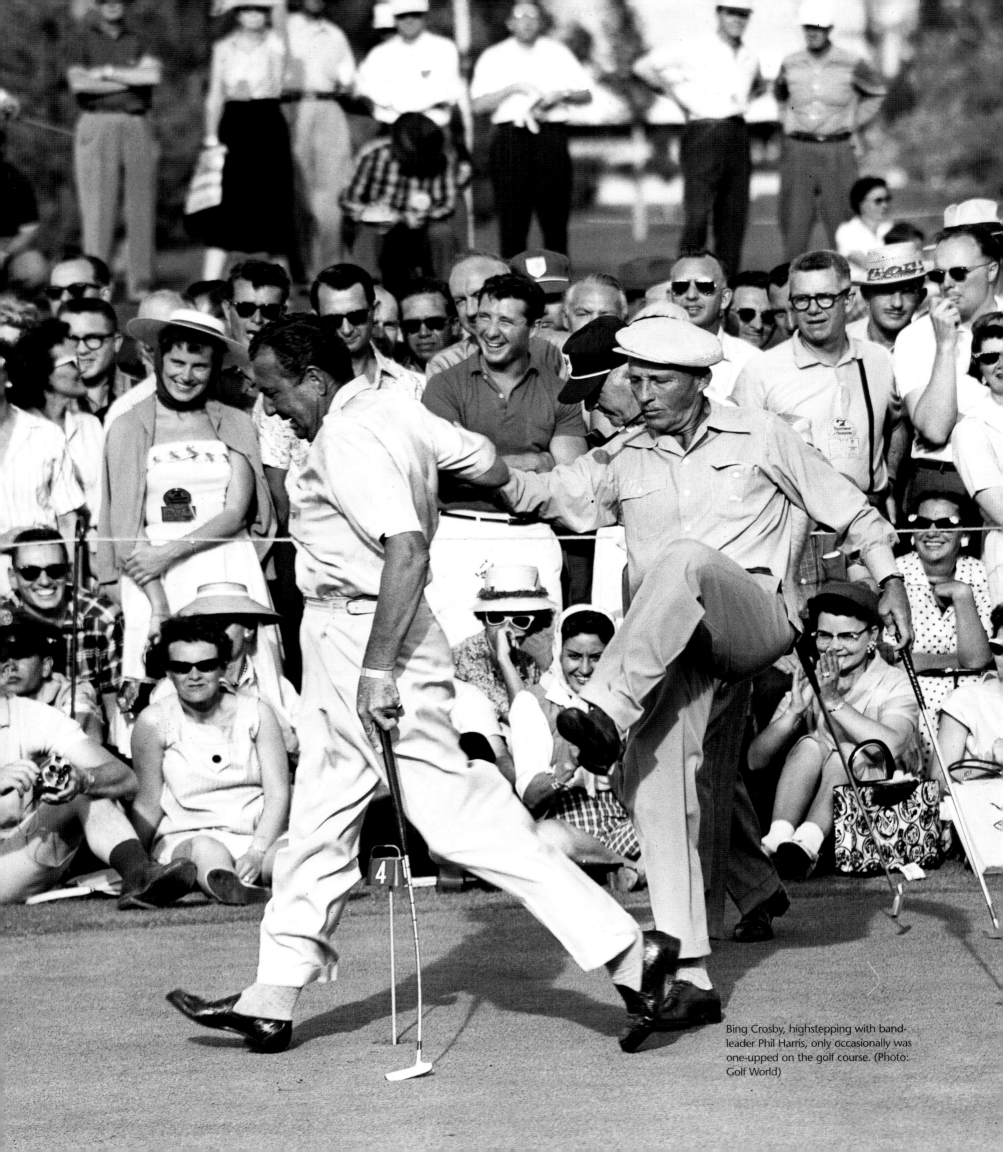

Bing Crosby, highstepping with band-leader Phil Harris, only occasionally was one-upped on the golf course. (Photo: Golf World)

We Found Him!

Despite stiff competition, Angelo Spagnolo is the worst of America's Worst Avid Golfers

by Peter Andrews

Arms and the man I sing, who, forced by fate,

To play golf all day and come home late.

Sliced and hooked along the Atlantic shore,

Long labors both by trap and green he bore.

To win the greenish coat, a sixty-six he made

On just one hole; and his caddie was sore afraid.

—(WITH PROFOUND APOLOGIES TO PUBLIUS VERGILIUS MARO, WHO NEVER SAW ANYTHING LIKE IT IN HIS LIFE.)

Well, that was some kind of shootout deserving of a bit of epic verse. And if Virgil is spinning softly in his grave, you can imagine what the troubled spirit of Harry Vardon is doing along about now. GOLF DIGEST's search for America's Worst Avid Golfer finally came to an end on the treacherous confines of the Tournament Players Club in Ponte Vedra Beach, Fla., and when the final stroke was tallied the name of Angelo Spagnolo led all the rest. In a tight match that could have gone a number of ways right up until the 17th hole, Angelo pulled himself together and squeaked past his nearest opponent by 49 shots. It was the kind of garrison finish of which sports legends are made.

It wasn't easy. The extent of Angelo's prowess was tested to the full by three fine challengers. Out of some 627 nominations the final four shook down to Jack Pulford, a restaurant owner from Moline, Ill.; Joel Mosser, a stock broker from Aurora, Colo.; Kelly Ireland, an attorney from Tyler, Tex., and Angelo, a grocery store manager from Fayette City, Pa. Four men from different parts of the country bound by a sense of sportsmanship and an abiding love for the game of golf matched only by their inability to play it. Together, they compiled in one afternoon a set of statistics that are likely to stand for as long as people keep score:

■ They had a combined score of 836.

■ They made 17 whiffs, put 102 balls in the water and were assessed 124 penalty strokes.

■ They hit no greens in regulation scoring no pars, one bogey, eight double-bogeys and 63 "others."

■ Angelo took a 66 on the par-3 17th water hole. After that, he admitted, "The wheels came off a little" and he took a 22 on the 18th for a grand total of 257.

■ Angelo's final score equaled the tour-record-low 72-hole score of 257 set by Mike Souchak in 1955.

■ If Angelo had played in that tournament, he would have missed the second-day cut by the 14th hole of the first day, when he still had 111 shots more to play.

All in all, it was quite a day.

THE PRACTICE ROUND

What had started out as a lark six months before when their friends and partners had first nominated them as possible Worst Avid Golfers (WAGs), turned serious on the afternoon of June 18. To simulate actual tournament playing conditions, GOLF DIGEST had arranged for the contestants to play a practice round; following that, they underwent the ritual flogging known as the pretournament press conference.

Joel flopped in a chair and began by saying, "I have just had a very difficult day. I shot 146 plus two Xs, and I only have one golf ball left."

Kelly also seemed stunned by the difficulty of TPC. "I've never seen anything so hard in my life," he said. "On the 11th [529-yard par 5] I used every club in my bag and was hitting 24 before I got on the fairway."

All four were convinced they would shoot better tomorrow—in fact, they all shot worse—and all were determined to come in with the lowest score. "If I wanted to become notorious," said Jack Pulford, "I'd sneak past the guards at the White House. I'm here to

After Spagnolo's 66 on the 17th, the path to the green became known as "Angelo's Alley."
(Photo: Jim Moriarty)

Tough day: Kelly Ireland, Jack Pulford and Joel Mosser (left to right), along with Angelo Spagnolo, accounted for a combined 18-hole score of 836, 17 of which were whiffs. (Photos: Jim Moriarty)

be the best . . . [pause] . . . of the worst." They all agreed that something around 140 should be good enough to win the next day and the conference broke up.

Afterward, I chatted with Joel for a while. He is a quiet man, who loves golf the way a wino loves muscatel. He knows it's nothing but trouble for him, but he can't get enough of it.

"It isn't always a picnic to play as badly as I do," he said. "But it's the guys I play with who make it fun. All of my regular foursome from Colorado have come down here just to cheer me on. Can you imagine that? We have a terrific time. We go away in the winter to some place warm and then we go to the prettiest part of town, which is always the golf course, and we play. Why shouldn't I love the game?"

Joel had to stick around for a television interview with a local station in Colorado. While he was nervously waiting for the camera to pan in on him, one of his regular foursome slips behind and starts to depants him. The tournament pressure is building.

That evening, our GOLF DIGEST instructional braintrust tried to analyze the contenders' swings:

■ Angelo gives a new dimension to the word "deliberate." He settles slowly, slowly down in his stance like a nesting chicken and just as the egg is about to drop, he lashes quickly at the ball, sending his woods arching straight into the air while his irons rarely get more than shoulder high. As one pro I spoke to said, "His grip is too strong, his stance is too closed and his visor is too low."

■ Kelly, a small man who plays in a cloth cap, looks like Spanky McFarland in an old Our Gang comedy. He does not have a bad swing, but he rushes it terribly, as if he were stealing apples from Farmer Brown's orchard and wants to get out of there before he gets caught.

■ Joel, on the other hand, takes his time. He stares at the ball as if it were the last one in Christendom, and he seems loath to put it in the air lest it disappear, taking the entire game of golf away with it.

■ Jack's swing, in some ways, is the most puzzling of the four. It looks terrific. In fact, Jack looks terrific. Dressed in the orange and blue of the Fighting Illini with a golf bag to match, Jack looks every inch the accomplished golfer. His waggle and practice swings are

excellent. But just before the moment of impact, it is as if inside his body a spare needle has been inadvertently left behind by an indifferent acupuncturist. Swing turns to spasm and the ball flies off at an oblique angle.

In case you might think that any of the players were sandbagging it and wanted to come in last, I can assure you they did not. The proof was in the most incontrovertible form imaginable—cash. Each contestant arrived with an entourage, and there was considerable betting between them on low score. The rivalry between Colorado and Texas was particularly keen. There was, as we used to say in gaming circles, "serious money" on who would make the lowest score—$2,500 that I knew about.

It is unlikely that anyone slept late the next morning. As the contestants met for breakfast, the air was still and quiet, broken only by the sound of equipment out on the course traversing the greens, mowing, mowing, mowing.

THE FINAL MATCH

The tournament got under way shortly before noon in front of a good-sized crowd, including 14 television camera crews. Each contestant had his vocal cheering section. Angelo's group wore T-shirts proclaiming "Angelo's Army," and Kelly was well represented by Texas' "We Beat Kelly Ireland Fan Club." Since there hardly is anyone in Tyler who hasn't, the membership roll of the club is large. Joel was supported by the members of his foursome, and Jack arrived on the tee with a group of his friends, including his golf professional from Moline, his mother and his ex-wife, Karen, who told me, "I've come here to watch Jack make a fool of himself, and I know he won't let me down."

PGA Tour Commissioner Deane Beman had seen to it that the TPC was arranged in its most menacing posture. The tees were as far back as the local alligators who live on the course would permit, and the pin placements were Sunday difficult. The players were split into two pairs with Joel and Angelo leading off while Kelly and Jack trailed behind. Each pairing had an official scorekeeper and two representatives from the PGA Tour to call the rules. Beman made a graceful speech and bid the games begin.

Angelo was first up and set the tone for the long day's work ahead. He settled in over the ball and let fly with a long, high drive—a career shot—straight into the water hazard. We could not know it at the time, but that was the high-water mark of excellence for the first hole. Joel's tee shot had good line but not quite the distance he had hoped for. He came to rest in the sawgrass that frames the tee area. Two shots later, he had made it perhaps 40 yards into the sand and was still 130 yards from the fairway with a smallish finger lake to the right. As Joel lined up his fourth swing, one of his Colorado foursome sidled up to me and whispered, "Water shot coming up. I've seen him hit this shot a thousand times."

He proved to be a good forecaster as Joel pumped

his ball into the lake. The Texas crew was back on the first tee watching all this, and when an envoy from Colorado came back to see if they would be willing to talk terms about the side bet, they just laughed.

As Angelo and Joel began to rumble down the first fairway, Jack and Kelly took their turns. Jack showed us the first of his infinite variety of shanks and winged one directly into the woods to the right. Kelly took careful aim and bounced a drive into the grass bleachers to the left of the first tee. He was given a free drop and hit into a ground-under-repair area. He got another drop and hit into another ground-under-repair area and got still another drop. In what was to be one of the many minor records that day, Kelly had taken three shots, had three free drops and was still just shy of the ladies' tee. A man from Colorado raced back to the stands and told the Texans they could go to hell.

The game would take many turns before the

afternoon was out, but that established the pace for most of the day. Angelo was up and down finding water like a dowser while Joel and Kelly bootlaced left and right and Jack dashed through the woods as if in perpetual search for a shaded Port-o-john.

Jack's group, except for Karen, who seemed to be enjoying herself hugely, was disconsolate. Jack's mother, a sweet, white-haired lady, rooted Jack on with quiet urgency. "Be careful, Jack," she whispered. "Oh, don't lift your head, Jack . . . oh, s---, Jack."

By the time we got to the turn, two races had developed—one for first place and one for last. Joel had fired a nifty 75 and was leading Kelly by 14 shots. At the other end of the scale, Jack was holding on to last place with a 104, but Angelo was slowly squandering shots.

It's amazing how easily a person can adjust to the role of celebrity these days. As the players came off the

Below: *There are lessons to learn from "the worst of the worst." (Photos: Jim Moriarty)*

Do not try this at home

Angelo Spagnolo embodies the problems of many amateur golfers. And those problems all emanate from his position in **Frame 1**: Angelo's grip is disastrously strong. Both hands are much too far to his right, his right hand curled under the shaft, his left pulled over on top of it.

Like many golfers with strong grips, Angelo seeks to compensate by playing the ball forward and pushing his hands even farther forward, almost outside his left leg, as a hedge against a duck hook. His head, angled to the left, keeps him from swinging his arms freely around his body.

Frame 2: Angelo's body is static as he starts the club back with his hands. This often happens when the address position is too tense, i.e., lacking a waggle or other preswing movement to relieve tension, a problem shared by all four WAG finalists.

Frame 3: Once Angelo does put his body in motion, his right leg collapses and his right knee bows outward, giving

him nothing to turn against on the backswing or drive off of during the forward swing.

Frame 4: Here is the culmination of all the Frame 1 errors. The clubface is pointing skyward, meaning it is dead shut, at the top, and Angelo's head has moved seven or eight inches rearward. This excessive lateral movement makes it a game of chance for him to return the clubhead to the ball squarely and on the desired path.

Frames 5 and 6: Of the four finalists, Angelo looks the best at the finish of the swing. But to prevent a duck hook, he must "block" the shot with his hands. Depending on the effectiveness of his "block," he will hit the ball varying degrees to the right. When his hands do release and he fails to block the shot, he smother-hooks the ball. In short, Angelo is paying for his faulty grip and his poor ball, hand and head position at address with highly unpredictable shot results.

—ANDY NUSBAUM, DIRECTOR, GOLF DIGEST SCHOOLS

front nine, Joel was grabbed by a television crew for a quick interview. Did he think his 14-shot lead could hold up? What was his strategy for the back nine? Joel smiled diffidently and admitted that, "the ball has been bouncing my way so far." He allowed how Kelly was a strong player and couldn't be counted out. "I'll just have to keep up the pressure."

Joel paused for a moment to sign a few autographs before heading for the 10th tee. Fuzzy Zoeller, who knows a thing or two about being charming, could not have been more gracious.

Joel refused to wilt on the back nine. He threw out a drumfire of 8s and 9s and 10s and by the 15th still held a comfortable eight-shot lead. Then it happened.

THE TURNING POINTS

The 15th is a sleepy 426-yard par 4, but it requires a needle-sharp carry over 150 yards of sand and water to get to the fairway guarded by trees on the left. Joel put his first in the water, then his second, then his third. You know how it is when you've had a terrific front nine and you begin to feel the ground slipping out from under you on the back? It tightens the nerves. Hitting seven, Joel put a ball into the muddy bank. He hit again but the ball stayed roughly where it was. Then he took a penalty. From there on the libretto gets a little murky, but by the time Joel was hitting 10 he was essentially back at the tee. He finally got his ball on dry grass in 16 and wound up with a 25.

"You should have hit into the trees and bounced it along," hissed one of his foursome.

"I was *trying* to hit it into the trees," Joel hissed back.

The golfer's tragedy. You rely on a duck-hook all day and then just when you need one the most what you get is a case of the chronic straights. It can happen to anyone.

Coming up behind Joel, Kelly found himself getting the same advice to cut his way through the arboretum. But the battle of San Jacinto was not won by Texans who skulked into the woods, and Kelly wouldn't have it. He went for it and hit a peach, which fell just a shade short in the water. Of course, San Jacinto wasn't won by men who were entirely stupid, either. Kelly then hit into the forest and emerged with a 12 for the hole. A 13-stroke swing! Kelly had the lead and the affair was in hand—if he could only negotiate the 132-yard par-3 17th.

As it turned out, Kelly would have to wait at the 17th tee for almost an hour while Angelo was caught up in his own passion play. All told, there were three whiffs recorded and 27 balls in the water. Unfortunately, a hip-high wedge shot, which is the basic building block of Angelo's short game, is of but limited use in trying to both carry water and stick on a small green. Angelo actually put seven shots on the lawn, but they all skipped over.

It is part of the human condition to live in hope, but as regular golf balls had already given way to the striped range variety, even the fiercest aspiration had to yield to prudence. Sorrowfully, he dropped a ball on the cartpath and began to putt down the road, over the bridge and finally onto the green—where once on the dance floor he three-putted for a 66. But let me tell you something about Angelo Spagnolo. In enduring perhaps 40 minutes of public humiliation, he did not wince or cry aloud. At no time did a single whispered blasphemy escape his lips. He took a 66 without a curse. Angelo Spagnolo has either the makings of a Christian saint or the most limited vocabulary of any man who has ever played golf.

If there is any consolation to scoring 63 over par on a single golf hole, it was supplied by Commissioner Beman. Henceforth, Beman declared, the cartpath of the 17th hole at TPC will be known as "Angelo's Alley."

Angelo solidified his hold on last place with a neat 22 on the 18th. Joel carded a 10 and could do nothing except sit in the clubhouse and hold his breath and hope that Kelly could not manage the last two holes in 37 or less.

Kelly steeled himself for the challenge and with only seven balls in the water and a bounce whiff, he two-putted his way to an 18 on the 17th. Teeing off on the final hole he said, "I have my strategy. Stay out of the water and the sand." Good thinking, and it paid off. Kelly, the only of the four to shoot the back in under 100, got to the 18th green in five and then drained a glorious 24-foot putt for a 6 and victory as "best of the worst."

There was the inevitable post-tournament press conference and Angelo, who had come so far to take the title of America's Worst Avid Golfer, was asked what he was going to do next.

He thought for a moment and then smiled broadly. "Take lessons."

THE EPILOGUE

But wait. Like it says in the television commercial, there's more. Since the tournament, Angelo has become an authentic media figure. He has given out press interviews without number and appeared on television more frequently than Claus von Bulow. He is thinking about writing a golf book. And he has secured the services of an attorney to help him negotiate a possible spot for a Miller Lite beer commercial where his chief function would be to make Rodney Dangerfield look good in plus-fours. Then there are the personal appearances to make.

And now there is talk of an international match to determine the World's Worst Avid Golfer. Again the competition is likely to be swift. So, stay as you are, Angelo. Don't take any lessons. Your country needs you.

Editor's note: Almost from the day of the tournament, the "Worst Avids" have held reunion tournaments, always to raise money for charity. Bad golfers from all over the country and the world have participated, raising more than $1 million for worthy causes. Way to go, guys!

> "The ball has been bouncing my way so far," said Joel Mosser. Prematurely, as it turned out.

Pete Dye's water-lined 16th and 17th holes
at the TPC have proved the undoing of
tour professionals and duffers alike. But
its ultimate victim was Spagnolo.
(Photo: Chris John/PDI)

"It was not the way the hole
was designed to be played."

—WORST AVID GOLFER ANGELO SPAGNOLO, ON WHY HE
RESISTED PUTTING UP THE PATH TO THE 17TH AFTER
DUMPING 27 BALLS IN THE WATER.

December 1991

Fields of Dreams

The Armchair Architect winners: When we build them, they will come

by Ron Whitten

GOLF DIGEST has held two Armchair Architect contests attracting almost 30,000 entries. The 1991 contest offered entrants a choice of a par-3, par-4 or par-5 design.

Every envelope contained a dream, every box a chance at immortality. More than 7,200 entries were mailed in to GOLF DIGEST's latest Armchair Architect Contest, containing everything from a quick sketch on a napkin to detailed three-dimensional models.

The challenge was to design the best possible hole on any of three actual topographic maps. The judging was handled by real golf course designers. The reward was the ultimate stuff of armchair architect dreams—dirt, grass and irrigation pipe. Actual, full-size golf holes will be constructed from the winning entries.

The Armchair Architect Contest was irresistible to any golfer who'd ever doodled on a scratch pad or envisioned a golf hole in the rumpled folds of a sweater. "I don't enter many contests, but I couldn't let this one go," wrote Vincent Sarno of Lima, Ohio. "I mean, where else can I dictate what the prize will be?"

The winning dream designs are now in hand, and the victorious par-3 design in Michigan has already been built and grassed. The construction of the other two holes has been delayed by environmental issues.

Our latest Armchair Architect Contest reminded us that golf architecture is a global passion. It prompted designs from a doctor in Zimbabwe, a parts manager in the Netherlands, a student in India and a draftsman in Australia.

We heard from an interpreter in the U.S. Embassy in Moscow and a sound-control engineer from Hamburg, Germany. There were politicians, pastors, nuclear-plant bosses, lawyers and prison guards. We heard from building architects in Scotland, Italy and Pakistan. We even got an entry from an insurance executive in North Pole, Alaska.

A recurring theme was the Persian Gulf War, which erupted just about the time we announced our contest last February. Lieut. Raymond F. Topp, a U.S. Army company executive officer, marveled at the proposed sites and wrote, "How I wish I had some water to contend with during Operation Desert Storm." Jay Abbott, of Covington, Va., scattered "Gulf War bomb-crater bunkers" between the tee and green on his par 3. Bryan Underwood, of Golden, Colo., dubbed the prominent hill on the par-3 site, "Saddam's Nose." And Robert M. Logan of Roseville, Mich., offered "The Mother of All Par 5s," a 664-yarder.

But the ultimate reality was that only three contestants could win this edition of GOLF DIGEST's Armchair Architect Contest. For the thousands of others, dreams remain dreams. At least until our next contest.

The par 3: A mirror image

If the course grows in as expected, some time early next summer Joe Kropiewnicki, 22, will become the first armchair architect to ever extract a divot from his own fantasy. For a devoted 10-handicap public-links player, it seems fitting that Kropiewnicki's design will become part of a public facility.

His par 3 was chosen by Michigan golf architect Jerry Matthews to serve as the second hole on his new Greystone Golf Club in the Detroit suburb of Romeo, Mich. It will play from a high spoil mound downhill to a green set in the basin of an old gravel pit, flanked by wetlands and an elaborate bunker complex.

Golf design, like politics, is the art of compromise. What began as a par-3 site with almost unlimited potential was reduced to a narrow north-and-south corridor by the demands of an essential housing development on the property, but Matthews took the new site restraints in stride.

Course construction at Greystone began even before all the envelopes had been opened, and it moved so rapidly that Matthews' client clamored daily for the winning entry to finish the layout. "I'm looking for someone who uses the land to the utmost and then does something creative with it," Matthews announced as he sifted through entries.

"Everything he's done I like," he said as he examined the entry from Harrisburg, Pa. Kropiewnicki scattered several tee boxes down the side of the huge "superdune," the earthen mound that remained following the gravel excavation. He also liked Kropiewnicki's use of existing wetlands as a lateral hazard; and his proposed green, while heavily bunkered, was accessible and had both easy and hazardous pin placements.

"It's accented with a huge bunker, not something that's my style, but it's certainly attention-grabbing without adding a great deal of additional expense," Matthews said.

The design actually had to be flip-flopped and its mirror image constructed to protect players from errant balls off an adjacent hole already built.

For years Kropiewnicki's hobby has been drawing golf developments, entire golf communities with housing lots and access roads as well as fairways and greens. While the Penn State graduate student is studying hospitality management, Kropiewnicki now says he'd really like to pursue a career in golf course architecture.

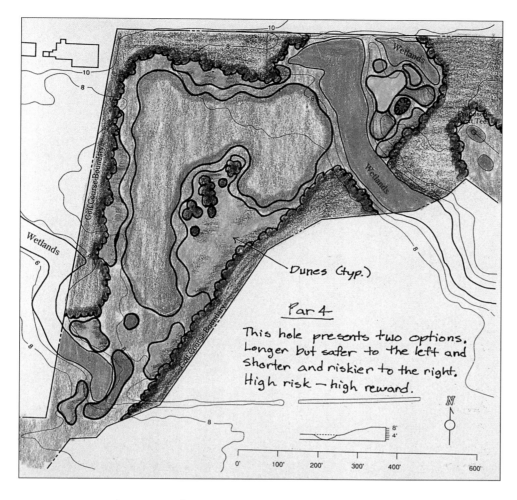

Par 4: Dean Bennett's design, one of several double fairways submitted, won over judge Tom Clark with its "risk-and-reward philosophy." It is to be part of a Virginia course still held up in 1999 by environmental and zoning concerns.

The par 4: Alternative routes

Maryland's Tom Clark, president of the American Society of Golf Course Architects, selected a double-fairway par 4 by 25-year-old Dean Bennett, of Golden, Colo., to appear as part of the 36-hole Accawmacke Plantation Golf Club on the shores of the Chesapeake Bay near Cape Charles, Va. Bennett's dogleg right will taunt us with a treacherous shortcut over dunes and a longer safe route to the left around a cluster of trees. Construction could begin next summer or fall, depending upon some zoning questions.

Hearings to obtain proper zoning have delayed construction, much to the dismay of Clark, at age 43 the youngest of our three architect/judges. Clark was not eager to commit to a design that would require additional environmental studies and permits. His ideal was an outstanding hole that didn't touch the existing wetlands. As much as he liked many designs that converted the wetlands into a pond, stretched it along one side of the fairway or wrapped it around a green, he was fearful that such a hole might involve another year of red tape or, worse yet, never get built at all.

Clark was intrigued with the many double fairways offered for his site, perhaps the most out-of-the-ordinary designs he received. "The trouble with alternate fairways," Clark cautioned, "is that unless there's a good reason for some people to use each of the fairways, you end up with one fairway never in play."

The double-fairway design Clark kept coming back to was Dean Bennett's. Others were more graphic or artistic, but Bennett's contained the features Clark thought essential.

"I like his risk-and-reward philosophy," Clark said during the judging. "If you hit it over a complex of sand dunes, you have a flip shot to the green. If you hit it out to the left, you have a longer shot to the green.

"I also like the fact that he gives average players who can't carry the wetlands in two a place to lay up. On many designs, the longer route seems to encounter more of the hazards. Length is problem enough for the average player."

Winner Bennett was especially pleased that Clark took notice of his greenside areas. He envisions them as grassy hollows, chipping areas mown at fairway height, dropping away from the green collar so that errant balls will roll farther away but not into serious trouble.

It didn't bother Clark that his pick looked like a right-angle dogleg, because it won't really play like one. And the cluster of trees left growing out of the dunes complex, far from interfering with play, set up strategic situations from the various tees.

Word of his winning entry gave Bennett, an assistant pro at Lakewood Country Club near Denver, special satisfaction. He keeps a sketchbook with him, and in his spare time he's forever doodling redesigns of the holes at Lakewood. "Now maybe they'll take a look at them," he said of his members.

The par 5: The beach hole

Golf architect Arthur Hills, of Toledo, Ohio, supplied the par-5 location, a sandy stretch along the Intracoastal Waterway at the proposed Bear Branch Resort in Myrtle Beach, S.C. To fill it, Hills picked a par 5 designed by John Percival Jr., a 32-year teaching professional at an indoor practice facility in Warren, Mich. The Percival par 5 will play from a high tee toward the waterway, then turn right and flow along its banks. A serpentine bunker will hug the left side and wrap around the front of the green. Bulldozers will be on the site as soon as environmental impact studies are completed.

Hills brought word of new site restraints at his course when he appeared for the judging. Red-cockaded woodpeckers, an endangered species, inhabit portions of the Bear Branch site in Myrtle Beach, he told us. No golf holes can be built in those areas. So the wide rectangle between the Intracoastal Waterway and a pine bluff he had set aside for our par 5 must now accommodate two or three golf holes. That effectively dashed the chances of many entries with marvelous double-fairway par-5 holes.

There was more. The developer decided to convert a pond at one end into a yacht basin with direct access to the adjacent Intracoastal Waterway. This meant rejection of many other fine designs. Hills was

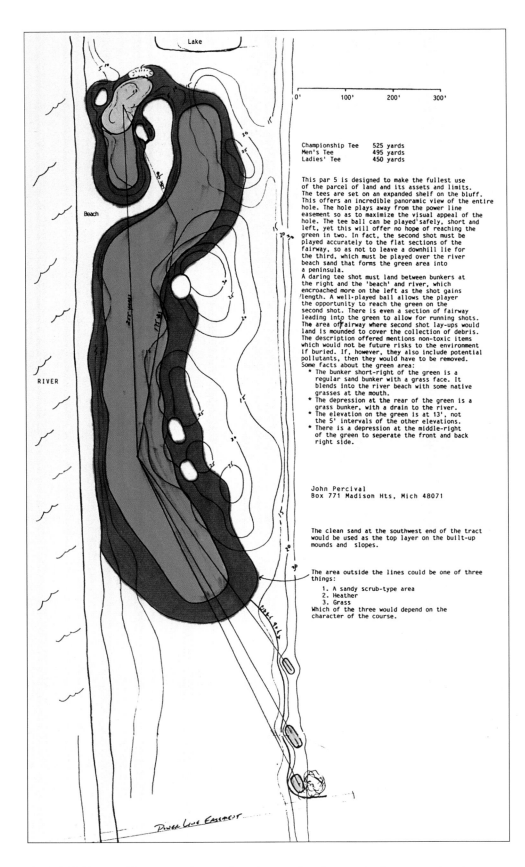

Lake

Beach

RIVER

0'	100'	200'	300'

Championship Tee   525 yards
Men's Tee   495 yards
Ladies' Tee   450 yards

This par 5 is designed to make the fullest use of the parcel of land and its assets and limits. The tees are set on an expanded shelf on the bluff. This offers an incredible panoramic view of the entire hole. The hole plays away from the power line easement so as to maximize the visual appeal of the hole. The tee ball can be played safely, short and left, yet this will offer no hope of reaching the green in two. In fact, the second shot must be played accurately to the flat sections of the fairway, so as not to leave a downhill lie for the third, which must be played over the river beach sand that forms the green area into a peninsula.
A daring tee shot must land between bunkers at the right and the 'beach' and river, which encroached more on the left as the shot gains length. A well-played ball allows the player the opportunity to reach the green on the second shot. There is even a section of fairway leading into the green to allow for running shots. The area off fairway where second shot lay-ups would land is mounded to cover the collection of debris. The description offered mentions non-toxic items which would not be future risks to the environment if buried. If, however, they also include potential pollutants, then they would have to be removed.
Some facts about the green area:
* The bunker short-right of the green is a regular sand bunker with a grass face. It blends into the river beach with some native grasses at the mouth.
* The depression at the rear of the green is a grass bunker, with a drain to the river.
* The elevation on the green is at 13', not the 5' intervals of the other elevations.
* There is a depression at the middle-right of the green to seperate the front and back right side.

John Percival
Box 771 Madison Hts, Mich 48071

The clean sand at the southwest end of the tract would be used as the top layer on the built-up mounds and slopes.

The area outside the lines could be one of three things:
1. A sandy scrub-type area
2. Heather
3. Grass
Which of the three would depend on the character of the course.

POWER LINE EASEMENT

Par 5: A Michigan teaching pro, John Percival Jr., designed the winning par 5 for a Myrtle Beach course. Percival's use of sand to create a "beach" along the Intercoastal won over judge Arthur Hills.

apologetic over the changes in the game plan, but those are precisely the sorts of things that force any designer back to the drawing board.

To Hills, the Intracoastal Waterway is the most impressive aspect of this particular site, and any contender had to incorporate it in some manner. That was no easy task, since there would be very little chance of altering the straight bank of the waterway. When he sorted through entries, Hills especially liked those holes that cleverly worked a straight shot of river frontage into play on the hole.

It finally came down to four entries. Percival's design had immediately caught Hills' eye. He liked the way in which a long strip bunker, "the beach" as it came to be known, tied the straight run of the waterway into the wavy fairway. Hills gave Percival points for using "a transitional element that is native to the site."

Percival's key was to incorporate a beach all along the fairway and wrap it strategically around the green.

Golf design has always been Percival's first love. As a teenager, he spent 2,500 hours building a painstaking scale model of an imaginary golf course. Golf course architects, it appears, do not dream in miniature.

NOW, ON TO THE REWARDS FOR OTHER DREAMERS.

Best animal attraction—Military policeman Robert Wagers of Leesburg, Va., shaped his par-3 green to look like a giant frog. Patrik Maran, a Swedish landscaping student, designed a par 3 with long, tentacled bunkers he called "The Octopus."

There were other aquatic escapades. Harry Dashiell, a Salt Lake City geologist, designed his par 4 with both fairway and mounds shaped like leaping dolphins. John C. Miller of Kenmore, N.Y., created a "jellyfish bunker" on his par 4.

But nothing tops the special "chicken tee markers" Michael Kennedy, of Eugene, Ore., created for players too hesitant to try his all-water-carry tee shot.

The Abe Lincoln Award—Shared by Steve Carlton of Brewster, N.Y., who sketched his entry on the back of his envelope, and Anthony Mull, a Muncie, Ind., graduate architect who sent in his entry penned on a paper napkin.

Model entries—Perhaps the most impressive aspect of the contest was the number of excellent scale models mailed in by contestants. Among the most striking ones were two white plaster sculptures by David Gastrau, of Los Angeles, built with the geometric precision of a PacMan board.

The three models of Carl Longdo, a Mount Tabor, N.J., promotion manager, were so realistic in their detail that overhead photographs of them looked eerily like aerial photos of the actual sites.

But no modeler worked harder this year than Dan Nalepa of Oak Ridge, Ill. His model par 3 featured an electric recycling waterfall sprung from atop the superdune poured down around the greens.

Two guys who should be teamed up—What are the chances Mark Mendonca, of Ipswich, Mass., designed his par-4 green in the shape of a human footprint, with the green being the pad of the foot and five bunkers being the toes. Meanwhile, John Brannigan, a retired toolmaker from La Grange, Ill., designed his par 4 with the fairway in the shape of the sole of a shoe.

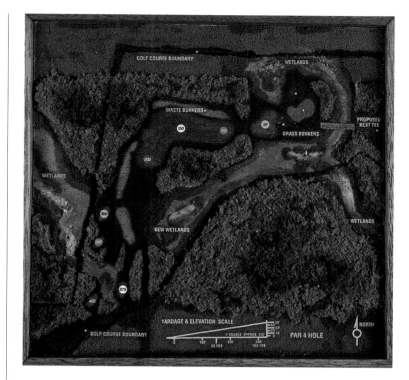

Among 7,200 entries in 1991 were holes shaped like a dolphin, a frog and an octopus. There were jellyfish bunkers and chicken tee markers. There were sketches on napkins, incredibly detailed overhead maps (top left), a working waterfall model (top right) and a dazzling 3-minute video with soundtrack (bottom).

Of the 22,000 entries in the 1991 contest, one winning design, a par 3, was built in Michigan. Two other designs were incorporated into Myrtle Beach, S.C., and Cape Charles, Va., course plans, but those courses have been delayed by environmental and zoning issues, respectively, to this day.

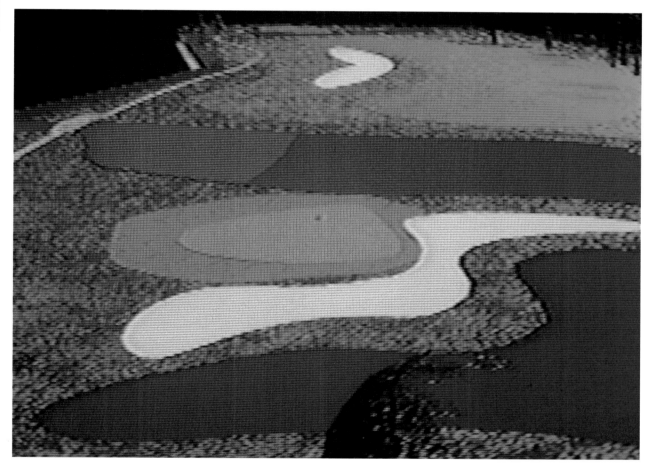

Speaking of big—Proof they do things big down in Texas: Larry E. Crane of Houston sent in a par-5 entry that, when unrolled, measured a full six feet long.

No. 1 with a bullet—Of the dozen videotape entries, by far the most entertaining was by Jonathan Rochelle, a systems analyst from Brooklyn, N.Y., whose three-minute, dazzling state-of-the-art computer graphics featured simulated helicopter fly-overs of his hole and a theme song called "Revenge." Forget golf design, Jonathan, your future is in music videos.

As to the future of the winning golf holes, we will be keeping tabs on their progress. When the grass is full and the greens are ready, the victorious new architects will be paraded before our cameras for ceremonial first divots.

A game for everyone. A young Irish foursome enjoys a round of pitch and putt. Real golf was never this much fun. (Photo: Jim Moriarty)

Crusades

An examination
of GOLF DIGEST's efforts
to keep the game growing

PASSIONS & CRUSADES

by Robert Carney,

Executive Editor, Special Projects

You may have heard the one about the club member who, intent on giving his favorite caddie a little added income, invites him home to paint the back porch. The caddie reports back in about an hour. "All finished?" asks the benevolent member. "Yes, sir," replies the caddie, "and by the way, it wasn't a porch, it was a BMW."

Folks, you can't tell a story like that about a golf cart, which is one of the reasons why our editors love caddies and only tolerate carts. Dave Anderson, The New York Times columnist and GOLF DIGEST contributing editor, put it another way: "You don't interview a golf ball." People, not equipment (no matter how advanced), make golf what it is. They create golf's laughs, lore and sometimes even literature.

And that's why every so often GOLF DIGEST gets on its high horse and undertakes what we unassumingly call a crusade.

Crusades are our campaigns. If most of the time we're helping readers improve their games, occasionally we feel obligated to try to improve the game. Crusades help us keep golf the way it ought to be, in our humble opinion. And how is that?

Well, frankly we like our golf on foot, over natural-looking courses, played crisply and within the rules, give or take a mulligan off the first tee only. We like presidents who play, pros who don't pout, and munies that let kids take a swing. We hate slow play, people who don't replace divots, stuffy clubs and anyone who forces us to ride. We despise tricked-up courses, multiple practice swings, haughty single-digit handicappers and hackers who plumb bob. We're already weary of cell phones and overwatered courses named Gleneagles something.

And so, over the years, our crusades were born:

- *Stop Slow Play!*
- *Play the Ball Down!*
- *Support Junior Golf!*
- *Take a Caddie!*
- *Bring Back Walking!*

Our first campaign involved a button we sent to President Dwight D. Eisenhower that read, "Don't Ask What I

Shot." Ike, a bit of a hacker, wore it proudly and so did 20,000 golfers who asked us for a copy.

That button taught us a lesson about crusades. Before giving the button to Ike, Press Secretary Jim Hagerty removed the words "Read GOLF DIGEST" from it. We learned that you're best at promoting the game when you're not also trying (too hard) to promote yourself.

Ike's button encompassed the one true thing in all of our crusades: Make golf a game for everyone. No matter what you shoot, no matter where you play, whether you walk or ride, this game's for you. Male or female, white or black, young or old, if you love the game we have room for you.

When we attacked slow play (endlessly and in vain, it seems) it was to keep the game growing. Why? Because the most common excuse offered by those who quit the game is, "It takes too long." (That recalls Henry Longhurst's description of the typical American four-ball round, in which all players hole out on every hole, as "an infinitely dreary business taking a minimum of four hours and being one of the greatest wearinesses of the flesh ever voluntarily imposed upon man in the name of recreation.")

When we pushed, again and again, for the right to walk, it was so the traditionalists and the fitness-minded would continue to play. And what better way to bring people into the game and preserve golf's traditions than through caddie programs and junior clinics? Our most recent campaign, promoting pitch-and-putt courses, was one more way of saying: C'mon in, you've got the time and we've got a course that fits your game.

In sum, if you're willing to show respect for the game's traditions and consideration for your fellow players, GOLF DIGEST wants you in the game. These mostly recent stories embody that 50-year-old theme: J. L. Briggs' declaration of walking independence and David Bamberger's heartfelt piece on caddies. The best of our efforts, perhaps, was the 1989 Marcia Chambers two-part investigation of discriminatory private club practices. When, weeks after her first story appeared, the Shoal Creek crisis developed, reporters at the PGA Championship went scrambling for reprints. Those stories won the American Bar Association's Silver Gavel Award. Her reports since, including her 1995 book, *The Unplayable Lie*, published by GOLF DIGEST and Pocket Books, have changed the game at a time when it desperately needed to change. Not through crusading, this time, but through reporting.

Another lesson learned.

Above: *GOLF DIGEST has long lead the crusade against slow play, as this October 1965 cover can attest.*

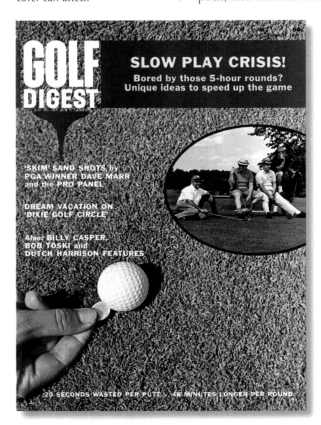

May 1990

Let's Get Back to Real Golf

One of our eloquent readers speaks out about our basic liberties—especially the right to walk

By J.L. Briggs

I hear a lot about my First Amendment rights to free speech, a free press and free this and that, but why doesn't it apply on the golf course? My right to play golf the way it should be played is not being protected.

There are few private clubs and fewer resort courses where you can insist on walking without being regarded as either a freak or a troublemaker.

The usual policy at these clubs is that if there are no caddies available, you must take a cart. And of course there are no caddies; they're as scarce these days as poor investment bankers. So you wind up with a cart or you don't play.

I don't object if the aged and infirm ride in carts. I don't even object if a whole generation of golfers prefers to haul their developing paunches

Illustration: Arnold Roth

around on four wheels, in the belief that walking on a golf course is just an act staged by touring pros on television. But I object vehemently when I am compelled to ride a cart and play a perverted version of what was once a healthful game. I can play tennis, squash, basketball, hockey, soccer and Ping-Pong the way those games are supposed to be played. But not golf. To compound my fury, I know that money is the reason I'm forced to ride. Clubs and resorts want the cart revenue.

They say carts speed up play. Baloney. Anywhere in Great Britain, where they regard golf "buggies" as a ridiculous American invention, golfers play weekend rounds far faster on their feet than Americans on their behinds. I am just recovering from a local member-guest shotgun that took $5\frac{1}{2}$ hours. Can golf sink any lower?

Some golfers protest that they can't pull or carry their bags because they're too heavy. Of course they are, and that's part of the problem. Buy a light Sunday bag and walk. Your game won't suffer, either, if you leave three or four clubs behind.

Golfers who favor carts overlook two major shortcomings. One, the secret of golf is tempo. If you're placid and relaxed, your swing tends to be the same. If, on the other hand, you zigzag across the course in a cart from ball to ball you do not have an opportunity to mentally prepare for the next shot. Two, golf is not merely hitting a ball. It is also the joy of breathing clean air and communing with nature, or conversing amiably with members of your group as you walk. Your spirits need rejuvenation after a hard week at work and your heart is crying out for exercise.

Isn't it time we help build bodies instead of revenues?

Caddies

Golf Digest launches a crusade to restore golf's oldest profession

by Michael Bamberger

A golfer making the turn during a recent round asked his caddie if he would like a refreshment from the snack stand. "Yeah," said the looper. "Coke. Plenty of ice."

If caddies had flawless manners, if they read greens perfectly, if they routinely put the right club in your hand, they would be no fun at all. The fact is, they are wholly unpredictable. A caddie may say, "Whatever you do, don't hit it O.B." He (or she) may shake his head in vigorous disgust as you snap-hook another one. He may lag 50 yards behind you. He may call you "Ma'am" or "Sir" eight times on a single green. He may be wholly unskilled at searching for a ball in the rough. He may identify the line of your putt with the toe of his sneaker. He may yell, "Fly, golf ball, fly," when the ball is already sailing way over the green without any verbal encouragement.

In other words, golf is enriched by the presence of caddies. Caddies provide the game with conversation. They provide the game with diversion. They provide the game with humor, with lore, with witnesses. They integrate the game. They make the game better.

The men's tour and the women's tour, thankfully, still require players to take caddies. A few good clubs—

your Winged Foots, your Seminoles, your Merions—still require players to take caddies. But these are rarefied golf environments. These are the exceptions.

Evidence, anecdotal and otherwise, suggests that each year the number of rounds worked by caddies at private clubs decreases, a decline that began in earnest in the middle 1960s. The number of American resort courses and public courses that make caddies available has become, as they say in the polling business, statistically insignificant. The sad fact is that the role of the caddie is in demise. Golf Digest is committed to reversing that trend.

This magazine seeks instead the demise of the caddie's replacement, the golf cart—the rough-flattening, noise-creating, air-polluting, exercise-robbing, path-requiring blight upon the golf landscape. Our hope is to rejuvenate the demand for caddies, and thereby diminish the demand for carts at golf courses of every stripe—private, public and resort. We realize that club pros often have their income tied to the cart business, but a management or membership committed to caddies could restructure the pros' compensation. And we realize that some golfers would be unable to participate in the game without the use of carts; obviously we have no objection to those riders. But our chief hope is for golf to return to its roots as a walking game. We want there to be the opportunity for thousands of people, of every imaginable background, to make money while being introduced to a very great game. Old Tom Morris learned to play golf as a caddie. So did Francis Ouimet, Gene Sarazen, Charlie Sifford, Sam Snead, Byron Nelson, Ben Hogan, Seve Ballesteros and scores of others. Will there ever be another champion to emerge from the caddie yard? The game will be poorer if there is not.

The game's humor is developed in the caddie shack, too. We know a caddie who describes himself on his business card as a specialist in "windages and yardages." A famous British caddie called Mad Max used to insist that certain putts were "slightly straight." The late Lee Lynch, who caddied on the men's tour for more than 40 years, used to interpret a putt's "overhaul break." It was a caddie whose name has been lost to the sands of time who, upon being asked by his boss what to do with a certain oversized divot, responded, "Take it home and practice on it."

The paving of caddie yards has led to the corruption of the title of the men who once ran them. The "caddiemaster" these days is the guy who keeps the carts running. This is an abomination. We eagerly await the day when the role of caddiemaster will return to its original, honorable purpose: to train and keep busy a stable of caddies; to explain the game's etiquette, with-

Golf is enriched by the presence of caddies. (Photo: Dom Furore)

Bobby Jones with caddie Dale Donovan at Interlachen, 1930. (Photo: Golf World)

"I expect to see dogs used universally in the future. With a dog as your caddie, there is no one to hear you swear and no one to make fun of your play."

—ANONYMOUS LABRADOR RETRIEVER OWNER DURING BRITISH CADDIE SHORTAGE IN 1914.

out which golf has no future; to teach the value of keeping your eyes and ears open and your mouth shut. It is only the caddiemaster who can explain the subtle and proper ways for a caddie to pursue a last-hole salary drive. Caddiemasters are amazing. We have never met anybody who ever carried as a kid who did not remember in every detail the physical and personal characteristics of the caddiemaster who for a period dictated the quality of the person's life. Caddieing is not about money. It's about learning how the world works.

In this vein, we hope never again to hear a young, well-pressed golf committee chairman at a swanky club where sandwiches are served without crust refer to a barn crowded with carts as "a profit center." This is not what the founding fathers had in mind when they invented the game. To any course manager who says, "We need the cart revenue," we say, raise your green fees, use less fertilizer, use less water, charge more for tees, don't pave cartpaths. Cart revenue? The truth is that carts cost, and their cost is incalculable.

There is now an entire generation of fitness kooks, people who spend hours going nowhere fast on exercise bicycles, who have trained the so-called caddiemaster at their club to strap their bag on the back of a cart immediately upon arrival at the course. Many of these people were introduced to the sport at golf "academies" where caddies are nonexistent. They'll say, "Gotta play a quick 18 today, Teddy, gonna cart it." They slip Ted a fiver and chug off. Somehow, they have convinced themselves that golf is faster in a cart. This is not the case. The five-hour round was unknown throughout golfdom until carts came on the scene. In Scotland, golf is still fast and carts are unheard of. Caddies, properly trained, help improve the pace of play mightily: One caddie stays on the tee and points out the line of flight to a colleague, who, positioned in the fairway, spots the incoming ball. Caddies also rake bunkers, replace divots, fix ball marks, tend pins. They help maintain the course; they keep the game moving.

The worst thing about the cart is that it cheats you of the chance to feel your shot and to feel the game. Having a caddie in your employ enhances your golfing sense. There is a satisfaction in standing in the middle of the fairway—150 yards from the hole, downhill, into the breeze, green soft—and saying to your caddie, "Whaddaya think?" There are few pleasures in golf more rewarding than crouching behind a 12-footer for a win on a putt for which you cannot find the line and hearing your caddie whisper confidently, "Ball and a half on the left and firm," and then holing it. "Good stroke," he says. "Good read," you respond.

If you have never taken a caddie, we urge you to try one. If they are unavailable at your club or course, we suggest you bring your own. You may have to petition the pro or the golf committee chairman to do this. Do this. You will be sowing the seeds of revolution. You will be creating a job. You will be improving your golf. You will be improving your club. Having an able caddie helps you play better. Having an experienced and involved caddie helps you play considerably better.

Having a truly professional caddie can help you raise your game to another level.

The presence of a caddie will help you concentrate on the task at hand, executing the shot that awaits you to the best of your ability. With a caddie on your bag, you don't have to worry about getting the cart over to your partner, in the rough, on the other side of the fairway. You won't throw out your back bouncing down a bumpy trail. You won't strain your shoulder by carrying your own bag. You don't have to search the horizon for your ball immediately after making contact. You can, as the old-time teaching pros used to say, keep your head down, as you're supposed to.

With an experienced caddie, you can have a little discussion about the length of the shot, the nature of the lie, the direction of the wind, the firmness of the ground, the line of the putt. The caddie who is involved in your game helps you focus on the unique and specific requirements of your shot in a way you might not do otherwise.

Having an expert caddie on your bag is like playing with a teaching pro. He may tell you that you are not following through, or you're gripping the club too tightly, or you need to take a deep breath and relax. It is a fact that bad rounds can be avoided with good on-course counseling. Given what you pay for a lesson, the $25 to $40 you spend on an expert caddie for a four-hour playing lesson is a fantastic value. The pro may take 45 minutes trying to explain the proper way to play a fairway bunker shot. Expert caddies have a knack for making things simple: dig in, choke up, top the ball.

It has been said that lack of caddies has caused the demise of the caddie. This is putting the cart first. With the economy lackluster and millions of people out of work, the caddie ranks would be swelling if there were sustained demand for their services. Caddies are not necessarily youngsters eager to play the game. The truth is, the caddie has no one face. The caddie is a fresh-scrubbed teenager hoping to earn a college scholarship and make some money for a Saturday night date. He's an unemployed steelworker trying to keep food on his family's table. He's a pensioner wearing galoshes, carrying a copy of the Daily Racing Form in his back-right pocket and a cigar in his front left.

Their mutual home, the caddie yard, is the place where a middle-aged black man with gold in his teeth shows a white kid from the suburbs how to play gin rummy while discussing whether the second-round leader at Augusta has a chance to hold on through Sunday.

It is in the caddie yard where they know if the pro is on the outs with the club president, if the peculiar pin placement on 11 was done in a spirit of playfulness or out of spite, and if Mr. Smith, recently separated, has taken up residence in the clubhouse. It is in the caddie yard where they can analyze your game, and your psyche, with more insight and more candor than you are likely to get from your pro or from your playing partners. Caddies see the game, they feel the game, they live the game. It is in the caddie yard where fervor for the game takes root.

June 1990

Knocking on the Clubhouse Door

America's private clubs face challenges from women and minorities. How they respond will change the way the game is played in the 1990s

by Marcia Chambers

Marcia Chambers' stories on private club discrimination changed the face of American golf. Her 1990 series won the American Bar Association's Silver Gavel Award.

Some miles inland from San Francisco lies the Peninsula Golf and Country Club, a typical country club for families and children—with Saturday night dances, tennis courts and golf tournaments amid ancient sycamores.

For 11 years, Mary Ann Warfield was a "family" member. She and her husband joined the 350-member club in 1970. There was never any question when they divorced in 1981 that Mary Ann and her two children would get the golf membership.

Golf had been her life. Her father, a pro in Oregon, taught her the game. She entered her first tournament at age 9. She integrated the all-male golf team in high school, earning a letter every year. And her wedding present was a set of woods. Her handicap was once as low as 6 and her dream was to play the LPGA Tour. While a member at Peninsula, she was active in interclub competitions. Golf and the country club were central to her life. She had been the women's club champion.

A few months after she was awarded the country club membership in her divorce settlement, the board of directors cited club bylaws and said she was not entitled to her husband's equity membership. Peninsula, like many of the nation's 3,500 equity clubs, awards adult males the voting and equity status in the club. What this meant was that Warfield could not be a club shareholder and, therefore, could not derive the market value of her shares if she resigned or died or if the club sold its land to a developer.

The value of the Warfield membership, purchased for $10,000 in 1970, is roughly $50,000 now, said Kevin R. McLean, Warfield's attorney. Many women, he said, use a club's facilities as spouses, only to discover at divorce that they do not hold a co-ownership, even though the membership was paid for by both of them with community property funds.

The board of directors terminated the Warfield membership after Mr. Warfield said he no longer wanted to be a member; it offered Mrs. Warfield a redemption fee, which she refused to accept. It also offered her daily golfing privileges without an equity membership.

"I told the board I am not that dumb," she said. "I love golf, and I had represented Peninsula for over 10 years [in interclub matches], and this was their response. I said there's something wrong here." When the board refused to reconsider, she filed a suit in California Superior Court. She argued that the state's civil rights Unruh Act entitled her to sue for an equity membership because the club was a business establishment and it discriminated against her on the basis of gender. (The Unruh Act prohibits discrimination in public accommodations and in "all business establishments of every kind whatsoever.")

Robert E. Kane, a former state judge and a member of Peninsula, has mounted a two-pronged argument in his defense of the club. He maintains that as a private club, Peninsula is not a business and is therefore exempt from the Unruh Act. He also argues that as a private club, Peninsula may discriminate as part of its right of free association under the First Amendment.

The case has been in litigation for nearly 10 years. Last year, an intermediate California state court gave Warfield the right to sue under the Unruh Act. The court said that associational privacy is not without qualification. It cited three major U.S. Supreme Court decisions that in recent years have upheld the laws of three states barring discrimination in service and private clubs where business activities take place.

In January the California Supreme Court upheld the intermediate court's decision, which sent shivers through the state's country-club world because it marked the first time the state's highest court held that a country club qualified as a business establishment and was subject to the state's discrimination laws under the Unruh Act. The Warfield case is also significant because it opens the door in California to the issue of male-only equity memberships.

Warfield now plays on public courses. She says once she filed her lawsuit, she was persona non grata at the club. Soon her business declined.

"I was in the real-estate business at the time, and the club was very important to my business," she said. "I have suffered extreme backlash, from people I thought were my best friends at the club. It was unbelievable to me. This was a small community. Once one friend invited me to play, but another woman took her aside and said, 'Don't invite Mary Ann, the lawsuit is still going on.' "

Not all clubs react like Peninsula. In Los Angeles, the Bel-Air Country Club, an equity club, was faced with a similar situation and decided to admit the woman as a member. In 1988 the club admitted aviator Brooke

Discussing gender discrimination is easy, but you enter a shadowy nether world when you talk about race.

Chambers' October 1990 report, "After Shoal Creek," reported on private club changes. One: Ron Townsend's admission to Augusta National. (Photo: Art Stein)

Knapp as a regular woman member after she and her husband divorced. Knapp, who lives on Bel-Air's 13th fairway and had an 8 handicap, said she "applied to be a regular member to continue my lifestyle as I had known it for the last 14 years." It took the club six months to admit her as a regular member with full voting and equity privileges. It may have helped that Los Angeles has an ordinance similar to New York City that bans discrimination in private clubs.

Warfield said that eventually she wants to bequeath her membership to her daughter or son, whom she taught to play golf. Bequeathing memberships to daughters is not yet possible at Peninsula. But some clubs have taken the lead in changing inheritance policies.

In 1987 Hillcrest Country Club, a Jewish club in Los Angeles, changed its bylaws to enable fathers to bequeath memberships to daughters as well as to sons. The club also decided to admit women members.

ACCESS TO THE CLUB

Litigation against clubs doesn't cease when membership and property rights have been resolved. Once you get in, there is the question of full and equal access to the facilities your membership has purchased.

Many women now work full time, often in executive posts and, like their male counterparts, find it difficult to play golf except on weekends. For them the Tuesday morning ladies group won't work. They want weekend morning play, yet often find that those times are set aside for men.

But women have found that in asserting a human right, they are defying a customary practice deeply ingrained in the culture of the private club. Efforts to change traditional weekend tee times have set off some of the fiercest emotional battles clubs have ever known.

Both men and women who have lived through the experience say the tee-time issue has the capacity to bring out the worst in the nature of both sexes.

The clubs that have been forced to move the most quickly to change their discriminatory tee times have been those that receive substantial tax abatements under so-called "open space" law. This type of law provides a country club with property tax breaks if the club agrees to keep its land free of development. But to benefit from the state's tax abatement, the club must comply with state laws, including laws barring discrimination.

In the last two years, three states have used tax abatements or tax write-offs to lead the attack on discriminatory tee times.

Most recently, California has targeted at least 50 country clubs as potentially discriminatory in their designated tee times. The state's Tax Franchise Board, which oversees state income taxes, has warned in letters to the clubs that unless preferred tee times are changed, club members will lose deduction of golf costs as a business expense on their state taxes.

Minnesota and Maryland, the two states in the nation with the toughest open-space laws, have launched major investigations to force some 30 clubs in each state to give equal access to women.

"This was one of the most emotional issues I have ever encountered," said Warren Rebholz, executive director of the Minnesota Golf Association. He said about 30 private clubs in the Minneapolis-St. Paul area have revamped tee times in response to legislation that equalizes tee times on weekends. The Minnesota law does recognize the need and desire for single-sex golf. It permits the clubs to hold women's- or men's-only play twice a week during weekdays and one weekend each month.

Rebholz said he found it was better to try to have a say in helping to draft the legislation than to draw firm opposition against it. The clubs, he added, are "getting used to it. It's the trend of the future. To buck it is not very perceptive."

In Maryland, the state's tax department launched an inquiry into possible discriminatory tee times after the Maryland Court of Appeals ruled against all-male Burning Tree, saying the club either had to admit women or pay full taxes.

Kaye Brooks Bushel, counsel to the Maryland Department of Assessments and Taxation, conducted the inquiry, reviewing the practices regarding tee times at 32 clubs that have accepted "open space" designation and where tax abatements are substantial. For example, one club in Montgomery County with a 281-acre course pays taxes on $14 million—not $61 million, its full value.

Bushel found that virtually every club denied women equal access to the course as a result of segregated weekend tee times for men and women. In less than a year, the policies were changed at these clubs, including some prominent ones like Congressional Country Club in the Washington, D.C., area.

"Many made whatever changes were necessary. Others needed a little bit of prompting from me," Bushel said. "It was common sense. Women who work will play on the weekends; women who don't will play on weekdays when it's less crowded. It's really a simple issue."

One of the clubs sent a letter to their members saying men and women would retain their bowling leagues, but members were entitled to join either one. "This shows the difficulty of government getting involved in these issues," she said. But it hasn't kept her out of them.

One club, the Lakewood Country Club in Rockville, Md., devised an innovative plan, which was approved by Bushel. The board decided that a couple would elect on a onetime only basis the "Preferred Time Golfer" and the "Non-Preferred Time Golfer."

It came as no surprise that most men preferred themselves; as of last count, of the 560 club members, only 13 wives were given the coveted weekend time slot. Thomas R. Smith, associate editor at National Geographic, and his wife, Mary, also an editor at the magazine, designated Mary as the preferred golfer. He hoped the designation "would enable the old-timers to give way and open the club equally, as it should be." The Smiths had been led to believe, they said, that the designated golfer would be the designated member. But that turned out to be false. Mary Smith gets to play early on weekends, but she doesn't get to vote.

Nor is legal pressure restricted solely to tee times. On

Jan Bradshaw (right) filed a lawsuit against the Yorba Linda C.C., Orange County, Calif., because of restricted tee times for single women. During the course of litigation, the club changes several of its policies towards women members.

Women want the same access to a club as their male counterparts, and if clubs are slow to change their ways, they act.

the line in Maryland, by virtue of its statute, is the issue of putting a membership in a man's name, holding Men's or Ladies' Day (but not Member's Day or Spouse's Day) and operating a men's grill.

On this latter issue, Maryland is by no means unique. Over the years there have been battles over women seeking access to a grill, a taproom, a dining room, a men's porch or a veranda. Grills are also on this year's legislative agenda in Minnesota.

In the 1950s and early '60s, issues of gender simply weren't recognized. Wives of members played golf at designated times and usually did not hold memberships in the club. Although many of these women are unsympathetic to the plight of the executive female golfer, the younger generation of women are in their corner. Many are rising in the business and professional world. They want the same access to a club as male counterparts, and if clubs are slow to change their ways, they act.

Some have filed grievances before their home states' human rights commissions. And often they have won. So far, women have filed teetime or grill discrimination claims against country clubs in Washington, D.C., Virginia, Connecticut, New Hampshire, Massachusetts, Minnesota, California and New York.

Others, frustrated by the refusal of their boards to change tee-time schedules on the weekends, have gone directly to state court. Jan Bradshaw, a 42-year-old interior designer, purchased a full membership at Yorba Linda Country Club in Orange County, Calif., following her divorce.

Bradshaw's job allowed her to play in the early mornings, and she wanted to continue that pattern on weekends. But she found the course closed to her until 11 a.m. on Saturday. Under the club's rules in 1988, when she filed a lawsuit asserting discrimination under the Unruh Act, single women could play only after the men and the couples had finished teeing off on Sunday at noon or 1 p.m.

Bradshaw is a devoted golfer who once played daily and had a 15 handicap. As a Mormon and the mother of three, she said she is stunned to find that wives and widows now view her as a "troublemaker. The women treat me as if I had leprosy. I am deeply ashamed of them."

Her lawsuit, she said, has uncovered the darker side of human nature. She said she has been ostracized: "My name on the sign-out sheet has been erased, my photographs on the bulletin board were mutilated and no foursome will play with me." She said widows, who pay half price, receive better treatment than divorcees, who pay full price. "Death is OK, divorce is not."

Her lawyer, Gloria Allred, the feminist attorney, said, "She paid the same membership fees as a man paid, but she received fewer benefits and rights, solely because she is a woman."

Bradshaw wants to settle her case. The atmosphere at the club has forced her out, she said. Postscript: During the course of the litigation, the club changed its weekend teetime schedules and gave women members the right to vote and to run for seats on the board.

By far the strangest tee-time incident occurred last

October at Long Island's Cedarbrook Club and led to the filing of criminal harassment charges against Ronald Forman, current chairman of the golf committee.

The Nassau County District Attorney's office brought the case on behalf of Mrs. Lee Lowell, who had filed a complaint against Forman. At a nonjury trial, the club's tee time policies were analyzed: weekend mornings were reserved first for male members, then male members with male guests, and then "lady" members with or without female guests. Mrs. Lowell had informed club officials that unless she was given early weekend tee times, she would take legal action. Under this threat, one of the club's owners gave her permission to tee off at 9:30 a.m. on weekends and holidays.

She quickly ran into trouble, she said, when her assigned male players refused to play with her. She testified that she was confronted by Forman at the second tee, that he cursed her, kicked her golf ball and threw a golf ball at her. At one point, there was a brief golf cart chase, she said, and at another point several men in golf carts sought to block her way.

Forman maintained that he did not harass Lowell. He said when he arrived that morning he heard a number of complaints from fellow golfers concerning Lowell's presence on the course. He and other members of the club decided she would have to leave. She refused. At that point, Forman decided to halt all play on the course until, as the judge put it, "the question of Lowell's gender invasion could be resolved." It was on his quest to stop all play that he encountered Lowell and accused her of driving a ball that narrowly missed hitting him.

The judge acquitted Forman of the criminal charge, finding a reasonable doubt as to whether he intended to harass Lowell. The judge, however, took the unusual step of researching the state privacy law, and he wrote a nine-page decision, finding the golf club's policies "repugnant and offensive," but, under current New York law, legal.

Forman's attorney, John R. Lewis, said Lowell had a choice: "If she didn't like the rules, she didn't have to join." As it turned out, the club did not renew her membership. She then sued the club before the state's Human Rights Division. Although in February that division informally notified the club's attorney that it was in violation of the state's antidiscrimination law, by mid-April no official action had been taken.

CLUBS AND RACIAL MINORITIES

Discussing gender discrimination is easy, but you enter a shadowy nether world when you talk about race. Race tends to be a hush-hush topic. Few country clubs would want to be known as avowedly racist, but of all the private clubs in the nation, many have no black or Hispanic members and many others have only a token one or two.

It is difficult to know the precise dimensions of the problem because no one keeps records: not the National Golf Foundation, the U.S. Golf Association, the National Club Association or the country clubs themselves. In part because of stress on such subjective qualities for admission as "kindred spirits," in part to avoid a possible basis for litigation, there are remarkably few solid figures to document the extent of the problem.

Women have made far greater strides in a shorter time than have racial minorities, largely because almost any white male has an immediate relative of the opposite sex, often one who has played golf at the club for years. But that is not the case with race. And unlike gender, where exclusion of 50 percent of the population makes it pretty hard to deny discrimination, a small club in a middle-sized community can always argue that they don't discriminate, it's just that they have very few blacks to choose from and they haven't found the "right" ones yet.

Although changes have occurred since the civil rights movement of the '60s, specifically the deletion in bylaws of "white males only," those advances are modest indeed. They are limited in part by club policies that are not explicitly racist, but work to frustrate any inquiry into a club's decision making.

The National Club Association (NCA), in its materials to member clubs, urges that clubs not accept applications but admit members by invitation only. If there is no applicant pod, then one cannot establish a differential rate of acceptance by race. It suggests using subjective criteria for selection, such as congeniality rather than objective criteria like gender or race. Further, the NCA urges that, when necessary, clubs "sanitize" records and that they leave no record of discussion by a membership committee "to avoid compulsory production by subpoena or in pretrial discovery."

For all these reasons, even if one wanted to sue, it would be extremely difficult to get a satisfactory record to begin a lawsuit. This is one reason for the lack of litigation. It's hard to attack a bowl of jelly.

But who wants to litigate anyway? Unlike employment discrimination cases, where the person may be fighting for money and a job and may not care whether the employer regards him or her fondly, the essence of private club life is sociability and congeniality. To begin that relationship by having to force one's way in through a lawsuit is a daunting prospect. This is Catch-22 for serious black golfers who love the game and can afford the costs of one of the better private courses.

Jack Jones is the black personnel director for Xerox's Americas Operation, which includes South and Central America, Mexico, the Middle East, North Africa and Canada. He learned how to play golf as a child, went on to be a caddie and now has a 10-handicap. He would like to be admitted into a private club in Fairfield County, Conn., where he has lived for the last five years, or in nearby New York.

At 51, Jones is financially able to join an expensive club. "As you move up the ladder, it would be nice to be able to do that," he said. Three other black golfing friends, all top executives at New York corporations, and all with decent handicaps, have made a concerted effort in the last three years to get into a private club, and one, George Lewis, vice president and treasurer of Philip Morris, was just admitted to St. Andrew's Golf Club in Hastings on Hudson, N.Y.

"You don't just knock on the door," said Jones. "You want it to be a natural selection. You don't walk up to someone and say, 'sponsor me.' You sure don't want to file a lawsuit. When you start filing lawsuits then you become a pariah."

In any private club a big issue is sociability. The proof of sociability is sponsorship—a member who says this is a good guy, someone you'll all enjoy. But if all the members are white, how many are on friendly enough, co-equal terms with a black golfer to be in a position to sponsor him? And if a member is friendly with a black golfer who fits the club's subjective criteria, will he be strong enough to overcome pressure from prejudiced members?

Besides the obvious social reasons for joining a club, there are also business reasons. Darwin Davis is senior vice president at the Equitable Financial Companies. He wants a private club for his family and for himself, but also to entertain clients.

"I feel blacks get hurt badly in a business situation," he said. "I'm at a disadvantage with my competitor. If I want to take the state controller out for a round of golf because I want to talk to him about a bond issue, the best I can do is take him to the public course I play in Stamford, Conn. The best I can feed him is a hamburger. My opponent takes him to his country club where he has a great lunch, with a bar, and he gets to use a locker room with a shower and have his shoes shined.

"On the family level, my white counterpart and his 12-year-old son both get to practice at their country club course. When the white 12-year-old gets to be a businessman, he is admitted to his father's club. My kid is still behind. It is a continuous cycle."

If business is so important, one might imagine that high-level corporate executives would use their leverage to open the country club doors to leading black businessmen. Some have, but it isn't easy.

Tom Shropshire was senior vice president for Miller Brewing Company, a subsidiary of Philip Morris, when he retired five years ago. Shropshire said that when he first arrived in Milwaukee in the early 1970s, the top brass at Miller, members of Milwaukee Country Club, made inquiries about Shropshire becoming a member. The club, the most exclusive in the area, had no blacks then or now, he said. Despite the role in the community, Miller's executives were told Shropshire would not be accepted. "When you cut people at that level, it hurts," he said.

Perhaps with that experience in mind, a few years later Miller Brewing wanted to build a brewery in Eden, N.C., but stipulated that any black executive had to be admitted to the local country club. With so many jobs at stake, the deal was accepted.

Now living in Los Angeles, Shropshire has been sponsored at Riviera, which has four black members, including O.J. Simpson, but memberships have been suspended following the purchase of the club by a group of Japanese investors. He is now considering membership in Wilshire Country Club, which has one black member.

He says corporate executives must take the initiative at their own clubs to pave the way for their black executives. The companies with the commitment to blacks—

Is there any hope for a genuinely integrated country club, where ethnic and racial dimensions are submerged and where all can enjoy the country club life without regard to skin color or religion?

like Xerox, Philip Morris, American Express, IBM—whose executives have moral as well as financial clout, could push firmly for a re-examination of club policies.

OTHER FORMS OF DISCRIMINATION

Clubs are expensive and many black golfers lack the money for high initiation fees. Some avoid the older clubs altogether, finding it easier to purchase new homes that are part of golf course developments. There the only color that is supposed to count is green. Some report less discrimination at golf course developments in the Sunbelt and elsewhere.

When discrimination does occur, golf memberships in these developments have been construed as a "property" interest. In one major case, the Court of Appeals for the Fourth Circuit held in 1980 that a Salisbury, Va., residential development had violated Federal civil rights laws when it denied a golf membership to a black couple who had purchased a home in the development. The court awarded the couple damages.

There are many black golfers who aren't looking for membership in any sort of private club. But they still face discrimination.

Dennis Morgan is the promotional director of the United Golfers Association, an organization of amateurs formed in 1925 when blacks were barred from playing on virtually all private courses. Morgan, a cost analyst for Detroit Edison, said that he and his golfing buddies may not have the funds for steep initiation fees, but they occasionally get together for a golf tour package to Florida.

A few years ago he arranged a trip for 60 golfers at a Florida club. The group played on a Monday and had a great time. The next year they wanted a return visit, only this time they wanted to play the course on Wednesday. Morgan said he was told by the golf pro that his group could play Monday, not Wednesday.

"I asked why," Morgan said. "And after beating around the bush, he finally said, 'It's because you're a black group.' Monday, he told me, was maintenance day and that's the day we could play. Then I realized that the year before there had been no one else on the course. We were all alone out there. It sent cold chills through my body."

THE PRICE OF MEMBERSHIP

Race or gender discrimination does make a difference to a club member when that member faces the loss of a prestigious public job because of his membership in an elite club. In the last few years, there have been several notable resignations.

Anthony Kennedy resigned from San Francisco's Olympic Club when he was nominated to become a justice on the U.S. Supreme Court. John Dunne, a former New York State Senator, recently resigned from the all-male Garden City Golf Club, when he was nominated to head the U.S. Justice Department's Civil Rights Division. And most recently Richard Phelan, who won a political post in Cook County, in Chicago, was forced to resign his membership at all-male Bob O'Link Golf Club in Highland Park, Ill. One of Phelan's opponents, R. Eugene Pincham, a black, held a rally outside the club, calling

Phelan's liberal credentials "hypocritical." Phelan said he made a mistake, but this mistake dogged his campaign.

It is sometimes the case that a prestigious club will accept a few black members. Olympic finally admitted its first two blacks in 1987, after the city filed its lawsuit against the club. In 1983 a Burning Tree executive told legislators that the club had only one black member because "those people, they don't play golf." At the time, Burning Tree had six Hispanic members and several Asians, most of whom were diplomats.

Now Burning Tree has another black member, Bryant Gumbel, the "Today" show host. He is NBC's weekend TV golf anchor and a member at Whippoorwill in New York.

Celebrity figures may well get in, although some clubs are known to be snippy about celebrity members of whatever race because of the visibility they bring the club. It is perhaps for this reason that President Reagan reportedly has been given an "honorary" membership at Los Angeles Country Club, where he is now taking lessons from the pro.

But for the noncelebrity black business executive, entry remains a problem. Tom Shropshire may get in a Los Angeles club. Jack Jones and Darwin Davis are still waiting in the New York area. Although Davis was the first black admitted to the exclusive Duquesne Club in Pittsburgh in 1981, that doesn't help him a lot in Connecticut. At age 57, he said: "I have worked hard and that's the American way. But one's efforts should bring rewards. My family ought to have the same opportunities as white families. I make enough money to do it; I'm a gentleman, a family man. I love golf. There is nothing about me except the color of my skin that keeps me from a club."

OTHER MINORITY PROBLEMS

Black golfers are not alone in experiencing discrimination. Virtually every ethnic or racial minority has been through something similar at some point. Indeed many of the clubs that are sites of the nation's major golf tournaments have a history of discrimination against both blacks and Jews. In 1968, when Richard Nixon was running for the Republican Presidential nomination, he was asked how he could lay moral claim to the White House when he belonged to Baltusrol, an exclusionary club in Springfield, N.J. At first he said he would seek change from within the ranks. But that didn't go over too well with the club membership. After he was nominated, Nixon decided to resign from Baltusrol, the site of the 1993 U.S. Open.

The situation of Jews is similar to that of blacks in that there are still many clubs that do not have Jewish members or, if they do, only a token few. And in some that do, there is still a kind of social segregation; often it is said that Jews socialize with each other and are not really woven into the social fabric of the club.

It is different in that unlike blacks, Jews in major urban areas have been better placed financially and, in the early part of the century, had the wherewithal to purchase the land to construct their own clubs when faced with exclusion from others. Each major metropolitan area has

After Ann Warfield was awarded the family membership at Peninsula G. & C.C., the club informed her that she was not entitled to her husband's equity membership. Warfield sued. In January 1990, the California Supreme Court upheld a lower court ruling that a country club was a business establishment and subject to state discrimination laws.

Across the country, there is little doubt that private clubs are undergoing the greatest challenge to their authority since they first opened their doors.

one or more Jewish club and they, too, tend to discriminate against blacks.

The latest ethnic trend is the purchase of golf courses and golf resorts by Japanese corporations. Although these are largely business ventures, the Japanese are passionate about golf, and given the costs in their own country, they can fly here and play more easily than staying at home. Increasingly, Asians are buying memberships in American clubs.

Is there any hope for a genuinely integrated country club, where ethnic and racial dimensions are submerged and where all can enjoy the country club life without regard to skin color or religion?

There is at least one. The Mill River Club, located in Upper Brookville, Long Island, is now 26 years old. It was the brainchild of one man, William S. Roach, a lawyer whose vision was a club unmarked by racial or religious segregation. The club's policy is to maintain an integrated membership. Currently it is roughly 50 percent Jewish, 50 percent Christian and others, including some half-dozen black Americans, four West Indians and four Orientals.

Leonard Pearlman, the president of the board of directors, said the club has been "enormously successful" in achieving its policies of nondiscrimination. Mill River's 127 acres, purchased in 1961 for $550,000, are owned by its 400 members. "We are very proud," he said.

But this success story does not yet extend to matters of gender. On weekend mornings the men's-only tee times appear to be sacrosanct. The club recently did change its bylaws to admit a divorced woman with full membership privileges, but only if her former spouse gives up his membership.

Roach, who is now retired and lives in Florida, was a former president of the National Club Association. He said he believes strongly that clubs should set their own policies and not be coerced by legislation.

LOOKING AHEAD

Across the country there is little doubt that private clubs are undergoing the greatest challenge to their authority since they first opened their doors. And it is the states and cities that are leading the movement to end discrimination in private clubs.

But regardless of associational claims, it appears that a state is not obligated to assist discriminatory clubs in obtaining state benefits, other than the essentials such as police and fire protection. Liquor licenses and tax abatements are not considered essential.

It took the city of San Francisco three long years and a heavy investment in public funds and time to get Olympic Country Club to consider opening its doors to women. Was it worth it, we asked George Riley, the city's lead attorney?

His answers come from the framework of the civil rights movement in the South: "You have to look at those struggles. And if you said, is it worth it to put all this emphasis on integrating a luncheon counter? People will go to jail and there will be all these lawsuits, is it worth it? If we thought that way then nothing would ever have been done."

There is, of course, a difference between the places of public accommodation that provided the settings for the civil rights battles of the '60s, and the private clubs that figure in today's litigation. The task of the courts, legislatures and private clubs in the last decade of the 20th century is to figure out just what that difference is.

in our view:
THE FIRST STEP IS TO TALK ABOUT THE PROBLEM

Editors Note: The editorial that accompanied Chambers' 1990 story may seem mild by today's standards, but the message remains true: When it comes to the problem of discrimination, clubs have to address it to redress it. Here is an excerpt.

If the Berlin Wall and Drexel Burnham Lambert could collapse in only six months, what does this new decade hold in store for golf? Private clubs are going to change in the 1990s, and it will be better for all of us if the changes come from within.

Should men retain exclusive tee times on Saturday and Sunday mornings? Should there be a men's-only grill? Should there be men's-only clubs? What does the Constitution guarantee? What rights do you give up for a lower tax rate or a liquor license?

If you are a private club member, you need to make sure that your leadership doesn't have its head in the sand. This means talking to your fellow members about issues that they usually don't want to talk about: race, religion and gender. There are no easy solutions that work for every membership. Part of the difficulty is that private clubs tend to be governed by officers elected to short terms. There are long-range problems that take several years to unravel. Clubs should lengthen the term of office to give their boards continuity in dealing with such complicated issues.

In the final analysis, many of these questions have more to do with morality than the law. Ask yourself: Are the policies and practices of your club fair? If the answer is yes, you have no problem. If the answer is no, the next question is "Why?"

—*THE EDITORS*

President Dwight D. Eisenhower wears a big smile and a GOLF DIGEST "Don't Ask What I Shot!" button during a round of golf with Senator Robert Taft of Ohio at Augusta National G.C., April 1953. (Photo: AP/Wide World)

The Rest of The Best

Chronology, covers,
America's greatest courses,
editors, contributors,
firsts, bests, and all the rest

Giving Voice to the Game:

Fifty years in the life of GOLF DIGEST —compiled by Cliff Schrock

SPRING 1950
William H. Davis, Howard R. Gill and Jack F. Barnett launch GOLF DIGEST. The first issue is a 16-page, digest-sized regional publication. Price: 15 cents.

MAY 1952
GOLF DIGEST goes to nationwide distribution and bills itself the "only newsstand golf magazine in America."

JULY 1952
Introduces national Hole-in-One service.

JULY 1953
President Dwight Eisenhower appears on the cover as part of the "Don't Ask What I Shot" promotion. (The only other President to ever appear on the cover is George Bush, September 1990.)

APRIL 1954
Betsy Rawls and Cary Middlecoff join as members of the GOLF DIGEST Advisory Staff.

JUNE 1954
Sam Snead appears on the cover for the first time.

JULY 1955
Introduces national Most Improved Golfer program.

MARCH 1956
Publishes first 100-plus-page issue (132 pages).

AUGUST 1957
Arnold Palmer appears on the cover for the first time.

1960
Reaches circulation of 100,000.

JUNE 1960
The GOLF DIGEST Pro Panel is formed with Horton Smith, Paul Runyan, Johnny Revolta and Jackson Bradley.

OCTOBER 1960
Ben Hogan appears on cover of 10th anniversary issue.

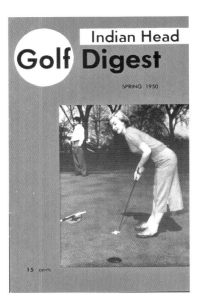

The first issue of GOLF DIGEST is published from the "home office" of Bill Davis in 1950. The price is 15 cents.

"I'll be at a seminar on stress."

David Harbaugh's "Rub of the Grin" cartoons have run for 20 years. (Art: David Harbaugh)

Sam Snead: first pro mentioned in pages of GOLF DIGEST and early member of the Golf Digest Pro Panel.

MARCH 1961
The Golf Digest Book Club is introduced.

OCTOBER 1961
Jack Nicklaus appears on cover for the first time, with Deane Beman.

JANUARY 1962
Page dimensions increase from digest-sized 8¼ by 5½ to conventional 8¼ by 11⅛.

FEBRUARY 1962
Issue price increases to 50 cents.

NOVEMBER 1962
Editorial offices moved from Evanston, Ill., to Norwalk, Conn.

FEBRUARY 1963
Palmer and Nicklaus appear on the cover together for the first time.

MAY 1963
Sam Snead joins GOLF DIGEST's Pro Panel.

1964
Start-up of trade magazine, Club Operations; title later changed to Golf Shop Operations.

OCTOBER 1966
GOLF DIGEST's first course ranking, America's 200 Toughest Courses. It later becomes America's 100 Greatest Golf Courses as ranked by GOLF DIGEST.

DECEMBER 1968
Lee Elder is the first African-American to appear on the cover.

MAY 1969
Sale of GOLF DIGEST to The New York Times Co. is announced.

1970
Reaches circulation of 500,000.

JANUARY 1970
20th anniversary issue.

1971
Starts the Golf Digest Schools, the first national golf school program in the world.

1974

First year that all 12 issues are each 100 pages or more.

1975

Start up of the National Long Driving Championship.

JANUARY 1975

Tom Watson appears on the cover for the first time.

AUGUST 1975

Arnold Palmer appears on the cover of the 25th anniversary issue; price for a single-issue copy increases to $1.00.

MARCH 1977

Publishes "A Golf Primer."

AUGUST 1977

Jack Nicklaus joins as Playing Editor.

FEBRUARY 1978

Tom Watson joins as Playing Editor.

SEPTEMBER 1978

Nancy Lopez joins as Playing Editor.

1980

Debut of the GOLF DIGEST Commemorative Pro-Am, which helps popularize the senior tour.

JANUARY 1980

Reaches circulation of 1 million.

MARCH 1981

Initial listing of America's 50 Greatest Public Courses.

JANUARY 1982

Tom Kite joins as Playing Editor.

MAY 1982

Jack Nicklaus named Chief Playing Editor.

NOVEMBER 1982

Charles Price joins as Contributing Editor.

FEBRUARY 1984

Initial listing of America's Best New Courses; price for a single-issue copy increases to $1.95.

AUGUST 1984

Reaches circulation of 1.2 million.

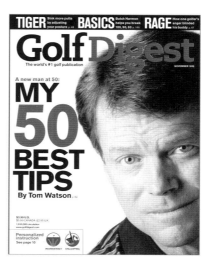

Tom Watson appears on cover for the first time in 1975 and joins as a Playing Editor in 1978. Watson again makes the cover for the November 1999 issue.

Nancy Lopez joins as a Playing Editor in 1978. (Photo: Lynn Sugarman)

When Dan Jenkins joined GOLF DIGEST in 1985 as Contributing Editor, he had more than 30 years of golf coverage experience. Here is Jenkins with Arnold Palmer after the 1962 British Open. (Photo: London Observer)

Hail to the Chief: Jack Nicklaus is named Chief Playing Editor in 1982. (Photo: Frank Gardner)

David Leadbetter joins the Professional Advsory Staff in 1990.

APRIL 1985

Dan Jenkins joins as Contributing Editor.

1985

Golf Digest Schools features teaching powerhouse of Dick Aultman, John Elliott, Jim Flick, Hank Johnson, Peter Kostis, Davis Love Jr., Jack Lumpkin, Tom Ness, DeDe Owens, Paul Runyan and Bob Toski.

AUGUST 1985

35th anniversary issue.

SEPTEMBER 1985

Editorial offices move from Norwalk to Trumbull, Conn.

OCTOBER 1987

Publishes first listing of The Best Golf Courses in Each State.

JANUARY 1988

Reaches circulation of 1.3 million.

JULY 1988

Seve Ballesteros joins as Playing Editor; price for a single-issue copy increases to $2.50.

OCTOBER 1988

Publishes first listing of America's 75 Best Resort Courses.

JANUARY 1989

Unveils major redesign and increased page size of 9 by 10⅞; The New York Times purchases Golf World, a weekly, placing the three leading golf publications in their fields under the same ownership. The three are marketed as "The Golf Company."

MARCH 1989

Publishes "The New Primer," a revised version of the March 1977 primer.

JANUARY 1990

David Leadbetter joins Professional Advisory Staff.

MARCH 1990

Publishes "The Advanced Golfer."

APRIL 1990

Selected as National Magazine Awards finalist in Special Interests category by the American Society of Magazine Editors.

AUGUST 1990
40th anniversary issue.

OCTOBER 1990
Nick Faldo joins as Playing Editor.

FEBRUARY 1991
Reaches circulation of 1.4 million.

APRIL 1992
Start of three-part investigative series on Deane Beman and the PGA Tour.

MAY 1992
Harvey Penick appears on the cover, which helps his *Little Red Book* become the all-time biggest selling golf book.

JUNE 1992
Mark O'Meara joins as Playing Editor; price of a single-issue copy increases to $3.50.

1993
Annual Places to Play guide expands to include reader comments and becomes stand-alone book.

FEBRUARY 1993
Phil Mickelson and Nick Price join as Playing Editors.

MARCH 1993
Reaches circulation of 1.45 million.

AUGUST 1993
Jack Nicklaus appears on cover for 47th time, the most of anyone.

JUNE 1994
Arnold Palmer appears on cover for 27th time, third most of anyone.

SEPTEMBER 1994
Sam Snead appears on cover for 21st time, fourth most of anyone.

NOVEMBER 1994
Tiger Woods appears on the cover for the first time.

FEBRUARY 1995
Publishes a new, third version of "The Golf Primer."

MARCH 1995
Reaches circulation of 1.5 million.

NOVEMBER 1995
GOLF DIGEST Extra for Women debuts.

JANUARY 1996
500th issue.

Harvey Penick kept notes on his thoughts on golf and teaching golf for more than 40 years. He shared these with the world in his Little Red Book in 1992. (Photo: Dom Furore)

Two golf greats improve on their records of cover appearances: Nicklaus (his 47th in 1993) and Palmer (his 27th in 1994). (Photo: Lester Nehamkin)

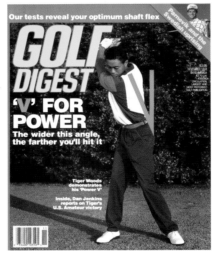

Exactly 13 years after his first appearance in GOLF DIGEST, Tiger gets his first cover, November 1994. His cover count now stands at nine.

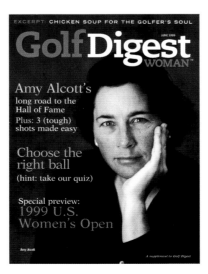

GOLF DIGEST WOMAN was published as a separate magazine in April 1998. Before launching, it was published as a special section in GOLF DIGEST since 1995. Amy Alcott was featured on the June 1999 cover.

FEBRUARY 1996
Publishes "The Power Primer."

APRIL 1996
Selected as National Magazine Awards finalist in Special Interests category by the American Society of Magazine Editors.

APRIL 1997
Ernie Els joins as Playing Editor.

AUGUST 1997
Tiger Woods joins as Playing Editor.

JANUARY 1998
Justin Leonard joins as Playing Editor.

FEBRUARY 1998
Reaches circulation of 1.55 million.

MARCH 1998
Debut of bonus instruction pullout Pocket Tips.

APRIL 1998
GOLF DIGEST WOMAN launches as a separate magazine.

JUNE 1998
Unveils major redesign and increases service reporting.

SEPTEMBER 1998
Places new key phrase on cover: "How to Play, What to Play, Where to Play."

JANUARY 1999
Se Ri Pak joins as Playing Editor; price for a single-issue copy increases to $3.99.

FEBRUARY 1999
Places personalized instruction icons on cover for first time.

JUNE 1999
Publishes first 300-page issue; Tiger Woods appears on cover for eighth time.

OCTOBER 1999
Sergio Garcia appears on cover for the first time.

NOVEMBER 1999
Tom Watson appears on cover for 33rd time, second most of anyone.

DECEMBER 1999
Publishes the 557th issue of GOLF DIGEST for a total of 72,538 pages.

The Cover of a Magazine Is Like an Honest Face

by John Barton

Producing a winning cover isn't a science, and it may not even be an art. At best it's educated guesswork.

It tells you so much about what's going on inside. A cover is a window into a magazine's identity, its personality. It's a magazine's way of saying hello to the world.

In its first 50 years, GOLF DIGEST's 557 covers have spanned the waterfront. We've shown legends old (Bobby Jones in April 1960) and new (19-year-old Sergio Garcia in October 1999). Dean Martin has made an appearance (May 1953) and so has Sylvester Stallone (August 1995). We've featured Dwight Eisenhower (July 1953) and George Bush (September 1990).

Our covers have been graced by the likes of Perry Como, Howard Cosell, Bing Crosby, Bob Hope, Michael Jordan, Danny Kaye, Jerry Lewis, Jayne Mansfield, Leslie Nielsen, Debbie Reynolds, O. J. Simpson and Ted Williams. A chimp appeared on the cover in August 1954, and again in July 1987, the latter time sitting on Payne Stewart, with the cover headline: "How Payne Stewart Got the Monkey Off His Back." (The only other animal to grace our front cover was Byron Nelson's horse in August 1955.)

The first time we featured Ben Hogan on the cover was in September 1953; the most recent occasion was October 1997 (we're sure that won't be the last).

In the early days, GOLF DIGEST could be a lot more experimental with its covers. The December 1969 issue bore surely the most bizarre cover in the magazine's history: three golfing Barbie dolls being watched by a lecherous Ken doll in a black trenchcoat, with the cover headline: "Hidden Hazard on Ladies' Tour." The introduction to the story inside said: "Watch out, you housewives, that 'dirty old man' lurking about the ladies' pro tour could be your husband."

Another cover, in January 1971, showed a chubby fellow in a sauna clutching a load of well-positioned golf balls about his midriff. "Warm Golf Balls Do Go Farther!" declared the headline.

Nowadays, however, like all magazines, we have to concentrate on producing covers that sell. The magazine business has become highly competitive—with something like 5,000 titles sold on newsstands in this country, it's become harder and harder to stand out in the crowd. Having a really eye-catching cover—and a strong brand name—is more important than it has ever been. It's not just on the newsstand that covers are important, either—90 percent of GOLF DIGEST's 1.55 million circulation comes from

subscriptions, and when the magazine lands in your mailbox along with junk mail, solicitations from various charities and credit card companies and letters from Auntie May, we want GOLF DIGEST to be the thing you turn to first.

At any magazine, the actual process of putting together the cover is a closely guarded secret. It usually involves a group of people huddled around a computer screen for hours at a time, sometimes days, poking, prodding and otherwise tweaking what appears on the screen in front of them. What if we made that word bigger? What would it look like if we made his shirt red? Shouldn't we put an exclamation point after the word "Slice"?

Producing a winning cover isn't a science, and it may not even be an art. At best it's educated guesswork, but nevertheless we've developed plenty of theories over the years about what works and what doesn't. The theories are always being challenged, altered, and replaced by new theories. We'd tell you what our favorite current theories are, but we don't want to give all our secrets away. The most obvious one, however, is that instruction-related covers sell well, especially those that offer a cure for those afflicted with a slice, golf's equivalent of the common cold.

In the first 10 years of the magazine's history, feature-related covers outnumbered instructional cover stories by a ratio of more than 5 to 1. Nowadays, practically every cover we produce is instruction related, the rare exceptions being when we have a particularly compelling tale to tell, such as our October 1997 search through the jungles of Vietnam for Tiger Phong, the war friend of Earl Woods who disappeared in a "re-education camp" in the mid-1970s.

So, what's our best-selling cover of all time? With a newsstand "sell-through" of 59.71 percent and total newsstand sales of 195,000, it was July 1997, when the cover featured an illustration of a spinning golf ball bearing the words "How to Fix your Slice." Did it work? All we can say is that, after all these years, we are all still trying to fix our slices. But at least we now have a better idea why we slice.

And who has graced our covers the most over the past half century? In reverse order, they are Billy Casper (16 covers); Sam Snead (21); Arnold Palmer (27); Tom Watson (33) and, in runaway first place with 47 cover appearances, who else but Jack Nicklaus.

The GOLF DIGEST Cover

Spring 1950

The GOLF DIGEST cover has not only reflected changes in the game during the last 50 years, but changes in the magazine's editorial focus. From 1950 to the late 1970s, GOLF DIGEST's covers were most likely a feature subject. The magazine spotlighted the glamour of the game, from the players and celebrities to places to play. By the end of 1977, the magazine had run 178 feature covers and 108 instruction covers.

But the focus changed in the late 1970s. Even though the magazine had always included instruction in its content, teaching its readers how to play became the primary cover subject. GOLF DIGEST started running more instruction covers to such an extent that by the end of 1998, instruction covers had overtaken features, 314 to 224.

GOLF DIGEST COVER SUBJECTS THROUGH 1999

Name (number of covers): Dates

Todd Anderson (1): August 1997

Paul Azinger (4): August 1987, October 1989, August 1991, August 1994

Seve Ballesteros (6): April 1977, February 1981, April 1984, December 1986, April 1988, October 1988

Jerry Barber (1): May 1962

Alice Bauer (1): August 1953

Marlene Bauer (4): August 1953; as Marlene Hagge: Dec/Jan/Feb 1956, March 1957, May 1973

Laura Baugh (1): May 1976

George Bayer (1): August 1963

Frank Beard (2): July 1970, December 1974

Chip Beck (2): July 1988, September 1991

Deane Beman (4): October 1961, March 1973, April 1992, May 1992

Debbie Bensmiller (1): March 1963

Marlyn Bensmiller (1): March 1963

Patty Berg (1): March 1958

Susie Berning (1): May 1974

Jane Blalock (3): January 1972, May 1975, May 1977

Tommy Bolt (4): April 1956, August 1958, March 1959, June 1962

Julius Boros (5): December 1952, August 1956, November 1963, February 1964, June 1964

Gay Brewer (2): January 1967, August 1967

Jack Burke (3): July 1956, March 1957, March 1996

George Bush (1): September 1990

Mark Calcavecchia (2): March 1990, September 1991

Harold Callaway (1): March 1960

Joe Campbell (1): June 1966

JoAnne Carner (Gunderson) (1): February 1963

Billy Casper (16): May 1958, March 1959, August 1959, June 1962, February 1963, March 1964, August 1965, January 1966, February 1966, July 1966, February 1967, February 1969, October 1969, May 1970, April 1971, April 1972

Bob Charles (1): July 1964

Bobby Cole (1): September 1969

Perry Como (1): June 1959

Chuck Cook (6): March 1989, September 1989, November 1989, November 1990, December 1992, March 1996

Howard Cosell (1): April 1973

Henry Cotton (1): May 1957

Fred Couples (3): June 1990, July 1992, April 1993

Bruce Crampton (1): August 1973

Ben Crenshaw (7): July 1974, June 1976, February 1977, June 1979, September 1985, March 1990, October 1995

Bing Crosby (1): June 1953

John Daly (4): November 1991, August 1992, November 1995, February 1996

Barbara Darrow (1): April 1954 (actress with Doug Ford)

Scott Davenport (4): March 1989, November 1991, December 1994, February 1995

Laura Davies (1): February 1996

William H. Davis (1): Spring 1950

Dave Debusschere (1): July 1970

Deena the chimp (1): July 1987

Jimmy Demaret (1): June 1956

Jim Dent (1): November 1974

Jack DePalo (1): March 1971

Bruce Devlin (2): October 1964, May 1965

Joe Dey (1): April 1973

Gardner Dickinson (1): June 1986

Roy Doty (1): January 1988

Dale Douglass (1): February 1971

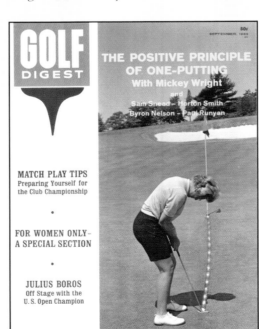

September 1963

September 1964

October 1957

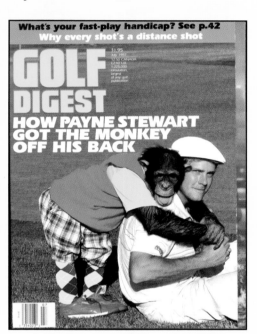

April 1977

September 1978

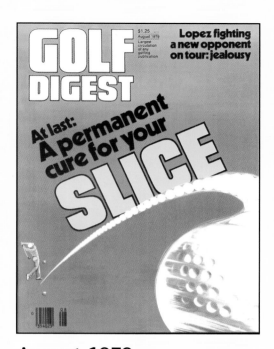

August 1979

July 1987

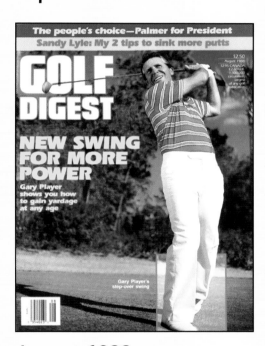

August 1988

December 1989

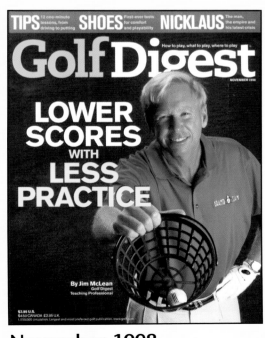

June 1997

November 1998

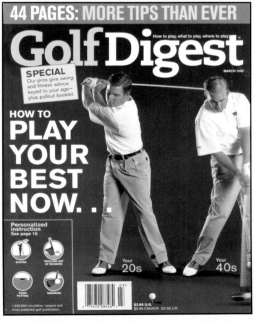

March 1999

to play and what to play. Invented course rankings.

ROBERT DEDMAN Patriarch of the giant Club Corporation of America, which saved Pinehurst and changed the course of course management.

JIMMY DEMARET This three-time Masters winner became one of the game's pioneer commentators and founded the precursor to the Senior PGA Tour.

JOSEPH C. DEY During 35 years with the USGA and five as the first commissioner of the PGA Tour, Dey established standards we live by today.

PETER DOBEREINER For thirty years "Dobers" was golf's most prolific, droll and elegant voice, on both sides of the Atlantic, and in our pages.

PETE DYE With bold use of waste bunkers and railroad ties, he brought Scotland to America and changed the way courses are designed.

DWIGHT D. EISENHOWER The "Golfing President" legitimized the game for the masses, demonstrating that golf was a game not just for the idle rich.

TOM FAZIO If Pete Dye specialized in the diabolical, Fazio brought finesse and a more playable, natural look to course architecture.

TIM FINCHEM Finchem reorganized Beman's empire, recognized the game's new global nature and established the World Golf Championships.

DAVID FOSTER The Colgate executive who brought money, prestige and television to the LPGA Tour when he helped launch the Dinah Shore.

LEO FRASER The son of a professional, Fraser spent a lifetime in the game and, as PGA President, settled the bitter dispute with tour pros in 1968.

JOE GIBBS The visionary who created The Golf Channel and gave us our favorite sport 24 hours a day.

BEN HOGAN The game's most precise shotmaker, he made serious practice de rigueur for pros and mesmerized the public with his superb play.

BOB HOPE Sponsor, fan and tireless promoter of the game, he carried a club wherever he went, spreading the gospel of golf around the globe.

DAN JENKINS First in *Sports Illustrated* and then in GOLF DIGEST, Jenkins gave a uniquely American voice to the sport—and we all laughed and tried to talk like he wrote.

ROBERT TRENT JONES He raised course architecture to its present stature, built 400 courses around the world and gave the public "country club" golf.

DAVID LEADBETTER Golf's leading instructor transformed the games of stars like Nick Faldo and in the process made teaching a business.

NANCY LOPEZ She was to women's golf what the Beatles were to popular music. Her nine wins in 1978 put the LPGA Tour on everyone's map.

GEORGE S. MAY Promoter, innovator and tournament sponsor generous with prize money, he was first to allow a black golfer to play in a PGA event.

MARK McCORMACK The Pied Piper who led golfers into the big money started with Arnold Palmer and became the most powerful man in the game.

GERALD MICKLEM The most effective post-World War II administrator in Great Britain, he returned the British Open to major status.

BOB MOLITOR The R&D man at Spalding who invented the two-piece ball which gave the average golfer both distance and durability.

JACK NICKLAUS Winner of more majors than any golfer in history, he "played a game with which we're not familiar," and founded an immensely successful course design business.

HARVEY PENICK Penick's *Little Red Book* sold millions and his minimalist, understated method changed the way the game is taught.

ARNOLD PALMER Golf's leading ambassador and one of its most savvy businessmen, he helped launch many enduring golf enterprises, from the senior tour to The Golf Channel.

GARY PLAYER Won more than 100 tournaments around the world, including major championships 19 years apart. He brought fitness and trans-continental flights to golf.

FRED RAPHAEL TV producer who fathered Shell's *Wonderful World of Golf* and the Legends of Golf, which set in motion the Senior PGA Tour.

Rivals and friends, Jack and Arnie detonated golf's boom.

RICHARD W. REES DuPont chemist who invented Surlyn, the uncuttable synthetic material that greatly increased the life expectancy of golf balls.

CLIFFORD ROBERTS Chairman of the Masters Tournament from the beginning, Roberts set a standard for running championships that is still unequalled.

CHI CHI RODRIGUEZ The crowd-pleasing pro who, through his play and his work with youth, changed the face of golf and the lives of thousands of kids.

CHARLES SIFFORD First African-American to compete full-time on the Tour, he suffered unheard-of abuse, but paved the way for players of color who came after him.

SAM SNEAD Snead's style and tempo are the ultimate model, and have helped him win more than 84 times and compete well into his 70s.

KARSTEN SOLHEIM Brilliant inventor and marketer who produced the first investment-cast, heel-and-toe weighted clubs, making golf easier for hackers everywhere.

FRANK THOMAS USGA equipment chief credited with (and blamed for not) protecting the integrity of the game in the face of an onslaught of technological change.

PETER THOMSON Player, architect, writer, administrator, Thomson won five British Opens and helped launch the Far Eastern tournament circuit.

LEE TREVINO His rags to riches story inspired thousands, but his great gift to the game was reminding us how much fun it can be.

RICHARD S. TUFTS One of the Pinehurst Tufts, he became USGA president, enlarged its Green Section and helped make the rules of golf uniform worldwide.

TOM WATSON An eight-time major tournament champion, Watson dominated the game in the 1970s and '80s and used his fame to promote the USGA.

EDWIN WATTS Entrepreneurial retailer and ex-pro who taught American golfers to buy their equipment mail-order.

HERBERT WARREN WIND Our leading golf journalist and historian, Wind wrote the definitive book on golf here: *The Story of American Golf*.

TIGER WOODS A Masters Champion at 17 and golf's first 100 million-dollar man, Tiger is the game's magnet and magician, the face of its future.

MICKEY WRIGHT Possessor of perhaps the best swing ever, she won 44 tournaments in a 4-year span and totally dominated the young LPGA Tour.

BABE DIDRIKSON ZAHARIAS A multi-sport athlete and founding member of the LPGA, she led the money list from 1948 to 1951, then entered the Hall of Fame.

 # Nongolf celebrities

Personalities who have appeared in GOLF DIGEST

Don Adams, June Allyson, Morey Amsterdam, Eddie Arcaro, Richard Arlen, Desi Arnaz, James Arness, Fred Astaire, Lauren Bacall, Rick Barry, Ethel Barrymore, Jack Benny, Milton Berle, Yogi Berra, Larry Bird, Joey Bishop, Humphrey Bogart, Ray Bolger, Pat Boone, Omar Bradley, Jack Brickhouse, Don Budge, George Burns, Richard Burton, George Bush, James Caan, Hoagy Carmichael, Art Carney, Johnny Carson, Don Carter, Oleg Cassini, Fidel Castro, Wilt Chamberlain, Happy Chandler, Cyd Charrisse, Bill Clinton, Ty Cobb, Claudette Colbert, Perry Como, Sean Connery, Chuck Connors, Gary Cooper, Bing Crosby, Dizzy Dean, Yvonne DeCarlo, Phyllis Diller, Dom DiMaggio, Joe DiMaggio, Celine Dion, Jimmy Dorsey, Kirk Douglas, The Duke of Windsor, Jimmy Durante, Leo Durocher, Barbara Eden, Dwight D. Eisenhower, Mamie Eisenhower, Jose Ferrer, Eddie Fisher, Joan Fontaine, Gerald Ford, Glenn Ford, Tennessee Ernie Ford, Henry Ford, Whitey Ford, Judy Garland, James

Garner, Dave Garroway, Greer Garson, Jackie Gleason, George Gobel, Paulette Goddard, Arthur Godfrey, Leo Gorcey, Robert Goulet, Betty Grable, Billy Graham, Otto Graham, Cary Grant, Dick Groat, Bryant Gumbel, Buddy Hackett, Alan Hale, Phil Harris, Rita Hayworth, Horace Heidt (bandleader), Audrey Hepburn, Katharine Hepburn, Hootie and the Blowfish, Bob Hope, Delores Hope, Rock Hudson, John Huston, Dennis James, David Janssen, George Jessel, Van Johnson, Danny Kaye, Buster Keaton, Howard Keel, John F. Kennedy, Ralph Kiner, Sandy Koufax, Jack Kramer, Bert Lahr, Frankie Laine, Burt Lancaster, Steve Lawrence, Janet Leigh, Vivien Leigh, Jack Lemmon, Bob Lemon, Jerry Lewis, Joe E. Lewis, Joe Louis, Ida Lupino, Fred MacMurray, Gordon Macrae, Jayne Mansfield, Mickey Mantle, Rocky Marciano, Ann Margret, Dean Martin, Groucho Marx, Harpo Marx, Zeppo Marx, Willie Mays, Roddy McDowall, Victor McLaglen, Robert Merrill, James Michener, Ray Milland,

Carmen Miranda, Cameron Mitchell, Robert Mitchum, Johnny Mize, Marilyn Monroe, Garry Moore, Terry Moore (actress), Ed Morrow, Bill Murray, Joe Namath, Ricky Nelson, Bob Newhart, Richard Nixon, Tip O'Neill, Dick Powell, Tyrone Power, Elvis Presley, Johnny Ray, Donna Reed, Don Rickles, Phil Rizzuto, Jimmy Rodgers, Sugar Ray Robinson, Mickey Rooney, Jane Russell, Babe Ruth, Robert Ryan, Jill St. John, Pierre Salinger, Carl Sandburg, Randolph Scott, Willie Shoemaker, Phil Silvers, O.J. Simpson, Frank Sinatra, Red Skelton, Tris Speaker, Bart Starr, Casey Stengel, Inger Stevens, Adlai Stevenson, Ed Sullivan, Bill Talbert, Ralph Terry, Danny Thomas, Lowell Thomas, Forrest Tucker, Lana Turner, Johnny Unitas, Robert Wagner, Fred Waring, John Wayne, Johnny Weissmuller, Raquel Welch, Lawrence Welk, James Whitmore, Ted Williams, Paul Winchell, Walter Winchell, Jonathan Winters, Shelley Winters, Smokey Joe Wood, Jane Wyman

When it comes to politicians, GOLF DIGEST is a non-partisan employer. Speaker of the House Tip O'Neill and President Gerald Ford were both subjects of the magazine's celebrity swing sequences. (Photo: Stephen Szurlej)

The All-time America's Greatest Courses

Since 1966, GOLF DIGEST has ranked the greatest courses in America biennially. Here are all the courses, listed alphabetically, ever included in the 18 rankings.

Alamance C.C., NC
Annandale G.C., MS
Arcadian Shores, SC
Aronimink G.C., PA
Atlanta A.C., GA
Atlanta C.C., GA
Atlantic G.C., NY
Atlantic C.C., NJ
Augusta National G.C., GA
Aurora C.C., OH
Baltimore C.C. , MD
Baltrusrol G.C. , NJ
Barrington Hills C.C., IL
Barton Creek C.C., TX
Bay Hill C., FL
Beechwood G.C., IN
Bel-Air C.C., CA
Belle Meade C.C., TN
Bellerive C.C., MO
Benson Park G.C., NE
Berry Hills C.C., WV
Bethlehem C., NY
Bethpage State Park (Black), NY
Beverly C.C., IL
Big Foot C.C., WI
Black Diamond Ranch, FL
Blackwolf Run G.C. (River), WI
Blue Hills C.C., MO
Bob O'Link G.C., IL
Bonita Bay C., FL
Boyne Highlands Resort, MI
Branch River C.C., WI
Briarwood G.C., IL
Broadmoor G.C. (West), CO
Brook Hollow G.C., TX
Brookridge C.C., KS
Brown Deer C.C., WI
Buena Vista C.C., NJ
Butler National G.C., IL
C.C. of Birmingham (West), AL
C.C. of Darien, CT
C.C. of Detroit, MI
C.C. of Indianapolis, IN
C.C. of Jackson, MS
C.C. of Miami, FL
C.C. of New Seabury, MA
C.C. of North Carolina (Dogwood), NC
C.C. of Orangeburg, SC
C.C. of Rochester, NY
C.C. of Virginia, VA
California C.C., CA
Camargo C., OH
Canoe Brook G.C. (North), NJ
Canterbury G.C., OH
Carlton Oaks C.C., CA
Cascades G.Cse., VA
Castle Pines G.C., CO
Cedar Ridge C.C., OK
Cedar Rock C.C., NC
Century C.C., NY
Champions G.C. , (Cypress Creek), TX

Champions G.C. (Jackrabbit), TX
Charlotte C.C., NC
Cherokee C.C., WI
Cherry Hills C.C., CO
Chicago G.C., IL
Cog Hill G. & C.C. (No.4), IL
Coldstream C.C., OH
Colonial C.C., TX
Colonial C.C. (South), TN
Columbia C.C., SC
Columbine C.C., CO
Concord G.C. , NY
Congressional C.C. (Blue), MD
Coral Ridge C.C., FL
Cottonwood C.C., CA
Country C., MA
Country C. (Open), MA
Country C., UT
Crooked Stick G.C., IN
Crosswater, OR
Crystal Downs C.C., MI
Cypress Lakes C.C., FL
Cypress Point C., CA
Dallas Athletic Club C.C., TX
Desert Forest G.C., AZ
Desert Highlands G.C., AZ
Desert Inn C.C., NV
Desert Mountain (Cochise), AZ
Desert Mountain (Renegade), AZ
DeSoto Lakes G.C., FL
Disney World G.C. (Palm), FL
Doral C.C. (Blue), FL
Double Eagle C., OH
Dub's Dread G.C., KS
Dunes G. & Beach C., SC
East Lake G.C., GA
Edgewood Tahoe G.C., NV
Eisenhower G.C., CO
El Niguel C.C., CA
Elcona C.C., IN
Eldorado C.C., CA
Elmwood Park G.C., SD
Emeis Park G.C., IA
Equinox C.C., VT
Estancia C., AZ
Eugene C.C., OR
Fairway Farms G.C., TX
Fargo C.C., ND
Fenway G.C., NY
Finkbine G.C., IA
Fircrest G.C., WA
Firestone C.C. (South), OH
Fishers Island C.C., NY
Flossmoor C.C., IL
Forest Highlands G.C. (Canyon), AZ
Fox Chapel G.C., PA
Garden City G.C., NY
Gates Park G.C., IA
Golden Horseshoe G.C., VA
Golden Valley G.C., MN

Golf Club (The), OH
Goodyear G. & C.C. (Gold), AZ
Grand Cypress G.C. (North/ South), FL
Grand Forks C.C., ND
Grandfather G. & C.C., NC
Green Valley C.C., SC
Greenbrier C. (Old White), WV
Greenville C.C. (Chanticleer), SC
Grenelefe G. & Racquet C., FL
Haig Point C. (Calibogue), SC
Happy Hollow C.C., NE
Harbour Town G. Links, SC
Harding Park G.C., CA
Hardscrabble C.C., AR
Hartford G.C., CT
Hattiesburg C.C., MS
Hazeltine National G.C., MN
Hershey C.C. (West), PA
Hickory Hills C.C., MS
Hillcrest C.C., IL
Hillcrest C.C., NE
Hiwan G.C., CO
Holmes Park G.C., NE
Holston Hills C.C., TN
Homestead (Lower), VA
Honors Cse., NC
Hot Springs C.C. (No. 3), AR
Houston C.C., TX
Incline Village C.C., NV
Indian Hills C.C., AL
Indian Spring C., MD
Innisbrook (Copperhead), FL
Innisbrook (Island), FL
Innisbrook G. & C.C., FL
Interlachen C.C., MN
International C.C., VA
International G.C., MA
Inverness C., OH
Inwood C.C., NY
Isle Dauphine G.C., AL
JDM C.C. (East), FL
Jupiter Hills C. (Hills), FL
Kanandaque G.C., NY
Kansas City C.C., KS
Kauai Lagoons (Kiele), HI
Kebo Valley C., ME
Kemper Lakes G. Cse., IL
Kenwood C.C., OH
Kittansett C., MA
Knollwood G.C., IL
Kutschers C.C., NY
La Costa C.C. (T. of C.), CA
La Quinta (Mountain), CA
Lake Nona G.C., FL
Lakeview C.C., WV
Lakewood C.C., LA
Lancaster C.C., PA
Laurel C.C., MS
Laurel Valley C.C., PA

Lindsey G.C., KY
Links at Spanish Bay., CA
Lochland G.C., NE
Long Cove C., SC)
Longwood C.C., IN
Los Angeles C.C. (North), CA
Lost Tree G.C., FL
Loxahatchee C., FL
Maidstone C., NY
Mauna Kea G. Cse., HI
Mayacoo Lakes C.C., FL
Meadow Brook C., NY
Medinah C.C. (No. 3), IL
Memorial Park G.C., TX
Memphis C.C., TN
Merion G.C. (East), PA
Meriwether C.C., OR
Metropolis C.C., NY
Milwaukee C.C., WI
Minikahda C., MN
Minneapolis G.C., MN
Moon Valley C.C., AZ
Moraine C.C., OH
Moselem Springs G.C., PA
Muirfield Village G.C., OH
Naples National G.C., FL
National G. Links, NY
NCR C.C. (South), OH
Newport C.C., RI
North Shore C.C., IL
Northland C.C., MN
Noyac G. & C.C., NY
Oak Cliff C.C.,TX
Oak Hill C.C. (East), NY
Oak Tree G.C., OK
Oakland Hills C.C. (South), MI
Oakmont C.C., PA
Oaks C.C., OK
Ocean Cse., SC
Ocean Forest G.C., GA
Ohio State University G.C. (Scarlet), OH
Old Baldy C., WY
Old Marsh G.C., FL
Old Warson C.C., MO
Old Waverly G.C., MS
Old Westbury G. & C.C., NY
Olympia Fields C.C. (North), IL
Olympic C. (Lake), CA
Oneida G. & Riding C., WI
Otter Creek G.C., IN
Oyster Harbors G.C., MA
Palmetto C.C., SC
Palmetto Dunes (Fazio), SC
Pasatiempo G.C., CA
Pauma Valley C.C., CA
Peachtree G.C., GA
Pebble Beach G. Links, CA
Pecan Valley C.C., TX
Pekin C.C., IL
Penobscot Valley C.C., ME
Pete Dye G.C., WV
PGA National G.C. (East), FL

PGA West G.C. (Stadium), CA
Philadelphia Cricket C., PA
Pine Needles G.C., NC
Pine Tree G.C., FL
Pine Valley G.C., NJ
Pinehurst C.C. (No. 2), NC
Plainfield C.C., NJ
Plantation G.C., ID
Pleasant Valley C.C., MA
Plum Hollow G.C., MI
Point O'Woods G. & C.C., MI
Portland G.C., OR (1)
Portsmouth C.C., NH
Prairie Dunes C.C., KS
Preston Trail G.C., TX
Prestwick C.C., IL
Prince Cse., HI
Princeville G.C., HI
Princeville Makai G. Cse. (O. & L.), HI
Pumpkin Ridge (Ghost Creek), OR
Pumpkin Ridge (Witch Hollow), OR
Purdue University G.C. (North), IN
Quail Creek C.C., OK
Quail Hollow C.C., NC
Quaker Ridge G.C., NY
Quarry at La Quinta, CA
Rainbow Springs G.C. (Big Moraine), WI
Red Fox C.C., NC
Rhode Island C.C., RI
Ridgewood C.C. (East/West), NJ
Rio Pinar C.C., FL
River Oaks C.C., TX
Riviera C.C., CA
Robert Trent Jones G.C., VA
Rosswood G.C., AR
Royal Kaanapali G.C., HI
Royal New Kent G.C., VA
Royal Oaks C.C., WA
Runaway Brook C.C., MA
Sahalee C.C. (South/North), WA
Salem C.C., MA
San Francisco G.C., CA
San Juan G.C., WA
Sanctuary G.C., CO
Sand Hills G.C., NE
Saticoy C.C., CA
Saucon Valley C.C. (Grace), PA
Sawgrass G.C. (East & West), FL
Scioto C.C., OH
Sea Island G.C., GA
Seaview C.C. (Pines), NJ
Seminole G.C., FL
Sewickley Heights G.C., PA
Shadow Creek G.C., NV
Shadow Glen G.C., KS
Sharon C., OH
Shawnee C.C., PA

Sherwood C.C., CA
Shinnecock Hills G.C., NY
Shoal Creek, AL
Signal Point C., MI
Skokie C.C., IL
Soboba Springs C.C., CA
Somerset Hills C.C., NJ
Southern Hills C.C., OK
Spring Valley C.C., KY
Spring Valley C.C., SC
Spyglass Hill G. Cse., CA
Stanford University G.C., CA
Stanwich C., CT
Sunny Jim G.C., NJ
Sycamore Hills G.C., IN
Tam O'Shanter C.C., IL
Tamarisk C.C., CA
Tamiment-in-the-Poconos, PA
Tannenhauf G.C., OH
Tarry Brae G.C., NY
Terrace Park C.C., OH
Texarkana C.C., AR
Timber Point C.C., NY
Timberlane C.C., LA
Torrey Pines G.C. (South), CA
TPC at Eagle Trace, FL
TPC at Sawgrass (Stadium), FL
Troon G. & C.C., AZ
Troon North (Monument), AZ
Tucson National G.C., AZ
Turtle Point Yacht & C.C., AL
University of Michigan G.C., MI
University of New Mexico G.C., NM
Valhalla G.C., KY
Valley C. of Montecito, CA
Village Greens C.C., KY
Vintage C. (Mountain), CA
Wade Hampton G.C., NC
Wakonda G.C., IA
Wannamoisett C.C., RI
Warren AFB G.C., WY
Warwick Hills C., MI
Wee Burn C.C., CT
West Bend C.C., WI
West Point Officers G.C., NY
Whaling City C.C., MA
White Bear Yacht C., MN
Whitemarsh Valley C.C., PA
Wild Dunes (Links), SC
Willamette Valley C.C., OR
Wilmington C.C. (South), DE
Winchester C.C., MA
Winged Foot G.C. (East), NY
Winged Foot G.C. (West), NY
World Woods G.C. (Pine Barrons), FL
Wykagyl C.C., NY
Wynstone G.C., IL
Yale University G.C., CT
Yellowstone C.C., MT
Yorba Linda C.C., CA

 **Firsts & First Mentions**

Innovations and people the first time they appeared in
GOLF DIGEST, *listed chronologically*

Male tour pro name: Sam Snead,
  Spring 1950

Female tour pro name: Marlene and
  Alice Bauer, Spring 1950

Cover blurbs: "How to Drive" and "Slicing,
  by Sam Snead," Summer 1950

Ad: For Gene Sarazen's book *30 Years of
  Championship Golf,* for $3 in Spring 1950;
  Motorola ad, Spring 1950

Instruction article: How to Putt, a synthesis
  by the staff of GOLF DIGEST, Spring 1950.

Personality feature: Jackie Burke Jr.,
  Spring 1950

Swing sequence: Sam Snead, Summer 1950

Putting sequence: Lloyd Mangrum,
  Spring 1950

Photo credit: "Acme Photo," for picture of
  Ben Hogan, Spring 1950

Celebrity name: Bing Crosby, Spring 1950

Cartoon: Spring 1950

Jimmy Demaret hat shot: Summer 1950

Women's instructional tip: Spring 1950

Equipment piece: How to Buy Golf Clubs,
  Early Spring 1951

Letters column: Early Summer 1951

Nationwide distribution: May 1952

Contents page: May 1952

Travel article: Pinehurst, May 1952

Doug Sanders, August 1952

Mickey Wright, December 1952

Ken Venturi, June 1953

Judy (Torluemke) Rankin, September 1953,
  won National Pee Wee Golf

Most Improved Male Award:
  February/March 1954

Harvey Penick, May 1954

Arnold Palmer, December/January 1954

Most Improved Female Award:
  February/March 1955

Performance Average Rating: April 1955

Reader survey: August 1955

Bob Toski instructional piece:
  December/January 1955

Annual issue: March 1956

Amateur rankings: March 1956

JoAnne Gunderson, March 1956

Dan Jenkins, May 1956

Jack Nicklaus, Dec/Jan/Feb 1956

Moe Norman, Dec/Jan/Feb 1956

Gary Player: March 1957

Arnold Palmer on cover: August 1957
  (shared with Wiffi Smith)

Jack Nicklaus picture: March 1958

Kathy Whitworth: March 1958

Bill Stewart, Payne's father: March 1958

Dave Marr: April 1958

Titanic Thompson: June 1958

Insert subscription card: July 1958

Jack Lumpkin: July 1958

Year and month on cover: August 1958

Davis Love Jr.: September 1958

Howard Gill subscription letter:
  November 1958

Rookie of the Year Award: November 1958

Booklet offered with subscription: "6 lessons
  from Johnny Revolta," March 1959

Carol Mann: March 1959

100,000 circulation: July 1959

Full golf hole picture: Minneapolis Golf
  Club, November 1959

One dollar issue: February 1960 annual

Dave Stockton: February 1960

Harvey Penick piece: May 1960

Byron Nelson booklet: July 1960

Publisher's Scorecard column: August 1960

Ray Floyd: November 1960

Bob Charles: February 1961

Arnold Palmer swing sequence: Feb. 1961

Records and Rarities listing: February 1961

Billy Graham: May 1961

Jay Sigel: October 1961

Full year of 12 issues: 1962

Advent of color pictures: January 1962

Jack Nicklaus swing sequence: January 1962

The Digest: February 1962

Eddie Pearce: October 1962

Places to Play: December 1962

Hale Irwin: February 1963

Jack Nicklaus instruction: February 1963

Tom Weiskopf: February 1963

First major piece on Big 3 of Palmer,
  Nicklaus and Player: July 1963

Lanny Wadkins: September 1963

Fairway Fables title: October 1963

Henry Longhurst: September 1964

Johnny Miller: October 1964

Tom Strange: February 1965

Joe Dey rules column: April 1965

Gatefold: July 1965

Nick Seitz article: December 1966

Article Reprint service: December 1966

Renee Powell: February 1966

Lee Trevino: February 1966

John Elliott: March 1966

Walt Zembriski: September 1966

Mancil Davis: November 1966

John Brodie: November 1966

Laura Baugh: December 1966

Joey Sindelar: December 1966

Nancy Lopez: January 1967

Jim McLean: February 1967

Andy North: February 1967

Gatefold cover: Titleist ad, May 1967

Tom Kite: October 1967

Jim Flick: January 1968

Pat Bradley: February 1968

Ben Crenshaw: February 1968

Tom Watson: February 1968

Mac O'Grady (Philip McGleno): July 1968

Gil Morgan: August 1968

African-American on cover: Lee Elder,
  December 1968

Bruce Lietzke: January 1969

African-American in ad: Lee Elder,
  May 1969

Lee Trevino on cover: June 1969

Use of illustrations for instruction pieces:
  June 1968 (photos used until this time)

Joe Jemsek: September 1969

Anthony Ravielli art for one-page instruction:
  September 1969

Dave Anderson piece: October 1969

Double gatefold: Florida boom,
  December 1969

Ad insert: William Joyce shoes, June 1958

Metal wood ad: March 1981

Tiger Woods: November 1981

Canadian and UK prices on cover:
  July 1983

Web address on cover: May 1997

Golf Digest A word from our sponsors

Date listed is the first ad run in GOLF DIGEST.

Acushnet/Titleist, February 1954

Acushnet putters, March 1957

Adjustable club, April 1963

Air-conditioned cap, May 1961

All-Star Glove with Arnold Palmer, January 1962

Amana, September 1969

Big 3 golf on TV, February 1965

Browning Bag Boy, April 1960

Buick, July 1962

Bulls Eye, July 1957

Cadillac, November 1963

Carling Black Label, September 1964

Champion glove, May 1956

Cushman cars, May 1955; with Ben Hogan, March 1958

Distance ball wars, Spalding, Sept. 1957

Doral, December 1961

Dunlop Maxfli, July 1953

Early Times Whiskey, August 1967

Eastern Air Lines, December 1962

Etonic, June 1953

Eyeball balls, December 1961

E-Z-Go, August 1955

Faultless with Lee Trevino, April 1969

Fiberglass shaft, May 1955

First golf school ad, Cyril Wagner, Oct. 1957

Foot-Joy, May 1953

Ford cars, September 1964

Golf gadgets, October 1960

Golf Genie, December 1953

GolfPride, July 1953

Gone with the Wind, December 1967

Haig Ultra, May 1958

Harley-Davidson golf cars, November 1962

Hogan, January 1962

Ben Hogan Roll-out Golf Green, May 1953

Hogan ball, August 1961

Hogan clubs, October 1968

Hogan golf shoes, June 1958

Hush Puppy, February 1968

Izod, July 1960

Jamaica golf, December 1961

Jantzen sportswear, June 1960

Jockey with Tony Lema, May 1965

Johnson & Johnson baby powder, July 1967

Kent cigarettes, September 1965

Lamkin grip, June 1961

Lazy Bones shoes, March 1966

Lifesavers hole-in-one trophy ad, September 1964

MacGregor first ad with Nicklaus, October 1962

MacGregor, May 1953

Maxfli ball, February 1962

George May ads, early 1950s issues

Mercedes Benz, November 1963

Mercury with Arnold Palmer sweepstakes, June 1967

Miller High Life, first beer ad, May 1955

Munsingwear, April 61

Nadco pullcart, July 1958

Newport, first cigarette ad, January 1964

Jack Nicklaus *Golf is My Game* book, December 1960

Old Hickory bourbon, March 1958

Arnie's Own, July 1968

Arnold Palmer aluminum shafts, March 1968

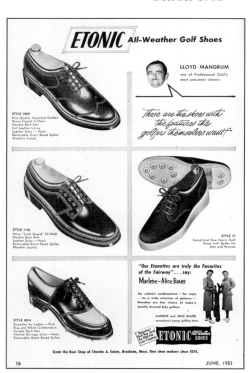

The first advertisement run in GOLF DIGEST was in the first issue, Spring 1950. It was for Gene Sarazen's book Thirty Years of Championship Golf.

Etonic has been making shoes since 1876 and advertising in GOLF DIGEST since June 1953.

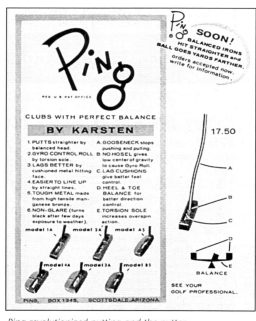

GOLF DIGEST ran this Miller High Life ad in May 1955. It was the first beer advertisement in the magazine.

Ping revolutionized putting and the putter industry, running its first ad in the February 1961 issue of GOLF DIGEST.

Arnold Palmer golf clubs, April 1964

Arnold Palmer golf shoes, June 61

Arnold Palmer Indoor Schools, April 1966

Arnold Palmer enterprises, April 1966

Arnold Palmer putters, September 1964

Arnold Palmer sportswear, May 1962

Pan Am, December 1961

Paper tee, December 1957

Pepsi, August 1963

Pinehurst Resort, December 1955

Ping, December 1961

Gary Player driving net, July 61

Pontiac, December 1964

PowerBilt, May 1953

Ram ball, May 1959

Rangefinder model, December 1961

Ray Bans with Arnold Palmer, July 1969

RCA record club, March 1969

Rolex, May 1964

Seagrams whiskey, June 1968

Sears golf cart, May 1956

See-brella, May 1961

7-Up, May 1967

Shag bag, September 1957

Shell Wonderful World of Golf, February 1965

Kenneth Smith, March 1960

Spalding clubs, April 1954

Spalding ball, June 1953

Spalding Dot, May 1954

Steel-centered ball, July 1958

Teacher's Highland Cream, first whiskey ad, June 1954

Titleist ball, July 1958

True Temper shafts, May 1956

United Air Lines, first airline ad, October 1960

U.S. Rubber, December 1955

Victory grip, November 1957

Wham-O practice tee, December 1957

Wilson, May 1953

Wilson with Arnold Palmer, July 1958

Wilson ball with Arnold Palmer, July 1960

Wilson with Billy Casper, June 1967

Wilson Staff, November 1963

Top Left: *From this ad, the first by Buick in July 1962, it would seem as though you could drive out of the worst bunker lie imaginable.*

Left: *An early E-Z-Go golf cart debuts in October 1960*

Above: *Spalding hatched this marketing campaign in June 1960*

Top right: *The Ben Hogan Co. started marketing its clubs to the largest golf audience in March 1970.*

Right: *Golf may never go out of style—but some of its fashion might.*

 # Editorial Staff 1950–1999

Titles and the staffers who filled them, listed chronologically

EDITORIAL DIRECTOR: Ken Bowden, Nick Seitz, Jerry Tarde

EDITOR: William H. Davis, John Barnett, Howard R. Gill, Richard Aultman, Nick Seitz, Jerry Tarde

EDITOR IN CHIEF: William H. Davis, Nick Seitz

EDITOR IN CHIEF EMERITUS AND FOUNDER: William H. Davis

CHAIRMAN EMERITUS AND COFOUNDER: Howard R. Gill Jr.

EXECUTIVE EDITOR: Dick Aultman, Nick Seitz, John R. McDermott, Jerry Tarde, Roger Schiffman

MANAGING EDITOR: Gordon E. Smith, John P. May, Larry Sheehan, Jay Simon, Roger Schiffman, Lisa Furlong, Mike O'Malley

ASSISTANT MANAGING EDITOR: Roger Schiffman, Guy Yocom, Cliff Schrock

SENIOR EDITOR: John P. May, Larry Dennis, Dwayne Netland, Jerry Tarde, Ross Goodner, Peter Andrews, Lew Fishman, Robert Carney, Don Wade, Jaime Diaz, Chris Hodenfield, Peter McCleery, John Huggan, John Barton, Guy Yocom, Mike O'Malley, Ed Weathers, Scott Smith

SENIOR WRITER: Guy Yocom, Pete McDaniel, Bob Verdi, Tom Callahan, Dave Kindred

EDITOR AT LARGE: Nick Seitz

WRITER AT LARGE: Dan Jenkins

FEATURES EDITOR: Nick Seitz

ASSOCIATE EDITOR: Dick Aultman, Gerald J. Pfarr, William D. Brooks, Leo Coughlin, Larry Sheehan, Cal Brown, Nick Seitz, Larry Dennis, Hubert Mizell, Dwayne Netland, Marven Moss, Ross Goodner, Don Wade, Jerry Tarde, Roger Schiffman, Robert Carney, Peter McCleery, Guy Yocom, John Huggan, Lois Hains, John Barton, Mike Stachura, Liz Comte Reisman, Topsy Siderowf, Scott Smith, Hunki Yun, John Strege

ASSISTANT EDITOR: Gloria Luchenbill, Kathy Jonah, Jeff Pomerantz, James McAfee, Jerry Tarde, Nick Romano, Peter McCleery, Lois Hains, Geoff Russell, Lorin Anderson, Topsy Siderowf, Mike Stachura, Hunki Yun, Matthew Rudy

INSTRUCTION EDITOR: Billy Casper, Robert Carney, John Huggan

TECHNICAL AND ADMINISTRATIVE EDITOR: Larry Dennis

CHIEF TECHNICAL EDITOR: Lew Fishman

EQUIPMENT EDITOR: Ed Weathers, Peter Farricker

TECHNICAL EDITOR: J. Victor East, John W. Baymiller, Guy Yocom, Art Chou

ART DIRECTOR: Irwin J. Lilla, John Scussel, Walter Skibitsky, Richard Ference, Ron Meyerson, John Newcomb, Pete Libby, Nick DiDio

ASSOCIATE ART DIRECTOR: John Kennedy, Gretchen Bruno, Nancy Graham, Al Nakas, Mary Lou Newman

ASSISTANT ART DIRECTOR: David C. Folkman, Pete Libby, Dorothy Geiser, Kim Miller, Lori Bruzinski, Kathleen Burke, Al Nakas, John Meier, Doug Wheeler

ART ASSOCIATE: Richard M. Ference, John Meier

ART ASSISTANT: Barbara Bell, David C. Folkman, Andrea Flagg, Laura Duggan

EUROPEAN EDITOR: Ken Bowden

GOLF DIGEST SPECIAL PROJECTS/EXECUTIVE EDITOR: Robert Carney

CHIEF OF RESEARCH: Hope Johnson, Kathy Stachura

RESEARCHER: Topsy Siderowf

COPY EDITOR: Hope Johnson, Melissa Yow

EDITORIAL PROJECT COORDINATOR: Sue Sawyer

EDITORIAL ADMINISTRATOR: Pat Richards, Jan Costello, Hillary Common, Sharan Smith, Kathleen Stachura, Pam Lato, Lorraine Blohm

EDITORIAL ASSISTANT: Caroline Stevens, Maureen Hickey, Patricia Warner, Ann Eden, Linda Lind, Joanne Graham, Barbara Kelly, Francine Delphia, Sue Glover, Nancy Morris, Lois Hains, Lynne Trout, Joan Urban, Dan Lockwood, Venetia Demson, Susan Irvine, Pat Sosnowski, Pat Richards, Carole Bogdany, Hope Johnson, Susan Irvine Smayda, Susan Malizia, Jan Van Munching, Rick Walter, Penny Sippel, Hillary Common, Elaine Conti, Mary Jane McGirr, Topsy Siderowf, Karen Bairstow, Margaret Farnsworth, M. Kathryn Wright-Stook, Larry Cafero, Laurie Arsenault, Chris Jerman, Joanne Wlodarczyk, Lisa Sweet, Gail McGarry, Melissa Lausten, Pam Lato, Tlona Coward

SENIOR STAFF PHOTOGRAPHER: Steve Szurlej

STAFF PHOTOGRAPHER: Steve Szurlej, Larry Petrillo, Dom Furore

ARCHITECTURE EDITOR: Ron Whitten

FASHION EDITOR: Barbi Zinner, Eileen Rafferty Broderick

FASHION DIRECTOR: Rose Mary Strafaci, Polly Noe

FASHION AND WOMEN'S ACTIVITIES CONSULTANT: Jane Stark

ASSISTANT FASHION EDITOR: Maureen Hickey

EDITOR GOLF DIGEST WOMAN: Liz Comte Reisman, Rona Cherry

WOMEN'S GOLF EDITOR: Sharron Moran

CONTRIBUTING EDITOR: Jerry Claussen, Lincoln A. Werden, Larry Sheehan, Ken Bowden, Dick Aultman, Hubert Mizell, Peter Dobereiner, Dave Anderson, Frank Beard, Dave Marr, Charles Price, Jolee Edmondson, Peter Andrews, Mickey Herskowitz, Jay Simon, Dan Jenkins, Ron Whitten, John May, Marino Parascenzo, Peter Thomson, Barry McDermott, Tom Callahan, Joseph C. Dey, Jaime Diaz, Marcia Chambers, Frank Hannigan, Robert Green, Dwayne Netland, Michael Bamberger, Ross Goodner, Bud Shrake, Dave Kindred, Larry Dorman, Lew Fishman, David Owen, Don Wade, John Huggan, Michael M. Thomas, Lisa Furlong, Dean Knuth

CONTRIBUTING ARTIST: Anthony Ravielli, James McQueen, Stan Drake, David Harbaugh, Elmer Wexler, Marcus Hamilton, Paul Szep, M. Greg Rudd, Roy Doty, Dom Lupo, Ed Acuna, Paul Lipp

CONTRIBUTING PHOTOGRAPHER: Anthony Roberts, Brian Morgan, Jim Moriarty

CONTRIBUTING WRITER/PHOTOGRAPHER: Jim Moriarty

EDITORS ON TOUR: Deane Beman, Dave Stockton, Lincoln A. Werden

CHIEF PLAYING EDITOR: Jack Nicklaus

PLAYING EDITOR: Sharron Moran, Billy Casper, Dave Stockton, Frank Beard, Lanny Wadkins, Jack Nicklaus, Al Geiberger, Jerry Pate, Tom Watson, Sam Snead, Hale Irwin, Nancy Lopez, Gary Player, Andy Bean, David Graham, Tom Kite, Amy Alcott, JoAnne Carner, Hal Sutton, Patty Sheehan, Bernhard Langer, Peter Thomson, Seve Ballesteros, Paul Azinger, Nick Faldo, Mark O'Meara, Nick Price, Phil Mickelson, Jane Crafter, Meg Mallon, Ernie Els, Gary McCord, Tiger Woods, Justin Leonard, Johnny Miller, Wendy Ward, Liselotte Neumann, Se Ri Pak, Bob Duval

SENIOR PLAYING EDITOR: Sam Snead

SENIORS' GOLF EDITOR: Sam Snead

PROFESSIONAL TEACHING PANEL: Horton Smith, Paul Runyan, Cary Middlecoff, Johnny Revolta, Jackson Bradley, Sam Snead, Eddie Merrins, John Jacobs, Jim Flick, Bob Toski, Davis Love Jr., Peter Kostis, DeDe Owens, Gary Wiren

TEACHING PROFESSIONALS/GOLF DIGEST SCHOOLS: Dick Aultman, John Elliott, Jim Flick, Hank Jonson, Peter Kostis, Davis Love Jr., Jack Lumpkin, Tom Ness, DeDe Owens, Paul Runyan, Bob Toski, Chuck Cook, Scott Davenport, Andy Nusbaum, Dick Drager, Tim Mahoney, Tom Paxson, Mark Wood, Charlie Epps, Gale Peterson, Todd Anderson, Mike LaBauve, Sandy LaBauve, Jim Goergen, Mark Winkley, Connie DeMattia, Don Hurter, Josh Zander

TEACHING PROFESSIONALS: Janet Coles, Jim McLean, Kay McMahon, Todd Anderson, John Elliott, Tom Ness, Hank Johnson, Josh Zander

PROFESSIONAL ADVISORY STAFF: Betsy Rawls, Cary Middlecoff, Frank Beard, Dave Marr, Byron Nelson, Sam Snead, DeDe Owens, Dr. Bob Rotella, Don Greene, Peter Kostis, David Leadbetter, Bill Mallon, Jim Flick, Dean Reinmuth, Bob Toski, Hank Haney, Johnny Miller, Harvey Penick, Paul Runyan, Hank Johnson, Butch Harmon, Judy Rankin, Renee Powell, Rick Smith, Randy Smith

ART DIRECTOR/GOLF DIGEST WOMAN: Kathleen Felix, Jennifer Cole

MANAGER, LIBRARY RESOURCES: Mary Rung

TECHNICAL ADVISORS/EQUIPMENT PANEL: Robin Arthur, Bob Bush, John Calabria, Art Chou, Dan Kubica, Howard Lindsay, Clay Long, Gene Parente, Dick Rugge, Carl Scheie, Tom Stites, Mike Sullivan, Harry Taylor, Tom Wishon

STAFF STATISTICIAN: Sal Johnson

ON-LINE PRODUCER: Jack Russell, Roy Astar

PRESIDENT: William H. Davis

PUBLISHERS: Howard R. Gill, John Barnett, William H. Davis, James FitzGerald, David Ferm, Tom Brown

ASSOCIATE PUBLISHER: Paul Menneg, John R. McDermott

Golf Digest Contributors

DAVE ANDERSON's column, "Sports of the Times," won the 1981 Pulitzer Prize for distinguished commentary, capping a 50-year-career in New York sports journalism, which continues to this day. He joined GOLF DIGEST as a regular contributor in 1973.

PETER ANDREWS has written for nearly every major magazine in America, including *Playboy*, *Esquire* and *American Heritage*. He is the author of several histories, including *A Reluctant Hero*, the story of World War I hero, Sgt. Alvin York. He has been a regular contributor to GOLF DIGEST since 1984.

The holder of 11 PGA Tour and one Senior PGA Tour victories, FRANK BEARD is one of golf's most articulate player-commentators. He authored a GOLF DIGEST column from 1970 to 1983, and still contributes occasional columns to *Golf World*.

CAL BROWN brought his intellectualized sense of humor, honed from an education on the streets of Chicago and at Princeton and from playing money games on golf courses around the world, to GOLF DIGEST in 1967. He was an Associate Editor of the magazine until 1975.

A GOLF DIGEST Contributing Editor since 1984, TOM CALLAHAN was the columnist or chief sports writer at various times for the Big 3—*Time*, *Newsweek* and *U.S. News and World Report*.

MARCIA CHAMBERS, long-time legal affairs reporter for the *New York Times* Sports Section, has been Contributing Editor to GOLF DIGEST since 1989. Her golf coverage awards include the Silver Gavel Award for Outstanding Public Service from the American Bar Association and the Silurian Award for Best News Feature Story from the Deadline Club of New York.

From 1965 to 1995, PETER DOBEREINER was arguably the best-read writer in golf, with more than 200 million readers of the *Manchester Guardian*, the *London Observer*, and from 1978, GOLF DIGEST. He was a deft, erudite writer whose witty and wise essays place him in the pantheon of Bernard Darwin, Henry Longhurst and Pat Ward-Thomas. He died in 1996 at the age of 70.

FRANK HANNIGAN spent 28 years with the U.S. Golf Association, beginning as public information manager and rising to senior executive director. Since 1989 he has served ABC Sports as rules interpreter and commentator. His contributions to GOLF DIGEST began in the 1970s. His memoir, *Guilty of Golf*, is due out later in 2000.

A sports columnist for the *Houston Chronicle*, MICKEY HERSKOWITZ is the author of more than 30 books, including collaborations with Dan Rather, Howard Cosell, Mickey Mantle and Tom Kite. Herskowitz made his first contribution to GOLF DIGEST in 1975.

After 23 years at *Sports Illustrated*, DAN JENKINS joined GOLF DIGEST in 1984, writing a monthly column and essays on the major championships. Jenkins is the author of 16 books, including such classics as *Semi Tough*, *Dead Solid Perfect* and *Baja Oklahoma*. His countless awards and honors include admission into the Texas Golf Hall of Fame alongside friends Ben Hogan, Dave Marr and Byron Nelson.

DAVE KINDRED has a distinguished career as a sports writer during which he has won the Red Smith Award for career achievement in sports journalism (1991) and the National Sportswriter of the Year (1997). Kindred is a leading columnist for *The Sporting News* and joined GOLF DIGEST as a Senior Writer in 1997.

Teacher to the game's great players, including Nick Faldo, Nick Price and Ernie Els, DAVID LEADBETTER is golf's leading swing guru. He is author of numerous books, including *The Golf Swing*, and the owner of a worldwide chain of instruction schools. He joined the Golf Digest Pro Panel in 1991.

A former member of Parliament who took up golf in his teens, HENRY LONGHURST gained more fame as a writer and broadcaster of the game than major winners do. He wrote 21 years for London's *Sunday Times*, moved to the *Evening Standard* and became a broadcaster both in the U.K. and the U.S. He wrote a GOLF DIGEST column from 1970 to 1976.

The "Pro from 52nd Street" was a GOLF DIGEST contributor and columnist throughout his career as a player—DAVE MARR was the 1965 PGA champion—and TV commentator, for ABC, the BBC and NBC. As elegant a writer as he was a commentator, Marr died in 1997 at age 63.

Formerly deputy editor of *The New Yorker*, CHARLES MCGRATH is now editor of *The New York Times Book Review*. He is a frequent contributor to *The New York Times Magazine*, writes often about golf and hockey and, since 1995, has been a contributor to GOLF DIGEST.

DWAYNE NETLAND joined GOLF DIGEST as an Associate Editor in 1974, after 17 years as golf editor of the *Minneapolis Tribune*. A semi-pro baseball player, who took up golf as a college student, Netland served as Travel Editor and Features Editor during his tenure at GOLF DIGEST.

DAVID OWEN is a Contributing Editor to GOLF DIGEST who also writes regularly for *The New Yorker*. A former Contributing Editor to *Atlantic Monthly* and Senior Writer for *Harper's*, Owen has written and edited several books on golf including *My Usual Game* and *The Making of the Masters: Clifford Roberts, Augusta National, & the World's Most Prestigious Tournament*.

The author of the game's most famous instruction books, beginning with the *Little Red Book* in

1992, HARVEY PENICK was mentor to some of the game's greats, including Tom Kite and Ben Crenshaw. After more than 70 years on the practice tee, Penick died in 1996.

One of golf's great raconteurs, CHARLES PRICE contributed stories and columns to GOLF DIGEST from 1982 until his death in 1994. The author of the *World of Golf* and *Golfer At Large*, Price was founding editor of *Golf Magazine* in 1959 and later a frequent contributor to *Golf World*. He was a close friend and authority on Bob Jones.

Sports Pyschologist BOB ROTELLA has counseled some of the game's great players, including Nick Price, Pat Bradley, Tom Kite and Davis Love. The former Director of Sports Psychology at the University of Virginia, Rotella is the author of *Golf is Not a Game of Perfect*, and *Golf is a Game of Confidence*. He is a consultant to professional teams and corportions around the country.

NICK SEITZ joined GOLF DIGEST in 1967 and became Editor in 1973, growing the magazine's circulation from less than 500,000 to more than a million. The author of many books and scripts about the sport, he was ESPN's first golf analyst. His work has won twelve annual Best Sports Stories awards. He retired as Editorial Director of the New York Times Co. Magazine Group in 1998.

JERRY TARDE joined GOLF DIGEST in 1977 as an intern and became Editor in 1984, at the age of 28. He has won writing awards for Best Newspaper Features, *The New York Times* (1988 and 1990) and Best Magazine Columns, GOLF DIGEST (1997).

The winner of more than 100 golf tournaments around the world, including five British Opens, PETER THOMSON is also one of the game's great spokesmen and statesmen. His columns and commentary appeared in GOLF DIGEST from 1971 to 1996.

The father of modern golf instruction, BOB TOSKI has contributed to GOLF DIGEST since 1955. As a player Toski won five tournaments, including the World Golf Championship, but he built a career on being able to teach both the game's both best pros and worst amateurs. In 1971 he founded the Golf Digest Schools with Jim Flick.

RON WHITTEN has served as Architecture Editor since 1985. Prior to joining GOLF DIGEST, Whitten practiced law in Topeka, Kan., for 12 years. He received the Donald Ross Award in 1996 from the American Society of Golf Course Architects.

The man who coined the phrase, "Amen Corner," HERBERT WARREN WIND is golf's leading essayist and historian. A longtime writer for *The New Yorker*, Wind's first contribution to GOLF DIGEST was his seminal treatise on golf course architecture in 1966.

I N D E X

Page numbers in *italics* refer to illustrations.

Aberdeen G.&C.C., Boynton Beach, Fla., 98, 109, *110, 111*
Adams, John, 91
Aitchison, Willie, 176
Alcott, Amy, 66
All-American Golf Tournament, *83*
Allenby, Robert, 90
Alliss, Peter, 100
Anderson, Dave, *114*, 174-177
Anderson, Willie, 168
Andrews, Peter, 16-21, 39-42, 114, 130, 194-197
Appleby, Renay White, 127-128, *128*
Appleby, Stuart, 127-128, *128*
Armour, Tommy, 91, 115, 135, 168
Augusta National G.C., Augusta, Ga., 12, 13, *16*, 16-17, *17*, *18*, 19, *20-21*, 31, 58, 106, *112-113*, 116, 125-126, 156-159, *160-161*, *162-164*, 162-164
Aultman, Dick, 64, 69-71
Austin, Debbie, 140, 141
Austin, Woody, 90
Azinger, Paul, 124, 157

Bader, Sir Douglas, 9
Baker-Finch, Ian, 100, 183-184
Ballesteros, Severiano, 54-55, 100, 114, 118, 124, 125, 130, 156, *160*, 167, 185
Ballybunion, Ireland, 12, 13, *23*, 23
Bamberger, David, 206, 208-209
Barber, Miller, 90, 138
Barnett, Jack, *8*, 8, 9
Barry, Mike, 124
Baugh, Laura, 140, 188, 190
Beard, Frank, 114, 116, *116*, 180
Beck, Chip, 90
Bel-Air C.C., Los Angeles, Calif., 192, 210-211
Beman, Deane, 120, 125, 130, 185, 195
Bennett, Dean, 201
Berganio, David, Jr., 81, *81*
Berning, Susan, 141
Beverage, Charlie, 151
Blalock, Jane, 140
Blanda, George, 147
Bolt, Tommy, 101, 191
Bondeson, Paul, 57
Boomer, Percy, 90
Boros, Julius, 60, 91, 157, 168-169, *169*
Bowden, Ken, 60-61
Braddock, Evelyn, 103
Bradshaw, Jan, 212, *212*
Brewer, Gay, 181
Briggs, J. L., 206, 207
British Open, 154-155, 171-177, 180-181
  1951, 25
  1972, *174*, 174-177
  1986, 185
  1988, 184
  1990, 184
  1991, 183-184
  1993, 183
  1994, *173*
  1995, 183
  1996, 182-183
  1999, 12, 182
Brown, Cal, 28-32
Brown, John Y., 149
Burke, Jack, Jr., 101-103, 117, 137
Burns, George, 44

Calcavecchia, Mark, 90
Callahan, Tom, 36-37, 114, 124, *124*, 130, 136-139
Callaway, Ely, 100
Campbell, Bill, 170
Carney, Robert, 206
Carnoustie, Scotland, 12, *172*
Carr, Simon, Rev., 36
Casa de Campo, Dominican Republic, *12*
Casper, Billy, 29, 90, 145, 159, *170*, 178, *190*, 190
Cedarbrook Club, Old Brookville, N.Y., 212
Chambers, Marcia, 206, 210-215
Chandler, Happy, 124
Chapman, Dick, 28
Chen, Tze-Chung, 185
Chirkinian, Frank, 138-139
Clampett, Bobby, 130
Clark, Tom, 201
Colbert, Jim, 91, 107, 124
Coles, Neil, 118
Congressional C.C., Bethesda, Md., *14*
Coody, Charlie, 108
Cook, Kevin, 130
Cooke, Alistair, 157
Cosell, Howard, *106*, 106, 179
County Louth (Baltray), Ireland, 24
Couples, Fred, 154
Crampton, Bruce, 179-180
Crenshaw, Ben, 62, 119, 124, 157, 158, 183
Crosby, Bing, 30, 47, 117, 188, 189, 192, *193*
  Bing Crosby National Pro-Am, 28
  1949, 31
  1963, 29
  1964, 29
  1968, 30
Crump, George, 36
Cypress Point C., Pebble Beach, Calif, 12, 17, 23, 28, *28*, 31-32, *32*, 43, 45, *46-47*, 106

Dahlby, Steve, 81
Dallemagne, Marcel, 89
Daly, John, 52, 53, 102-103, *103*, 157, 183, *185*
Danecki, Walter, 171-172
Daniel, Beth, 91, 109
Darwin, Bernard, 37, 52
Davenport, Scott, *51*
Davies, Laura, 91
Davis, Darwin, 213, 214
Davis, William H., *8*, 8, 9, 12, 188
Dawson, Johnny, 28
Del Monte Forest, Calif., 28, 30
Demaret, Jimmy, 12, 19, 32, 117, 131
Dennis, Larry, 80-82
De Vicenzo, Roberto, 188
Devlin, Thomas R., 149
Dey, Joe, 31, *106*, 106, 138, 166
Dickinson, Gardner, 132, 135
Dickinson, Jimmy, 176
Dobereiner, Peter, 9, 22-25, 114, *114*, *118*, 118-119, 130, 154, 171-173
Donovan, Dale, *209*
Douglass, Dale, 29
Dromoland, Ireland, 23
Drum, Bob, *143*, 143-146, 191, *191*
Dudley, Ed, 82
Duval, David, 91, 98
Dye, Peter, 12, 198

Eagle Creek, Naples, Fla., 138
Egan, Chandler, 28
Eggeling, Dale, 90
Eisenhower, Dwight D., 156, 188, 206
Elder, Lee, 159
Elkington, Steve, 90
Elliott, John, *50*, 64, 65
Els, Ernie, 90, 130, 156, 166, 183
Estes, Bob, 91
Evans, Chick, 28

Faldo, Nick, 101, 118, 124, 167, 183, *185*
Faulkner, Max, 25
Fazio, Tom, 35, 36
Feherty, David, 110
Fezler, Forest, 30
Finsterwald, Dow, 146, 181
Fleck, Jack, 60, 143, 188, 191
Flick, Jim, 53, 80
Flitcroft, Maurice, *171*, 171-173
Floyd, Ray, 138
Forman, Ronald, 212
Furgol, Ed, 52

Gallagher, Jim, Jr., 90
Galway Bay, Ireland, *24-25*
Gibson, Leland (Duke), 59
Gill, Howard R., Jr., 8, *9*
Goalby, Bob, 131, 135
Goodman, Johnny, 28
Goodner, Ross, 163
Grant, Douglas, 27, 28
Green, Ken, 130
Greystone G.C., Romeo, Mich., 12
Grout, Jack, 104

Hagen, Walter, 49, 55, 114, 115, 135, 168, *168*, 169
Hall, Charlie, 89
Hannigan, Frank, 114, 165-170
Hardin, Hord, 125-126, *126*
Harlow, Bob, 135
Harmon, Butch, 78, 84
Harmon, Claude, 43, 44, *84*, 84-85, 135
Harris, Allen, 86
Harris, Phil, *193*
Harris, Robert, 129
Havlicek, John, 45
Heard, Jerry, 180
Hebert, Lionel, 181
Hemmer, John, 34
Hendrix, Johnny, 144
Herbert, Ross, 127
Herskowitz, Mickey, 130
Hill, Dave, 180
Hills, Arthur, 201-202
Hinkle, Lon, 124
Hogan, Ben, 8, 12, 31, 36, 43, 45, 49, 53, 55, 57, 60, 62, *68*, 68, *72-74*, 80, *90*, 91, *97*, 98, 107, 108, 114, 117, *130, 131*, 131-135, *132*, 133, *134*, 137, 139, 143, 144, *146*, 156, 159, *165*, *166*, 166, 168, 191
Hogan, Valerie, *132*
Hollins, Marion, 31
Hope, Bob, 142, *189*, 192
Hoskins, Clayton, 17
Huggan, John, 92-95

Inkster, Juli, 90-91
Inman, Joe, 148-149

Ireland, Kelly, 194-197
Irwin, Hale, 157, 169, *170*
Iverson, Becky, 91

Jacklin, Tony, 91, 104, *174*, 174-177
Jacobus, George, 82
Jamieson, Jim, 180
January, Don, 138
Jenkins, Dan, *114*, 114, *123*, 123, 130, 143-146, 155, 182-185, 191
Johnson, Hank, 52
Johnson, Leslie (Johnny), 16
Johnston, Harrison, 28
Jones, Bobby, 21, 28, 31, 48, 49, 55-56, *72-74*, *88*, 88-89, 104, 115, 116, 121-122, *122*, 137, 143, 154, 156, 157, 159, *165*, *167*, 168, 170, 189, *209*
Jones, Grier, 180
Jones, Jack, 213, 214
Jones, Robert Trent, 23, 30, 31, 110, 165
Jordan, Michael, 53

Keeler, O.B., 143
Kelly, Claribel, 133
Kerdyk, Tracy, 91
Kessler, Kaye, 132, 143
Kieman, John, 36
Kindred, Dave, 114, *127*, 127-128, 156-159
Kite, Tom, 52, 62, 90, *102*, 102, 183
Knapp, Brooke, 210-211
Knight, Bobby, 147
Kostis, Peter, *51*, 53, 104
Kropiewnicki, Joe, 200

LaBauve, Mike, *50*, 64, 65
Lacey, Charles, 89
Laffoon, Ky, 82
Lahinch, Ireland, 23, 24
Lane, Barry, 91
Langer, Bernhard, 108, 118, 185
Laoretti, Larry, 90
Lapham, Roger, 31
Leadbetter, David, 68, 92-95, 104, 188
Lehman, Tom, 90
Lema, Tony, 60
Leonard, Justin, 90
Leonard, Marvin, 132
Lietzke, Bruce, 90
Little, Lawson, 28
Little, Sally, 140, 142
Littler, Gene, 36, 138, 143
Longhurst, Henry, 9, 25, 114, *115*, 115, 177, 206
Lopez, Domingo, *141*, 141, 142
Lopez, Mariana, 141, 142
Lopez, Nancy, 130, *140*, 140-142, *141*, *142*
Loudermilk, Hardy, 63
Love, Davis, III, 90, 99-100, *100*
Love, Davis, Jr., *50*, 52, 53, 82, 100
Lowell, Lee, 212
Lumpkin, Jack, *50*, 53, 64
Lye, Mark, 139
Lyle, Sandy, 118, 124, 185

Macdonald, C.B., 49
Mackenzie, Alister, 21, 26, 31, 47, 49, 116
Mackenzie, Keith, 172
Mahoney, Tim, *50-51*

Maiden, Stewart, 104
Mallon, Meg, 91
Maltbie, Roger, 91
Mangrum, Lloyd, 36, 117
Marr, Dave, 109, 114, *117*, 117,
   178-181, *179*, *180*
Marsh, Graham, 119
Marshall, Jean, 122
Masters Tournament, 16, 17, 116, 154,
   156-159, 162-164, 180-181
   1956, 136-137
   1958, 137, 163-164
   1960, 137
   1963, *61*
   1971, 108
   1984, 139
   1986, 124, 125
   1990, 184
   1992, 154
   1995, 183
   1996, 182
   1997, 182, *182*
Matthews, Jerry, 200
May, John, 53
Mayfair, Billy, 91
McCleery, Peter, 154-155
McCord, Gary, 156
McCormack, Mark, 145-146
McCumber, Mark, 91, 124
McDaniel, Pete, 78
McDermott, Johnnie, 169
McGrath, Charles, 33-35
McNamara, Dale, 142
McSpaden, Jugs, *96*
Melnyk, Steve, 180
Merion G.C., Ardmore, Pa., 8, 12, *48*,
   48-49, *49*, 108
Merrill, Hans, 32
Metz, Dick, 82
Mickelson, Phil, 90
Middlecoff, Cary, 53, 55, 56, 82,
   143
Miller, Johnny, 27, 108, 130, 143, 157
Mill River Club, Upper Brookville, N.Y.,
   215
Mize, Larry, 91, 174
Mizener, Addison, 45
Moody, Orville, 90, 108, 143, 175
Morgan, Dennis, 214
Morrison, Alex J., 90, 91
Morse, John, 90
Morse, Samuel F. B., 28, 30
Moss, Donald, 162
Mosser, Joel, 194-197
Muirfield, Scotland, 173-177, *192*, 192
Muirhead, Desmond, 98, 109-111
Murphy, Bob, 30, 91, 180
Myrtle Beach, S.C., 8

Nagle, Kel, 175
Nakajima, Tommy, 130, 185
Nary, Bill, 31
Nelson, Byron, 29, 53, 57, 71, 80-82,
   83, *97*, 103, 135, 137
Netland, Dwayne, 130, 140-142
Neville, Jack, 27, 28
Newton, Jack, 119
Nicklaus, Charlie, *99*
Nicklaus, Jack, 19, *19*, 27, 28, 31, 36,
   44, 52, 55-57, 60-61, 66, *67*, 67,
   75-77, *99*, 99, 101, 104, 108, 114,
   117, 118, *122*, 124, 125, 143, *145*,
   145, 154, 156, 168-170, *174*,
   174-177, 178, 179, 181, 185
Nicolette, Mike, 119
Nicoll, John, 40
Norman, Greg, 101, *101*, 114, 118-
   119, *119*, 124, 156, 157, 174,
   183, 185
North, Andy, 148, 167, 185

Oak Hill C.C., Rochester, N.Y., *14*
Oakley, Annie, 33
O'Connor, Christy, 118
O'Grady, Mac, 130, 188, 190
Old Head, Kinsale, Ireland, *22*
Oliver, Porky, 32
Olmsted, Frederick Law, 33-35
O'Malley, Mike, 188
O'Meara, Mark, 91
O'Neill, Tip, 53
Ouimet, Francis, 28
Owen, David, 114, *126*, 126
Owens, DeDe, *51*, 53

Packard, Larry, 138
Palmer, Arnold, 24, 29, *56*, 56,
   57, 60, 66, *72-74*, 114, 117,
   125, 126, 130, 137, 138, *143*,
   143-146, *144*, *145*, *146*, 148, 156,
   163-164, 169, *170*, 175, 178, 179,
   181, 191
Parascenzo, Marino, 130
Parnevik, Jesper, *190*
Patton, Billy Joe, 159
Pavin, Corey, 126
Pebble Beach G. Links, Calif., 12, 13,
   26-27, *28*, 28-31, *29*
Peete, Calvin, 90
Penick, Harvey, 52, 62-63
Peninsula G.&C.C., San Francisco,
   Calif., 210, 211
Percival, John, Jr., 201-202
Peskin, Hy, 8
Peterson, Gale, *50-51*
PGA Championship, 154, 155,
   178-181
   1986, 185
   1988, 185
   1989, 184
   1990, 184
   1991, 184
   1998, 182
Picard, Henry, 44
Pinehurst Resort & C.C. (No. 2), N.C.,
   12, *33*, 33-35, *34*, *35*, 43
Pine Valley G.C., N.J., 12, 13, *36*,
   36-37, *37*
Pittman, Jerry, 44
Player, Gary, 60, 100, 103, 124, 130,
   146, 156, 177, 179, 181
Portmarnock, Ireland, 24
Prairie Dunes C.C., Hutchinson, Kan.,
   14
Price, Charles, *114*, 114, *121*,
   121-122, 154, 161
Price, Nick, 90, 124, 157, *173*, 185
Pulford, Jack, 194-197

Quick, Smiley, 28
Quinn, Brennan, 130

Ransom, Henry, 32
Rarick, Cindy, 90
Renner, Jack, 120
Rice, Grantland, 168
Riegel, Skee, 28
Robbins, Kelly, 91
Roberts, Clifford, 16, 126, 137, 159
Rodriguez, Chi Chi, 91, 102
Rosburg, Bob, 28, 99, 144
Ross, Donald, 14, 33-35, 43, 44, 49
Rosses Point, Ireland, 23-24
Rotella, Bob, 66
Royal County Down, Ireland, *22*, 25
Royal Dublin, Ireland, 24
Royal Portrush, Ireland, 25
Runyan, Paul, 53, 64, 65
Russo, Marty, 149

Ruth, Babe, 37
Ryan, Allan, 43
Ryder Cup Matches, 98, 155
   1987, 185
   1993, 183
   1995, 183

St. Andrews, Scotland, 12, 13, *38*,
   39-42, *40-41*, *42*, *152-153*
Salinas, Albert, 100-101
Sanders, Doug, 181, 191
Sand Hills G.C., Mullen, Neb., *13*, 14
Sarazen, Gene, 57-58, *112*, 115, 156,
   159, 166, 168, *168*, 169
Schiffman, Roger, 130
Scully, Vin, 192
Seitz, Nick, 8, 98, 114, *129*, 129-135
Seminole G.C., N. Palm Beach, Fla., *43*,
   43-45, *44-45*, *46*
Senior, Pete, 90
Shady Oaks C.C., Fort Worth, Tex.,
   131-132
Sheely, Gene, 133-134
Shinnecock Hills G.C., Southampton,
   N.Y., *15*, 120, 165, 166
Shropshire, Tom, 213, 214
Sifford, Charlie, 159
Sigel, Jay, 90
Simpson, Scott, 185
Singh, Vijay, 90
Sligo, Ireland, 23
Sluman, Jeff, 185
Smith, Alex, 169
Smith, Macdonald, 169
Smith, Scott, 98, 111
Smith, Willie, 169
Snead, J.C., 130, *147*, 147-151, *148*
Snead, Sam, 8, 53-60, 69, *96*, 98,
   106-107, *112*, 115, 125, *129*, 129,
   137, 143, 144, 147-151, *148*, *169*,
   169-170
Snead, Sue Bryant, 147, *148*, 150
Souchak, Mike, 144
Spagnolo, Angelo, 188, *194*, 194-199,
   196
Spander, Art, 143
Spyglass Hill G. Cse., Pebble Beach,
   Calif., *28*, 28, 30-31, *31*
Stachura, Mike, 72, 77
Stacy, Hollis, 142
Stadler, Craig, 101, 107
Stephens, Jack, 159
Stephenson, Jan, 110
Stewart, Payne, 52, 90, *155*, 183
Stewart, Walter, 143
Stone Harbor G.C., Cape May, N.J. 110
Stout, Bill, 89
Stranahan, Frank, 28
Strange, Curtis, 139, 157, 167, *185*
Summerall, Pat, 138, 139
Sutton, Hal, 90
Swann, Lynn, 45
Sycamore Hills G.C., Fort Wayne, Ind.,
   10-11

Tarde, Jerry, 9, 114, *125*, 125-126
Tewell, Doug, 17
Thacker, Frank, 30
Thomson, Peter, 109, 114, 119, *120*,
   120
Tillinghast, A.W., 49
Tolley, Cyril, 28, 89
Toski, Bob, *51*, 53, 69-71, 104, *105*
Tournament Players Club at Sawgrass,
   Ponte Vedra Beach, Fla., 120, *120*,
   194, 194-197, *198-199*
Trevino, Lee, 58-59, 66, *67*, 67, 86-87,
   100, 100-102, 108, 141, 144, 157,
   169, *170*, *174*, 174-177, 181

Tschetter, Kris, 91
Tufts, James Walker, 33, 34
Tufts, Richard, 166
Tupling, Peter, 175
Tway, Bob, 91

U.S. Open Championship, 165-170,
   180-181
   1929, *88*, 89
   1950, 8, 36, 135
   1954, 170
   1960, *61*, 144
   1964, *138*
   1972, 29, 154
   1980, 61, *61*
   1983, *154*
   1985, 185
   1987, 185
   1988, 184
   1989, 184
   1991, *155*
   1992, 183
   1993, 183
   1994, 183
   1995, 183
   1999, 12
U.S. Senior Open Championship 1994,
   33
U.S. Women's Open Championship
   1975, 141

Van de Velde, Jean, 172, 182
Vardon, Harry, 117
Venturi, Ken, 103, 130, *136*,
   136-139, *137*, *138*, *139*, 143, 144,
   163
Verdi, Bob, 98

Wadkins, Lanny, 180
Waldorf, Duffy, 90
Walker, Colleen, 90
Ward, Bud, 28
Ward, Harvie, 136
Warfield, Mary Ann, 210, 211, *214*
Washam, Jo Ann, 142
Waterville, Ireland, 23
Watson, Tom, 23, 52, 59, 102, 106,
   124, 168, 188
Weibring, D.A., 90
Weiskopf, Tom, 17, 107, 108, *109*,
   180
Weisman, Emanuel, 16
Whitaker, Jack, 138
Whitten, Ron, 12-15, 98, 200-203
Whitworth, Kathy, 140, 141
Williams, Ted, 98, 106-107, 147,
   150
Wilson, David, 41
Wind, Herbert Warren, 12, 43-45, 62,
   135, 144, 162-164
Woodbridge, Natasha, 128
Woodbridge, Todd, 128
Woods, Tiger, *75-79*, 78, 129, *182*,
   182
Woosnam, Ian, 185, *185*
Wright, Mickey, *75-77*, 103, *103*, 107
Wyeth, Marion, 43
Wysong, Dudley, 28

Yocom, Guy, 52-53, 86-87
Yorba Linda C.C., Calif., 212
Young, Donna Caponi, 140
Yun, Hunki, 89

Zaharias, Babe Didrikson, 58
Zembriski, Walt, 91

Nurtured Under Golf's Melodic Line

Peter Dobereiner, December 1986

My dear grandson:

Here is the scheme. First, I amass a huge amount of money (details of how this is to be achieved are slightly hazy, but press on) and then I create a wondrous golf course. New courses take time to mature, but by the turn of the century the saplings should have grown to a useful golf stature, and you as well. However, in the nature of things men do not have much time to spend with their grandsons. By the time you can reach the corner of the doglegs with your driver my ashes may well be redressing a potash deficiency on one of the greens. Since I cannot be sure of being around to explain why you should not hook your ball out of the cup with your putter, or smirk when I miss a short one, it might be prudent to commit a little nagging to paper in advance.

I suggest that you prepare yourself for golf with a simple spiritual exercise—an exciting one, really, and quite dangerous. What you do is make a firm vow to yourself when you wake up one morning that you will not tell a lie before lunchtime. This does not mean just not telling whoppers. It also means confronting dishonesty wherever you find it. If somebody says, "Have a nice day" in the mechanical tones of an answering machine, you must reply firmly: "Save your breath because I know well enough that you do not care what kind of a day I have." When a woman in your office invites you to admire the flowers on her desk you say: "This obsession with reproductive organs is sick, Miss Fortescue." Get the idea?

You will probably tell me that life is not like that, that life is lubricated by harmless white lies, the fudging of abrasive issues and the pretending not to see unpleasantness. Quite so. But golf is not life; it is a world of make-believe. You have to believe that your ball is lost even though you know it is sitting in front of you somewhere on the fairway as plain as day. If your ball moves after you have addressed it you have to accept without question that you caused it to move as surely as if you had nudged it with your club, even though this is palpably untrue. Worse, you have to insure that the people you are playing with conform to the same upside-down honesty. Playing the truth game will get you into practice for suspending your faculties of logic and common sense for as long as it takes to play a round of golf.

The second half is not quite so straightforward. Let us start by writing down some words: Amazing grace how sweet thou art, that saved a wretch like me. Put like that, baldly in cold print, those words do not mean much, if anything, the kind of banality that a drunk might say to the driver of the last bus. Not quite in the gibberish class

of the first rule of golf but hardly inspiring. But set those words to music and put them in the mouth of a single-figure soprano and everything makes beautiful, harmonious sense.

So it is with golf. It all comes together once you put the right tune to the words. Where can you learn that tune? Well, you can pick it up at clubs such as Sunningdale and Pine Valley, but it is not so easy to analyze the melodic line. Consideration is a large part of it. There is a pompous preamble to the Rules of Golf under the quaint old title, Etiquette, which boils down to an exhortation to show consideration to other players. Sportsmanship is part of the tune, and that means doing everything possible to enable your opponent to play his best golf while denying yourself the benefit of any doubt in fringe situations. Playing the game for the sake of it is part of the tune, and I must stress that this does not mean playing less than your hardest. There is a vast gulf between playing to win and winning at all costs.

My own grandfather, that is your great-great-grandfather, had his own private word for people who did not conform to his Victorian ideas of behavior. Unusually for that era, he was totally unconscious of class distinctions and anyone, from high or low estate, who was boring, boorish or ignorant was castigated as a 'dung-starter.' My grandmother, greatly to my secret amusement, used to have fits of the vapors whenever he used that dreadful expression.

Manners change with the times, of course, and I have no way of guessing how a dung-starter will be defined in the 21st century. My guess is that failure to wear a tie in the club dining room will not qualify a man as a dung-starter 20 years from now, but only time will tell. You, I feel sure, will have an acute perception of what constitutes a dung-starter and the final element of the tune of golf is not to be one.

I have not said anything about the technique of playing golf, and I shall confine myself to the sage advice given by Deacon Palmer to his son, Arnold: Learn to grip the club properly and then go out and knock the hell out of the ball.

The rest is up to you. If you want to become a great champion then you have my blessing provided that you can pull off the rare trick of doing so without becoming a dung-starter. If you want to be a happy hacker, then that is fine by me, too. A high handicap is not a badge of shame. But however far you care to pursue this game, always remember that it is a game and the object is to enjoy it.

With love, Grandfather

Illustration:
Debbie Chute